*Practical Suggestions
for Teaching with*

The Bedford Guide
for College Writers

EIGHTH EDITION

Practical Suggestions
for Teaching with
The Bedford Guide
for College Writers
EIGHTH EDITION

X. J. Kennedy, Dorothy M. Kennedy, and Marcia F. Muth

Prepared by

Dana Waters
Dodge City Community College

Sylvia A. Holladay

Shirley Morahan

Bedford/St. Martin's   Boston ◆ New York

For information, write: Bedford/St. Martin's, 75 Arlington Street, Boston, MA 02116
(617-399-4000)

ISBN-10: 0–312–46931-4

ISBN-13: 978–0–312–46931–3

Instructors who have adopted *The Bedford Guide for College Writers,* Eighth Edition, as a textbook for a course are authorized to duplicate portions of this manual for their students.

Preface

We have revised the eighth edition of *Practical Suggestions,* the instructor's manual for *The Bedford Guide for College Writers,* with busy classroom instructors in mind. We know that as you prepare for classes, confer with students, and evaluate writing, along with the many other tasks instructors must fit into their schedules, you will find the explanations and activities we have included here a welcome resource. You will find advice based on the most recent research in composition, along with approaches and strategies we have used successfully in our own classrooms. We hope the advice and practical suggestions we have provided will help you and your students build a successful writing community.

Practical Suggestions is organized into two parts. Part One contains advice on the logistics of teaching, such as how to structure your own course, what to do on the first day of class, how to forge a writing community with your students, and how to integrate technology into your teaching. We have provided a variety of syllabi to use as course models. These suggest how you might design your course with a specific emphasis or within a certain time frame. Acknowledging the time constraints of any busy instructor's schedule, we offer advice about how to individualize your instruction when students need it most, through student conferences, both in and out of class.

This section also addresses broader concerns such as how to encourage your students to think and write critically and how best to help underprepared students without jeopardizing the progress of other students. You will find a wealth of advice on assessing student writing, including suggestions on using a portfolio approach in your classroom and on evaluating and grading your students' writing. The suggestions in these chapters are flexible and can be adapted to fit most classroom situations.

Part Two offers specific, chapter-by-chapter advice on using *The Bedford Guide.* For each chapter you will find descriptions of how the readings, the writing assignments, the steps to engage the writing process, and the suggestions for self-evaluation might work in your classroom. You will find advice about how to use the activities for peer response, collaborative writing, and e-writing in each of these chapters. In revising *Practical Suggestions,* we have aimed to make this edition even more practical. In response to instructor feedback, we have added more handouts and "Here's an Idea" boxes, with activities to aid and reinforce learning.

This revision of the instructor's manual owes much to the instructors who provided their thoughtful feedback on the seventh edition of *Practical Suggestions:* Nada Ayad, Fullerton College; Dipo Kalejaiye, Prince George's Community College; Phil Martin, Minneapolis Community and Technical College; Lori Spillane, Indiana University-Purdue University Indianapolis; Matt Van Boening, Friends University; and Jill Zasadny, St. Cloud State University. We would especially like to thank Kathleen Beauchene of Community College of Rhode Island for providing thoughtful teaching suggestions for the selections in *A Writer's Reader.* And thanks to everyone at Bedford/St. Martin's who helped to develop and produce this manual, including Beth Castrodale, Stephanie Naudin, and Lindsay DiGianvittorio.

Contents

Preface   v

PART ONE   Designing and Teaching the Composition Course   1

1. Planning Your Course   1

   WHAT TO DO THE FIRST WEEK   2
   RESOURCES IN *THE BEDFORD GUIDE*   6
   SAMPLE SYLLABI   6

2. Creating a Writing Community   33

   STARTING A CONVERSATION ABOUT WRITING   33
   PEER RESPONSE   37
   STUDENT CONFERENCES   40
   PUBLISHING STUDENT WRITING   41

3. Teaching Critical Thinking and Writing   46

   THREE VIEWS OF COGNITIVE DEVELOPMENT   46
   RESOURCES IN *THE BEDFORD GUIDE*   52

4. Providing Support for Underprepared Students   54

   DEVELOPMENTAL WRITERS   54
   ESL STUDENTS   59
   RESOURCES IN *THE BEDFORD GUIDE*   61

5. Using Technology in Your Composition Course   65

   GETTING STARTED   65
   SOLVING COMMON PROBLEMS   67
   TEACHING WITH COURSE MANAGEMENT SOFTWARE   69
   USING ONLINE TUTORING SERVICES   72
   TECHNOLOGICAL RESOURCES IN *THE BEDFORD GUIDE*   72
   TECHNOLOGICAL RESOURCES ACCOMPANYING *THE BEDFORD GUIDE*   74

6. Assessing Student Writing   77

   PORTFOLIOS   77
   RESPONDING TO STUDENT WRITING   79
   EVALUATION AND GRADING   83
   INSTITUTIONAL ASSESSMENT   86
   A WORD ABOUT PLAGIARISM   87
   RESOURCES IN *THE BEDFORD GUIDE*   88

PART TWO   Using *The Bedford Guide* in Your Course   98

7. Teaching *A Writer's Guide*   **98**
   THE FOUR PARTS OF *A WRITER'S GUIDE*   **98**
   HOW TO USE *A WRITER'S GUIDE*   **100**

A COLLEGE WRITER'S PROCESSES   **102**

Chapter 1: Writing Processes   **102**

Chapter 2: Reading Processes   **103**

Chapter 3: Critical Thinking Processes   **104**

A WRITER'S SITUATIONS   **105**

Chapter 4: Recalling an Experience   **105**

Chapter 5: Observing a Scene   **115**

Chapter 6: Interviewing a Subject   **122**

Chapter 7: Comparing and Contrasting   **131**

Chapter 8: Explaining Causes and Effects   **139**

Chapter 9: Taking a Stand   **146**

Chapter 10: Proposing a Solution   **157**

Chapter 11: Evaluating   **166**

Chapter 12: Supporting a Position with Sources   **175**

SPECIAL WRITING SITUATIONS   **183**

Chapter 13: Responding to Literature   **183**

Chapter 14: Writing in the Workplace   **194**

Chapter 15: Writing for Assessment   **197**

A WRITER'S STRATEGIES   **203**

Chapter 16: Strategies for Generating Ideas   **203**

Chapter 17: Strategies for Stating a Thesis and Planning   **213**

Chapter 18: Strategies for Drafting   **221**

Chapter 19: Strategies for Developing   **225**

Chapter 20: Strategies for Revising and Editing   **230**

Chapter 21: Strategies for Designing Your Document   **237**

Chapter 22: Strategies for Understanding Visual Representations   **240**

8. Teaching *A Writer's Reader*   **243**

   USING *A WRITER'S READER* TO TEACH CRITICAL READING   **243**

   Chapter 23: Families   **246**

   Chapter 24: Men and Women   **259**

   Chapter 25: Popular Culture   **272**

   Chapter 26: E-Technology   **284**

   Chapter 27: Education   **296**

9. Teaching *A Writer's Research Manual*   **308**

   Important Features of *A Writer's Research Manual*   **308**

   Introducing Students to the Researching and Writing Process   **309**

   Chapter 28: Planning and Managing Your Research Project   **311**

   Chapter 29: Working with Sources   **322**

   Chapter 30: Finding Sources in the Library, on the Internet, and in the Field   **324**

   Chapter 31: Evaluating Sources   **331**

   Chapter 32: Integrating Sources   **333**

   Chapter 33: Writing Your Research Paper   **336**

   Chapter 34: Documenting Sources   **345**

10. Teaching with *A Writer's Handbook* and the Appendices   **349**

   Important Features of *A Writer's Handbook*   **349**

   Using *A Writer's Handbook* to Teach Grammar   **350**

   Using the Appendices to Teach Grammar and Research   **351**

   Using Ancillaries to *The Bedford Guide* to Teach Grammar   **352**

Answers for Lettered Exercises   **353**

Answers for Numbered Exercises   **361**

APPENDIX A: *The Bedford Guide* Readings at a Glance   **371**

APPENDIX B: Ancillaries to *The Bedford Guide for College Writers*, Eighth Edition   **384**

PART ONE   Designing and Teaching the Composition Course

CHAPTER 1

Planning Your Course

The question "How?" will occupy you for most of the first year you teach writing. Many of your answers will come from the process of teaching — stepping back and looking at teaching and learning, recalling good teaching you've observed, talking with other writing teachers, reading about writing theory and pedagogy, and, of course, using your imagination. Teaching, like writing, is a recursive process. Even as you shape one assignment you are also revising the last one you gave, so that next time it will work better for your students. In the middle of reading student writing, you'll catch yourself also inventing some strategy to improve class discussion.

This chapter contains the advice we wish someone had given us before we first stepped into a composition classroom, along with several sample syllabi, each designed for a different course length and focus. Once you decide on your course objectives — or learn what objectives have been established for the course by the writing faculty on your campus — one of the syllabi at the end of this chapter will help you design your own course.

If you have questions this manual or the instructor's annotated edition of the text doesn't answer, don't hesitate to ask other writing teachers for guidance. Some of the best teaching tips — recalled, observed, or improvised — come from talking with colleagues. Journals in the field will also show you a wide variety of practice and theory about ways to teach writing. You might want to look for these particularly useful academic journals from the National Council of Teachers of English: *College Composition and Communication, Teaching English in the Two-Year College,* and *College English.* Also consider consulting *Teaching Composition: Background Readings,* Third Edition, an ancillary that accompanies this text and includes readings collected from journals on different topics related to composition.

We found that George Hillocks Jr. provides a good overview of teaching practices in "What Works in Teaching Composition: A Meta-Analysis of Experimental Treatment Studies" (*American Journal of Education* 93 [November 1984]). One of the most effective ways to teach writing is to use what Hillocks classifies as an "environmental" mode of instruction. This method combines a focus on writing-as-process with collaborative learning and individualized instruction. He recommends class activities such as invention strategies, in-class drafting and redrafting, peer evaluation, and small-group discussion, so that both teacher and students have responsibility for what happens in the course. *The Bedford Guide* is structured to encourage a writing-as-process pedagogy by guiding students through planning, drafting, developing, and revising each writing assignment and by providing opportunities for peer evaluation and group learning. You'll also find specific strategies for teaching students the writing process in each chapter of *Practical Suggestions.*

WHAT TO DO THE FIRST WEEK

Begin to learn at least your students' first names on the first day of class. This task might seem daunting, but if you pay particular attention during icebreaking activities and study your students carefully as you call the roll the first week, you can do it. Engage the class in name activities for the first two or three class sessions if you need to. Explain to them that you have a number of students, and because they are important to you, you want to learn their names as quickly as possible. It is imperative that you show them this respect if you want to establish a rapport.

The first three class meetings should establish

- a working definition of "writing-as-process"
- guidelines for journal writing
- the importance of collaborative learning to students' growth as writers
- recognition of one another as members of a writing community
- the convenience of word-processing programs

It is important to establish these priorities the first week in order to persuade students to work with you to improve as writers. To do this, begin the first day by describing the course and its policies, introducing students to the writing process, and inviting them to join you in establishing a community of practicing writers. By the end of the first week, students should have a sense that they constitute a community of writers.

Describe the Course

When introducing the course to your students, be sure to specify

- the objectives for their growth as writers
- the workload they can expect
- an approximate pacing of that workload
- the overall design of the course
- your grading criteria and policy
- course Web site policy, if applicable

If you are specific and clear about these issues at the beginning of the course, students will have a sense of a "contract" being established. This information will give those who

---

Here's an Idea . . .

Begin with a student in the first row. Have him introduce himself ("My name is John Smith"). The student next to him must then introduce both herself and the student who came before her ("My name is Jane Doe, and this is John Smith"). Continue through the classroom. Each successive student must introduce him- or herself and all the students who have already introduced themselves. The last person (that should be you) will be introducing all the students in the class. If you can do this without taking notes, you are well on the way to remembering all of your students' names.

don't want to work within the guidelines of your contract the opportunity to drop your course and register for another. It will also protect you if a student later decides to dispute his or her grade.

As you list the objectives or competencies of the course, explain how the objectives enter into your evaluation of students' progress and final work, and describe how you hope students will develop as writers during the course. You might want to ask them to freewrite for ten minutes about what they hope to learn from the course, and then have them read their responses aloud or in groups. A syllabus will be new to some students, so go through it with them.

It is important to give students all of this information in writing. However eloquently you might present yourself and the course during the first class, most students experience an overload of information and stimuli that first week of school. They need something they can read five weeks into the semester when they start to ask, "Why are we doing this?" or "When is my revision due?" or "What's the portfolio policy?"

Provide a Schedule

Give students a calendar of class activities and writing assignments. Because they are juggling several courses, the more they know about what to expect in your course and when to expect it, the better they can organize their time. Remember that many of your students will be overwhelmed by all the new responsibilities of college life.

When setting students' deadlines, take into account the assignments' complexity as well as the campus calendar of events and holidays. Also keep in mind your own workload: Space deadlines at least a few days apart so that you won't be overwhelmed by a deluge of papers. If you teach more than one section, stagger the deadlines from section to section.

Be flexible. You will most likely need to revise the calendar as the course progresses, taking extra time for a particular assignment or a student-generated activity or even dropping a writing assignment. Remember your own experiences as a student as you plan the schedule or syllabus. It's better to build in a few extra activities in the beginning rather than to add them later. A colleague of ours gives his students the class schedule in three parts — one for each six weeks of the course. This practice allows him to assess his progress and revise dates as needed.

Similarly, give the class thorough information about your attendance and grading policies. Students must make adult decisions about attending class and participating in the course. They will be learning a great deal from one another in this course, so you'll want to carefully explain the responsibility and value of class participation. Make it clear that you are planning class activities that will directly apply to the goals of the course: Students will be generating ideas for writing, drafting, revising, and evaluating

---

Here's an Idea . . .

Give students a short quiz on the policies stated on your syllabus to ensure they have read and understand them. Pose hypothetical situations; for example, "Janice missed the midterm exam without notifying her instructor in advance that she would be absent. . . ." Then ask students to identify the consequences by answering fill-in-the blank, short-answer, or multiple-choice questions.

their writing in class. Also check whether your campus has a specific attendance policy that you must honor.

Explain Grading Policies

It is crucial that your grading policy be clear. Include a specific statement about any revision policy you have. Tell students everything about their performance that you will assess for the course grade. It's unfair, of course, to add requirements later, so establish at the start whether class participation, peer editing, or missed deadlines and assignments will affect students' grades. Also explain to them the gravity of plagiarism, and how it can undermine all their efforts. Later in the semester, you might want to give out the criteria for a grade of A, B, C, D, or F, along with examples of papers that would receive each grade. On the first day, you only need to give an overview with specifics about course goals and policies.

Read over your grading policy carefully, paying particular attention to tone. You don't want to sound authoritarian, cynical, legalistic, or punitive, but you do want to establish your standards clearly.

Introduce Portfolios

If you are asking students to assemble a portfolio, discuss it on the first day of class. Make clear your requirements, especially ones that will affect students' final grade. If the students' grades hinge on completion of a certain number of papers, be sure they understand what is required and the consequences of failing to meet the requirements. If students are to include drafts or early versions of their papers in their portfolios, tell them not to destroy these versions as they revise. To be safe, ask students to keep any version of an assignment that has written comments from you or a peer. Include this information in your syllabus. For more on using portfolios in your course, see pages 77–79.

Introduce the Course Web Site

If your course includes an online component (through a course management system, for example), guide students through the course Web site on the first day of class. Give students clear guidelines about what kind of online participation you expect from them. How much of the course will be Web-based? Will assignments be posted online? Will you grade students' participation in online discussion boards? Will you participate in the discussions? Answering these kinds of questions early in the semester will help prepare students for a smooth transition between the physical classroom and the online learning environment. If you are using electronic ancillaries such as *The Bedford Guide* Web site or e-book, you may also want to walk the class through these resources early in the course. (For more on the electronic ancillaries available with *The Bedford Guide*, see pages 74–76 of this manual. For more on teaching with course management systems, see pages 69–72.)

Ask Students to Write

Before you begin grading a student's writing, it's important to have already read a variety of writings from him or her. It is crucial that your students write during the first class so that you can assess their abilities. If you will be using portfolios and asking students to include reflective writing, focus their attention right away on themselves as writers: Ask them to write about their successes, their failures, their strengths, and their concerns. Or ask them to write a letter introducing themselves and describing what you

Here's an Idea . . .

Bring in a recruiting poster or an ad from your university depicting a college scene. Ask students to write for an entire class period in response to the following prompt:

> Study this poster, which the university sends prospective students, and respond in an essay to the following questions: What image of itself is the university establishing with this poster? What elements of the poster's composition and design support this image? From your own experience and what you've observed this week, is that self-image accurate? Why, or why not?

This assignment requires analysis and evaluation and possibly classification, comparison, contrast, and description. Read the essays to establish their strengths and whether the writers accomplish these three tasks:

- make a general claim
- support the claim with specific examples
- think about their experience and evaluate the claim

This is a lot to ask early in the semester, but it does show students where you want them to be by the end of the course: thinking at a complex level and moving from general claims to specific evidence and back. Explain this to students, and ask them to read a set of essays and rank them as responses to the assignment, using the criteria that you have given them for evaluation. The set of essays that you bring to class should be from another section, with students' names masked out.

need to know about them in order to work with them as writers. (We often ask students to write about one fear and one fantasy they have about the course.) Use the letters to get to know your students and to identify their writing concerns. Don't overlook comments by students who equate writing with handwriting and tell you that they can't spell. Most students respond to this request by giving you personal and useful information about their images of themselves as writers. Writing your own letter of introduction and reading it to students will also begin to establish the class as a community of writers.

Prepare students to spend a class period writing for assessment. Explain that you want to see how they handle a timed writing situation and that they will have an opportunity later in the course to further develop the draft, to shape and revise it. Although narration or description would be easier, give them an assignment that prompts critical thinking. Ask them to observe data, make generalizations, and evaluate their generalizations. This assignment will give you a sense of how well they understand the skills you will be asking them to use later in the semester. It will also allow you to make some broad observations about their cognitive readiness so that you can begin to individualize your instruction. For more about the connection between cognitive development and critical thinking, see Chapter 3 of this manual.

RESOURCES IN *THE BEDFORD GUIDE*

Walk your students through the text during the first week of class. *The Bedford Guide* has numerous built-in learning aids, but many students will never find them on their own. Show your students specific places in the text that help guide them through the writing process. (For more about the writing process, see pages 102–04 in this manual.) The most important features to point out during the first week are

- the general guide to content in the inside back cover of the book and at the end of the first three chapters.
- the "How to Use *The Bedford Guide*" introduction
- the step-by-step directions for each stage of the writing process
- the models of student writing
- the checklists for each step of the writing process
- the tips for e-writers
- the questions for peer response
- the Draft Doctor charts
- the Quick Research Guide
- the Quick Editing Guide

You will need to remind students of these aids later on in the semester, but highlighting them in the beginning can help alleviate students' anxiety and encourage them to search for help on their own.

You might want to spend a few extra minutes explaining the Facing the Challenge section for each writing assignment and the Quick Research Guide and Quick Editing Guide at the end of students' textbooks. These features are designed to help students write successful, focused responses to the chapter's assignment. The Facing the Challenge sections suggest ways for students to handle the most difficult aspect of an assignment, whereas the Quick Research Guide offers students step-by-step pointers for writing from sources and succinct information on documentation. The Quick Editing Guide provides guidance on editing for common grammar and mechanics problems and comprehensive editing checklists. The Draft Doctor charts, a new feature in this edition, help students find and fix problems in their drafts. The charts are included in Chapters 9, 12, 17, 32, 34, and the Quick Editing Guide. Each chapter incudes additional charts and diagrams to help students with specific assignments and other writing tasks. Remind students that, when they are writing on their own, they can refer to these guides for help. For more about using these features and providing support for underprepared students, see Chapter 4 in this manual.

SAMPLE SYLLABI

These syllabi illustrate the flexibility that *The Bedford Guide* offers instructors. Because there are so many ways to organize a course, we've provided a wide variety of examples. The first eight syllabi assign specific chapters and assignments for each week of class:

- Process-Focused Syllabus: Fifteen- or Sixteen-Week Semester
- Process-Focused Syllabus: Ten-to-Twelve-Week Semester

- Critical Reading and Writing: Fifteen- or Sixteen-Week Semester
- Critical Reading and Writing: Ten-to-Twelve-Week Semester
- Writing Course with Research Component: Fifteen- or Sixteen-Week Semester
- Writing Course with Research Component: Ten-to-Twelve-Week Semester
- Process-Focused Course with Research Component: Two Seventeen-Week Semesters
- Writing across the Curriculum: Ten-to-Twelve-Week Semester

The last three models are variations written by instructors who use *The Bedford Guide*:

- Sequenced Syllabus
- Calendar Syllabus
- Introductory Syllabus

No matter which syllabus you use, it's best to make the information clear, complete, and brief. Many departments require that the objectives, grading, and attendance policies be included on the syllabus so that students receive them during the first class meeting. This may seem boring and tedious, but it serves to protect both you and your students. Examine the model syllabi in your department chair's office or ask your colleagues to share one of theirs.

PROCESS-FOCUSED SYLLABUS
Fifteen- or Sixteen-Week Semester

Week One
Reading Assignment   Ch. 1, Writing Processes. Ch. 2, Reading Processes. Ch. 21, Strategies for Designing Your Document.
Classroom Activities   Icebreaker activity. Activity to introduce writing process. In-class letter about the student as writer or in-class diagnostic essay. Hands-on introduction to computer/writing lab.

Week Two
Reading Assignment   Ch. 4, Recalling an Experience. Ch. 16, Strategies for Generating Ideas. Ch. 17, Strategies for Stating a Thesis and Planning.
Writing Assignment   Ch. 4, Recalling an Experience.
Classroom Activities   Assignment from Other Assignments (Ch. 4). Generating ideas focused on recall essay; planning strategies focused on recall essay.

Week Three
Reading Assignment   Ch. 17, Strategies for Stating a Thesis and Planning (reread). Ch. 18, Strategies for Drafting. Ch. 19, Strategies for Developing. Ch. 20, Strategies for Revising and Editing.
Classroom Activities   Revision of recall essay with focus on stating and developing a thesis. Peer evaluation training workshop.

Week Four
Reading Assignment   Ch. 5, Observing a Scene. Ch. 2, Reading Processes (reread).
Writing Assignment   Ch. 5, Observing a Scene.
Classroom Activities   Critical reading activity. Peer evaluation of Recalling an Experience essay. In-class macro-revision.

Week Five
Reading Assignment   Ch. 6, Interviewing a Subject.
Writing Assignment   Ch. 6, Interviewing a Subject.
Classroom Activities   Interviewing exercises. Assignment from Other Assignments (Ch. 6). Peer evaluation of Observing a Scene essay.

Week Six
Reading Assignment   Ch. 22, Strategies for Understanding Visual Representations.
Classroom Activities   Conferences on works-in-progress. Exercises on image analysis.

Week Seven
Reading Assignment   Ch. 15, Writing for Assessment.
Writing Assignment   Reflective essay on writing assignments.
Classroom Activities   Peer evaluation of Interviewing a Subject essay. In-class practice of timed writing.

Week Eight

Reading Assignment
Ch. 3, Critical Thinking Processes. Ch. 7, Comparing and Contrasting.

Writing Assignment
Ch. 7, Comparing and Contrasting.

Classroom Activities
Critical thinking activity.
Midterm evaluation conferences.

Week Nine

Reading Assignment
Ch. 8, Explaining Causes and Effects. Ch. 19, Strategies for Developing (reread).

Writing Assignment
Ch. 8, Explaining Causes and Effects.

Classroom Activities
Peer evaluation of Comparing and Contrasting essay. In-class revision of work-in-progress with focus on developing.

Week Ten

Reading Assignment
Ch. 9, Taking a Stand.

Writing Assignment
Ch. 9, Taking a Stand.

Classroom Activities
Peer evaluation of Explaining Causes and Effects essay. In-class drafting of letter to the editor with focus on audience.

Week Eleven

Reading Assignment
Ch. 10, Proposing a Solution. Ch. 18, Strategies for Drafting (reread).

Writing Assignment
Ch. 10, Proposing a Solution.

Classroom Activities
Peer evaluation of Taking a Stand essay. In-class revision of work-in-progress with focus on openings and closings and on emphasis.

Week Twelve

Reading Assignment
Ch. 11, Evaluating. Ch. 20, Strategies for Revising and Editing (reread).

Writing Assignment
Ch. 11, Evaluating.

Classroom Activities
Peer evaluation of Proposing a Solution essay. Evaluation of pop culture artifact or objet d'art.

Week Thirteen

Reading Assignment
Ch. 12, Supporting a Position with Sources.

Writing Assignment
Ch. 12, Supporting a Position with Sources.

Classroom Activities
Peer evaluation of Evaluating essay. Exercises in quoting, paraphrasing, summarizing, and documenting sources. Conferences on revising works-in-progress.

Weeks Fourteen and Fifteen

Classroom Activities
Peer evaluation of Supporting a Position with Sources essay. Self-assessment letter about the student as a writer-in-progress. Revision workshops.

Week Sixteen

Final exams or portfolio deadline.

Week One

Reading Assignment | Ch. 1, Writing Processes. Ch. 2, Reading Processes. Ch. 21, Strategies for Designing Your Document. Ch. 4, Recalling an Experience.

Writing Assignment | Ch. 4, Recalling an Experience.

Classroom Activities | In-class diagnostic essay. Hands-on introduction to computer/ writing lab.

Week Two

Reading Assignment | Ch. 5, Observing a Scene. Ch. 16, Strategies for Generating Ideas.

Writing Assignment | Assignment from Other Assignments (Ch. 5).

Classroom Activities | Peer evaluation training workshop. Peer evaluation of Recalling an Experience essay.

Week Three

Reading Assignment | Ch. 6, Interviewing a Subject. Ch. 17, Strategies for Stating a Thesis and Planning.

Writing Assignment | Ch. 6, Interviewing a Subject.

Classroom Activities | In-class redrafting of diagnostic essay, with focus on stating and developing a thesis. Conferences with student writers. Interviewing exercises (starting on p. 122 of this manual).

Week Four

Reading Assignment | Ch. 7, Comparing and Contrasting. Ch. 3, Critical Thinking Processes.

Writing Assignment | Ch. 7, Comparing and Contrasting.

Classroom Activities | Peer evaluation of redrafted diagnostic essay. Peer evaluation of Interviewing a Subject essay. Critical thinking activity.

Week Five

Reading Assignment | Ch. 8, Explaining Causes and Effects. Ch. 18, Strategies for Drafting.

Writing Assignment | Ch. 8, Explaining Causes and Effects.

Classroom Activities | Peer evaluation of Comparing and Contrasting essay. Mid-term evaluation conferences.

Week Six

Reading Assignment | Ch. 9, Taking a Stand. Ch. 19, Strategies for Developing.

Writing Assignment | Ch. 9, Taking a Stand.

Classroom Activities | Peer evaluation of Causes and Effects essay. Revision workshop with focus on developing.

Week Seven

Reading Assignment | Ch. 10, Proposing a Solution. Ch. 20, Strategies for Revising and Editing.

Writing Assignment | Ch. 10, Proposing a Solution.

Classroom Activities | Peer evaluation of Taking a Stand essay. Conferences with student writers.

Week Eight
Reading Assignment   Ch. 11, Evaluating.
Writing Assignment   Ch. 11, Evaluating.
Classroom Activities   Peer evaluation of Proposing a Solution essay. Revision work-
                        shop with focus on revising for audience, structure, and pur-
                        pose.

Week Nine
Reading Assignment   Ch. 12, Supporting a Position with Sources.
Writing Assignment   Ch. 12, Supporting a Position with Sources
Classroom Activities   Peer evaluation of Evaluating essay. Exercises on quoting,
                        paraphrasing, summarizing, and documenting sources.

Week Ten
Reading Assignment   Ch. 22, Strategies for Understanding Visual Representations.
Classroom Activities   Peer evaluation of Supporting a Position with Sources essay.
                        Conferences on revising works-in-progress.

Week Eleven
Reading Assignment   Ch. 15, Writing for Assessment.
Classroom Activities   Conferences on revising works-in-progress. Revision work-
                        shop with focus on editing.

Week Twelve
Classroom Activities   Reflective essay on the student as writer-in-process. Revision
                        workshop. Final exam or portfolios due.

Week One

Reading Assignment   Ch. 1, Writing Processes. Ch. 2, Reading Processes. Ch. 21, Strategies for Designing Your Document. Ch. 4, Recalling an Experience: Robert G. Schreiner, "What Is a Hunter?"

Writing Assignment   In-class diagnostic essay analyzing "What Is a Hunter?"

Classroom Activities   Self-assessment letter about student as writer and reader. Journal entries focused on experiences in reading Chs. 1 and 2. Hands-on introduction to writing center/computer lab.

Week Two

Reading Assignment   Ch. 4, Recalling an Experience. Ch. 16, Strategies for Generating Ideas.

Writing Assignment   Ch. 4, Recalling an Experience.

Classroom Activities   Peer evaluation training workshop. Critical reading activity. Journal entries: Why have the authors organized the chapter this way? What would you revise?

Week Three

Reading Assignment   Ch. 5, Observing a Scene. Ch. 17, Strategies for Stating a Thesis and Planning.

Writing Assignment   Ch. 5, Observing a Scene.

Classroom Activities   Peer evaluation of Recalling an Experience essay. Journal entries: Describe what you're reading and writing for other courses. Analyze a chapter of a textbook that presents problems for you.

Week Four

Reading Assignment   Ch. 6, Interviewing a Subject. Ch. 18, Strategies for Drafting.

Writing Assignment   Ch. 6, Interviewing a Subject.

Classroom Activities   Interviewing exercises (starting on p. 122 in this manual). Peer evaluation of Observing a Scene essay. Journal entries: Analyze the kinds of conversation in your classes. Interview a senior in your field about "survival strategies."

Week Five

Reading Assignment   Ch. 3, Critical Thinking Processes. Ch. 22, Strategies for Understanding Visual Representations.

Writing Assignment   Short essay analyzing an image.

Classroom Activities   Peer evaluation of Interviewing a Subject essay. Journal entries: Analyze the appeal used in a television commercial, a magazine ad, a political speech, or a blog.

Week Six

Reading Assignment   Ch. 7, Comparing and Contrasting. Ch. 19, Strategies for Developing.

Writing Assignment   Ch. 7, Comparing and Contrasting.

Classroom Activities   Student conferences on reading strategies. Journal entries: Compare and contrast course work and study problems in this and other courses.

Week Seven

Reading Assignment	Ch. 8, Explaining Causes and Effects. Ch. 20, Strategies for Revising and Editing.
Writing Assignment	Ch. 8, Explaining Causes and Effects.
Classroom Activities	Peer evaluation of Comparing and Contrasting essay. Journal entries: Analyze the causes of your successes and failures in relation to your course work this semester and to your overall academic goals.

Week Eight

Reading Assignment	Ch. 15, Writing for Assessment.
Writing Assignment	Midterm self-assessment of critical reading and writing.
Classroom Activities	In-class essay exam on readings from Ch. 8. Journal entries on readings and on preparing for essay exams. Midterm evaluation conferences.

Week Nine

Reading Assignment	Ch. 9, Taking a Stand.
Writing Assignment	Ch. 9, Taking a Stand.
Classroom Activities	Peer evaluation of Causes and Effects essay. Journal entries on the reading selections in Ch. 9.

Week Ten

Reading Assignment	Ch. 10, Proposing a Solution.
Writing Assignment	Ch. 10, Proposing a Solution.
Classroom Activities	Peer evaluation of Taking a Stand essay. Group exercises in problem solving. Journal entries: solutions for time management problems, class participation problems, and study problems.

Week Eleven

Reading Assignment	Ch. 11, Evaluating.
Writing Assignment	Ch. 11, Evaluating.
Classroom Activities	Peer evaluation of Proposing a Solution essay. Journal entries: Evaluate a favorite television show and movie. Timed in-class essay using evaluation.

Weeks Twelve and Thirteen

Reading Assignment	Ch. 12, Supporting a Position with Sources
Writing Assignment	Ch. 12, Supporting a Position with Sources.
Classroom Activities	Peer evaluation of Supporting a Position with Sources essay. Exercises on preparing bibliography entries and using and citing sources. Journal entries: Evaluate each of your sources for its contribution to the academic exchange.

Weeks Fourteen and Fifteen

Reading Assignment	Ch. 13, Responding to Literature. Ch. 15, Writing for Assessment: Writing for Portfolio Assessment. Ch. 20, Strategies for Revising and Editing (reread). Quick Editing Guide.

Weeks Fourteen and Fifteen (continued)

Writing Assignment	Ch. 13, Responding to Literature: Literary Analysis.
Classroom Activities	Peer evaluation of Literary Analysis essay. Begin preparing a portfolio of your writing that is most representative of your abilities to think critically; due week sixteen. In-class conferences about portfolio decisions. Journal entries: Reflect on the process of analyzing literary works; give reasons for portfolio choices.

Week Sixteen

Classroom Activities	Portfolio revision. Journal entry: self-assessment of the student as critical reader and writer. Portfolio due or final exam.

Week One

Reading Assignment | Ch. 1, Writing Processes. Ch. 2, Reading Processes. Ch. 21, Strategies for Designing Your Document. Ch. 4, Recalling an Experience: Robert G. Schreiner, "What Is a Hunter?"

Writing Assignment | In-class diagnostic essay analyzing "What Is a Hunter?"

Classroom Activities | Self-assessment letter about student as writer and reader. Journal entries focused on experiences in reading Chs. 1 and 2. Hands-on introduction to writing center/computer lab.

Week Two

Reading Assignment | Ch. 4, Recalling an Experience. Ch. 16, Strategies for Generating Ideas.

Writing Assignment | Ch. 4, Recalling an Experience.

Classroom Activities | Peer evaluation training workshop. Journal entries: Why have the authors organized the chapter this way? What would you revise? Critical reading activity.

Week Three

Reading Assignment | Ch. 5, Observing a Scene. Ch. 17, Strategies for Stating a Thesis and Planning.

Writing Assignment | Ch. 5, Observing a Scene.

Classroom Activities | Peer evaluation of Recalling an Experience essay. Journal entries: Describe what you're reading and writing for other courses. Analyze a chapter of a textbook that presents problems for you.

Week Four

Reading Assignment | Ch. 6, Interviewing a Subject. Ch. 18, Strategies for Drafting.

Writing Assignment | Ch. 6, Interviewing a Subject.

Classroom Activities | Interviewing exercises (starting on p. 122 in this manual). Peer evaluation of Observing a Scene essay. Journal entries: Analyze the kinds of conversation in your classes. Interview a senior in your field about "survival strategies."

Week Five

Reading Assignment | Ch. 3, Critical Thinking Processes. Ch. 8, Explaining Causes and Effects

Writing Assignment | Ch. 8, Explaining Causes and Effects

Classroom Activities | Peer evaluation of Interviewing a Subject essay. Group exercises on problem solving through causal analysis. Journal entries: Analyze the causes of successes and failures in your coursework this semester and in meeting your overall academic goals.

Week Six

Reading Assignment | Ch. 9, Taking a Stand. Ch. 19, Strategies for Developing.

Writing Assignment | Ch. 9, Taking a Stand

Classroom Activities | Peer evaluation of Explaining Causes and Effects essay. In-class development of works-in-progress. Journal entries: Respond to reading selections in Ch. 9.

Week Seven

Reading Assignment	Ch. 10, Proposing a Solution. Ch. 20, Strategies for Revising and Editing.
Writing Assignment	Ch. 10, Proposing a Solution.
Classroom Activities	Peer evaluation of Taking a Stand essay. Midterm evaluation conferences. Journal entries: solutions for time management problems, class participation problems, and study problems.

Week Eight

Reading Assignment	Ch. 11, Evaluating
Writing Assignment	Ch. 11, Evaluating
Classroom Activities	Peer evaluation of Proposing a Solution essay. Journal entries: Evaluate an advertisement, television show, or movie.

Week Nine

Reading Assignment	Ch. 12, Supporting a Position with Sources.
Writing Assignment	Ch. 12, Supporting a Position with Sources.
Classroom Activities	Peer evaluation of Evaluating essay. Exercises on preparing bibliography entries and using and citing sources. Journal entries: Evaluate each of your sources for its contribution to the academic exchange.

Weeks Ten and Eleven

Reading Assignment	Ch. 13, Responding to Literature.
Writing Assignment	Ch. 13, Responding to Literature: Literary Analysis.
Classroom Activities	Peer evaluation of Literary Analysis essay. Prepare a portfolio of your writing that is most representative of your abilities to think critically; due week twelve. Journal entries: responses to readings in Ch. 13; reflections on process of analyzing literature; give reasons for portfolio choices.

Week Twelve

Classroom Activities	Revision workshop. In-class conferences about portfolio decisions. Journal entry: self-assessment of the student as critical reader and writer. Portfolio due or final exam.

| WRITING COURSE WITH RESEARCH COMPONENT |
| *Fifteen- or Sixteen-Week Semester* |

Week One

Reading Assignment — Ch. 4, Recalling an Experience. Ch. 16, Strategies for Generating Ideas. Ch. 17, Strategies for Stating a Thesis and Planning.

Writing Assignment — Ch. 4, Recalling an Experience.

Classroom Activities — Drafting of letter about the student's writing and research background.

Week Two

Reading Assignment — Ch. 21, Strategies for Designing Your Document. Ch. 18, Strategies for Drafting. Ch. 19, Strategies for Developing.

Classroom Activities — Hands-on introduction to writing/computer lab. Peer evaluation training workshop. Library research project (see p. 313 of this manual for a scavenger hunt and other projects).

Week Three

Reading Assignment — Ch. 3, Critical Thinking Processes. Ch. 28, Planning and Managing Your Research Project. Ch. 29, Working with Sources.

Writing Assignments — Ch. 28, Planning and Managing Your Research Project: Writing from Sources (paper due week ten). Annotated bibliography for research paper-in-progress.

Classroom Activities — Research journal entries on three possible topics for research paper-in-progress. Office conferences with individual writers about topics for research. Peer evaluation of Recalling an Experience essay. Critical thinking activity.

Week Four

Reading Assignment — Ch. 29, Working with Sources (reread). Ch. 30, Finding Sources in the Library, on the Internet, and in the Field.

Classroom Activities — Drafting of critical evaluation of literature or other reading. Include quotes and paraphrases. Peer discussion of research project. Orientation on library databases.

Week Five

Reading Assignment — Ch. 31, Evaluating Sources. Ch. 17, Strategies for Stating a Thesis and Planning: Outlining.

Writing Assignment — Research journal entries on causes and effects of some aspects of topic for research paper.

Classroom Activities — Interview expert in the field of research project.

Week Six

Reading Assignment — Ch. 32, Integrating Sources.

Classroom Activities — Exercises on quoting, paraphrasing, and summarizing one article from a local paper and one from a scholarly journal.

Week Seven

Reading Assignment — Ch. 33, Writing Your Research Paper.

Classroom Activities — Peer evaluation of interviews for research project.

Week Eight

Reading Assignment Ch. 34, Documenting Sources. Ch. 20, Strategies for Revising and Editing.

Classroom Activities Discussion of documentation problems for individual research papers. Peer evaluation of introductions to research papers-in-progress. Exercises on documentation and proofing research paper. Peer-editing workshops with final rough draft of the research paper. Timed in-class essay for midterm exam or assessment.

Week Nine

Classroom Activities Evaluation conferences with individual writers about research papers.

Week Ten

Reading Assignment Ch. 20, Strategies for Revising and Editing (reread); Quick Research Guide; Quick Editing Guide.

Writing Assignment Research paper due.

Classroom Activities In-class revising and editing.

Week Eleven

Reading Assignment Ch. 8, Explaining Causes and Effects.

Writing Assignment Ch. 8, Explaining Causes and Effects.

Classroom Activities Conferences on the research process and paper.

Week Twelve

Reading Assignment Ch. 9, Taking a Stand.

Writing Assignment Ch. 9, Taking a Stand.

Classroom Activities Peer evaluation of Causes and Effects essay.

Week Thirteen

Reading Assignment Ch. 10, Proposing a Solution.

Writing Assignment Ch. 10, Proposing a Solution.

Classroom Activities Peer evaluation of Taking a Stand essay.

Week Fourteen

Reading Assignment Ch. 11, Evaluating.

Writing Assignment Ch. 11, Evaluating.

Classroom Activities Peer evaluation of Proposing a Solution essay. Timed in-class essay evaluating a subject.

Week Fifteen

Reading Assignment Ch. 22, Strategies for Understanding Visual Representations.

Writing Assignment Written letter of evaluation of the student as writer and researcher.

Classroom Activities Exercises on analyzing images. Revision workshops.

Week Sixteen

Final exams or portfolio deadline.

Week One
Reading Assignment   Ch. 4, Recalling an Experience. Ch. 16, Strategies for Generating Ideas. Ch. 21, Strategies for Designing Your Document.
Writing Assignment   Ch. 4, Recalling an Experience.
Classroom Activities   Drafting of letter about the student's writing and research background. Hands-on introduction to writing/computer lab.

Week Two
Reading Assignment   Ch. 3, Critical Thinking Processes. Ch. 28, Planning and Managing Your Research Project. Ch. 17, Strategies for Stating a Thesis and Planning.
Writing Assignment
Paper due week ten.   Ch. 28, Planning and Managing Your Research Project.
Classroom Activities   Peer evaluation training workshop. Peer evaluation of Recalling an Experience essay. Critical thinking activity.

Week Three
Reading Assignment   Ch. 29, Working with Sources. Ch. 30, Finding Sources in the Library, on the Internet, and in the Field. Ch. 5, Observing a Scene. Ch. 18, Strategies for Drafting.
Writing Assignment   Ch. 5, Observing a Scene.
Classroom Activities   Library orientation tour. Assignment from Other Assignments (Ch. 5).

Week Four
Reading Assignment   Ch. 31, Evaluating Sources.
Writing Assignments   Ch. 31, Evaluating Sources. Annotated bibliography of readings for a research essay-in-progress. Research journal entries evaluating readings for a research paper-in-progress.
Classroom Activities   Peer evaluation of Observing a Scene essay.

Week Five
Reading Assignment   Ch. 6, Interviewing a Subject. Ch. 32, Integrating Sources.
Writing Assignment   Ch. 6, Interviewing a Subject.
Classroom Activities   Office conferences with individual writers about topics and research-in-progress. Exercises on quoting, paraphrasing, and summarizing articles from local paper or research project.

Week Six
Reading Assignment   Ch. 8, Explaining Causes and Effects. Ch. 19, Strategies for Developing.
Writing Assignment   Ch. 8, Explaining Causes and Effects.
Classroom Activities   Peer evaluation of Interviewing a Subject essay. In-class writing exploring causes and effects of some aspect of research topic.

Week Seven
Reading Assignment   Ch. 9, Taking a Stand.
Writing Assignment   Ch. 9, Taking a Stand.
Classroom Activities   Peer evaluation of Causes and Effects essay.

Week Eight
Reading Assignment   Ch. 33, Writing Your Research Paper.
Writing Assignment   Drafting of research paper.
Classroom Activities   Peer evaluation of Taking a Stand essay. Peer evaluation of introduction to research papers.

Week Nine
Reading Assignment   Ch. 10, Proposing a Solution. Ch. 17, Strategies for Stating a Thesis and Planning: Outlining. Ch. 22, Strategies for Understanding Visual Representations.
Writing Assignment   Assignment from Other Assignments (Ch. 10).
Classroom Activities   Exercises on formal outlining (p. 215 of this manual). Analysis of images.

Week Ten
Reading Assignment   Chapter 34, Documenting Sources.
Writing Assignment   Research paper due at end of week.
Classroom Activities   Exercises on documentation. Documentation workshop.

Week Eleven
Reading Assignment   Ch. 20, Strategies for Revising and Editing. Ch. 11, Evaluating.
Writing Assignment   Assignment from Other Assignments (Ch. 11).
Classroom Activities   Evaluation conferences with individual writers about research papers. Portfolio revision.

Week Twelve
Reading Assignment   Ch. 20, Strategies for Revising and Editing (reread). Quick Research Guide. Quick Editing Guide.
Writing Assignment   Revising of research paper. Written letter of evaluation of student as writer and researcher.
Classroom Activities   Revision workshops. Final exam or portfolio deadline.

PROCESS-FOCUSED COURSE WITH RESEARCH COMPONENT
Two Seventeen-Week Semesters

First Semester: Composition I

Week One

Reading Assignment	Ch. 1, Writing Processes. Ch. 2, Reading Processes. Ch. 4, Recalling an Experience. Ch. 21, Strategies for Designing Your Document.
Classroom Activities	Drafting of in-class reflective essay on the student as a writer or diagnostic essay. Hands-on introduction to writing/computer lab. Exercise introducing the steps of the writing process.

Week Two

Reading Assignment	Ch. 4, Recalling an Experience (reread). Ch. 16, Strategies for Generating Ideas.
Writing Assignment	Ch. 4, Recalling an Experience.
Classroom Activities	Peer evaluation training workshop. Activities to generate ideas focused on Recalling an Experience essay.

Week Three

Reading Assignment	Essay from *A Writer's Reader.*
Writing Assignment	Journal Prompt from an essay in reader.
Classroom Activities	Group work on analyzing essay from reader. Peer evaluation workshop on presenters' Recalling an Experience essay.* Peer evaluation of Recalling an Experience essay.

Week Four

Reading Assignment	Essay from reader. Ch. 17, Strategies for Stating a Thesis and Planning.
Writing Assignment	Revised draft of Recalling an Experience essay due. Assignment from Journal Prompts or Suggestions for Writing following essay.
Classroom Activities	Group work on analyzing essay from reader. Planning activities focused on stating a thesis and organizing ideas.

Week Five

Reading Assignment	Ch. 5, Observing a Scene. Essay from reader.
Writing Assignment	Ch. 5, Observing a Scene.
Classroom Activities	Observation exercise from Other Assignments (Ch. 5). Group work on analyzing essay from reader. Collect observation data for essay. Stating a Thesis and Planning activities with focus on Observing a Scene essay.

Week Six

Reading Assignment	Essay from reader.
Writing Assignment	Reflective essay on drafts of Recalling an Experience and Observing a Scene essays.
Classroom Activities	Group work on analyzing essays from reader. Peer evaluation workshop on presenters' Observing a Scene essays. Peer evaluation of Observing a Scene essay.

*For an explanation of such workshops, see p. 38.

Week Seven
Reading Assignment   Ch. 18, Strategies for Drafting. Essay from reader.
Writing Assignment   Observing a Scene essay revised draft due. Assignment from Journal Prompts or Suggestions for Writing following essay.
Classroom Activities   Group work on analyzing essay from reader. Drafting activities focused on introductions and conclusions. Conferences on works-in-process.

Week Eight
Reading Assignment   Ch. 6, Interviewing a Subject. Ch. 19, Strategies for Developing.
Writing Assignment   Ch. 6, Interviewing a Subject.
Classroom Activities   Activities focused on interviewing skills. Peer evaluation of interview questions. Class visit by professional journalist.

Week Nine
Reading Assignment   Essay from reader.
Classroom Activities   Group work on analyzing essay. Check working portfolio. In-class essay: midterm reflection on student's writing in this course. Midterm exam.

Week Ten
Reading Assignment   Ch. 22, Strategies for Understanding Visual Representations.
Writing Assignment   Short essay analyzing an image.
Classroom Activities   Analysis of images. Peer evaluation workshop on presenters' Interviewing a Subject essays. Peer evaluation of Interviewing a Subject essay.

Week Eleven
Reading Assignment   Ch. 3, Critical Thinking Processes. Ch. 7, Comparing and Contrasting. Ch. 20, Strategies for Revising and Editing.
Writing Assignment   Revised draft of Interviewing a Subject essay due. Assignment from Other Assignments (Ch. 7).
Classroom Activities   Conferences on works-in-process. Revision workshop: Ch. 20, Strategies for Revising and Editing: Revising for Structure and Support.

Week Twelve
Reading Assignment   Ch. 8, Explaining Causes and Effects. Essay from reader.
Writing Assignment   Ch. 8, Explaining Causes and Effects.
Classroom Activities   Group work analyzing essay from reader. Class activity on causes and effects. Revision workshop: Ch. 20, Strategies for Revising and Editing: Revising for Purpose and Thesis, and Revising for Audience.

Week Thirteen
Reading Assignment   Ch. 12, Supporting a Position with Sources.
Writing Assignment   Ch. 12, Supporting a Position with Sources.
Classroom Activities   Peer evaluation of Explaining Causes and Effects essay. Exercises on quoting, paraphrasing, and summarizing.

Week Fourteen

Reading Assignment	Ch. 15, Writing for Assessment.
Writing Assignment	Timed in-class essay from Suggestions for Writing in reader. Revised draft of Explaining Causes and Effects essay due.
Classroom Activities	Peer evaluation workshop on presenters' Supporting a Position with Sources essays. Peer evaluation of Supporting a Position with Sources essay.

Week Fifteen

Reading Assignment	Essays from reader.
Writing Assignment	Revised draft of Supporting a Position with Sources essay due. Reflective essay on Interviewing a Subject, Comparing and Contrasting, Explaining Causes and Effects, and Supporting a Position with Sources essays.
Classroom Activities	Group analysis of essays from reader. Revision workshop.

Week Sixteen

Writing Assignment	Final reflective essay to be included in presentation portfolio.
Classroom Activities	Revision and editing workshop. Conferences on selection and revision for presentation portfolio.

Week Seventeen

Writing Assignment	Presentation portfolio due.
Classroom Activities	Portfolio workshop; final exam.

Second Semester: Composition II

Week One

Reading Assignment	Part One: A College Writer's Processes.
Classroom Activities	Introduction/ice breaker activity. Drafting of in-class reflective essay on student as writer and class goals. Hands-on introduction to writing/computer lab. Activity from Ch. 2, Reading Processes.

Week Two

Reading Assignment	Ch. 28, Planning and Managing Your Research Project.
Classroom Activities	Library orientation tour. Library orientation exercise. Activities from Ch. 3, Critical Thinking Processes.

Week Three

Reading Assignment	Ch. 9, Taking a Stand: Recognizing Logical Fallacies. Ch. 30, Finding Sources in the Library, on the Internet, and in the Field.
Classroom Activities	Exercises on recognizing logical fallacies. Library orientation exercise due. Assignment of college library hunt exercise (see p. 313 of this manual). Activity to evaluate Internet sites.

Week Four

Reading Assignment	Ch. 34, Documenting Sources. Essay from reader.
Classroom Activities	College library hunt exercise due. Exercises on documentation. Group analysis of essay from reader.

Weeks Five and Six
Reading Assignment   Ch. 9, Taking a Stand. Essay from reader.
Writing Assignment   Ch. 9, Taking a Stand.
Classroom Activities   Group work on analyzing essay from reader. Generating ideas and planning activities for Taking a Stand essay.

Week Seven
Reading Assignment   Essay from reader. Ch. 10, Proposing a Solution.
Writing Assignment   Ch. 10, Proposing a Solution.
Classroom Activities   Group work on analyzing essay from reader. Generating ideas and planning activities for Proposing a Solution essay. Peer evaluation of Taking a Stand essay.

Week Eight
Reading Assignment   Ch. 11, Evaluating. Essay from reader.
Writing Assignment   Ch. 11, Evaluating. Revised draft of Taking a Stand essay due. Short reflective writing on Taking a Stand essay.
Classroom Activities   Group work on analyzing essay from reader. Generating ideas and planning activities for evaluating essay. Peer evaluation of Proposing a Solution essay.

Week Nine
Reading Assignment   Ch. 28, Planning and Managing Your Research Project (review).
Writing Assignment   Ch. 28, Planning and Managing Your Research Project: Writing from Sources. Revised draft of Proposing a Solution essay due.
Classroom Activities   Generating ideas for research topic. Peer response to Evaluating essay. Midterm reflective essay on the student's writing in this course. Midterm exam.

Week Ten
Reading Assignment   Ch. 20, Strategies for Revising and Editing.
Writing Assignment   Revised draft of Evaluating essay due. Short reflective writing on Proposing a Solution and Evaluating essays.
Classroom Activities   Three general research topics phrased as questions due. Individual conferences to select research topic. Preliminary search. Revision activities on Taking a Stand, Proposing a Solution, and Evaluating essays.

Week Eleven
Reading Assignment   Ch. 29, Working with Sources. Ch. 30, Finding Sources in the Library, on the Internet, and in the Field (review). Ch. 31, Evaluating Sources.
Classroom Activities   Approved research question due. Library research lab. Annotated bibliography cards due. Preliminary outline due.

Week Twelve
Reading Assignment   Ch. 32, Integrating Sources.
Classroom Activities   Exercises in quoting, paraphrasing, and summarizing. Library research lab. Note cards due.

Week Thirteen

Reading Assignment   Ch. 33, Writing Your Research Paper. Ch. 17, Strategies for Stating a Thesis and Planning (review sections on thesis statement and formal outline).

Classroom Activities   Exercises on thesis statement and outlining. Thesis statement and formal outline due. Individual conferences on thesis statement and outline.

Week Fourteen

Reading Assignment   Ch. 34, Documenting Sources.

Writing Assignment   Research paper rough draft (with outline and Works Cited).

Classroom Activities   In-class drafting of research paper. Individual conferences on research paper. In-class reflective writing on research project.

Week Fifteen

Reading Assignment   Ch. 20, Strategies for Revising and Editing (review).

Writing Assignment   Research paper rough draft due. Final reflective essay for inclusion in presentation portfolio.

Classroom Activities   Individual conferencing on research paper drafts. Revision workshop using the Quick Research Guide and the Quick Editing Guide.

Week Sixteen

Writing Assignment   Research paper final draft due.

Classroom Activities   Conferencing on portfolio selection and revision. Revision workshop.

Week Seventeen

Writing Assignment   Presentation portfolio due.

Classroom Activities   Revision workshop. Final exam.

Week One

Reading Assignment — Ch. 1, Writing Processes. Ch. 2, Reading Processes. Ch. 4, Recalling an Experience.

Writing Assignment — Ch. 4, Recalling an Experience.

Classroom Activities — Letter about the student's understanding of writing in his or her major. Drafting of diagnostic essay describing a controversy or critical issue in student's field of inquiry or interest.

Week Two

Reading Assignment — Ch. 21, Strategies for Designing Your Document. Ch. 5, Observing a Scene. Ch. 16, Strategies for Generating Ideas.

Writing Assignment — Ch. 5, Observing a Scene.

Classroom Activities — Peer evaluation training workshop. Peer evaluation of Recalling an Experience essay.

Week Three

Reading Assignment — Ch. 6, Interviewing a Subject. Ch. 30, Finding Sources in the Library, on the Internet, and in the Field. Ch. 17, Strategies for Stating a Thesis and Planning (emphasis on Stating and Using a Thesis).

Writing Assignment — Ch. 6, Interviewing a Subject.

Classroom Activities — Revision of diagnostic essay, with focus on stating and developing a thesis. Exercises on interviewing (starting on p. 122 of this manual). Peer evaluation of Observing a Scene essay.

Week Four

Reading Assignment — Ch. 2, Reading Processes (review). Ch. 7, Comparing and Contrasting. Ch. 30, Finding Sources in the Library, on the Internet, and in the Field. Ch. 34, Documenting Sources.

Writing Assignment — Ch. 7, Comparing and Contrasting, with focus on student's field of interest.

Classroom Activities — Find and analyze readings from the student's field of interest. Exercises on documenting sources using documentation style of student's discipline. Peer evaluation of Interviewing a Subject essay. Conferences about reading skills and writing-in-process.

Week Five

Reading Assignment — Ch. 3, Critical Thinking Processes. Ch. 31, Evaluating Sources. Ch. 32, Integrating Sources.

Classroom Activities — Exercises on summarizing and abstracting. Exercises on integrating sources using style of student's discipline.

Week Six

Reading Assignment — Ch. 15, Writing for Assessment.

Classroom Activities — Peer evaluation of Comparing and Contrasting essay. Timed essay exam on readings from *The Bedford Guide*.

Week Seven

Reading Assignment	Ch. 19, Strategies for Developing (with emphasis on Defining).
Writing Assignment	Drafting of essay defining key words in student's field of interest.
Classroom Activities	Exercises in extended definitions. Drafting of extended definitions. Midterm evaluation conferences.

Week Eight

Reading Assignment	Ch. 8, Explaining Causes and Effects.
Writing Assignment	Ch. 8, Explaining Causes and Effects, using a topic from student's field of interest.
Classroom Activities	Causal analysis exercises. Peer evaluation of Definition essay.

Week Nine

Reading Assignment	Ch. 9, Taking a Stand. Ch. 10, Proposing a Solution. Ch. 20, Strategies for Revising and Editing.
Writing Assignment	Ch. 10, Proposing a Solution.
Classroom Activities	Peer evaluation of Causes and Effects essay. Revising of works-in-process.

Week Ten

Reading Assignment	Ch. 12, Supporting a Position with Sources.
Writing Assignment	Ch. 12, Supporting a Position with Sources.
Classroom Activities	Peer evaluation of Proposing a Solution essay. Select cluster of readings in student's field.

Week Eleven

Reading Assignment	Ch. 11, Evaluating. Ch. 22, Strategies for Understanding Visual Representations.
Writing Assignment	Drafting of essay evaluating an image.
Classroom Activities	Analysis of image. Peer evaluation of Supporting a Position with Sources essay. Peer evaluation of essay evaluating an image.

Week Twelve

Classroom Activities	Portfolio revision and editing workshops. Final exam or portfolio deadline.

Instructor   Rita Hooks

Course   Composition I, Wed. 5:30 P.M.–8:30 P.M.

Course Description   This course was designed to develop composition skills. It emphasizes the development of the multiparagraph essay and includes practice in the selection, restriction, organization, and development of topics. It also offers the student opportunities to improve abilities with sentence structure, diction, and mechanics. Selected writing samples are examined as models of form and as sources of ideas for the student's own writing.

Required Texts

X. J. Kennedy, Dorothy M. Kennedy, and Marcia F. Muth, *The Bedford Guide for College Writers*, 8th ed.

A recent, college-level dictionary, such as *The American Heritage Dictionary*

Course Requirements

All assigned readings in *The Bedford Guide*

All assigned writings:

Diagnostic essay

In-class outlines (3)

In-class rough drafts (3)

Out-of-class formal essays (3)

Forty-five-minute timed writings (3)

Required departmental writing

Other in-class assignments

Grammar exercises (homework from *A Writer's Handbook*). You may choose to do additional grammar exercises on *The Bedford Guide* Web site at <bedfordstmartins .com/bedguide>.

Attendance   Because the success of each student in this workshop-style course depends on in-class writings, tests, discussions, and conferences with the instructor, attendance is mandatory. A student will be dropped after two unexcused absences or three late arrivals with a grade of "W." The last day to withdraw and receive a grade of "W" is Saturday, March 7.

Grading   The final grade will reflect the student's success after completing all of the course requirements.

Calendar

Week 1   Introduction to course
Diagnostic essay
Ch. 16, Strategies for Generating Ideas
Brainstorming, freewriting

Week 2   Ch. 4, Recalling an Experience
Narrative essay
Conferences

Week 3	Ch. 17, Strategies for Stating a Thesis and Planning
	Narrative essay revision (due at end of class)
Week 4	Ch. 6, Interviewing a Subject
	Group interviews
	Collaborative essay rough draft
Week 5	Collaborative essay (finished in class)
	Ch. 7, Comparing and Contrasting
	Formal topic outline
	Comparing and Contrasting essay outline and rough draft (in class)
	Sentence fragments
	Exercises 1–1 and 1–2 due
Week 6	Comparing and Contrasting essay rough draft due
	Ch. 20, Strategies for Revising and Editing
	Peer analyses
	Comma splices and fused sentences
	Exercises 2–1 and 2–2 due
	General rules for written assignments (handout)
	Criteria for evaluating essays (handout)
Week 7	Comparing and Contrasting essay due
	Forty-five-minute timed writing I
	Commas and semicolons
	Exercises 21–1, 21–2, 21–3, 21–4, 21–5, and 22–1 due
Week 8	Ch. 8, Explaining Causes and Effects
	Formal sentence outline
	Causes and Effects outline and rough draft (in class)
	Misplaced and dangling modifiers
	Exercises 10–1 and 10–2 due
	Conferences
Week 9	Causes and Effects essay due
	Ch. 5, Observing a Scene
	Paragraphs on photographs (in class)
	Parallel structure
	Exercise 13–1 due
Week 10	Spring break
Week 11	Ch. 15, Writing for Assessment
	Ch. 22, Strategies for Understanding Visual Representations
	Forty-five-minute timed writing II
	Incomplete sentences
	Exercises 11–1 and 11–2 due
Week 12	Ch. 9, Taking a Stand
	Topic for persuasive argument (due at end of class)
	Required departmental writing
	Refutation (in-class assignment)
	Mixed constructions and faulty predication
	Exercise 12–1 due

Week 13   Ch. 10, Proposing a Solution
               Thesis statement and opponent's strongest argument (due at end of class)
               Persuasive argument outline and rough draft (in class)
               Conferences

Week 14   Persuasive argument rough draft due
               Ch. 11, Evaluating
               Group evaluations
               Ch. 13, Responding to Literature

Week 15   Persuasive argument due
               Final exam
               Self-evaluation essay

CALENDAR SYLLABUS (excerpt)

Instructor David Hartman
Course Composition I, computer-assisted classroom

JANUARY

Sunday	Monday	Tuesday	Wednesday	Thursday	Friday	Saturday
		1	2	3	4	5
6	7 General course introduction.	8	9 **Diagnostic Timed Writing**	10	11 Freewriting and Brainstorming. READ Ch. 16.	12
13	14 Audience and Purpose. READ Chs. 1 and 2.	15	16 Paragraphs. READ Ch. 18.	17	18 Group orientation.	19
20	21 **MLK Day No Class**	22	23 Recalling an Experience. READ Ch. 4. Five-min. journal response. Questions to Start You Thinking, p. 59.	24	25 Recalling an Experience. READ Ch. 4. Five-min. journal response. Questions to Start You Thinking, p. 59.	26
27	28 Observing a Scene. READ Ch. 5. Five-min. journal response. Questions to Start You Thinking, p. 75.	29	30 Group response. Peer evaluation training. Recalling an Experience draft due.	31 Group response: Revision. READ Ch. 20.		

INTRODUCTORY SYLLABUS

Instructor   David Galaher

Course   Composition I

Required Textbooks

The Bedford Guide for College Writers, 8th ed.

Norton Anthology of Short Fiction

Attendance

ENG 102 is a writing, reading, and discussion course. Consequently, much of the course's value to the student will come from his or her interaction with both other students and the instructor. Students who are not in class will not be able to live up to their responsibilities to either themselves or to the rest of the class. Therefore, regular attendance is expected.

Grading

The student's grades in ENG 102 will be based primarily on the written work handed in. As the course progresses, we might also have a few short quizzes that, along with class participation, might contribute to the final grade. All papers will be graded according to divisional standards (attached) for expository writing. Students with perfect attendance will earn the right to an A grade, which might be used to replace the lowest grade in the course.

Goals

The specific goals and objectives for the course as well as the criteria for A, B, and C papers will be taken up during the first two weeks of the course. Once we have discussed the requirements of the course and defined the requirements for each letter grade, I will print out a second page to the syllabus.

Assignments

All written work will follow the General Rules for Themes guidelines. You must turn in all written work on time to receive full credit. Assignments may be turned in ahead of time, however. Get to know someone in class to contact about assignments and class work missed if you have to be absent from class. All out-of-class papers must be completed on a word processor or typed.

Conferences

My office number is _____. On my office door you will find my office hours posted. Please feel free to come by and discuss problems with your writing. My phone number is _____.

CHAPTER 2

Creating a Writing Community

One axiom of writing-as-process pedagogy is that writers learn from other writers. A writing community provides an accessible audience for the individual writer and can give an immediate response. As members of the community, students share prewriting and drafting strategies, advise one another about parts or the whole of a work, and write with one another in mind. A writing community collaborates so that each member can prosper.

Some theorists describe students as novices and initiates in an "interpretive community" (the phrase is borrowed from Stanley Fish's discussion of reader-response theory). Although members of the community share certain assumptions and conventions of thought and style, the novice does not yet know how to think within that community and might feel intimidated by the language the members share. The initiate, however, has learned the "secrets" of the community and responds to tasks appropriately, even if generally. Students who are still novices will say that they don't know "how to write," because they do not yet know the conventions of academic writing. Initiating students into the writing community in your course will give them a sense of belonging — and more confidence — in the larger academic community as well.

Another reason that writing-as-process focuses on the "community of writers" is to encourage the development of critical thinking and writing. Paulo Freire, the Brazilian educator and literacy activist, describes the best classroom as one in which teachers and students — "master-learners" and "learners" — investigate material together; generate themes for reflection, discussion, and action; and collaborate in naming what they learn. Freire believes that collaboration enables individuals to move from naive to critical consciousness. Freire's theory assumes a fundamental relationship between higher-order thinking and collaborative learning in a writing community.

Think of yourself as part of the writing community in your class. Let your students know what type of writing you do outside the classroom, and participate in freewriting exercises and in-class essay assignments. Your participation will show students that the writing process is similar for writers at all levels and that you take the process seriously. It's important for students to see your responses to the process as well. They will be heartened to find that even you are sometimes frustrated or disappointed with your work, and your enthusiasm about what you discover through your writing will inspire them.

This chapter discusses other strategies you can use to foster your students' writing community: starting a conversation about students' writing on the first day of class, using peer-response activities and student conferences throughout the course, and seeking out or establishing forums in which students can publish their writing from the course.

STARTING A CONVERSATION ABOUT WRITING

If you use an icebreaker on the first day of class, take this early opportunity to ask students about the strategies they use to learn names: note taking, associating a name with a fact or some article of clothing, and so on. This will encourage students right away to begin thinking reflectively about their thinking and learning processes.

Here's an Idea . . .

As an icebreaker, ask students to pair off with a classmate they don't know. Have them introduce themselves and tell each other three facts about themselves, one of which is a lie. Ask students to decide which fact is their partner's lie. Often, students guess wrong because their partner will reveal unusual, stranger-than-fiction facts.

Comment on their skills, and put them in the context of the writing process. Ask students which stages of the process they think would require these skills.

Use Reflective Writing and Journals

It's important to build into your course ways for students to talk frequently about their writing. While you will most likely talk about students' writing in class, you should also require them to write reflectively about their writing processes and to use journals as a resource for their writing.

Students can practice reflective writing in their journals, in class exercises, or in homework assignments. To get them started, ask them to talk or freewrite about what writing is like for them. Give them some metaphors that describe what writing is to different people ("My addiction and I need a daily fix"; "A lot like going to the dentist, not always pleasant but certainly necessary"; "Unwinding when I'm too uptight"). Of course, some students might be stymied by the idea of a metaphor, so prompt them with questions such as "Is writing something you enjoy or fear?" or "How does it make you feel?" This activity is also a safe way for students to express writing anxiety, and students will admire particularly clever or original metaphors.

Many students will begin the course with a great deal of anxiety about writing. One way to relax them during the first week is to read them student writing from the past semester. You might want to read the reflective writing that former students have written as the last assignment for the course because it focuses on students as writers. Reading excerpts of essays by students who completed the course successfully to those who are just beginning the course will establish a common ground and a sense of community.

Students might need additional encouragement to use journals as a tool. Many have become jaded with journal writing in high school. Redefine a journal as a daybook or notebook, as Donald M. Murray suggests, and share with students Murray's adherence to the ancients' advice *nulla dies sine linea,* "never a day without a line." They should understand the importance of recording their ideas and impressions daily — not just what happens, but how they respond to what happens. Encourage students also to write about their experience of writing, their struggles with the assignments, and anything else that pertains to the course. You might want to require them to write for at least fifteen minutes daily, responding to something you bring to read to them or using the questions that follow the readings in the text. This will help students learn to read more critically and prepare them for class discussions. For more about using journals in your course, see pages 206–07 of this manual.

Here's an Idea . . .

Read this excerpt aloud on the first day of class, and then ask students to respond to the question that the writer poses. Tell students that the writer is a young man, Terry Schramm, who wrote a case study of himself as a student in Peter Elbow's class. It was the last assignment of a Composition I course, and in one part he asks,

> What is a writer? Is it anyone who puts a pen to paper, or is it something more? Is a poet a writer? I think that a writer is someone who puts part of himself into the words he or she writes. I am an infrequent writer, but in my second stage of writing (college) I am more confident in my abilities. I know now that with time and many revisions, I can put something down on paper in a semi-coherent manner. I can't say that I am looking forward to it with glee, but at least I feel ready and prepared for the next course.

This testimonial offers students affirmation of the common ground they now share as members of a community of writers. It may also help to alleviate anxiety.

You might also want to keep a journal for yourself of your responses to what happens in class each day — what goes well and what flops, problem assignments and problem students, what you intend to do differently next time, and ideas for additional activities and assignments.

Encourage Responses

One of the most important tools for building community in your classroom is discussion. Discussion not only helps bring fuzzy thinking into focus by encouraging students to articulate their ideas, but it also shows students how new ideas emerge when they contribute their voices to a discussion.

Even as an undergraduate, you were probably aware that some students didn't read the assignment, some read it but weren't confident they understood it, and some were more than prepared for discussion. Encourage all students to come to class prepared for discussion by giving each student some responsibility for the reading. Divide the class into groups of four and assign each group a specific question about the reading that they should be prepared to discuss. Allow groups to confer during the first five minutes of class; then ask for their responses.

To begin a discussion, ask a broad question and wait. If no one responds, restate the question, perhaps narrowing it to give a clue. Many of the questions that follow the readings in the students' textbooks use this pattern. They ask about an aspect of the reading and then narrow it using more specific detail. Avoid beginning with "Can anyone tell me . . . ?" or "Does anyone know . . . ?" These kinds of questions tend to discourage students from participating because they are afraid of not knowing or looking stupid. If students still seem reluctant to respond, ask them to freewrite for five minutes about the question you've posed.

For variety, ask students to bring to class a question they have about what they've read or about how the reading connects to the writing assignment. Collect the questions at the beginning of class, sort them quickly, and use them to shape your discussion.

Here's an Idea . . .

Write each student's name on an index card. Following each question you ask in class discussion, draw a card. The student whose name you've drawn must respond to the question. Students read assignments more carefully and are more attentive in class when they realize they will be randomly selected to respond in class discussion. Variation: If a student can't answer the question, he or she may hand it off to another student of his or her choosing.

Resist the temptation to answer the questions yourself. Allow students to arrive at their own answers.

As often as possible, invite students to take responsibility for leading the class discussion. Ask two students to set up a point-counterpoint response to the reading. Or have three students divide an essay and take responsibility for asking the class one question about readers' responses and one question focused on the writing in each third of the essay. For more advice about how to encourage student participation, see the Quick Start activities in the Instructor's Annotated Edition of *The Bedford Guide*.

Respect Silence

What if you ask a question and no one responds? Wait. Many new teachers, unnerved by silence, jump in too quickly. This shows students that they really don't have to think about the question — the instructor will do the work for them. You might have posed a question that requires some complex thinking, recall, or review. Give students time. Thirty seconds can seem like an eternity when silence follows a question, but practice waiting at least that long.

Many students are also unnerved by silence. Someone will jump in eventually, if only to fill that silence. Be careful, however, that he or she does not become the class voice: "As long as Jen says something, we're off the hook." Open the discussion by asking other students to respond to the student's comment before you do. Often the student who speaks first will contribute the easy or obvious answer that needs elaboration. Direct some follow-up questions to the student who answered, but be sure to direct questions to the rest of the class as well.

Here's an Idea . . .

Pass out 4-by-6 index cards. Have each student write a question about the reading assignment on a card. Then collect and redistribute the cards. Ask each student to be responsible for discussing the question on the card he or she received. Give students ten minutes to work on an answer or to locate information in the text. This exercise pressures students to read carefully and think about what they have read. Remind them that they may not always be able to answer the question on the card they received. In fact, some questions have no simple answer. Emphasize that they must rely on the group to help them. To make this exercise less intimidating, you may want to ask pairs of students to work together.

Some students are naturally talkative; others sit in silence. You might need to teach students who are not active in the classroom how to participate. In their first conferences, quiet students often say they just never have talked in class. Tell them that you expect them to participate and that there are many ways they can do so. Be supportive of quiet students but try to pull them into discussion. Assigning collaborative activities for small groups might help. To begin discussion of a reading, assign questions to groups of students and ask them to present their answer to the class. Or ask each student to prepare either a question about the reading or a comment. When one student repeats what someone else has said, follow up with "OK, so you agree with Andrea?" This comment establishes that the second student's contribution is equally valuable. It also confirms that students share perceptions or beliefs and helps build the writing community.

Provide Confirmation

Always acknowledge a student who contributes to the discussion. Reinforcement can range from a nod to "Good" to "Thank you" to a restatement ("You think Baker's putting you on?") to a follow-up question ("Do you agree or disagree with Gwyn that this essay is funny?"). If this kind of interaction doesn't seem natural to you, then practice it. An instructor has the responsibility to draw students out: e + ducere, "to lead out of," is the root of education.

Most class discussion is intended to establish a range of opinion or evaluation as well as to help students negotiate consensus about issues in the reading or writing process. Most of the time you aren't looking for a "right" answer, but students often think you are because they have been socialized to regard the teacher as the authority. Use reinforcement to show students that you want to hear what they have to say. And when you are looking for a particular answer, be sure to tell your students.

PEER RESPONSE

All writers need a number of critical readers, and student writers are no exception. While your insight as an expert reader will be essential to students' progress, peer editors can also provide valuable criticism. Most students find their peers' remarks especially helpful and often more encouraging than an instructor's. You might doubt the usefulness of an inexperienced writer's advice. Don't. With a little guidance, peer editors quickly become irreplaceable readers. No one understands the challenges of a writing assignment the way a fellow student writer struggling with the same assignment does. For more about using peer editing, contact your writing center director; often he or she trains writing assistants to respond to student writing and might have additional advice for you to pass along to your students. At the end of this chapter you will find a handout to train students to take charge of their peer group critiques and use them effectively.

Your time will be well spent if you take some time to train your students to respond effectively before they begin peer editing. Explain that as readers they must give useful feedback and as writers they must actively seek the information they need to improve their drafts. Show them the hierarchy of revision. Also, remind them to state first what works well in a piece of writing and then to comment on weaknesses in the following order:

1. unclear meaning (general)
2. unclear presentation of information

3. sentences that don't work

4. words that are misused or that could be more accurate

One School's Example

Instructors at Dodge City Community College have increased the success of peer-response sessions by expanding them using an activity developed by Ralph Voss of the University of Alabama. Although the activity requires an additional class period for each writing assignment, instructors find it worth the time.

At the beginning of the semester, students draw numbers to determine which of the six required essay assignments they will present to the class. Three or four students present their essays for the same assignment. On the appointed day, student writers bring copies of their typed rough drafts for each member of the class and the instructor. Once the drafts are distributed, one writer reads his or her work aloud while the other students follow along on their copies. Each student must tell the writer one thing that works well in the essay and one thing that still needs attention. If a writer is misunderstood, he or she is probably not stating the issue clearly. The writing alone must communicate the student's ideas.

At first, some students are unsure of how to respond to a student writer's draft. Instructors should explain that peer responses might be as simple as identifying a word or phrase that the reader especially liked or didn't understand, but the comment must be specific. Generalizations such as "I liked the essay" won't do. Beginning comments usually focus on spelling and punctuation errors or other traditional concerns. But students quickly learn to move to deeper matters, such as clarity, content, and structure. Listening to the strengths and weaknesses identified by better writers helps those students with less revision experience move beyond superficial observations.

The advantages of these presentations are twofold: The papers that student writers present are often the strongest essays in their portfolios, and the public forum quickly teaches students how to give constructive critical comments.

At the beginning of the next class, students return the presenters' drafts to each of presenters, marked with more extensive comments than those the student offered in the workshop. The presenters can then spend the class period going through the responses and revising their drafts. At this point, they are free to ask for clarification of any peer reader's remarks. The other students work in groups of three or four to respond to one another's drafts. Taking turns, each student assumes the role of writer, providing drafts of his or her essay for each group member; the other group members take the role of reader. Conversation is important, because one group member's remarks may lead to questions or further comments from others. In this way, both readers and writers learn.

Resources in **The Bedford Guide**

The textbook includes several features to support peer editing and group learning in your classroom. See the Instructor's Annotated Edition of *The Bedford Guide* for Quick Start suggestions to use as collaborative classroom activities. These will help your students feel more comfortable working with one another and help to build a sense of community.

For further peer editing and group learning guidelines, refer students to the For Peer Response and For Group Learning activities throughout *A Writer's Guide*.

For Peer Response   These checklists guide students working on drafts with partners or in groups by providing specific questions to ask of their peers' writing. Some instructors copy the checklists and have peer editors attach their responses to each draft they read. In conferences, the instructor can then see how writers are using their peers' comments, whether they are misunderstanding or disregarding criticism or praise. This feedback also allows instructors to evaluate how the peer-response system is working in their courses.

In these activities, the authors mix "criteria-based responses," the basis that instructors use to evaluate the writing, with "reader-response descriptions," the reactions and intuitions that peers have to a piece of writing. To become effective peer editors, students need a mix of prompts. Long before peer editors can identify a pattern of organization or word choice and evaluate that pattern, they can tell whether the parts of a draft feel connected and whether certain words are "just right" or "confusing." Ask students to suggest questions to add to the peer-response checklists, and encourage them to invent both criteria-based and reader-response questions. You might also want to suggest that students use the revision checklists throughout the book for additional peer-editing questions.

When you prepare students to begin working in small groups responding to one another's drafts, raise their awareness of the impact of their remarks in peer-group critiques. Ask them to write about positive and negative experiences that have influenced their writing and to share them with the class. Insist that students be both honest and kind with one another. Encourage them to identify what works well in their peers' writing, however small, in addition to what needs more attention. As your students talk in their groups, circulate and work with them, encouraging them to make specific, constructive comments. Sit with each group for a few minutes, but don't let your visit be intrusive: Don't dominate the discussion. Gently remind students to stay on track with their discussion.

For Group Learning   These activities not only help to establish a sense of community in your course but also encourage active learning and, as a result, stronger critical thinking and writing skills. If you plan to grade collaborative assignments, remember that not all students work willingly in groups. Highly competitive students often resist collaborative projects and might challenge a "group grade." Explain to those students that teamwork and collective projects are very much a part of many professions; encourage them to negotiate roles and responsibilities with other group members. If you are uncomfortable giving a group grade, ask each student to fill out an assessment of other members in his or her group and then average these points into each student's project grade.

Ancillaries to The Bedford Guide

In addition to the features in the textbook, several ancillaries also support peer editing and collaborative learning.

Companion Web site.   The Web site for *The Bedford Guide*, at <bedfordstmartins.com/bedguide>, includes peer response worksheets for all the types of writing covered in Part Two of the text. The Web site also includes other resources, such as "Ask the Draft Doctor," to help students improve their writing whether they are working independently or in a peer group.

PeerSpace.   This premium resource, available on *The Bedford Guide* Web site, includes confidence-building activities that teach best practices for peer review. It offers models, exercises, assignments, and an interactive simulation game.

Comment.   This peer-review software, also available through *The Bedford Guide* Web site, lets students share and comment on their writing. Instructors can create comments that link directly to specific passages in *The Bedford Guide e-Book*. (For more information on the e-book and other electronic resources for *The Bedford Guide,* see pp. 74–76.)

STUDENT CONFERENCES

Conferences give students the chance for a one-on-one conversation about writing, focusing on their individual concerns as writers. We encourage you to experiment with a range of individualized instruction techniques during the semester and develop a method that works best for you and your students. Often different classes and groups of students require different conferencing strategies. At times, a longer meeting in your office is necessary, but don't underestimate the value of two-minute in-class conferences while students are working in groups. Asking writers for an immediate response to "What's working and what isn't?" is an effective way to focus their revision process.

Initial Conferences

Meet with each student for twenty minutes sometime during the first month to talk about his or her perceptions of the general strengths and weaknesses of his or her writing. Have on hand the work the student has done so far: the diagnostic essay, reflective writing, in-class freewriting exercises, or the first formally submitted essay. Ask students to decide the direction and focus of the conference by preparing questions or concerns they would like to discuss with you. Prepare some of your own questions that will require students to reflect instead of answering yes or no. In their twelve years of schooling, what have students learned about their writing strategies? Let them talk while you ask questions and take notes. You might want to combine your notes from student conferences with your journal in a new notebook each semester.

The goals of the first conference are

- to discuss what students have observed about their own writing processes
- to discover whether you are providing specific, clear, helpful, and fair descriptions of their writing in your written responses
- to find out how they see their work as peer editors and how they're using peer evaluation
- to learn what you can do to make them more comfortable or confident in the course
- to establish or strengthen rapport with them

Don't be surprised if some students seem nervous or if some want to stay longer than planned. Remember that this might be their first and only experience working one-on-one with a college teacher. Encourage them to talk to you about their work-in-progress; tell them you'd rather talk with them about their work while they're stuck than after they've nearly given up because they've gotten stuck.

Midterm Conferences

Schedule midterm conferences to review students' progress to date and to talk about their writing behaviors and attitudes. One way to prepare is to ask students to write a self-assessment describing what they've learned so far and what they hope to accomplish by the end of the semester. Ask them to turn in their assessments before they meet with you so that you have a chance to read them and decide on a focus for the conferences. You'll find a sample self-assessment questionnaire on page 90 of this manual.

In the conferences, give students an evaluation of their overall course work as well as specific comments on pieces of writing. Review students' goals for the remainder of the term and discuss topics or strategies for writers to develop. If you have a revision policy, discuss the decisions students have made about what and how to revise. A checklist of student progress and work is particularly useful to have at this conference.

Short Conferences

Try to schedule shorter conferences throughout the semester. Although conferencing takes time, it is an invaluable teaching strategy in a composition course. Students learn about the writing process from your responses to their writing — something a simple red letter at the top of a page does not accomplish. Conferencing is the most effective tool for elaborating or clarifying the comments you make on papers or in class. Having conferences with students while they are drafting an assignment is particularly helpful. Ask them to bring their drafts to the conference and choose the thesis or one paragraph to read with you. Then comment on what you see the student doing and ask what he or she plans to do; this will help the student to identify the purpose and method informing the draft and to generate additional, related ideas.

During class periods when students are freewriting, brainstorming, drafting, revising, or working in small groups, take the opportunity to hold quick mini-conferences with individual students. Three to five minutes is enough time for writers to check out a topic, a writing strategy, or a revision problem with you. Some writers will want and be able to work independently; others will want more frequent feedback and advice from you. The opportunity to meet with you during class will give these students the extra help they need. You might also want to designate office hours on particular days during the semester for mini-conferences.

Written Conferences

One instructor we know confers with her students in writing. She lays the groundwork by asking students to attach a preconference worksheet to the drafts they submit to her. On the worksheet, students respond to the following questions:

1. What problems did you have when planning or writing?
2. What works best in the paper?
3. What needs attention and revision?
4. What questions do you have for me about your paper?

She then comments on the students' responses to the questions and gives her own reading of the paper, with specific suggestions for revising. Written conferences can be conducted via e-mail if you wish.

PUBLISHING STUDENT WRITING

Why should you encourage and assist students to publish their writing? Because some of the benefits that student writers experience include increased competency in problem solving, in evaluating writing, in editing as advising, and in working collaboratively. Writers establish community and exchange ideas by publishing their work. If in your academic career you had the exhilaration of having your work published, you understand the importance of being heard and you appreciate how much can be learned by participating in a conversation among colleagues. Students feel the same sense of accomplishment when their work is approved and esteemed by others.

Students, like the most seasoned author, get excited whenever they see their names in print. Students who have poor images of themselves as writers, however, will dread the thought of submitting their work. These students will be jolted to revise those images when their writing is selected for publication. We have observed extreme timidity in the finest writers. Don't be afraid to nudge your students a bit. Think about what kept you from submitting work and try to anticipate those fears and that hesitation in your writers.

Students who understand that they must submit a piece for publication as part of the course requirements will look at their work with a more critical eye. When they focus on writing as a means of communicating with an audience larger than their teacher and classmates, they will understand why it's important to consider purpose and style. As they repeatedly revise a draft to bring it to publication standards, they will gain a deeper appreciation for the hard work and persistence required for good writing. Students who didn't previously believe in the importance of rewriting are often the ones who spontaneously revise a draft many times to bring it to publication quality. In this way the possibility of publication will often inspire students to exceed the expectations of a mandatory first-year writing course.

What resources can you use to help writers publish their work? Most immediately, you can make publication a group project. Locally and regionally, you can work with colleagues to initiate or continue a publication of expository student writing. Nationally, you can help students investigate opportunities for publication in magazines, newspapers, journals, and online magazines. One caution: You need to do more than recommend that "you try to get this published."

Note: The editors of *The Bedford Guide* are always looking for good student papers to include in the book. Please send promising papers — with the students' contact information so that we can request permission — to: *Bedford Guide* Essay Search, Bedford/St. Martin's, 75 Arlington Street, 8th Floor, Boston, MA 02116.

Classroom and Campus Publication

Classroom publication is possible with a shoestring budget. Take advantage of your campus's computer and printing services. Have students decide on the criteria for publication and evaluate the writing themselves.

Will the publication be a miscellany of student writing, or should the publication be juried in some way? If a miscellany, each student should submit at least one piece of writing. This requirement makes each writer review and assess all of his or her writing to decide what to submit, much like a portfolio. If the publication is juried, the students should come to consensus about the kinds of writing, features of writing, topics, formats, editorial policy, selection of jurors, and procedures for the selection and editing of writings.

Will the publication be a class activity, a volunteer activity, or an activity of the instructor with secretarial support? If this is a volunteer activity, you need to consider whether to give extra credit or perhaps to permit publishing activity to substitute for some other course assignment. If this is a class activity and everyone has a specific role, you need to think about how to weight the class-participation aspect of your grade and how to evaluate the performance of the members of the publishing community.

Regardless, we recommend that you not agree to take full responsibility. This is the kind of hands-on learning that students need.

Encouraging students to begin or to participate in an established campus publication of student writing is another way to elicit, nurture, and improve student writing. An academic institution should create opportunities for students to publish and should celebrate quality writing and successful student writers. Campus publications enhance the academic culture at your institution by showing that writing is valued by the institution, across the curriculum, and throughout professional careers.

Of course, most colleges and universities have student publications such as the newspaper, the literary magazine, and the yearbook, but we're talking about something more: a collection of student expository writing that has been juried by writing specialists, that carries a bona fide royalty or prize, that is published for use in composition classes on campus, and that becomes so strong a campus tradition that it's listed among achievements and publications when a student first drafts a résumé.

If your school doesn't already have one, you won't be able to initiate such a publication by yourself. You will need to work with your colleagues to launch it, and your institution will have to provide support — from outright funding to secretarial assistance to desktop publishing facilities to access to printing services. If you want to recommend such a campus publication, anticipate and be ready to answer your colleague's questions. Be prepared to defend your reasons why a journal of expository student writing is necessary when some textbooks include student writers. Point out to your colleagues that as professional writers, they understand how reading the work of their peers spurs them as writers. When student writers judge their writing only against professional models, they can easily conclude, "I can't reach that far." When they set their writing against the published writing of their peers, however, the reaching seems more possible.

If your colleagues are still hesitant, mention that first-year writers might connect more immediately with student models because of references to local settings and events. Cite the positive effects of being able to invite those published writers into your class to talk about their own writing and rewriting processes that led to the published essays. (Students are always encouraged by the opportunity to ask published writers how they "got it," how they started, what made them persist, and so on.)

Once the publication has been approved, ask interested faculty members to serve as the first "publishing board," working through the first publication. That board needs to decide (1) the purpose of the publication (Will instructors use it in their classes and, if so, as a required or recommended text? Who should receive teaching and complimentary copies? How large a printing will be needed?), (2) what writers are eligible to submit material (Should they be only students in a specific course, or could they be members of the first-year class who write in any of their courses?), and (3) what funding must be negotiated and how the publication should be distributed.

Don't overlook the possibility that your department can fund the publication of a limited number of copies. If you can garner institutional funding or even grants, you might be able to save money with private printing companies. Research the policies of your campus in your earliest discussions about publication. Finally, check with your campus bookstore management about their policies on selling the publication.

Distribution might be tied to funding decisions. Regardless, be sure to distribute the publication to members of the campus community who support your endeavors: academic officers such as deans of instruction, vice presidents of academic affairs, members of writing-across-the-curriculum programs, the writing center, the library (copies both for browsing and for the archives), and so on. The public relations office of your institution might include a story or notice in the alumni magazine.

With the nuts and bolts of your publication in place, you should decide whether apparatus (headnotes, questions, and so on) is needed. This apparatus might discuss the writer's process in inventing, shaping, and drafting the piece published. Study questions that focus on reader response and rhetorical analysis are always useful. You can perhaps learn from the writer which rhetorical effects were the result of inspiration and which resulted from perspiration.

Regional and National Publication

Many regional and state essay contests send out calls for manuscripts to English departments. Ask the director of your writing program to post announcements about writing competitions, and have these announcements routinely sent to all campus media for news briefs or public-service announcements. Arrange to include those announcements in the school newspaper or on the school Web site or online newsletter.

Ask students to research online magazines and journals and report back to class with a list of Web addresses. A good place to start is the Arts & Letters Daily (<www.aldaily.com>), which lists hundreds of links to print and online journals, magazines, and newspapers. Advise your students to pay close attention to submission guidelines; they vary for each publication.

Students don't have to wait for journals or magazines to publish their work. They can publish on their own Web page, which many schools will sponsor. Once students learn HTML, the language of the Web, they can be as creative and personal as they want, using images, sounds, and links to their favorite sites.

Don't overlook the letters-to-the-editor section of the college or city newspaper. Begin by discussing in class several letters to the editor and the articles or events on which they are based. Then get students writing and peer-editing a letter on a current event. You might be surprised at how many students actually have their work published.

Once students know about regional and publisher-sponsored competitions and opportunities for publication, encourage them to submit manuscripts. Many of our colleagues who emphasize sending works out for publication give extra credit for published work. Ultimately, though, publication is its own reward.

RESPONSIBILITIES IN THE WRITING WORKSHOP

Responsibilities of the Reader

Read through the whole draft before commenting.

Offer advice that you would find helpful.

Be honest, but be tactful.

Tell the writer what you like about the text as well as problems you have with pieces.

Be specific. Point out in the text examples of what you say.

Suggest possible ways to make the text better, but don't tell the writer what to do.

Help the writer see different ways of looking at the writing.

Remember that you are not responsible for fixing the text; you are offering a reader's view.

Listen to the writer without interrupting.

Let each group member speak; engage in a conversation about the text.

Responsibilities of the Writer

Provide each member of the group a copy of your draft.

Take charge of your workshop. Ask questions about your draft, and get the information you need for revision.

Remember that group members are talking about the writing, not about you.

Appreciate your group's efforts to help you improve your text.

Don't argue or explain. Listen and ask questions.

Ask for specific examples of readers' comments. Have them show you in the text.

Repeat back to the reader what you've heard; make sure you understand the comment.

Take notes on your draft for later reference.

Remember, this is YOUR writing. You are not obligated to make any suggested changes. However, do consider reader's comments carefully.

CHAPTER 3

Teaching Critical Thinking and Writing

In first-year composition, you will meet students with a wide range of skills. Some will be more than enthusiastic and ready for the tasks that you set and that *The Bedford Guide* encourages. Others might be enthusiastic to work with you but might become uneasy as they grapple with discussion and writing tasks. Some might be highly anxious about the course because they fear that they cannot think through and write about the issues presented. Others might feel out of place because they see their peers responding more quickly and easily to the writing prompts. Take heart from the fact that writing is, as Janet Emig first named it, a mode of thinking. Remind students that through the process of writing they all will become more critical thinkers regardless of where they begin. Trust that students have the ability to think critically if we provide them with a foundation and a context and then give them the time to practice and develop those abilities.

Critical thinking and active learning are inextricably linked. Students will develop strong critical thinking skills in an environment that both challenges and supports them. The best critical thinkers have some sense of their own worth and have experienced success in their undertakings through active learning. By focusing on writing-as-process pedagogy, collaborative learning, and peer editing, *The Bedford Guide* provides a variety of ways to incorporate active learning into your course. These strategies have grown out of what educators have learned from research in cognitive development. Understanding how theorists classify and describe the learning process will help you to identify where students are in their thinking and learning processes and to adapt your teaching to fit the individual student's needs. Accordingly, this chapter contains both an overview of three basic theories of cognitive development — with suggestions for using them to teach critical thinking and writing — and a description of resources in *The Bedford Guide* that can help your students think and write more critically.

THREE VIEWS OF COGNITIVE DEVELOPMENT

Studying theories of cognitive development can help instructors examine their teaching practices and build into their courses new ways of helping students become better writers and more critical thinkers. Three theorists who have fundamentally influenced how we think about teaching writing are Jean Piaget, William G. Perry, and Benjamin Bloom. While each describes the stages and process of learning somewhat differently, they all offer insights that can be directly applied to teaching writing as a process and to developing students' critical thinking skills.

Piaget's Four Stages

If you've studied educational or cognitive psychology, you are probably already familiar with the work of Jean Piaget, who observed that children interact with their world by organizing mental structures or thinking stages. Piaget classified four basic developmental stages that occur in an observable sequence:

- the sensorimotor stage
- the preoperational stage

- the concrete operations stage
- the formal operations stage

According to Piaget, in the sensorimotor stage (birth to age two), children create mental structures egocentrically, thinking about the world and structuring their perceptions about it in terms of its connection to the self. In the preoperational stage (age two to seven), children begin "decentering," moving away from the self and from their egocentric frame of reference. Children at this stage ask incessant questions and make up stories as they attempt to begin to understand other people's thoughts and feelings and the world around them.

During the concrete operations stage (age seven to eleven), children begin to understand their experience of the world in a more general and abstract way. Their writing tends to be linear and narrative. They can give examples but not definitions. They can list facts but find it difficult to take a perspective on them or make a generalization about them.

The movement from concrete operations to formal operations (beginning around age eleven) is a major change. Adolescents (and adults) in the formal operations stage can deal logically with the world around them, can sort out probability and improbability, and can form hypotheses and make connections between causes and effects. They can abstract from specifics and generalize to a truth. They develop problem-solving and "problem-finding" abilities. As they become increasingly aware of alternatives to their own way of structuring the world, they become less egocentric. In the early stage of formal operations, however, adolescents have difficulty separating their selves from their opinions.

The transition from concreteness to abstractness, from simplicity and absolutism to complexity and relativism, and from egocentrism to decentrism can be roughly classified as a transition from "lower-order" to "higher-order" thinking. It is higher-order thinking that we elicit, value, and reinforce in college. As formal-operational adolescents approach adulthood, they are increasingly able to separate their selves from their opinions and can reflect on those opinions. In fact, the central accomplishment of the undergraduate years might simply be that students develop the ability to construct a context in which their opinions can be the object of reflection and rethinking.

Following Piaget's earliest publication, educators assumed that individuals moved into the stage of formal operations during adolescence. They assumed that college-age students, far along in adolescence, are therefore formal thinkers who can use purely verbal, symbolic, and abstract processes to understand what they encounter in their readings and courses. Researchers in the 1970s, however, found that many first-year students are often in a transition between operating concretely and operating formally. First-year college students might reason formally in areas that particularly interest them or in which they have experience, but not in other areas. In fact, when students talk about their writing, they are quick to say that it is easier for them to write about something that interests them. This is both an obvious fact and a statement about the cognitive tasks that are easier at that point for them. In areas that don't interest them or that contradict their previous concrete structures for explaining their world, the same students might feel lost and fall back on simpler skills such as memorizing the text or narrating, listing, and cataloging rather than analyzing or synthesizing.

You are likely to find that even though students will succeed with critical writing, many of them, if given the choice, would prefer to write personal narrative and descriptive essays. Sustaining an interest in writing critically might be difficult because those students are not yet entirely comfortable with college-level demands for analysis. Such behaviors challenge you as the instructor to develop a course that provides both opportunity for personal writing and guidance in writing critically. A few highly apprehensive students prefer, however, not to write about personal experiences. They would rather write about more objective topics that do not require them to look inside themselves and reveal their thoughts and feelings. As an instructor, you will need to provide topic options for both groups of students.

Basic writers seem at best "transitional" and often operate only from the stage of concrete operations. In *Errors and Expectations: A Guide for the Teacher of Basic Writing* (New York: Oxford UP, 1982), Mina Shaughnessy discusses the critical thinking problems that are connected to patterns of error in writing, concluding that basic writers have not yet developed cognitive strategies that their peers already practice in writing. Andrea Lunsford has studied the connections of egocentrism and basic writing and has concluded in "The Content of Basic Writers' Essays" (*College Composition and Communication* 31 [October 1980]) that basic writers have difficulty decentering and are consequently less able to form abstractions and concepts crucial to analyzing and synthesizing in writing.

Transitional writers experience a discrepancy between their abilities to assimilate and to accommodate. They can assimilate, take in new information, and fit it into their present understanding of the world. They find it difficult, however, to accommodate their thinking to deal with new, even contradictory, ideas. Often they simply ignore new information. When writers are troubled by new information and feel a discrepancy, Piaget calls the reaction "disequilibrium," which can cause both discomfort and excitement. You will see this response in writers when you challenge them to analyze an idea opposed to one they cherish. When writers suddenly find a way of accommodating their thinking so that they can assimilate the information into a changed understanding of the world, "equilibration" occurs.

As writing instructors, we try to increase the likelihood that equilibration will happen. We offer support — through specific assignments and discussion, through collaborative learning, through evaluation of the writers' multiple drafts, through clear explanation of our expectations. We try to offer complex yet accessible support and to build a rich writing environment, because these moments of equilibration happen more often in a writing community in which students feel safe to expose themselves.

Piaget suggests that hands-on learning is crucial to cognitive development. In a writing course, this means frequent writing at all stages, and researchers in composition add that it also includes intervention from an expert advisor in all aspects of the process. Theoretical discussion of writing must always be anchored in actual writing practice and tied to writers' discussions about their writing. Terminology should follow, not precede, extensive experience of the process or strategy to which it is applied. Structured problem-solving class activities and writing assignments are necessary to give concrete thinkers many points of contact with what they already know. They need a firm structure to stand on while they try out the unfamiliar.

According to their cognitive readiness, students will have various expectations of the instructor and the classroom. Transitional thinkers will look to someone else to evaluate and judge their writing rather than to themselves as writers. They will expect the instructor to somehow complete their thinking and writing, often by telling them what they need to do. The more confident formal operators bring the instructor in as a consultant or as a resource in the process of generating or thinking back and re-creating the writing, and this is the point to which we try to bring all student writers. Transitional thinkers can be devastated by an instructor's criticism; the more ready writers do not as often see criticism as a violation of the self. Transitional writers responding to evaluation might conclude that they have failed, that an evaluation is unfair or idiosyncratic, or that their opinions are being judged and rejected. Transitional thinkers watch their selves through others' eyes and write so that their ideas will be validated by others. The more ready thinkers use writing as an expression of the self and as a part of their own psychological systems. You will need to think about these almost predictable responses of the transitional student when you comment on drafts and essays as well as when you evaluate writing.

Perry's Study of College-Age Students

Piaget's work did not stretch into late adolescence or early adulthood. Only recently have cognitive psychologists looked more carefully at college-age individuals. One such researcher, William G. Perry, began his career teaching English at Harvard University and eventually directed a counseling center for students with study problems. Over two decades he observed and conversed with students about their reflections on their "knowing" and coming to know. Whereas Piaget and many cognitive psychologists suggest that cognitive development is a natural and inevitable process that can be anticipated, Perry has focused on the socialization that furthers cognitive development and on the way in which the educational environment assists cognitive development. Perry has classified his observations into nine stages, or "schemes," of cognition. We can condense those nine schemes into four major stages: absolutist, dualistic, multiplistic, and relativistic.

Often college students are moving away from simple absolutist thinking into "either-or" or dualistic structures. Dualistic thinkers believe that every question has one simple answer. They believe that there is a right way and a wrong way, and that if they are assiduous in seeking out authorities, they will receive answers. Dualistic thinkers in your writing class want you to tell them exactly how to write. They are very concerned with what you want even when you make it clear that you want writers to discover what they themselves need or want to say. Dualistic thinkers are more than willing to revise to "get it right" as long as you tell them what to "fix."

Multiplistic thinkers are willing to entertain the idea that there might be uncertainty — for a while. They still think that knowledge is absolute, but they acknowledge that sometimes it takes some process of thought to arrive at the absolutes. These thinkers can talk about gray areas, but they believe that with enough discussion or research, authority figures will be able to make that grayness into a sharp contrast of black and white. Although multiplistic writers might not believe that their writing has intrinsic value, they participate in writing processes such as generating ideas because the instructor has made it clear that he or she values those behaviors. Even if unwittingly, they might be stretching as writers and thinkers. Because a composition course generates writing and thinking, both dualistic and multiplistic thinkers are changing their attitudes and writing and thinking behaviors even though they might not be aware of those changes.

With attention to students' stages of development, you will encourage and assist both dualistic and multiplistic students to develop further and become relativistic thinkers. These thinkers realize that there is no absolute knowledge or truth and that what you as the instructor think and value depends a great deal on where you stand to look at things. They realize that grayness and not being able to reach certainty are the order of the world. Some relativistic thinkers conclude that every opinion is as good as any other. Consequently, they might decide that your evaluation is "only your opinion" and challenge your grading. They might resist evaluation from you and their peers, or they might accept other opinions and work seriously to shape "reader-based prose." They might even espouse nihilism and remain unmotivated to work with you in a writing community. They might also, however, regard teachers as no longer absolute authorities but as people who know how to use cognitive strategies to make some sense of uncertainty, and they might work enthusiastically in a writing community. Relativistic writers are usually willing to work with assignments where the outcome is unclear — a situation that intimidates dualistic thinkers.

How do you assist writers in their transition from dualistic to multiplistic to relativistic thinking? First, recognize that dualistic students' classroom requirements are different from those of relativistic students. The former have a strong need for structure in assignments, tasks, and evaluation. Relativistic thinkers appreciate freedom to invent assignments, reorganize and initiate tasks, and evaluate. They appreciate a variety of class activities. Because you will have both kinds of students in your writing classroom, you need to organize a syllabus that provides structure for students who need structure and freedom for students who need freedom.

Perry believes that the educational environment assists students' development in college and that a student is socialized to grow as a critical thinker. Thus, the more we can assist students to participate in a community of writers, the more likely we will help them change as thinkers. The more students engage with peers and instructors and observe them as thinkers in situations that prompt analysis and critical thinking, the more they value and practice higher-order thinking. For specific suggestions about fostering the community of writers in your course, see Chapter 2 of this manual.

Bloom's Taxonomy

Benjamin Bloom organized a taxonomy, or hierarchy, of cognitive skills (and a taxonomy of affective skills) that you might use to understand and encourage critical thinking in your students. Bloom's taxonomy, in short, consists of the following skills, given in order of increasing complexity:

- knowledge
- comprehension
- application
- analysis
- synthesis
- evaluation

Specifically, Bloom lists knowledge of terms, of specific facts, of process, of conventions, of trends, and of classifications as preceding knowledge of criteria, methodology, universals in a field, principles, and theories. Students know — recall, recognize, identify, acquire, distinguish, and define — facts before they comprehend them. After students operate with those kinds of knowing, they move to translation, interpretation, extrapolation, application, and analysis — first of elements, then of relationships, and finally of organizational principles. Higher on the taxonomy, Bloom lists synthesis, production of a unique communication, production of a plan, derivation of a set of abstract principles, evaluation, and judgment in terms of external criteria.

Any writing assignment requires more than one of these cognitive abilities. If you ask for a cognitive task requiring skills high on the taxonomy, you need to structure either the assignment or the generating of ideas (ideally both) so that students can draw on the cognitive resources they already have as they stretch their abilities. Basically, students can respond comfortably to a cognitive task that is one step beyond the level at which they habitually perform successfully. Conversely, students might become bored if you ask them to continually use cognitive skills below those they habitually use. This is one reason the "drill and practice" approach to grammar has little effect on the grammatical competency demonstrated in writing. Students long since "knew" grammar. Only by focusing on a pattern of grammar as it combines with other parts of writing to create meaning will you engage the student at an appropriate cognitive level. Grammar should be taught in the context of the students' own writing.

What has all this classifying of cognitive tasks to do with writing in the classroom? If you want your students to analyze relationships, you must be sure that they can first classify, generalize, and illustrate. You might need to give them hints about using some of those strategies to generate an analysis. If you want them to exercise higher-order judgment in terms of external criteria, you must be sure that they can first classify, generalize, analyze, synthesize, deduce, and compare and contrast. This approach might seem too reductive — clearly, a writer might be able to synthesize without being equally confident at deduction. But as you frame assignments, think about the level of difficulty of cognition that you're asking of writers and check for cognitive readiness in the writers as you make assignments. Fortunately, many students will be vocal about "not understanding what the assignment means." Others might be intimidated; they don't want to appear "stupid" in a classroom where others obviously know what to do. Follow the text's example when you introduce an assignment to your students. Check for their understanding of what's expected. Describe many examples of appropriate responses to the assignment. Suggest ways to generate ideas, to shape drafts, and to "think about their thinking" when they revise.

Structuring critical thinking skills for underprepared students helps to lead them through unfamiliar processes and empowers them as thinkers. You can supply this structure by writing sequences of assignments, using verbs that are specific to the cognitive task. Bloom's taxonomy lists verbs that signal each level of cognitive development. These are useful to keep in mind as you think about the level at which you would like your students to respond:

- knowledge: *characterize, define, describe, distinguish, explain, identify, name, recall, recognize, specify, state*

- comprehension: *conclude, demonstrate, differentiate, draw, explain, give in your own words, illustrate, interpret, predict, rearrange, reorder, rephrase, represent, restate, summarize, translate*

- application: *adapt, apply, classify, develop, generalize, imagine, organize, relate, restructure, speculate, transfer*

- analysis: *analyze, categorize, compare, contrast, deduce, examine*

- synthesis: *combine, conclude, constitute, derive, document, formulate, modify, organize, originate, relate, specify, summarize, synthesize*

- evaluation: *appraise, argue, decide, evaluate, judge, rate, sum up*

If you discuss essay exams, remind students to use the verbs in the question's prompt to decide how to answer. Similarly, if you are writing an assignment or prompting a discussion in which you want students to practice a particular level of thinking, use verbs that indicate that level. Articulate for yourself the kind of thinking in which you want students to engage before you write the assignment and before you begin your assessment of student responses. Also think about whether one mode of discourse — such as process analysis — demands higher- or lower-order cognition than another — such as causal analysis — and sequence your writing assignments accordingly.

If you ask questions during class discussion on just one level of thinking, students will most likely respond only on that level. If you ask a question that challenges students to a higher level of cognition, such as asking them to "grow a metaphor," you might need to help them by backing up and restating questions, by drawing on a series of cognitive tasks that lead them to the more complex challenge. For example, questions about comparing and contrasting two things would redirect students' attention and help them generate materials that could be combined and recombined into metaphor. You might want to audiotape a class discussion and then analyze how students respond to the level of cognition your questions require of them. Take notes on the kinds of questions that elicit effective critical thinking, and practice using those questions in class.

RESOURCES IN *THE BEDFORD GUIDE*

A Writer's Guide, A Writer's Reader, and *A Writer's Research Manual* all contain resources that help students to develop critical reading and writing skills. The following is a list of specific resources with references to pages in this manual where you will find advice about using them in your course.

- Part One, "A College Writer's Processes," in *A Writer's Guide* (pp. 5–50), pages 102–04 in this manual. This introduction presents students with an overview of strategies for writing, reading, and critical thinking, and discusses in detail types of evidence, how to select and test evidence, and kinds of appeal. Refer students to this information for help with constructing arguments and selecting and testing evidence for their essays. Note that charts at the end of each Part One chapter refer students to helpful writing, reading, and critical thinking resources in the text and online.

- Paired essays in *A Writer's Reader* (pp. 437–584), pages 243–307 of this manual. Appearing at the end of each chapter in the reader, the paired essays give students the opportunity to examine how two different writers address a similar subject. Each essay in these groupings is followed by a Link to the Paired Essay question that asks students to compare and contrast or synthesize the two writers' ideas. At least one of the pair's writing assignments asks students to write an essay in which they draw on both of the paired selections.

- Responding to an Image. Chapter 22, "Strategies for Understanding Visual Representations," in *A Writer's Guide* (pp. 418–35), pages 240–42 of this manual, provides students with ways to read a visual text. In addition, each of the nine assignment chapters in the rhetoric and the five chapters in the reader begins with an image and a series of questions to prompt critical reading of that image. See, for example, page 55 in *A Writer's Guide* and page 105 of this manual.

- Web Search activities in *A Writer's Reader*, page 244 of this manual. These prompts, at the beginning of each chapter in the reader, ask students to locate specific information on the Internet and to use critical thinking skills to evaluate the material they find. Use these assignments to show students the importance of critically evaluating not only Internet material but all research sources.

- Reading Critically questions in *A Writer's Reader*. These questions, following each selection in the reader, focus on critical thinking and reading strategies covered in Part One of *A Writer's Guide*. Suggest that students refer to Part One for help, especially with the questions that focus on kinds of appeal and types of evidence.

- Chapter 31, "Evaluating Sources," in *A Writer's Research Manual* (pp. 650–62), pages 331–32 of this manual. This chapter contains checklists and questions for thinking critically about library, field, and Internet sources. If your students' textbooks include *A Writer's Research Manual*, refer them to this chapter for help with evaluating any reading material they draw on for their essays.

- Quick Research Guide, page 63 of this manual. This appendix, included in all versions of *The Bedford Guide*, offers more advice on critically evaluating sources, as well as succinct information and checklists to help your students think critically throughout all steps of the research process, from searching for sources to writing a paper that defines and supports their thesis. Refer them to this guide as they make decisions about how to respond to their investigation and construct their drafts.

CHAPTER 4

Providing Support for
Underprepared Students

Most composition students enter our classrooms armed with the skills to process what we will teach them in the next few weeks. Not all of them, however, are prepared to succeed in a college composition course. After years of elementary and high school English classes, many students still lack basic writing skills. Some have simply not paid attention and fallen behind. Others have lagged because of nonattendance or migratory lifestyles, have struggled with learning disabilities, or, for some other reason, have fallen through the cracks. Nontraditional students' skills might have become rusty through disuse. Many composition students are nonnative speakers of English in various stages of mastering a foreign language. Whatever the reason, you will probably encounter underprepared students in your composition classroom.

Working with underprepared students demands extra time, extra energy, and lots of patience, but if we leave them to fend for themselves, they will probably be defeated. Because they struggle with the simplest tasks, they need a lot of praise and encouragement. Celebrate small victories; for these students, such accomplishments are no small matter. Regardless of the amount of work required, helping underprepared students achieve success can be one of the most rewarding of our tasks as teachers.

In this chapter, we discuss how to provide extra support for both underprepared students who are considered developmental writers and those who have difficulty with writing because English is their second language. Although students in these two groups might share certain difficulties, in general the obstacles they encounter are very different, and you will need to address them differently in your course.

DEVELOPMENTAL WRITERS

Developmental implies that writers can develop cognitive skills that they have not yet acquired. Although all students are in various stages of "development," developmental writers often regard themselves as "stupid" and believe they are the only ones in class who don't understand. As a result, they often lack the confidence to ask questions. Encourage them, of course, but let them know that they can also come to you outside of class with any questions. Make sure they understand that in peer-group sessions, their reaction as a reader is valuable to the writer; they don't need to know how to fix the problem. Because they lack confidence, developmental writers are satisfied with a lower grade and see little use in revision; they are much more likely to feel they can improve their papers if you respond without grading them.

Developmental writers often

- are weak in basic grammar, punctuation, and syntax skills
- lack organizational skills
- suffer from low self-esteem that has come from repeated failure in English studies
- lack critical thinking skills
- lack motivation

- are prone to erratic attendance
- are prone to procrastination

Of course, not all developmental writers will exhibit these problems. Many recognize the need for strong communication skills and just need help to catch up. Others might be struggling with learning disabilities and find it difficult to follow directions, or they might be slow writers with short attention spans.

These students need flexibility within structure and clear directions about what to do and how to do it. Require that writing assignments be typed or printed out. Poor handwriting makes writing difficult both to read and to revise. The convenience of revising on a computer will make the process seem much more manageable. Also, don't underestimate the aesthetic factor. Seeing their writing neatly printed on a white sheet changes it dramatically. It looks professional; it encourages students to see themselves as real writers. If students must handwrite assignments, have them write on every other line so that their papers will be easier to read and to revise.

When planning course work, design writing assignments and prewriting, drafting, and revising activities that allow basic writers to practice modes of writing and thinking that will lead them to analyzing and synthesizing. Shape a learning environment centered on student writers; writing and sharing with other students and talking about the writing process will help developmental writers learn to generalize from a group of specific details or to classify a list of facts. Developmental writers are capable of making broad leaps in critical thinking during a writing course. See Chapter 3 of this manual for a discussion of the connection between cognitive development and critical thinking skills.

Diagnostic Essays

It is imperative that you ask students to write in class on the first day. You must know immediately if a student does not have the skills required to do the work in your course. (See Chapter 1 of this manual for specific suggestions about the kind of writing you should ask students to do during the first week.) If you determine that students are underprepared, you will need to decide whether to shift them to more appropriate writing courses or to adapt your course to address their skill levels. Your college has most likely designed composition courses especially for students without the skills to survive in the regular composition classroom; such courses might be called Basic English, Developmental Composition, or Preparatory Composition.

Check to see whether your school's admission policy requires tests of students' writing skills. If a student's scores fall below the appropriate range for your course, ask an administrator whether the student should be moved to another course. If for some other reason the student has been placed in your course, then you need to know right away that the student will be struggling to overcome weaknesses and that you must provide extra help. Sometimes students choose to take a regular composition class despite low skill levels. In this case, talk with the student and determine what his or her weaknesses are and why he or she has chosen to take your class. Be frank about your expectations and what it will take for the student to overcome deficiencies and to succeed. Then devise a plan together for providing the extra help the student will need.

If you are teaching a developmental composition course, or if you determine that you have a number of underprepared students in your class, you should also administer a diagnostic grammar test to identify areas that will most likely cause them problems. Diagnostic tests can be found on Bedford/St. Martin's *Re:Writing* resource at <bedfordstmartins.com/rewriting>, under Exercise Central: Diagnostics. More tests are available on *Testing Tool Kit*, a CD that is available for free to adopters of *The Bedford Guide*.

Help Students to Organize

Many developmental writers lack organizational skills. To address this problem, in your first conference, help students set specific long- and short-term goals and to devise a means of measuring their progress. You might want to ask them to track their progress in reflective writing or in journal entries.

When you make an assignment, give students an idea of how long it might take them to complete it. Remember, it will take developmental writers much longer, so they need help budgeting their time carefully. Give assignments both orally and in writing. Some students will respond well to only one of these methods of delivery. Don't expect students to remember what you tell them. Write everything down either in the syllabus (remind them where), on the chalkboard, or in handouts. If you have a course Web site, you might consider making your assignments and handouts available online. Ask students to use calendar organizers to record due dates for each assignment.

Begin class with an outline of what you will cover and end with a summary of key points. Write these down, too. Some students learn holistically; they become confused by individual parts. They need to have an idea of the whole picture — the lesson, the unit, even the course — in order to focus on the steps. They need to see how the new material relates to previous lessons. Beginning with an overview will help these students. Be sure to provide time for questions and answers, and wait long enough for students to think about what they need to ask.

Here's an Idea . . .

At the beginning of each class period, list objectives and key points on the far left side of the board. On the right side, list assignments for the next class period. Use this information to orient students as you move through the lesson. Be sure to erase what you've written in the middle of the board before you write new information. Underprepared students have a tendency to get lost amid the clutter.

Developmental writers function better if you break assignments into parts. Teaching writing as a process works well for them because it allows them to focus on one step of an assignment at a time without being overwhelmed. The checklists for each part of the process, in Chapters 4–12, are invaluable for developmental writers. You might want to copy these and have students attach them to their drafts. The assignments in Part Two, "A Writer's Situations," help developmental writers build on each previous assignment, sequentially moving into increasingly difficult tasks.

Although writing instructors generally abhor fixed patterns such as the five-paragraph essay, developmental writers might not be ready to throw away this crutch. They function well with narrative patterns, so use these to show basic writers how to organize other kinds of information. Once they grasp this concept, explain that while this is one way to organize an essay, there are many other ways to handle the same information.

Here's an Idea…

Working with a draft of an old paper from your files, demonstrate to developmental students one or two alternative ways they might organize the information in the paper. Then hand out copies of the paper and ask students to reorganize the information in a different way. They will need help getting started. Move around the room suggesting patterns students might try. Then have them share their revisions to illustrate several ways to organize the information. Finally, ask the students to reorganize the information in a draft of their own.

Remember, developmental writers are just beginning to internalize skills that your other students have learned long ago. In fact, developmental writers might need to learn how to construct a paragraph, or even a sentence, before they build an essay. As they tackle the course material, you might need to arrange extra instruction in these most basic skills. Refer students to the information on building paragraphs in Chapter 18, "Strategies for Drafting," and on sentence skills in Chapters 35 and 36 of *A Writer's Handbook*. For more help, refer students to the additional handbook exercises.

Here's an Idea . . .

Encourage underprepared students to tape lectures. This will give them another chance to hear and process all of the information.

Find Resources on Campus

A regular classroom cannot provide all the extra help developmental writers need. Most campuses provide several additional means of support. Locate the resources on your campus and discuss them with your students. Start by looking for the following resources:

- Tutoring programs. Your students can set up appointments on a regular or as-needed basis for help with their writing skills. Talk to the director or the tutors. Inform them of your students' specific weaknesses that need attention or of assignments that have certain requirements. Alert them to the directions for assignments in *The Bedford Guide*. Your students will be less confused if tutors use the same terminology as the text. If your school has no tutoring program or writing center, consider looking into online tutoring services (for more on these services, see p. 72 of this manual).

- The writing center director. Again, make him or her aware of your students' specific needs and your requirements for assignments. Whereas writing assistants might be helpful, you will need to determine what level of service they can provide.

- Computers in the writing or tutoring center. Check to see if these are equipped with computer-assisted instruction software, which can provide helpful practice in certain skills.

- Support for students with learning disabilities. Ask counselors or your department chair if special services exist. For example, dyslexic students might receive tape-recordings of their textbooks. (If not, consider asking a student who reads well to tape reading assignments. Funding might even be available to the student as part of a work-study financial aid program.)

- A buddy system. Developmental writers benefit from the help of their better prepared peers, and their peers will learn from teaching. Tell students how to form study groups, or how to pair up and share responsibility for notes and assignments when one of them must miss class.

- Study skills workshops. Many schools offer these on campus, and some offer them online. Emphasize that all students need these skills to survive and succeed in college. You might also want to refer students to an excellent online resource, <howtostudy.org>.

Schedule Conferences

Meet with developmental writers frequently; they will need a lot of individual attention. In conference, wait for them to speak. Allow them to identify their problem areas and to guide the direction of the conference. Remember, hearing about all the weaknesses you find in their papers will overwhelm and defeat them. Help them to succeed by dealing with one problem at a time.

Often these students know what they want to say, but they have trouble putting it on paper. Ask them to tell you what they want to say. Then suggest they write down exactly what they just said to you. This is a new idea for many of them. If they still have trouble, try transcribing what they say as they speak.

Some poorly motivated students come to life when they are allowed to write about subjects they care about, but they need help in choosing topics in which they feel invested. Often they believe only deadly dull topics are appropriate for a writing class. They might also have trouble inventing ways to write about what interests them. Use brief conferences, in the classroom or in your office, as an opportunity to guide their invention techniques. Show them how to use the invention techniques in Chapter 16, "Strategies for Generating Ideas." If developmental writers are eager to communicate their ideas, they will be more willing to work on the skills to do that.

Handling Disruptive Behavior

Poorly motivated students can cause problems in the classroom. Because some of them have short attention spans and don't commit to the material, they become restless. You can avoid this by keeping them busy. Call on them frequently; vary the material, alternating instruction with activities that require participation. The more active the learning in your classroom, the less time students have to become restless.

If a student does become disruptive, stop what you are doing and deal with his or her behavior immediately. Tell the student that such actions are inappropriate and will not be tolerated, then move on with the lesson. After class, talk with the student privately to try to ascertain the cause of his or her behavior. Be understanding, but be firm. Make it clear that disruptive behavior will not be tolerated for any reason. Try to form a bond with the student. If students believe you really care, they will be less willing to give you grief.

If you continue to have problems with a student, talk to your department chair about what can be done. Other students in the classroom are entitled to a learning environment free from such distractions.

> *Here's an Idea . . .*
>
> Ask students to bring two copies of their drafts to a conference. Read the papers aloud, exactly as written. Read slowly, and wait while students make corrections on their copies. Often students will hear mistakes they don't see on the written copy. Suggest that peers help one another with the same exercise for each draft, and encourage writers to read all of their papers aloud.

ESL STUDENTS

There is no typical ESL student. Some are international students learning to adapt to a new culture as they learn a new language, but some have been immersed in the target language and culture all of their lives. Some are highly motivated to succeed; some are not. Some display specific writing problems characteristic of their native languages and cultures, while others have problems that are more difficult to identify and characterize. Many writing difficulties are universal to all second-language learners, regardless of native language or culture.

Every college student must acclimate to new learning situations and unfamiliar cultures. The ESL student faces the additional challenge of doing this in a second or other language. Problems with ESL students' writing might range from minor, easily correctable errors to major distortions of orthography, semantics, and syntax that cannot be considered acceptable Standard English. While intermediate and advanced ESL students emerge from their ESL classes with a basic understanding of semantics and syntax and varying degrees of familiarity with idiomatic and colloquial usage, they often continue to have difficulty with spoken and written English because they limit themselves to a literal decoding of the language. If students rely on semantics and syntax alone, they will regularly misunderstand language situations at all levels of college study.

If ESL students are enrolled in a first-year composition course, it is reasonable to assume that they are subject to the same requirements as other students enrolled in the same course. To expect less endangers the quality of the instruction and the integrity of the institution providing it. How those requirements are met, however, is often up to the individual instructor. It might not be effective or appropriate for an instructor to engage in individualized instruction for nonnative writers who are, after all, expected to meet the minimum requirements of the courses in which they are enrolled. An instructor of a regular composition course often does not have the resources of the developmental or ESL instructor and cannot be expected to perform those functions. There are, however, a variety of strategies you can use to encourage ESL students to succeed, without establishing an alternative set of requirements.

Two Types of Analysis

Two approaches have traditionally been used to understand second-language learning: contrastive analysis and error analysis. Familiarity with these methods might help you to identify students' patterns of error and individualize your instruction accordingly.

Contrastive analysis compares the structures of a student's native and target languages in order to explain or predict errors. This method assumes that errors are a result of "interference" from the learner's native language. Rather than simply contrasting discrete linguistic terms, contrastive analysis examines broader differences between languages, such as usage, cultural environments, and patterns of discourse.

Error analysis collects and classifies errors made by individual students, allowing for a more prescriptive approach to correcting systematic errors. This method identifies the following general categories of error:

- *Omission of grammatical morphemes* leaves out items that are not essential to the meaning of the sentence, as in "I buy some book," where past and plural markers are omitted.

- *Double marking* of a given semantic feature supplies two or more markers when only one is required, as in "She didn't wanted," where the past tense is marked more than once.

- *Regularization* ignores an irregular form of a word, as in "The police catched him," where the regular past tense marker *-ed* is used instead of the irregular caught.

- *Archiform* uses one form when several are required; for example, using the subjective for both subjective and objective pronouns, as in "She goes to town; I know she."

- *Alternating use of two or more forms* confuses usage that is still being internalized, as in the random alternation of *much* and *many* in "too much assignments" or "many homeworks."

- *Misordering* follows previously learned syntactical rules when a construction requires that items be reversed, as in "I don't know who is it," where *is* erroneously follows the rule for simple questions rather than embedded questions.

If error analysis is to be of value, it should be carried out with rigor and its results interpreted with caution. Beyond basic errors, students might be overproducing familiar structures or avoiding difficult ones. For ESL students enrolled in regular composition courses, you will most likely find a streamlined set of proofreading and correction symbols more useful than a complex taxonomy of errors. Be sure to direct your ESL students to the pages of symbols at the end of the textbook.

Adapting the Writing Process

Like developmental writers, ESL writers benefit from breaking the writing process into distinct steps. Focusing on one step of an assignment at a time turns an overwhelming project into a manageable one for them, so take every opportunity to make each step more concrete. Copy the revision checklists in Chapters 4–12, and ask students to attach them to their drafts. When necessary, refer students to the information on building paragraphs in Chapter 18, "Strategies for Drafting," and on improving sentence skills in Chapters 35 and 36 of *A Writer's Handbook*. Point out the boxed ESL guidelines throughout *A Writer's Handbook*; a convenient index to these guidelines is printed at the end of the version of the text that includes the Handbook.

Standard activities for generating ideas — such as brainstorming, freewriting, and clustering — allow ESL students to fulfill preliminary course requirements successfully and gain confidence before moving on to more difficult tasks. Once ESL students understand that prewriting and informal outlining are not graded, they will relax and often thrive during these stages of the process. ESL students also gain valuable experience from working with other writers on collaborative activities.

The opportunity to draft multiple versions of an essay and to receive nongraded responses is essential to ESL students' success. Because several drafts will most likely be necessary, nonnative writers should be made aware from the beginning of the course that additional drafts will be required of them. Working drafts enable ESL students to address their language problems within the context of regular instruction, in the same way that other students in the class are learning to write and to talk about their writing. Although drafts might be dense with errors, if you require a series of drafts from ESL students, you will not need to mark every error in each draft. Instead, you can decide to focus on a cluster of related skills — such as verb forms, verb tenses, and subject-verb agreement — for each round of drafts. This approach to responding to drafts can alleviate any pressure you might feel to be a comparative linguist or an ESL specialist. Identifying and clearly understanding specific objectives for ESL students' additional drafts will allow you to read and mark them quickly.

RESOURCES IN *THE BEDFORD GUIDE*

Numerous resources for underprepared students are built into the textbook, but many students don't know to look for them on their own. Early in the term, give them a guided tour. Take time to explain to the class how the book provides charts that show where students can find helpful resources in the text and online. These charts appear at the end of Part One chapters and in the back of the book. Also, new to the book are detailed charts, called "Draft Doctors," to help students identify and fix common problems in their drafts, such as weak thesis statements, poorly supported arguments, and poorly integrated sources. You might want to work through one or more of the Draft Doctors in class, using a paper from a former class with the student's name removed. This process will help students develop the habit of asking of their drafts the kinds of questions posed in these charts. In addition, the book provides examples and exact, step-by-step directions for each writing assignment. You might also point out the checklists for the stages of the writing process, including the Editing Checklists that help students identify and correct grammar problems. Call students' attention to the textbook's end sheets, and explain how to use them to answer grammar or punctuation questions. Remember, underprepared students might not have the terminology they need to locate information about their specific problems, so you will need to provide extra guidance for them as weaknesses emerge.

Although the text offers selections for a wide range of reading levels, some students might lack the reading skills necessary to fully comprehend even the most accessible pieces. *The Bedford Guide* offers stronger coverage of critical reading in Chapter 2, and "A Writer's Situations" (pp. 51–232) includes helpful annotations of the professional essays and critical reading questions in the margins of student essays. Point out to students that these annotations will help them become stronger readers, encouraging them to respond to the prompts as they work through the essays.

Remind students that even accomplished readers need to read through a piece of writing several times in order to understand its subtleties. The process of writing — of revising and refining an essay — also offers writers the opportunity to revise their ideas about what they've read. Encourage students who have difficulty with reading to focus their responses by answering the Meaning questions following the selections in *A Writer's Guide* and then to meet with you individually to ask their own specific questions. Also point out that students can use the As You Read questions in *A Writer's Reader* to focus their attention as they read through a piece the first and second times. Remind them that the vocabulary glosses can help them better understand the connotations of the more difficult words in a selection. Ask students to keep lists of new words they learn and to look for ways in which these words are used outside of the classroom — for example, in the newspaper, in conversations, and on television. You might even want to ask students to search for new words on the Internet and to write a journal entry about the results: How are the results related (or not) to the word's meaning?

A common obstacle for developmental writers is a lack of motivation. Several features in the textbook can help improve students' motivation. Using the models of student writing (including notes, outlines, and essays) emphasizes that first-year composition students can, in fact, take on challenging writing assignments and succeed. Incorporate activities that demonstrate the ideas in the Applying What You Learn sections in order to show students that the writing skills they are learning will be useful later — whether in college or the workplace. Remember, too, that teaching strategies that engage students in active learning, such as group collaboration or peer editing, also motivate students to improve their critical thinking skills.

While most students can benefit from additional help with writing, underprepared students in particular will find the following features useful as they respond to each chapter's writing assignment.

Facing the Challenge

These sections, following the main assignment in each chapter, alert students to the assignment's most challenging part and give them strategies for addressing it. Often the authors specify approaches, such as brainstorming or freewriting, and topics for students to think about. Consider using these suggestions to introduce the assignment to your students.

Here's an Idea . . .

Here are some activities to help students build basic skills:

- Have students list three to five key questions they have about their topic, trying to anticipate what the reader will want to know. Then have them arrange the questions in the order they think the reader would ask them. This order might depend on importance, what leads to what, saving the best for last, and so on. When students write, they simply answer the questions.

- Copy each sentence of a well-constructed paragraph. Mix the sentences up and have students arrange them in the best order. Have them consider topic sentence, order of information, and transitions. Have them justify their choices.

- Create a scavenger hunt to help students learn to use *A Writer's Handbook* in *The Bedford Guide*. Make up a sheet of sample questions — for example, when to use a colon — and have students find the answer using the handbook. Let them create their own scavenger hunt.

- Collect flawed sentences from your students' writing or other sources. Find ones that have the same errors you find in their writing. Ask students to talk about what is wrong, then revise to clarify meaning or improve style.

At the beginning of the semester, have students form groups of three (called "think tanks") and sign up to present an assignment's most difficult challenge to the class. A different think tank will be responsible for presenting the challenge for each week's assignment. In addition, ask the think tank to present a variety of ways to handle the challenge or to plan a class activity that demonstrates how to approach the challenge. Tell groups that they may come to you for help, but don't be surprised if, as the course progresses, students find creative and surprising ways to advise one another on their own.

After peer-evaluation sessions, have students freewrite about the most successful strategies they or their peers found for addressing the assignment's challenge or about aspects of the assignment that presented unexpected difficulties. Students can then incorporate this writing into reflective essays for their portfolios. With students' permission, collect and copy their freewriting to keep on file for future think tanks to use as a resource.

Quick Research Guide

Each version of *The Bedford Guide* includes a Quick Research Guide, which focuses on the most challenging aspects of writing source-based papers. When assigning any paper for which students are asked to draw on sources, suggest that they consult this guide for quick advice on defining their research goals, searching for and evaluating sources, incorporating source material effectively and fairly, and citing and listing sources according to MLA style.

This guide contains several checklists and charts aimed at helping students with little research experience understand their research goals and find the best sources to meet those goals. For example, it includes checklists that help students have in on the purpose for their research, find and evaluate sources, and cite sources properly; tables that describe the different types of evidence that students can draw on and that explain how to incorporate this information effectively; and charts that help students understand the best research applications of various print and electronic sources.

The guide also provides clear and accessible advice on quoting, paraphrasing, and summarizing. Writers who are unfamiliar with the conventions of incorporating (and citing) source material often plagiarize unintentionally, so be sure to alert students to resources in the Quick Research Guide that can help them avoid this serious problem.

Quick Editing Guide

Every version of *The Bedford Guide* also includes a Quick Editing Guide, which focuses special attention on students' most troublesome grammar and editing problems and includes an Editing Checklist for each one. Tell peer editors and writers that their final drafts are not complete until they have used this guide to edit them. Encourage students to keep a list, either in their journals or in a computer file, of their own most common grammatical and mechanical errors and to use their list to check each draft of their papers.

The Quick Editing Guide also contains For E-writers boxes, which offer important advice about the dangers and benefits of using grammar and spell checkers and suggestions for how to use the search-and-replace function to edit more effectively. Many instructors question the use of grammar and spell checkers. They believe that students receive too much assistance and unfairly score better than their non–computer-literate classmates. No computer program, however, can transform C or D papers into A

Here's an Idea . . .

Have students bring for class discussion any particularly difficult — or even comical — choices a word processor asks them to make.

---

papers. Many developmental students are such "creative" spellers that the spell check cannot give them an option for their misspelled words. And students must be able to choose which option is correct. With grammar checkers, students must be reminded that the computer cannot think or reason. Students themselves must analyze the sentences the computer program identifies to determine whether there really is a problem. Because grammar and spell checkers give students the opportunity to analyze their writing and make logical decisions on word choice and punctuation, students often spend more time in serious editing than they would if they didn't use the word processor's functions.

For a complete discussion of using *A Writer's Handbook* to help underprepared students with grammar, see Part Two, Chapter 10 of this manual, "Teaching with *A Writer's Handbook*" (p. 349).

Ancillaries to The Bedford Guide

In addition to the features in the textbook, several ancillaries also provide ways to help underprepared students improve their writing. *The Bedford Guide* companion Web site at <bedfordstmartins.com/bedguide> provides additional help and activities for every stage of the writing process. New to the Web site is the "Ask the Draft Doctor" feature, which gives students advice about common writing problems and refers them to relevant materials on the Web site, including exercises for every section of *A Writer's Handbook*. You can access your students' exercise scores and the time they did the exercises from the Instructor Resources link on the companion Web site. Additional help for ESL students includes exercises specifically geared to second-language learners. You also might point students toward the grammar tutorials on Exercise Central, <bedford stmartins.com/exercisecentral>. To test students' writing and grammar competency, consider using the *Testing Tool Kit* CD accompanying *The Bedford Guide*. It includes items written specifically for ESL students with questions available at two levels of difficulty. A chart correlating chapters in the text with items in *Testing Tool Kit* appears on the inside back cover of this book. For more details on the electronic supplements accompanying *The Bedford Guide*, see Chapter 5.

Study Skills for College Writers helps students who need extra guidance (and practice) develop the study skills necessary for a successful college career. Helpful tips and strategies for managing time, taking notes, taking tests, and accessing college resources are just some of the skills that are covered in this rich resource. Full of activities designed to help underprepared students improve their skills, *Study Skills for College Writers* could be of great value to your ESL students.

Also, throughout the Instructor's Annotated Edition of *The Bedford Guide*, you will find specific suggestions for ways to include ESL students in your class discussions and to address their particular needs.

CHAPTER 5

Using Technology in
Your Composition Course

Uses of technology in your course can range from requiring students to write and revise drafts using a word processing program to teaching a course online or through interactive television, where technology is the means of delivery. As a writing instructor, you will most likely be using technology in your course. In the opening address at the 1998 Conference on College Composition and Communication, Cynthia L. Selfe argued that regardless of whether we, as writing instructors, are enthusiastic fans or wary critics of using computers in the classroom, we have a responsibility to teach students to think critically about how they use technology. The impact of technology on the way we communicate is undeniable. Many students in your class will have used computers to write; some, especially older, returning students, may not have. Encourage all students to take advantage of your course as an opportunity to learn to write with computers, and you will be helping them gain access not only to a wider audience but also to potential job markets.

Begin by asking students to talk about their comfort level with technology —they might discover they know more than they had realized about writing with computers and online technology. In fact, some students (younger ones especially) may be more comfortable with technology than you are, and they may be a valuable resource. For students who are less comfortable with computers, you might ask questions like the following: At what point, if any, did students begin to resist the influence of computer technology in their lives? What aspects of technology do they wholeheartedly embrace, and why? Listen to students' fears about writing with computers or their overzealous endorsements of the Web, and turn these statements into questions for the class to investigate in print and online. Consider asking librarians or other local experts on computers and writing to present their views on the questions your students raise. Or ask students to arrange a panel discussion with guests from different segments of the workforce or media to address the influence of computers in their respective professions. With access to a computer network, students could conduct these interviews via e-mail or a listserv.

This chapter gives basic advice about getting started in teaching writing with computers, solving common problems in the computer classroom, and using *The Bedford Guide* and its online resources to help students write with computers.

GETTING STARTED

Many colleges provide computer labs for students. If your school does not, you will need to make other arrangements to help students get access to computers. Find out if the campus has computer classrooms (in the library or in another department) that are available during your class times. Not all courses require the use of computers for every class period, so you might trade off computer and traditional classrooms with a colleague for all or part of a semester. A shared arrangement can work with cooperation and a printed schedule for the students. Many colleges have computer labs even if they don't designate computer-assisted classrooms for specific disciplines. Contact the computer center personnel, and find out what kind of software is available, what hours the lab is open, and what kinds of services the lab offers. Try to arrange an orientation for your students with hands-on training.

If you don't feel comfortable teaching with computers, don't worry. Check with your college's computer services department to find out whether it offers professional development classes for college personnel. Continuing-education programs also offer inexpensive classes on using computers (sometimes free to faculty).

If you are a new instructor and find yourself assigned to a computer classroom, don't panic. Other teachers in your department are using computers in their classes, so ask to sit in. Most teachers in computer-assisted courses love to share their enthusiasm. They might also offer handouts and instruction. Plus, they are your best reference for what to expect with students as well as with the computers and printers.

Eddye Gallagher, of Tarrant County Junior College, offers the following advice to instructors who are new to teaching with computers:

- Arrive before the class is scheduled to begin. For early-morning classes, allow extra time to turn computers on.

- If computers are networked, don't position yourself in front of the classroom. Wander around the room to encourage students to interact with one another as well as with you.

- When you lecture and give instructions to be followed later, have students darken their screens so that they will listen to you. Otherwise, they may pay more attention to the computer screen than to you.

- Because students want to work on the computers rather than listen to you, help them out by providing detailed handouts (or e-mail) on assignments. Include specifics on what you want: type of writing, acceptable topics, due dates for drafts, peer editing, final copy, and materials to be submitted with final draft.

- Be patient with students who might need special orientation and help. If your computer or software has a built-in tutorial, have students use it. Students can progress at their own speed; slower students will not feel rushed or pushed.

- Go slowly. Blend writing and computer instruction. Introduce a little information at a time. Wait until students are comfortable with simple word processing before introducing more complex software.

- When introducing a new task on the computer, keep the class together. Be sure that each student is following your instructions. Don't let students work ahead. Have those students who finish early help others.

Emphasizing the importance of writing with computers in your course quickly establishes the sense of your class as a community of writers. Encourage students who are familiar with the software to assist you in answering other students' questions. Students will begin peer response right away as they ask one another for advice about using the word-processing software. Provide all students with a handout that includes when and where computers are available on campus, directions for logging onto the computer network, and guidelines for writing on a computer for your course.

Ask students to print out and hand in any prewriting they do on a computer. You may want them to save this work in a separate folder to use later. If they are feeling stuck during freewriting, have them open these files and scroll for phrases or images that catch their eye and inspire them to begin writing.

If students surf the Internet, they might be familiar with the lists of frequently asked questions (FAQs) that can be found on most Web sites. Some software packages also contain FAQ lists. (If students don't know what FAQs are, have them look up a few lists, print them out, and bring them to class; if students don't have Web access, print out a list for them.) Ask students to compile their own FAQ list for your course, either about using the computer to write or about the writing process in general.

After students have become comfortable with the basic word-processing skills they need to write for your course, encourage them to experiment with the software's various tools. For example, ask them to compare the thesaurus on the word processor with the different thesauri in your school's library and the local bookstore. Or have them evaluate the grammar checker on the computer by reporting three examples of errors that the grammar checker would not catch and three examples of when the checker might be helpful.

To help students think more reflectively about the writing process, take every opportunity to have them discuss in class or write reflectively about their experiences using computers to write. Take advantage of the computer's most valuable asset: the ability it gives writers to rearrange and save different versions of a draft. Encourage students — especially those who have problems generating text — to play with their writing on a computer (saving their files often). The invisible-writing exercise on page 299 of the textbook is especially helpful for students with high writing anxiety or writer's block. Before students begin the exercise, assure them that you will not mark errors in their invisible writing and that they will be producing writing they can use later.

SOLVING COMMON PROBLEMS

Two basic kinds of problems arise in a computer classroom: the usual difficulties students have generating ideas and drafting and the mechanical snafus they encounter when using computers. Even a computer-literate student might have a bad writing day and sit staring at the screen. If you notice a student just sitting, stop and chat. Try to determine what the problem is. Sometimes students zone out for a few moments because they're tired, thinking about a test in another class, or merely trying to figure out what to say next. If the student is struggling for correct words during the writing of a first draft, offer suggestions on how to continue — for instance, typing the first word that comes to mind or putting a string of question marks to indicate a word problem. Remind students that the draft isn't a final version. They will have plenty of time to revise and find the perfect word. If students haven't done the assigned preparation, suggest that they start at that point and return to the lab after class to catch up. Often students know what they want to write, but they can't think of a way to write it. If you have them tell you orally, you can then say, "OK, type what you just told me." Or you can suggest that the student just start typing — freewriting to see where the subject will go.

If students don't ask you for help, ask yourself why. Have you isolated yourself from the students by staying at your own computer? If so, walk around and perhaps read over a few shoulders. Making yourself more accessible can help students to become more comfortable about asking for assistance. Also, remember that some students don't need help. They are self-motivated and have done their homework, so when they get to class, they are ready to begin writing and want to be left alone. Those students will usually come to you when they hit a rough spot. In addition, some students prefer to ask the advice of another student rather than of the teacher.

Here's an Idea . . .

Suggest that students keep journals, "what if" lists, and random idea files on their computers. If you are in a computer-assisted classroom, set aside one computer for students to stop by and write a couple of sentences or comments on the day's assignment or activity.

Mechanical problems might be harder to deal with. You will be more comfortable in the classroom and save a tremendous amount of time if you learn everything you can about the computers. Work with your support staff to find out the typical problems that you might face (or read the computer manual's troubleshooting guide). Then ask for guidance on quickly correcting the problem. Some problems with nonworking computers or printers are relatively simple to solve:

- Check the power switch (it's amazing how many computers or printers start working when they are turned on).
- Check the cable connections (cords can come loose).
- Make sure the student is using the correct printer (sometimes students have printed three copies of a document because they thought the computer was connected to a different printer).

Unfortunately, not all problems are simple. A computer crash can fall into that category. If the crash was caused by a power surge or momentary power outage, then the computer will start working as soon as the power comes back on. However, anything that students have done since the last save will be lost. "Autorecover" features save a document at set intervals, automatically opening the last saved version when you reboot after a crash. If this feature is available, show students how to be sure that it is turned on. It is not fail-safe, however, so constantly remind students to save their documents frequently. Tell them that the few seconds the process requires can save them the frustration of trying to reconstruct an hour's worth of work after a power outage.

Occasionally, you will experience crashes that result from mechanical problems. These are not as easy to solve, and you will probably require the help of your computer support staff. Because help is not always readily available, you will need to move the student to a different computer. Just remain calm and reassure the student to alleviate his or her frustrations.

Other problems originate with disks. If CDs are severely scratched or cracked, they can stop working. Students tend to throw their disks in the bottom of a purse or back-

Here's an Idea . . .

When students begin to draft an assignment on the computer, ask them to make two separate files — one for the assignment itself and the other, called "Outtakes," for pieces of writing that they delete from their drafts but that they want to save. Encourage them to use this file as a resource for future freewriting or journal writing.

pack, forgetting how fragile they are. If students use CDs, encourage them to keep disks in protective carrying cases and to create a backup disk on which they save all of their documents. Better, steer them to a more reliable alternative to floppy disks: zip disks or flash drives. Zip disks — fatter, better constructed versions of floppy disks — are less easily damaged than floppy disks and also have more storage capacity. Flash drives, also known as thumb drives or memory sticks, are a bit more costly, but they are convenient, resilient, and capable of holding vast amounts of information in a very small format. Students can use one flash drive to store files for all their classes.

TEACHING WITH COURSE MANAGEMENT SOFTWARE

More and more colleges and universities are subscribing to e-learning systems such as Blackboard and WebCT. These sophisticated course management packages can be useful whether you are teaching a distance learning course entirely online or adding an online component to a traditional face-to-face class. With a course Web site, you can post essential documents, make announcements about class meetings and assignments, use discussion boards or chat rooms for interactive dialogue, enrich course content with links to related Web sites, and set up groups to work outside the classroom. These are just a few of the ways that online teaching can make your life easier and your teaching more effective.

Getting Started

If you are new to using a course management system, your first step in getting started should be to speak with your school's technology coordinator. He or she will generally set up your account, put up your Web site shell, issue your username and password, and put you in touch with faculty who already use the software and are willing to share strategies and techniques.

Take advantage of all the training you can get. Although course management software isn't complicated to use, it can be intimidating for first-timers. Learning as much as you can and practicing *before* you go "on stage" with students will make for a more seamless introduction of technology into your course. Your school may run training seminars or short classes, and if you teach in an urban school, there may be an area conference of users from other schools. Check with your department to see if it will cover training expenses.

The course management package itself may offer another good source of how-to information. Both Blackboard and WebCT have support pages for instructors and course developers. (Look for an FAQ or support link on the control panel of your home page.)

Here's an Idea . . .

In the middle of the semester, ask students to pull out papers from earlier assignments. Have small groups put together a short list of grammar and punctuation errors that come up frequently in their essays, creating a table in Word that contains the following columns: Error, Example, Why It's Wrong, How to Fix It, and Corrected Example. As a class, decide on the top ten errors and compile a master "ProofGoofs" table to post on the course site.

Don't underestimate the time you need to put up content and check it out. Test your links when you first post them, and continue to do so throughout the course. Also be sure to anticipate worst-case scenarios before you start. What happens if your students are taking an online quiz and the university server goes down? How will you reach students if spam filters on their personal e-mail servers block your messages? We recommend that you talk with other instructors to work out strategies for dealing with these problems before they occur.

Sweep often for viruses, and warn students to run a virus scan before uploading to or downloading from the site. It is extremely important to back up everything you put on your Web site or download from it. Keep files on a flash drive, on your home and/or school computer's hard drive, or in a series of postings to your private e-mail account.

Building Your Course Web Site

Before you begin creating your site, you may want to make a quick outline of the material you plan to post. You should also consider how often you will add information to the site. If you put up everything at once, you may intimidate students. On the other hand, if you rigidly post a module every weekend, with its corresponding assignment due a week later, you may well turn off learners who need flexibility in when and how they learn.

Take some time to decide which areas of the site will be most useful to you and to your students. If you are new to online course management, you might begin by using just a few major features of the software package. Blackboard and WebCT components that you may find particularly useful include the course information and course documents areas, external links, and discussion boards.

Course Information   In this area you can include your course schedule and syllabus, the school plagiarism policy, and other documents related to policies and procedures. In your syllabus (and on the first day of class), be sure to discuss the course Web site. Provide students with an outline of what they will find on the site and where they will find it, and establish your expectations for online participation.

Course Documents   Whether you organize the folders in this area by topic or by week, this is a good place to post handouts, checklists, and additional readings. Within your course documents, you might find it useful to include links to various exercises, examples, writing activities, and readings on the companion site for *The Bedford Guide*.

External Links   This feature is a great way to leverage your teaching. In addition to the companion site for *The Bedford Guide,* you might want to link to your school's or another school's online writing laboratory (OWL). Many OWLs offer handouts, checklists, and tutorials. Often, school librarians can help you create a list of other helpful Web and library resources that you can link to from your course site — book reviews, periodical

---

Here's an Idea . . .

You might begin the course by having students introduce themselves in a brief posting. They can write about their academic backgrounds, their families, their goals for the course — anything they would like to share with classmates. Ask students to read everyone's introductions and to comment on two or three of them.

Here's an Idea . . .

Set up two discussion board forums titled "Writing Strategies" and "Writing Challenges." Ask students to post in either, sharing specific writing tips, questions, and concerns. Those who post on the strategies board ("I'm pretty confident about doing X. My strategy is to . . .") can become mentors to their classmates. Those who post to the challenges board ("I have trouble with X . . .") can work with you and with classmates to work on their problem areas. The course management software lets you set up a climate in which students feel it's okay and safe to admit they're confused or want reassurance.

databases, online museum and library collections, and government sites are just a few of the types of links that students will find helpful.

Discussion Boards Threaded discussions, or series of online postings on particular topics, are an excellent way of getting students involved in the course. You can use discussion boards to set up forums on topics that you cover in class or to post open-ended questions for comment. Before students begin posting to the board, hold a class discussion on Netiquette: the dos and don'ts of responsible, courteous Internet behavior. Stress that you will not tolerate flaming (personal attacks), and encourage students to avoid posting in all capital letters (they're hard to read and indicate "shouting"). If you want students to post more than "Good job" or "I liked that," provide examples of strong and weak posts, and discuss the factors that contribute to the difference. Ideally, discussion boards help teach students the arts of asking open-ended, thought-provoking questions; of reflection; of realizing — and posting — new insights and explaining to others why they agree with a comment or how they see a particular topic differently.

Learn through experience when to jump in on the online conversation and when to let the students alone in their talking. Most course management packages include a control panel that allows you to sort posts easily, so you can track who's writing and who's lurking.

After you have become fluent in the easier-to-master components of online teaching, consider having your class interact in small online groups — perhaps through peer editing or online group presentations. You can set up a chat room for a full, real-time class lecture and discussion or for virtual office hours. A course site can also enable small groups to "meet" online in synchronous discussion, to post to a group discussion board, and to exchange files with each other. Another idea is to bring in a guest expert for an online chat session. Students can post pre-conference questions, and after the chat you might post the chat transcript.

Assessment is another useful feature of course management packages. You can write simple multiple-choice quizzes for students to take online, and the program will grade them and report the scores to you. You might also create a page where students can view their assignment grades throughout the course. Pebuilt tests, quizzes, and other content are available to *Bedford Guide* adopters who use course management systems. To preview and adopt content, visit <bfwpub.com/lms>.

Obtaining Feedback

Be sure to solicit feedback from your students on how useful your course site really is. You might ask students to turn in a quick reflection paragraph after a major assignment involving online research or collaboration. Ask them what worked and what didn't work technically and what challenges or successes they had with the assignment. Ask for success stories — not only with yes/no questions ("Did you use the online glossary I set up?"), but also with open-ended prompts ("To what extent did you use and learn from peer-editing online feedback?" "Please give a specific example"). Save those success stories, and share them with faculty and administrators.

USING ONLINE TUTORING SERVICES

Online tutoring services such as <smarthinking.com> or <tutor.com> are increasingly popular resources for students. Students who subscribe to a service can submit multiple drafts of their essays to professionally trained tutors, many of them moonlighting composition instructors, for feedback. Depending on the site, students can submit drafts by e-mail or fax; some services use chat rooms. Services train tutors not to "fix" papers for students but to report areas of weakness, ask questions, and suggest alternatives. Many services track resubmitted drafts throughout the process, and most provide a quick turnaround on each draft, billing students at an hourly rate for each submission. While online services tutor mostly students who have purchased their own individual service, some colleges have contracted with services to tutor blocks of their students. If your school has no writing center, recommending an online tutoring service can offer an alternative for students who need extra help. Students should be aware of turnaround times and all fees before they subscribe. Advise them to check the credentials of the tutor and to check the references provided. Sites such as <homeworktips .about.com> list top picks for online tutoring services. In addition to the commercial online services, many universities offer online writing resources for students. Sites such as Purdue University's Online Writing Lab at <owl.english.purdue.edu> provide a wealth of resources and links to help students with their writing.

TECHNOLOGICAL RESOURCES IN *THE BEDFORD GUIDE*

Throughout *The Bedford Guide* and its electronic ancillaries you will find resources both to improve students' understanding of current technology and to help you use computers to enhance your writing instruction. You may want to copy the following pages for your students so that they can keep track of all the electronic resources that are available to help them while they write. If your students know that these resources are there and can become familiar with them through your instruction and with a little outside experimentation, these tools will fast become the first place students go to get ideas or to get help.

Chapters on Writing with Computers

Throughout the text are guidelines for writing with computers. Chapter 21, "Strategies for Designing Your Document," provides tips on using word-processing programs for document design. Chapter 14, "Writing in the Workplace," illustrates the use of e-mail for professional correspondence and contains some practical ideas for using this medium. If your students' textbooks include *A Writer's Research Manual*, you can refer them to these chapters, which address the use of computers for research and research writing. The Quick Research Guide, in all versions of the text, also covers searching for, evaluating, and documenting electronic sources.

Here's an Idea …

Encourage students to create a podcast around one of the issues that you address in the course, such as the effects of iPods or text messaging on human interaction. Students can work in teams to script an editorial or to plan a set of interview questions to be asked of, say, a campus media expert. Outside of class or during an additional class session, they can record and edit their work. When students have finished, you might "broadcast" the podcasts during a class session, encouraging feedback from other students. It's usually possible to record podcasts directly onto a computer with free software such as Audacity. If you are unfamiliar with recording methods, ask for help from a more experienced instructor or from a representative of your campus computer center.

Reader Selections and Activities

New to *A Writer's Reader* is a chapter on electronic technology, added in response to reviewer requests. It explores such topics as the effects of iPods on the social fabric, the possibilities and consequences of online learning communities, and free speech and privacy issues in the age of MySpace. This chapter encourages students to think critically about technology and it provides many springboards for discussion, whether in traditional classrooms or in online learning environments.

A Writer's Reader also contains Web-based research and discussion activities. At the beginning of each chapter in the reader, a Web Search prompt suggests a question or topic for exploration and points students toward relevant Web sources. The activities are tied to the chapter topic and will give students practice finding and evaluating Web sources. You might want to use the activities as the basis for class discussion or for journal writing, or as springboards for paper writing. For more on this feature, see page 244 of this manual. Chapter 8 of this manual contains suggestions for using individual Web Search activities.

Web Tips

The Bedford Guide contains Web references (marked with a blue bullet) in the margins of the text, referring students to *The Bedford Guide* Web site for further practice, activities, instruction, and examples. These cross-references include keywords, marked with a magnifying glass icon, that students can type into the Web site, bringing them to the information they need.

For E-Writers Boxes

Throughout the text, the E-Writers boxes give students ideas for using their computers for specific assignments and activities. In the rhetoric and the research manual, these boxes suggest planning, drafting, developing, and revision techniques for specific writing assignments. Encourage students to try out at least one or two of these ideas early in the term; the book's index contains a complete list for students who would like to experiment with a variety of techniques.

TECHNOLOGICAL RESOURCES ACCOMPANYING
THE BEDFORD GUIDE

The first of the resources described below — the companion Web site, Re:Writing, and Teaching Central — are free and open.

The Bedford Guide for College Writers *Companion Web Site*

The companion Web site at <bedfordstmartins.com/bedguide>, offers a convenient home base for students and instructors using *The Bedford Guide*. Students can access additional activities, assignments, models, and examples. Instructors can access a rich array of additional resources for their courses, such as sample syllabi, PowerPoints, and other supplemental course materials.

The companion Web site is keyed to the content of *The Bedford Guide* itself, so it should be the first place you direct students for further help and activities. Keywords in the text's cross-references allow students to jump immediately to useful information on the Web site. In addition, a new "Ask the Draft Doctor" feature gives students advice about common writing concerns and refers them to relevant materials on the Web site. Your students will appreciate the straightforward and easy-to-navigate design of the site.

The Web site also offers access to Exercise Central, the largest collection of editing exercises available online. Practice is available for each topic in *A Writer's Handbook* — with immediate and helpful feedback. You'll find that even students who are clear on grammar concepts will want to use Exercise Central for practice. In addition, exercises cover such writing basics as identifying thesis and support, organizing support, identifying effective introductions and conclusions, integrating source material and avoiding plagiarism, and documenting sources. Also included are new ESL exercises. Students will appreciate Exercise Central's ease of use and clear design, as well as its immediate feedback function: It answers the question "why" when they make an error. You can access your students' scores through the Instructor Resources link on *The Bedford Guide* home page. For even more online exercises, refer students to <bedfordstmartins.com/exercisecentral>.

Re: Writing

This resource, at <bedforstmartins.com/rewriting>, collects Bedford/St. Martin's most popular and widely used online resources at a single address. It includes grammar exercises and diagnostics, research and documentation advice, model documents, tutorials on avoiding plagiarism and evaluating sources, visual analysis activities, instructor resources, and more.

Here's an Idea . . .

Have groups of students look up different schools' Web sites and evaluate them based on criteria established by the class. If your school has a Web site, have students compare and contrast it with one from a college in another part of the country. In what ways do the sites serve prospective students, currently enrolled students, and faculty differently? How are the purposes of the two sites similar? As an alternative, have students compare and evaluate the services offered by different online writing centers.

Teaching Central

Teaching Central, at <bedfordstmartins.com/teachingcentral>, includes all the Bedford/St. Martin's support for instructors, from the first-time teaching assistant to the program director. From this site, instructors can access landmark references (both print and online, such as *The Bedford Bibliography for Teachers of Writing*); teaching advice and blogs; collections of background readings; classroom materials such as handouts, assignments, and activities (including special material for adjuncts); and information about Bedford/St. Martin's-sponsored workshops on technology, assessment, visual rhetoric, and more.

Testing Tool Kit: A Writing and Grammar Test Bank CD-ROM

This CD allows you to create secure, customized tests and quizzes to assess your students' understanding of the writing and grammar concepts covered in *The Bedford Guide*. It contains nearly two thousand questions grouped into sets on specific writing and grammar topics — forty-seven in all. You can administer the sets as presented or mix and match them to create your own tests. Question sets are at two levels of difficulty so that you can pick the right level for your courses and goals. Also included are ten ready-to-administer diagnostic tests.

A chart at the end of this manual correlates chapters in *The Bedford Guide* with topic sets in *Testing Tool Kit*. For a demo, visit <bedfordstmartins.com/toolkit>. *Testing Tool Kit* is available for free to adopters of *The Bedford Guide*. To obtain a copy, contact your local sales representative.

The following items are premium resources for building online courses:

- **The Bedford Guide for College Writers *e-Book*.** The e-book offers the complete text of the print book, with built-in state-of-the-art tools and multimedia from the book's Web site. Students can highlight and annotate the readings, respond to writing prompts directly in the book, jump to interactive exercises, and bookmark sections for reference. Instructors can add their own materials —models, notes, assignments, course guidelines — and even reorganize chapters. For a Quick Start on using the e-book, see p. 76.

- *PeerSpace.* This resource includes confidence-building activities that teach best practices for peer review. It offers models, exercises, assignments, and an interactive simulation game.

- *Re:Writing Plus.* This growing collection of premium learning modules includes *i-cite online*, visual exercises for citing and documenting sources; *PeerSpace*; *Make-a-Paragraph Kit*, with an animated introduction to the writing process, grammar tutorials, and more; and *Write On* video tutorials on writing.

- *Comment.* This Web-based peer-review software lets students share and comment on their writing. Instructors can create comments that link directly to specific passages in *The Bedford Guide e-Book*.

- *CompClass.* This easy-to-use course management system integrates all the innovative media supporting *The Bedford Guide* — the e-book, *Re:Writing Plus*, *Comment*, the book companion site, and more — with course tools designed specifically for the reading, writing, practice, and discussion that writing instructors and students do.

A note about activation codes and access: Activation codes are required for the e-book, *PeerSpace, Re:Writing Plus, Comment,* or *CompClass.* Codes can be purchased separately or packaged with the print book at a significant discount. Once activation codes have been purchased, these resources can be accessed through *The Bedford Guide* Web site. For more information, visit <bedfordstmartins.com> or contact your local Bedford/St. Martin's sales representative.

Quick Start for *The Bedford Guide e-Book*

Students: Students can activate their e-book account using the instructions in the access code card they purchased, or log in with the information they received when they purchased access through the Bedford/St. Martin's Web site.

Instructors: After obtaining instructor access to the e-book via the Web form or your sales rep, log in with your e-mail address and password.

Once you are logged in, follow these instructions to get started.

Navigation

- Use the arrows at the top of each page to page through the book.
- Use the **Go to chapter** pulldown menu to select a specific chapter.
- Within chapters, use the chapter-level table of contents in the left sidebar to navigate the chapter and find related resources on the book's Web site.

Add your own notes to any page

1. Click the **Notes/Highlighting** link near the top of the right sidebar to open the **Notes/Highlighting Options** menu.
2. Click **Add Note** to open a new note.
3. Type your note in the blank text area of the box.
4. Click the **SAVE** icon in the right sidebar.

- To edit or delete a note, click the **EDIT** icon in the upper left corner of the note.
- To open a printable view of all of your notes, click the **Notes** link at the top of the left sidebar.
- To learn how to share notes with other users, open the help menu and read the sections on **Annotation Sets** and **Note Subscribing and Importing**.

Other Features

- Open the help menu by clicking the question mark (?) icon at the top of any page.
- To find out how to add custom material to the e-book, open the help menu and choose **Custom Sections**.

CHAPTER 6

Assessing Student Writing

If grades and writing had a direct and positive correlation, then after years of producing at least passing grades, students would enter our classrooms with the skills they need to write decent papers. We all know that this does not happen. Students have endured a wide spectrum of evaluation — from papers awash in red ink to having to write each misspelled word twenty times. We believe we owe them a different type of evaluation and a different way to think about "the grade."

In the past, we, the authors of this manual, graded almost every piece of student work that came across our desks — from rough and final drafts to reflective writing — and averaged them with quizzes and exams, but the more grades we assigned, the less students focused on writing. To emphasize the importance of writing as a process rather than as a product, we now ask students to save everything that has been part of the process — from scribbles to final drafts. Many instructors ask students to keep this writing in a portfolio — an especially effective way to evaluate students' writing processes as well as their final work. In this chapter, we provide information on using writing portfolios in your course and evaluating them. You'll also find references to student portfolios throughout this manual and a section on organizing and revising a writing portfolio in Chapter 15, "Writing for Assessment," of *The Bedford Guide*. Two additional Bedford/St. Martin's resources offer valuable advice on portfolios: *Portfolio Keeping* (for students) and *Portfolio Teaching* (for instructors).

Later in the current chapter we discuss three distinct ways to engage with student writing — responding, evaluating or grading, and assessing — all of which are essential to your course if students are to grow as writers. We hope this advice will help you to establish a system of evaluation that succeeds with your students.

PORTFOLIOS

We cannot recommend strongly enough using portfolios in your course. The minute you put a grade on a student's writing, the process stops. Portfolio evaluation enables you to detect problems and remediate them in an ungraded situation. When students revisit their writing over a longer period of time, the process of rethinking and revising allows them to produce much stronger work. By assembling portfolios and reflecting on the writing in them, students learn to think more critically about writing — both their own and that of others — and to see writing as a process. As a result, they become more autonomous writers.

Once you decide to use portfolios in your course, you must define

- your purpose
- the content you will require
- how to evaluate the content

Purpose

Composition instructors at Dodge City Community College chose to use portfolios because they show a truly representative sampling of a student's work. The student has ample time to develop his or her writing, fully engaging in the writing process and applying what he or she has learned throughout the course.

Using portfolios in your course shows students that good writing is the result of a process. Portfolios can lessen the stress of a task that many students consider troublesome and give them a greater chance for success. And you can be more confident of fair assessment when evaluating portfolios. For more on the benefits of using portfolios in your course, see *Portfolios: Process and Product*, by Pat Belanoff and Marcia Dickson (Portsmouth, NH: Heinemann-Boynton/Cook, 1991).

Content

Our students keep all of their writing — preliminary work, drafts of each essay, and reflective writing — for the semester in a *working portfolio*. This can be any type of expandable or pocketed folder. If students do not have all of their preliminary work in their working portfolio, we do not accept their presentation portfolio for grading at the end of the term. This ensures that students complete all of the assignments, not just the essays required in the presentation portfolio.

The *presentation portfolio* is a separate folder in which the students place their best work for grading at the end of the term. The contents of this portfolio determine the writing grade for the course. We require our students to select three essays from the six that they have written during the course to include in these portfolios. Other instructors we know also require students to include one timed, in-class writing assignment. In addition, students must write a final reflective essay to include in their presentation portfolios.

Reflective Writing

The inclusion of reflective essays distinguishes a portfolio from just another collection of essays. In reflective writing, we ask students to think critically about what they do and why they do it. Asking students to evaluate their own thinking and writing processes helps them to focus on their next step by looking at where they've been. Reflective writing teaches students to judge their work on their own, without relying on an instructor's evaluation.

Here are some topics you might want to ask students to consider in their reflective essays: where they were as writers when they began the course and where they are at the end; goals they have accomplished and how they have done so; problems they are still having and strategies they can use to overcome them; and what they consider difficult about writing, what they consider easy, and what makes it so. In their writing about selections for their presentation portfolios, ask students to discuss why they chose to include the essays they did and why they excluded others, or which writing they like best and which they feel is their most substantial. They might also discuss specific areas of their writing in which they were especially successful or areas in which they felt the writing did not work. You may want to assign the Self-Assessment Questionnaire included at the end of this chapter to help guide students' responses to their writing.

Be specific about the subjects that you deem out of bounds, such as the textbook, the instructor, or the time and effort a student spent on the assignment. Students must write about writing itself. It's a good idea to familiarize students with reflective writing before the end of the term by asking them to write about specific writing assignments throughout the course. These earlier reflective pieces can, of course, be included in their working portfolios and serve as a resource for producing the final reflective essay.

Evaluation

Students who are fixated on grades will become anxious not knowing their grades until the end of the course. One way to handle this concern is to give them a broad estimate at midterm. Do this only in a conference and not earlier than the middle of the semester. Make clear that this grade is subject to change as the student's writing evolves. This policy can help ease anxiety so that the student becomes more focused on the writing and less concerned with grades.

The week before students turn in their presentation portfolios, schedule conferences with them to talk about the pieces they have chosen to revise. Ask them to describe what they see as necessary revisions and to identify the remaining trouble spots in the selected drafts.

When it's time to evaluate the presentation portfolios, use the same criteria you would for evaluating individual essays: Look for the writer's ideas and content, organization and structure, and mechanics and usage. Explain these requirements in the syllabus or in a handout. Many students are not familiar with portfolios and will need to refer to this information throughout the course. Also, clearly state your expectations about what constitutes a complete portfolio — for example a student who does not do all the required writing will fail the course. This avoids unpleasant surprises at the end of the semester.

Many instructors resist using portfolios in their courses because they fear being overwhelmed with paperwork at the end of the term. This is not at all the case, however. Grading presentation portfolios requires less time because you have been working with the writer on previous drafts all semester. Having already responded to earlier work, you need only to award the presentation portfolio a holistic grade, without writing extensive comments on each draft. Ask students to highlight revisions on each new draft. This will not only help you follow the trail of their revisions throughout the semester, but it will also make evaluating the final portfolio easier and quicker. If your course includes a research component with a long paper, consider grading those papers earlier in the term and figuring those grades into the final grade for the presentation portfolio at the end of the semester.

One of our colleagues allows his students to continue to revise their assigned essays and submit drafts for critique until students are satisfied with their papers. At any time during the term, his students may submit a final draft for grading. As in other delayed grading approaches, this variation fosters the notion that a piece of writing is not finished until the writer is satisfied with it. Although many students still submit all of their final drafts at the end of the semester, with this approach, you can finish some grading early.

You might also want to consider exchanging your students' presentation portfolios with a colleague who uses portfolio evaluation. This will ensure a more objective reading of student essays that can sometimes feel too familiar to you because you've worked closely with the material during the course.

RESPONDING TO STUDENT WRITING

We use the term *responding* here to mean the act of making specific comments about student writing and describing what students have done well and what they need to do better. When we respond to student writing, we hide the red pen and sit on our hands. An instructor, of course, has the responsibility to grade students' writing, but grades hold little meaning for struggling writers if evaluations are not grounded in and accompanied by clearly stated and specific comments. Your responses will contribute an essential element to a student's writing process. Until students learn to think about and read their own work more critically, they rely on you to question and guide them.

To encourage students to succeed and to continue to stretch as writers and thinkers, concentrate on building into your course ways for them to receive responses on three levels:

- from peers
- from self-evaluation
- from the instructor

Receiving these responses at various stages of the writing process enables students to understand in a much more profound way their own process of critical thinking and writing. We emphasize the importance of the writing process by requiring students to submit rough drafts for each writing assignment, asking them to staple or clip their drafts together in reverse chronological order. We also insist that students type their final rough draft. Marking a typed draft makes the recursive nature of writing more explicit for students: Just because a draft is typed does not mean the essay is finished. We return these drafts with comments on content, organization, and mechanics, but without a grade.

If you are not using portfolios in your course, ask students to turn in the typed final paper with all of their intermediate drafts, peer-editing checklists, and prewriting materials so that you can see what is changing from assignment to assignment and what might be persistent problems for students. With such a quantity of writing, patterns of weaknesses emerge more easily, and students can work to revise them on their own or in class with peer editors.

Remember that not every piece of writing requires an extensive response from you. For some writing, peer editors will provide commentary; other pieces can be discussed briefly or at length in class or in conferences. For more about responding to student writing, see *Teaching Composition: Background Readings,* Third Edition.

Holistic Evaluation

Always read students' writing in its entirety first. Always. This sounds obvious, but too often writing teachers develop a habit of automatically reading students' work against a mental criteria sheet and ticking off "statement of thesis OK," "transition to paragraph 2 faulty," or "incoherent phrase here." It's important to articulate for yourself your first impression of the whole work so that you don't make partial judgments that do not hold true later in a student's essay.

A response to the work as a whole is called *holistic evaluation.* Holistic evaluators know that, as practiced readers and writers, they can recognize, almost intuitively, how the parts of a piece of writing are connected to the whole and how effective those connections are. Holistic evaluation always respects and rewards what is on the page. Atomistic evaluation — focusing on the parts without paying attention to the whole work — tends to critique student writing based on what it does not accomplish.

When responding to student papers, comment first on the writing as a whole: how much the work seems to be informed by a purpose, how much of it is developed with thought and feeling, and how accessible the writing is to you as a reader. Be sure to describe why the writing is successful or unsuccessful. Tell students —either in conferences or in writing — what works, what doesn't, and how to begin revisions.

Be specific; writing the word *good* at the top of a page does nothing to help improve the writer. Indicate which part or parts of the essay are effective and why, and which section or sections still seem to lack a focus or plan. If the writing is successful but not of the highest quality, describe what works well and what the student needs to do to improve the writing. If the work is not only successful but also particularly well done, tell the writer what aspects make it exceptional so that he or she can use that information in revising or in approaching future writing assignments. Remember that your purpose in commenting on students' writing is to help them improve their writing skills: be positive and specific.

For more about holistic scoring, see Karen Greenberg's essay in James McMillan's *Assessing Students' Learning* (New Directions for Teaching and Learning, 1988) and Edward M. White's *Teaching and Assessing Writing,* Second Edition (Jossey-Bass, 1994).

Some Guidelines for Responding

Students' most frequent complaint about feedback is "If you get a decent grade, the teacher doesn't tell you why." Even though responses take various shapes, the following rules of thumb might be helpful:

1. Always begin with praise or with a description of the writing's strengths. Know that students weigh the negative feedback three or four times more heavily than the positive feedback. If you give one comment that praises and one that suggests revision, the student will probably hear both as negative comments. Sometimes you might have to look harder for something to praise than for something to critique, but it's important to acknowledge that even an unsuccessful piece of writing took time and trouble. Remember to address specific areas of content or mechanics. Positive feedback can profoundly change attitudes about writing and increase student motivation.

2. Select a few specific areas to comment on. Students might be overwhelmed if you comment on everything. If you look at several drafts, be sure that in subsequent drafts you comment on the areas that you earlier suggested needed revision.

3. Avoid labels (abbreviations or symbols) in your response. You'll be tempted to use them because of the time involved in responding effectively, but don't. Many writing handbooks still offer charts with labels for categories of writing problems in syntax, grammar, and word choice. Don't use them. They communicate, if at all, to only the most assiduous student, and that student is usually a dualistic thinker, looking for ways to fix a product rather than ways to think about how his or her writing affects the reader and how to make it better. If a writer had realized a particular wording was "awkward," he or she most likely would have revised the wording. You need to explain with a concise statement why that particular wording is awkward and how it complicates or obfuscates meaning. If some students have a pattern of writing incomplete sentences in finished drafts, it's not likely that labeling them "s.f." or "frag" will help them break the habit. They need to know the logic behind "s.f." and "frag." Indicate problematic sentences with a bright highlighter and explain how the problem you've identified affects the meaning in one of the sentences. Encourage writers to think through how the other highlighted materials affect both the meaning and readers' responses. (Note that Comment, an online peer review tool, can make commenting on papers easier. See p. 75 for a description.)

4. Make responding with specific comments part of the drafting and revising process. Formalize this structure by scheduling office conferences or mini-conferences during in-class writing and revising sessions.

5. Encourage students to assess and comment on their own work in reflective writing, peer-response groups, and conferences. Whenever students submit writing to you, ask them to include a note about what particularly pleases and troubles them about it, and keep those concerns in mind as you respond. You might also want to ask students to use the Revision Checklists and For Peer Response questions in *The Bedford Guide* as guidelines for writing about their process. Use these self-assessment materials to prompt conversations with students about their process and progress. In conferences, ask students to tell you what they like best about a draft and what problems they see with it. If you encourage self-assessment at various turning points in the course, students will become more self-reflective and analytical writers.

Ranking Papers

Holistic evaluation is also a useful way to get an overview of the class. Read ten responses to an assignment, arrange them from strongest to weakest, and then rank them from 8 to 2, strongest to weakest. Be sure you have at least one essay for each level. You'll have more than one for some levels. Organize the essays into three ranges with 8 and 7 at the higher end of the scale; 6, 5, and 4 as the middle and average responses; and 3 and 2 as the weakest papers. Then read the remainder of the papers against this range to get a clearer picture of both relative success and what characterizes lower-, middle-, and upper-range papers. Share this information with your class as you return the essays.

Or ask students to perform their own holistic evaluation. Bring to class the papers that exemplify the levels of evaluation, and ask students in small groups to read the entire set and arrange them in order. (Use papers from another class section and mask out the names of the writers. Trade papers with colleagues if necessary to build a bank of papers to use in your classes.) Record students' evaluations on the board. You might be surprised at what happens. Although there will be some disagreement about specific rankings, there usually isn't much disagreement across the range of high, middle, and low rankings, because good writing is so easily recognized. If an essay does score across the range, ask students about their reactions: How do personal preferences about topic, style, or tone affect their responses to the essay?

Practicing holistic evaluation helps student writers begin to assess themselves by showing them how to revise, how to satisfy assignments more successfully, or how to develop their writing more richly. Because the ranking is descriptive, not a judgment carrying the weight of a grade, students will see, once again, that there is no one right way to respond but that successful writers are able to use a prompt to discover a purpose for writing and to shape a draft to a particular audience in a variety of effective ways.

Auditory Evaluation

Many instructors find auditory evaluation to be a useful method of responding to student writing. In conferences, ask students to read their writing aloud. Listen for strengths and weaknesses and take notes on which sections need revisions and which are working especially well. By reading their drafts aloud, students become more sensitive to the voice and tone they are using in their papers. They will often stop and revise, by changing words and phrases, while they are reading; they might even ask you to wait while they make notes on the draft. The experience of hearing their own language is a valuable editing tool. You might also want to ask students to read their drafts to peer editors, or to encourage students to read their papers aloud by themselves before handing them in.

EVALUATION AND GRADING

Ideally, we would be writing coaches rather than writing judges. For most of us, however, grades become necessary at some point. If responding focuses on describing the success of a writing process, grading focuses more directly on measuring the success of the process and the product. You will need to establish for students what each grade represents. Bring to class past essays and portfolios that have received an A, and ask groups of students to examine them. Also bring in B, C, and D papers so that students get a solid sense of what you expect.

Regardless of your grading procedure, you will need to monitor whether students are completing their drafts by the assigned deadlines. Students must practice the writing process in order to make progress in their writing. To help them keep track of deadlines, you might give students copies of the checklist on p. 91 of this chapter. Missing deadlines and falling behind in their assignments will only diminish the importance of the process. For this reason, some professors state in their syllabi that they will not accept a paper past the established deadline. Others lower the grade they give to the draft by ten points. Consider telling students that if an essay is not turned in on or before the deadline, they will lose points on their portfolio. Tell them, "If your body is not in class on the deadline, your paper should be." Place a check in your grade book as each assignment is collected to indicate that the deadline was met. Next to the names of the writers who are late, write the point penalty. Do not accept a portfolio from any student writer who has not completed all of the assignments.

Accompanying Grades with Comments

Grading can produce angst for both you and your students. We encourage you to allow students the option of revising their work even after you grade it. The purpose of your response and evaluation is to help students improve their writing, and they should be given that opportunity. Even if you don't allow students to revise once they've been given a grade, couch your comments in terms of how the writer might go on to further revise his or her work. This will reinforce the idea that a writer's process also continues from one assignment to the next.

Ideally, your letter or number grade should follow comments throughout the essay on the rhetorical and linguistic strengths and weaknesses of the piece, as well as a longer comment that sums up and praises the success of the writing by describing features that contributed positively and negatively to the grade. Remember, too, that asking a question instead of stating a criticism forces the writer back to the essay to find the answers. Here are examples of evaluative comments with grades:

OK! I'm impressed by the revisions of your categories for classification here. Now they don't overlap, and I can see good reasons for discussing each category. Overall, you explain the craziness of cab drivers clearly and with strength. I think the fourth paragraph contains powerful, connotative language. What keeps this paper from a higher grade? (1) Where did you lose sight of your audience? In fact, Joe Grant commented on this in his peer advice. What is the thesis of this essay? (2)

What problems do you see in your sentence structure and spelling? Why do your sentences seem to come directly from your thinking in a listlike way? How could you change the sentences I highlighted? You could work on both of these areas and submit a stronger essay. I encourage you to do so.

B

James: I'm more than persuaded that Novinger has a serious problem with drinking. I particularly enjoyed the anecdotes you used to demonstrate the problem. The statistics are well chosen. I had no trouble reading the essay and particularly appreciated the variety of sentence structure and of vocabulary here. Your proposal to open a dry nightclub is imaginative. Have you explained the proposal carefully enough? What could/would I do next if I were on the Novinger Betterment Committee? In addition, what are the other reasonable solutions? Look again at the peer-editing checklists; both peer editors suggested some alternative solutions that you might need to disqualify. If you were to work further with both these parts of your proposal, you not only would have a stronger grade but also would have a proposal you could be proud to send to the NBC. The proposal is so well stated that with more "guts" to the reasoned explanation, this will be an outstanding paper. See me if you have questions about how to generate more materials for your explanation or disqualification. *C*

Grading Revisions

Responding and grading in a course that focuses on writing-as-process might differ from other grading you recall or observe. Think carefully about how to coordinate your revision policy with your grading policy. Use your evaluations as well as your responses to acknowledge the revision process and help students to internalize criteria for successful writing. There are a number of different ways to account for students' revision process in their final grades: Some instructors grade both the final draft and the revision and average the two grades for each assignment. Some use the second grade only and weight the criterion of improvement heavily in assigning that second grade. And some grade all final drafts and give students the option of revising them. However you decide to evaluate revisions, it's wise not to accept revisions during the last week of classes. Students need to plan ahead, and you need ample time to read and evaluate their work.

Choose a revision policy that will best promote serious writing and best motivate students to take responsibility for meriting the grade. You know how often students talk about teachers "giving" them a grade. Through a clear, fair revision policy, you demonstrate that a writer works to achieve a higher level of competence and success — and in fact, grades himself or herself.

Most students appreciate the opportunity to work further with writing that has been commented on and graded. A few, however, abuse the opportunity. Either they don't work seriously during their composing process because they know they have a second chance or they procrastinate about revising until the panic of approaching finals sets in. You'll need to make clear to them that they must use the opportunity for revision wisely. Remind them that revising soon after the original drafting makes it more likely that they can re-create their composing process, identify problems with it, recall strategies from it, and work from abundance. Of course, you need to set deadlines for revisions. You also need to make it clear that revision doesn't automatically improve the grade. Otherwise, students will clean up surface errors but ignore your incisive recommendations about the ideas, the development, the effect on the audience, and other rhetorical aspects. Insist that good writing often results from serious rewriting.

Here's an Idea . . .

Have your students submit a blank cassette tape with their drafts. Mark places in the draft that you want to comment on with a number. Then, prefacing your remarks with a number, record the comments that refer to that number. This works especially well for students who are auditory learners, and it has the advantage of eliminating paperwork for you.

Establishing a Grading System

Regardless of whether you decide to grade based on letters or numbers, you will need to clearly describe for your students what qualifies for each grade level. Provide this information as soon as possible, either when you make an assignment or when you return the first set of graded papers. Some instructors give these descriptions along with examples of student papers for each grade. (If you do this, take the models from another class section.) Also, most departments will have a folder that is supplemented each semester with sample essays for each grade level.

Letter grading assumes that there are such things as A and F papers. Can you clearly define an A paper? Decide whether you are looking for certain A-paper characteristics in addition to specific criteria for success or a set of "primary traits" for each assignment. Tell students about both sets of your criteria. When you write an assignment or develop a prompt for an assignment you've chosen from *The Bedford Guide*, think about how you will evaluate and grade responses to the assignment. Share that information with students when you discuss the writing assignment.

Many educational systems have numerical rubrics that you can refer to, but we encourage you to develop your own and not to rely on one developed by someone who does not know your expectations and your students. One of our colleagues who uses a numerical grading system awards each paper up to 25 percent (or 25 points) for originality and logic of content; up to 25 percent for the development of ideas through a method of explanation or persuasion; up to 25 percent for style, which includes tone and awareness of audience; and up to 25 percent for expression, which includes diction, grammar, punctuation, and spelling. He weights the papers from the end of the semester more heavily than earlier ones. This kind of analytical scoring defines subskills and assigns a score to each one. Although this approach does not look at the success or failure of a piece of writing as a whole, it can be useful in identifying students' specific strengths and weaknesses, especially if you look for patterns emerging from several writing assignments.

Some states have adopted analytical guides for assessing the writing programs in public schools, and if students in your area have been assessed using a certain model, you might want to consider adopting similar criteria in your own classroom.

The Kansas model, outlined in detail in the handout at the end of this chapter, looks at six traits:

- content and ideas
- organization
- voice
- word choice

- sentence fluency

- conventions

Although this model was developed for assessment rather than grading, instructors have adapted it for grading by assigning points to each of the traits and weighting them according to which traits they want to emphasize. The traits are each rated on a continuum of 1 to 5. A 5 rating indicates a writer who is in control, a 3 indicates a balance of weaknesses and strengths in a particular trait, and a 1 indicates a prewriting, searching stage. See pages 92–97 of this manual for the handout "Six-Trait Analytical Assessment Model," describing for students a 1, 3, and 5 paper in each of the traits.

Using a commen set of descriptive terms facilitates discussion of skill areas and helps students to target specific skills for improvement. The six-trait model, or a similar one, can lighten the paper load when you respond to drafts because it allows you to focus extensive comments on one or two traits and to indicate others with just a rating. In early drafts, focus on ideas and content or on organization, and then as students progress, you can begin to evaluate language and conventional skills.

Revising Your Grading Policy

Grading is also a recursive process. Although you might be tempted to change your grading policy in the middle of a semester, don't. You can revise your policy the next time you teach the course; for the first semester, stay with the policy you've announced. You've made a contract with your students, and breaking it will only disrupt the learning process.

If you're feeling uncertain about your evaluation or grading, trade papers with a veteran writing instructor and ask him or her to grade them. Then sit down and discuss with your colleague why and how he or she grades in a particular way. Don't be afraid to discuss this. You will have insights to help your colleague as much as he or she will have some to assist you. Know that you must go through a recursive process to clarify to yourself what you're measuring, why, and how best to do so. As you gain more insight and confidence through the process, grading becomes easier. Don't let yourself agonize so long over grading that it interferes with your other teaching tasks.

Try quickly reading all of the papers at once to help you decide how to revise an assignment the next time you teach the course. Establish a strong sense of the class's overall response before you begin grading the papers individually. Many instructors grade the first papers they read either more leniently or more harshly than the last papers. Having a sense of the class's overall performance will keep you from revising your grading criteria as you work through the papers, and it will provide insight into whether the assignment itself is too difficult or unclear.

INSTITUTIONAL ASSESSMENT

Because faculty members believe strongly in their definitions of assessment, large-scale assessment can provoke heated departmental arguments. Read the professional journals in your library and you will discover that the debate is not limited to a few academic departments. Our students are continuously assessed: by the college, by the state, by their employers, and by individual instructors. In all contexts, assessment should be a valid and unbiased indicator of the students' skills and past experience. Its use should aid both student and instructor in learning, not ranking.

You will need to think about how to prepare your students for writing assessment beyond your classroom. Assign a diagnostic timed essay early in the semester and report back to students about how well they think on their feet. When you request a writing sample to use for assessment, tell students what criteria you will use to judge their writing. Although we would never advocate teaching to a test, students still need to prepare for those unavoidable written exams. Chapter 15 of *The Bedford Guide*, "Writing for Assessment," gives students suggestions that apply not only to exams but also to most writing situations. This chapter is useful in generating discussion of how students can approach large-scale assessment tasks successfully.

Your written program or university curriculum might require some kind of assessment for placement, for advising, or for course completion or graduation. If your school uses such assessment, be sure that the assessment has value for the students. Insist that its results be described to student writers in such a way that they can look again at their writing process and behaviors and improve as writers. If possible, discuss assessment results with each writer. If students were placed in your course as a result of assessment, use the assessment writing and its results as part of your first formal conference. Discuss with students whether the information from the assessment can help them shape their own course goals. Treat assessment results as an additional source of information about writing and as an additional perspective for thinking about ways to improve as a writer. Students should know whether their writing is competent and satisfactory, not just to check off another requirement but to decide whether, when, and how to rewrite differently — both in an assessed writing situation and in other writing situations. They need to know about the quality of their critical thinking in order to assess their skills and set additional learning goals.

A WORD ABOUT PLAGIARISM

Explaining plagiarism is a balancing act. You don't want students to feel you are accusing them a priori, but you do want to make clear that plagiarism is a serious offense with serious consequences. In most cases, plagiarism is unintentional. Students either don't know how to acknowledge a source, or they are just careless about doing so. In some cases, they don't recognize that what they are doing is plagiarism. Be sure to define plagiarism for them. One professor includes these examples in his syllabus:

- copying someone else's assignment or paper and submitting it as your own
- buying and submitting another student's work or a professionally prepared paper
- copying writing or parts of writing found on the Internet and submitting it as your own
- copying or paraphrasing words, phrases, sentences, passages, dates, or statistics without attribution
- using someone else's ideas without giving them credit
- collaborating on assignments without the permission of the instructor

Tell students that plagiarism is using someone else's ideas or words without acknowledging them, and that it is a form of cheating. Point out the department's policy on academic honesty. Find it in the student handbook or college catalog, or ask your department chair for a copy.

The best way to discourage plagiarism in student writing is to require students to provide all preliminary work and earlier drafts on demand and to submit this work with their drafts. Some instructors require students to hand in copies of their sources as well. If you suspect plagiarism, compare the student's draft with earlier writing, including in-class writing. If a draft seems markedly different, check further. The student may have enlisted the assistance of someone who has "helped" revise the draft so extensively that the student's own writing has disappeared. If this is so, earlier drafts of the assignment will reveal similarities in content. Sometimes a student borrows from another source extensively without realizing that she should have acknowledged the source. These types of plagiarism are not deliberate cheating and should not be treated as a moral failing. They require teaching the student to seek appropriate kinds of help or to document properly. Because standards for attribution are sometimes different in other cultures, you may find it necessary to explain the appropriate standards to international students.

Deliberate plagiarism, however, is a serious transgression that requires a disciplinary response. Most instructors have encountered plagiarism of one degree or another, so talk to your colleagues about how they have detected and handled the problem. Check your school's or department's policy regarding plagiarism and make the consequences of plagiarizing clear in your syllabus. If you know a student has deliberately plagiarized, allowing him or her merely to rewrite an assignment without further consequences makes cheating a game: "Can I get away with this now if I only risk having to do the assignment later?"

The Internet has exacerbated the opportunity for students to plagiarize, but it has also made detection easier. Often you can find plagiarized passages by typing a suspect line or phrase from the student's draft into a search engine such as <Yahoo.com> or <Google.com>. Enclose the line in quotation marks. If the passage — or the whole essay — was plagiarized, it may appear near the top of the list of search results. Many schools subscribe to programs written to detect plagiarism, such as <turnitin.com>.

If you find proof of plagiarism and believe that it was intentional, inform your department chair or dean to see how you should proceed. You may need to set up a conference with the student. Bring the essay in question and copies of the original source to the conference to show the student, but retain them for your file. Tell the student what you have found and explain the consequences, calling the student's attention to your syllabus and the department or college policy on plagiarism. Be direct and specific. After the conference, update the department chair or dean. Refer students to pages 663–66 in *A Writer's Research Manual*, or section D1 of the Quick Research Guide for more on plagiarism.

RESOURCES IN *THE BEDFORD GUIDE*

The Bedford Guide provides resources that help students prepare for assessment and help you to respond to and evaluate their writing. The following list includes references to pages in this manual, where you will find more information about using these resources in your course.

- Chapter 15, "Writing for Assessment" (pp. 277–90), pages 197–202 of this manual. Most college students will be required to take an essay exam at some point. Because of the time constraints, when faced with tests, students often forget everything they ever learned about the writing process. You can help them apply the writing skills they learn in your course to other forms of writing-based assessment by giving them the opportunity to practice their test-taking skills in your course. Chapter 15 also covers strategies that students can use to prepare for essay and short-answer exams.

Early in the semester, introduce students to the advice the authors give about assembling writing portfolios and including reflective writing about their work. Ask them to return to the list of questions on textbook pages 287–88 before their midterm evaluation or conference and before they hand in their final portfolio.

- *A Writer's Research Manual* (pp. 585–717), pages 308–48 of this manual. If your version of *The Bedford Guide* includes *A Writer's Research Manual*, direct your students to Chapter 32's advice on avoiding plagiarism. In addition, Chapter 33, "Writing Your Research Paper," and Chapter 34, "Documenting Sources," offer improved coverage that will help your students use source material responsibly.

- Quick Research Guide (pp. A-1–A-34), page 352 of this manual. Available in all versions of *The Bedford Guide*, this appendix helps students avoid plagiarism by providing clear advice on incorporating, citing, and documenting sources.

- Quick Editing Guide (pp. A-35–A-53), page 351 of this manual. Some instructors lower students' grades for grammatical or mechanical errors in their writing. Encourage students to refer to the Quick Editing Guide on their own to improve their final drafts and to increase their awareness of the kind of errors they are likely to make under the pressure of timed essay exams.

- For Peer Response boxes, page 39 of this manual. Through peer editing, students learn to revise and edit by modeling the kinds of questions instructors will ask of their papers in an evaluation. The peer-response boxes throughout the text focus students on these questions and emphasize the importance of revision to the writing process.

Ancillaries to The Bedford Guide

In addition to the features in the textbook, several ancillaries also support response and evaluation and help your students understand and avoid plagiarism.

- Comment for *The Bedford Guide*. This Web-based tool makes it easy for you to provide meaningful responses to student writing. Comment helps you focus on what to say rather than how to legibly squeeze it into the margins of a paper. It also allows you to link to specific parts of the *Bedford Guide e-Book*.

- Exercise Central. *Bedford Guide*-specific exercises are available through the companion Web site at <bedfordstmartins.com/bedguide>. Exercise Central helps you identify your students' most common grammar errors and lets you assign exercises that allow students to practice grammar, writing, and research skills at their own pace. Even more practices are available at <bedfordstmartins.com/exercisecentral>.

- Re:Writing. Available at <bedfordstmartins.com/rewriting>, this resource includes a tutorial on avoiding plagiarism, among other aids and activities.

- The *Testing Took Kit* CD-ROM. With more than two thousand test items, this resource allows you to create secure, customized tests and quizzes to assess students' writing and grammar competency and gauge their progress as the course progresses. A chart correlating test items with sections of *The Bedford Guide* appears at the end of this manual.

SELF-ASSESSMENT QUESTIONNAIRE

How would you describe your progress as a writer?

What writings have satisfied you most? Why?

What has been most difficult for you to master? Why?

What would you list as your strengths as a writer at midterm?

What do you see as problems to solve as a writer in the second half of the semester?

What goals are you setting for yourself?

Rate your success with reaching any of those goals.

What assistance do you most need from me, your instructor?

COMPOSITION I CHECKLIST

Writer _____ Section _____

	Topic	Prewriting	Draft	Peer Editing	Submitted Manuscript
Recalling an Experience					
Observing a Scene					
Interviewing a Subject					
Comparing and Contrasting					
Explaining Causes and Effects					
Taking a Stand					
Proposing a Solution					
Evaluating					
Suporting a Position with Sources					

Ideas and Content

5 This paper is clear, focused, and interesting. It holds the reader's attention. Relevant anecdotes, details, and evidence enrich the central theme or story line. Ideas are fresh and original.

- The writer seems to be writing from experiences and shows insight: a good sense of how events unfold, how people respond to life and to one another.

- Supporting, relevant, telling details and evidence give the reader important information that he or she could not personally bring to the text.

- The writing has balance: Main ideas stand out. Argument is cogent.

- The writer seems in control and develops the topic in an enlightening, entertaining way.

- The writer works with and shapes ideas, making connections and sharing insights.

3 The paper is clear and focused. The topic shows promise, even though development is still limited, sketchy, too general, or out of balance with main ideas.

- The writer is beginning to define the topic but is not there yet. It is pretty easy to see where the writer is headed, although more information is needed to "fill in the blanks."

- The writer does seem to be writing from experience, but he or she has some trouble going from general to specific observations.

- Ideas are reasonably clear and purposeful, even though they may not be explicit, detailed, personalized, or expanded to show in-depth understanding.

- Support is attempted but doesn't go far enough yet in expanding, clarifying, or adding new insights.

- Themes or main points seem a blend of the original and the predictable.

1 The paper has no clear sense of purpose or central theme. To extract meaning from the text, the reader must make inferences based on sketchy details. More than one of the following problems is likely to be evident:

- Information is very limited or simply unclear. Attempts at development might be minimal.

- The text is repetitious or reads like a collection of random thoughts from which no central theme emerges.

- Everything seems as important as everything else; the reader has a hard time sifting out what's critical.

- The writer has not yet begun to define the topic in a meaningful or personal way.

- The writer might still be in search of a real topic or a sense of direction to guide development.

Organization

5   The organization enhances and showcases the central ideas or theme. The order, structure, or presentation is compelling and moves the reader through the text.

- Details seem to fit where they're placed; sequencing is logical and effective.
- An inviting introduction draws the reader in and a satisfying conclusion leaves the reader with a sense of resolution.
- Pacing is very well controlled; the writer delivers needed information at just the right moment, then moves on.
- Transitions are smooth and weave the separate threads of meaning into one cohesive whole.
- Organization flows so smoothly that the reader hardly thinks about it.

3   The organizational structure is strong enough to move the reader from point to point without undue confusion.

- The paper has a recognizable introduction and conclusion. The introduction might not create a strong sense of anticipation; the conclusion might not leave the reader with a satisfying sense of resolution.
- Sequencing is usually logical. It might sometimes be too obvious or otherwise ineffective.
- Pacing is fairly well controlled, although the writer sometimes spurts ahead too quickly or spends too much time on the obvious.
- Transitions often work well; at times, though, connections between ideas are fuzzy or call for inferences.
- Despite a few problems, the organization does not seriously get in the way of the main point or story line.

1   The writing lacks a clear sense of direction. Ideas, details, or events seem strung together in a random, haphazard fashion — or else there is no identifiable internal structure at all. More than one of the following problems is likely to be evident:

- The writer has not yet drafted a real introduction or conclusion.
- Transitions are weak; connections between ideas seem confusing or incomplete.
- Sequencing, if it exists, needs work.
- Pacing feels awkward, with a lot of time spent on minor details or big, hard-to-follow leaps made from point to point.
- Lack of organization makes it hard for the reader to get a grip on the main point or story line.

Voice

5   The writer speaks directly to the reader in a way that is individualistic, expressive, and engaging. Clearly the writer is involved in the text and is writing to be read.

- The paper is honest and written from the heart. It has the ring of conviction.
- The language is natural yet provocative.

- The reader feels a strong sense of interaction with the writer and senses the person behind the words.

- The projected tone and voice give flavor to the writer's message and seem very appropriate for the purpose and audience.

3   The writer seems sincere but not genuinely engaged, committed, or involved. The result is pleasant and sometimes even personable, but it is not compelling.

- The writing communicates in an earnest, pleasing manner. Moments here and there amuse, surprise, delight, or move the reader.

- Voice might emerge strongly on occasion, then retreat behind general, vague, tentative, or abstract language.

- The writing hides rather than reveals the writer.

- The writer seems to weigh words carefully, to keep a safe distance between the writer and reader, to avoid risk, and to write what he or she thinks the reader wants.

1   The writer seems indifferent, uninvolved, or distanced from the topic or the audience. As a result, the writing is flat, lifeless, or mechanical; depending on the topic, it might be overly technical or jargonistic. More than one of the following problems is likely to be evident:

- The reader has no sense of the writer behind the words. The writer does not seem to reach out to an audience or make use of voice to connect with that audience.

- The writer speaks in a kind of monotone that tends to flatten all potential highs and lows of the message.

- The writing communicates on a functional level, with no apparent attempt to move or involve the reader.

- The writer is not yet sufficiently engaged or comfortable with the topic to take risks or share himself or herself.

Word Choice

5   Words convey the intended message in an interesting, precise, and natural way. The writing is full and rich, yet concise.

- Words are specific and accurate; they seem just right.

- Imagery is strong.

- Powerful verbs give the writing energy.

- Striking words and phrases often catch the reader's eye, but the language is natural and never overdone.

- Expression is fresh and appealing; slang is used sparingly.

3   The language is functional, even if it lacks punch; it does get the message across.

- Words are almost always correct and adequate (although not necessarily precise).

- Familiar words and phrases communicate but rarely capture the reader's imagination. The writer seems reluctant to stretch.

- The writer avoids experimenting with language; however, the paper might have one or two fine moments.
- Attempts at colorful language might seem overdone or out of place.
- A few energetic verbs liven things up now and then; the reader yearns for more.
- Images lack detail and precision.
- The writer might lean a little on redundancy or slip in a cliché, but he or she does not rely on these crutches to the point of annoyance.

1   The writer struggles with a limited vocabulary, searching for words to convey meaning. More than one of the following problems is likely to be evident:

- Language is so vague and abstract (for example, "It was a fun time," "It was nice and stuff") that only the most general message comes through.
- Persistent redundancy clouds the message and distracts the reader.
- Clichés or jargon serve as a crutch.
- Words are used incorrectly in more than one or two cases, sometimes making the message hard to decipher.
- The writer is not yet selecting words that would help the reader to a better understanding.
- Verbs are weak; "to be" verbs dominate; imagery is fuzzy.

Sentence Fluency

5   The writing has an easy flow and rhythm when read aloud. Sentences are well built, with consistently strong and varied structure that makes expressive oral reading easy and enjoyable.

- Sentence structure reflects logic and sense, helping to show how ideas relate. Purposeful sentence beginnings guide the reader readily from one sentence to another.
- The writing sounds natural and fluent; it glides along with one sentence flowing effortlessly into the next.
- Sentences display an effective combination of power and grace.
- Variation in sentence structure and length adds interest to the text.
- Fragments, if used at all, work well.
- Dialogue, if used, sounds natural.

3   The text hums along efficiently for the most part, although it might lack a certain rhythm or grace. It tends to be more pleasant or businesslike than musical, more mechanical than fluid.

- The writer shows good control over simple sentence structure, more variable control over complex sentence structure.
- Sentences might not seem skillfully crafted or musical, but they are grammatically correct and solid. They hang together and get the job done.

- The writer might tend to favor a particular pattern (for example, subject-verb, subject-verb), but there is at least some variation in sentence length and structure (sentence beginnings are not all alike).
- Fragments, if used, seem the result of oversight.
- Dialogue sometimes sounds natural, sometimes forced or contrived.
- Some parts of the text invite expressive oral reading; others might be a little stiff, choppy, or awkward. Overall, though, it's pretty easy to read this paper aloud if you practice.

1 The paper is difficult to follow or read aloud. Most sentences tend to be choppy, incomplete, rambling, or awkward; they need work. More than one of the following problems is likely to be evident:

- Sentences do not sound natural, the way someone might speak. Word patterns are often jarring or irregular, forcing the reader to pause or read over.
- Nonstandard English syntax is common.
- Sentence structure tends to obscure meaning rather than show the reader how ideas relate.
- Word patterns are monotonous (for example, subject-verb, subject-verb-object). There is little or no real variety in length or structure.
- Sentences might be very choppy, or words might run together in one giant "sentence" linked by "ands" or other connectives.
- The text does not invite expressive oral reading.

Conventions

5 The writer demonstrates a good grasp of standard writing conventions (for example, grammar, capitalization, punctuation, usage, spelling, paragraphing) and uses them effectively to enhance readability. Errors tend to be so few and minor that the reader can easily skim over them.

- Paragraphing tends to be sound and to reinforce the organizational structure.
- Grammar and usage are correct and contribute to clarity and style.
- Punctuation is smooth and guides the reader through the text.
- Spelling is generally correct, even on more difficult words.
- The writer might manipulate conventions — particularly grammar — for stylistic effect.
- The writing is sufficiently long and complex to allow the writer to show skill in using a wide range of conventions.
- Only light editing would be required to polish the text for publication.

3 The writer shows reasonable control over a limited range of standard writing conventions; however, the paper would require moderate editing prior to publication. While errors do not block meaning, they tend to be distracting.

- Paragraphing is attempted. Paragraphs sometimes run together or begin in the wrong places.

- Problems with grammar or usage are not serious enough to distort meaning.
- Terminal (end of sentence) punctuation is almost always correct; internal punctuation (commas, apostrophes, semicolons) might be incorrect or missing.
- Spelling is usually correct (or reasonably phonetic) on common words.
- The paper seems to reflect moderate but not extensive or thorough editing.

1   Errors in spelling, punctuation, usage and grammar, capitalization, or paragraphing repeatedly distract the reader and make the text difficult to read. More than one of the following problems is likely to be evident:

- The reader must read once to decode, then again for meaning.
- Paragraphing is missing, irregular, or so frequent (for example, every sentence) that it does not relate to the text's organization.
- Errors in grammar and usage are very noticeable and might affect meaning.
- Punctuation (including terminal punctuation) is often missing or incorrect.
- Spelling errors are frequent, even on common words.
- Extensive editing would be required to polish the text for publication.

PART TWO Using *The Bedford Guide* in Your Course

CHAPTER 7
Teaching *A Writer's Guide*

Unlike other kinds of writing instruction, *A Writer's Guide* focuses on the student's role in his or her own writing by emphasizing the writer's processes, the critical thinking and reading skills necessary to write effectively, the actual situations that will require students to write, and the strategies that guide students through the writing process. In this section we discuss the four parts of *A Writer's Guide* and explain the features that make the textbook particularly useful.

There is no single order in which to teach *A Writer's Guide*. Each chapter offers students a framework for experimenting with new ideas and ways to succeed in their efforts. All assignments are designed to show students that writing is a dynamic process. The authors make connections between the resources, strategies, and readings so as to encourage students to begin to see writing as a recursive process. Their description of the writing process emphasizes the re-vision and re-thinking inherent in writing. If your students think about the discrete subprocesses and clear-cut steps within writing, they might imagine it to be a linear rather than a recursive process. For some of your students, the most profound change during the semester will be understanding and experiencing for the first time writing as "thinking on paper."

Part One, "A College Writer's Processes" (p. 5) succinctly describes the processes of writing, reading, and thinking critically. To further the discussion of writing-as-process, ask students to draft a reflective essay about their writing process. Have them include one or two paragraphs describing what they think is the best thing they have written and explaining why this piece pleases them and how it pleases or displeases readers. Ask students to tell you everything you need to know to work with them effectively in a writing course. This kind of reflective writing is particularly useful because it gives you a sense of each student's history as a writer and provides a good focus for your first conferences with students. For more about reflective writing, see Chapter 2 of this manual. For more about using this assignment as a diagnostic in-class essay, see Chapter 4 of this manual.

THE FOUR PARTS OF *A WRITER'S GUIDE*

You should adapt the sequence in which you teach the chapters of *A Writer's Guide* to fit your course and your students' needs. For example, you might find that the writing process makes more sense to your students if you begin the semester with Part Four, "A Writer's Strategies," before you move on to the first essay assignment in Part Two, "A Writer's Situations." Or you might want to intersperse certain chapters from Part Three, "Special Writing Situations," with the chapters in Part Four. Take advantage of *The Bedford Guide*'s flexibility and experiment with your syllabus from semester to semester.

A College Writer's Processes

Part One is a special introduction to strategies for writing, reading, and critical thinking. (For more advice on teaching with these chapters, see pp. 102–04.) The critical thinking chapter not only defines this process but also explains how to use evidence and recognize types of appeals. Questions following the readings in The Bedford Guide often refer to this information, so you might want to ask students to mark this section for easy reference.

Note that each chapter in Part One ends with a chart that points to writing, reading, and critical thinking resources in the book and on the book's Web site. Students may want to refer to these charts throughout the course.

A Writer's Situations

Part Two shows students how to use recalling, observing, interviewing, and other methods as resources in their writing. By focusing on personal experiences as material for writing in the first part of the section, Part Two helps students build their confidence as writers before they move on to the more analytical writing tasks in the second part of the section. While students might use these resources in everyday interactions, they often have not learned how to use them when writing essays. To demonstrate how often effective writing relies on such resources, ask students to look for examples in other sources. The more students know about the techniques that other writers use, the more options they will have to strengthen their essays.

Part Two also challenges students to stretch their analytical abilities by comparing and contrasting, explaining causes and effects, persuading, evaluating and using sources to support a position. Chapters 7–12 are sequenced so that each chapter leads students through a critical thinking and writing assignment that is more difficult than the one before it.

Special Writing Situations

The three chapters in Part Three provide students with specific strategies for writing in college — beyond the composition course — and in the workplace. Chapters 13 and 15 introduce students to writing skills that they will need throughout their college careers. Chapter 13 shows students how to apply the critical thinking skills they've learned in Part Two to literary forms, while Chapter 15 provides methods that will enable students to write well under the pressure of timed essay exams and suggests ways to prepare for forms of writing assessment such as writing portfolios. Chapter 14 discusses the writing skills students will need to compete for a job and gives them guidelines for effectively communicating in business settings.

A Writer's Strategies

Part Four discusses in detail each step in the writing process — generating ideas, planning, drafting, developing, and revising and editing — as well as strategies for designing documents and understanding visual representations. Although all of these skills are introduced and reinforced in every chapter of A Writer's Guide, Part Four encourages students to focus more intently on them, providing more examples and more practice for each stage of the writing process.

HOW TO USE *A WRITER'S GUIDE*

The chapters in *A Writer's Guide* are structured to lead students through the process of writing an essay and to reinforce the connection between thinking and writing. What follows are descriptions of the chapters' features, with suggestions for how to use them in your course. For advice about how to use the Facing the Challenge sections, see Chapter 4 of this manual.

Most chapters in *A Writer's Guide* also contain boxes with activities for peer response, group learning, and e-writing (writing with a computer). For more about the collaborative learning activities, see Chapter 2 of this manual. For more about the activities for E-writers, see Chapter 5 of this manual.

Learning from Other Writers

Most chapters in *A Writer's Guide* include examples of professional and student writing. The student essays, in particular, will provide your students with the extra encouragement they need: proof that real students can and do write successful papers. Remember that some of your student writers will not have read as richly and extensively as others. Calling attention to key words and image patterns helps them as readers and as writers. The authors have annotated thesis statements in the professional essays — and the first points supporting these statements — to give students a better understanding of how experienced writers state and back up a main point. Later in the professional essays, "Analysis Tips" for instructors highlight additional features that might be helpful to point out to students. Also, questions in the margins of the student essays encourage close reading and analysis.

We urge you to use the Meaning and Writing Strategies questions following both essays in the chapter. These questions will help students become more critical readers and more observant of how a writer's choices affect meaning. While many students quickly dismiss such questions, encouraging students to grapple with them is valuable. The series of questions following each reading can be used to start class or small-group discussion. You might also want to use the questions as in-class writing prompts.

Learning by Writing

The assignments in *A Writer's Guide* lead students through the writing process step-by-step, focusing on the challenges specific to the assignment and then suggesting ways to generate ideas, plan, draft, develop, and revise and edit. Part Four, "A Writer's Strategies," contains even more guidance and examples for each step of the writing process.

The Other Assignments section in each chapter offers alternatives to the main assignment presented and discussed in the chapter. You might want to use these as shorter writing assignments to supplement the main assignment, or as a sequence of assignments on your syllabus.

Checklists

A Writer's Guide also contains three types of useful checklists for students. Discovery Checklists help students to generate ideas for each assignment, Revision Checklists help them to rethink their writing, and Editing Checklists help them to correct common grammar and punctuation problems in their essays. These checklists are invaluable. Copy them and ask students to attach them to their drafts, especially if students are struggling with a particular part of the process.

Boxes

Boxes throughout the text will help you and your students identify quick tips on peer collaboration (For Peer Response and For Group Learning), as well as advice on using computers to write (For E-Writers). Also of great help to students are the Facing the Challenge boxes that appear at the most crucial moment of an assignment. These boxes offer strategies and suggestions and also serve as a pep talk to students as they write.

Applying What You Learn

These lists identify the ways in which students will use the writing skills they have learned in the chapter — be it in another course, in the workplace, or in the community. Students often walk out of a composition classroom and into a sociology or a business administration classroom and forget to take what they've learned with them. Writing instructors, however, can help students to learn to understand writing as a way of making connections between different fields of study and different ways of thinking. The Applying What You Learn sections will help you do that.

A College Writer's Processes

Part One of *The Bedford Guide for College Writers* introduces students to writing, reading, and critical thinking processes that are essential to college-level work. The following advice and activities will help you make optimal use of these chapters.

CHAPTER 1: WRITING PROCESSES

In Chapter 1 the authors introduce the writing process and ask students to focus on their own processes through activities designed to make them reflect on how, exactly, they write. Writing is such an intrinsic process that most students have no idea how it occurs. Getting them to examine their own processes can generate a thoughtful class discussion that helps students begin to think of themselves as writers who are a part of a writing community. Taking the first or second class period to engage in such a discussion can be time well spent.

Introduce the writing process by having students go through the steps as you demonstrate them on the board. Direct students to fold a sheet of paper in half horizontally and then vertically, creating four sections. (As an alternative, you can hand each student four or five 4-by-6-inch index cards, in different colors if you prefer.) Filling a small space with writing will seem less intimidating to students who may be anxious about beginning a college writing course.

Demonstrate the section titled "Generating Ideas" by showing students how to brainstorm to find a topic. Write at the top of the board "An experience that had an important impact on my life," then brainstorm for five minutes. (This topic has the added advantage of preparing students for the "Recalling an Experience" assignment in Chapter 4.) Show students how you examine what you've written and choose the most promising topic for your paper. Think aloud so they can follow your process. Direct students to do the same brainstorming process in the upper left quadrant of their paper, and after they brainstorm, have them settle on the topic that seems most promising.

Then move on to "Planning." Demonstrate finding a thesis by writing the most important aspect of the experience, or the point you want to make about it. Sketch a thumbnail outline arranging the supporting points you might include. Have students do the same in the upper right section of their paper.

Next demonstrate "Drafting" by quickly writing an introduction, a conclusion, or part of the narrative. Again, have students do the same in the lower left section of their papers. Move on to demonstrate "Developing" by answering reporters' questions — who, what, why, when, where, and how — about your topic or by writing sensory details you recall. Have students complete this step of the process in the lower right quadrant of their papers. Finally, explain that the process would include "Revising and Editing" had they produced a draft. Point out that this exercise is a brief version of the writing process, and suggest that they keep their preliminary work to refer to as they begin their first assignment.

You also might want to discuss how a writer's purpose and audience affect the entire writing process. Point out Chapter 1's Audience Checklist and College Audience Checklist and encourage students to return to these as they write any paper.

CHAPTER 2: READING PROCESSES

Chapter 2 is an introduction to college-level reading and includes activities to help students advance their reading to levels necessary for college work. Begin by introducing students to the idea of reading for different purposes at different levels and speeds. We read a comic strip differently than we read a contract, for example. Invite them to talk about their reading habits. Don't be surprised if they don't read much beyond assignments. Sadly, many students rarely read, and they have no practice reading beyond a literal level. Ask them to think about what they are required to read for everyday life. What is the difference to them between that kind of reading and "critical reading"?

Explain to students that reading is a process of text construction, just as writing is. Rereading to grasp levels of meaning is like rewriting to clearly convey meaning — a necessary part of the process. To demonstrate the reading process, bring to class copies of a reading, or direct students to an essay from *A Writer's Reader*. Ask students to read the text three times, recording the level of their understanding after each reading on a scale of one to ten, with ten being the highest level of understanding. They should note what they understand, what they find confusing, how they tried to understand, and so on. Then ask them to write a few paragraphs describing the progress of their reading, including any questions they still have about the text. Most of your students will see the level of their understanding increase with each reading. Suggest that ideally, the reading process culminates in conversation. Other readers can always bring new insights to a text. This might be a good time to talk to students about the advantages of forming study groups for their classes.

Here's an Idea . . .

Ask students to bring in articles they are required to read in other classes. Be prepared to supplement their examples with readings from *The Bedford Guide* or from current issues of *The New Yorker, The Atlantic Monthly, Essence, Salon.com,* or *Slate.com.* Ask groups of students to skim the articles they brought in and choose one to analyze. Ask each group to read the article and to divide it into parts for individuals to analyze. Suggest that they practice the "active" reading demonstrated on page 24 by making marginal notations and queries, underscoring key passages, and so on.

Next have each group paraphrase one paragraph within the article and summarize the entire article. When the groups hand in their materials, skim the readings and comment on how effectively each group has read actively and practiced summarizing and paraphrasing.

For the next class, ask each group to decide how the parts work together to create the whole (that is, if the parts develop the main purpose or add some additional, related ideas), what they would omit if they evaluate the reading as "boring" or "repetitive," how the writer makes contact with the reader and whom the writer establishes as the "reader," and, finally, what strategies they can use to understand readings that were not written with first-year college students as the primary audience.

An alternative to this sequence is to select only one article from those submitted. After groups work through questions in class, have them report on their analyses and discuss their critical reading processes.

To help students move from summary to critical analysis of their reading, have them complete the following five-part exercise on an article from a journal or magazine or on an essay from *A Writer's Reader*:

1. Locate the author's thesis, or main point, and state it in your own words in a sentence or two.

2. Go through the article, paragraph by paragraph, and summarize the main point made in each paragraph in a sentence or two. Leave several lines of blank space after each of your summaries.

3. Locate the author's conclusion and sum it up.

4. In the blank space after your summary of each paragraph, list any evidence the author provides to support that point.

5. Finally, write your own response to each main point, clarifying whether you agree or disagree with the author's interpretation.

Advise students to use this exercise in any class where they must analyze a reading to fully understand its ideas or opinions. When your students are confident that they fully understand an author's viewpoint, they will be more likely to challenge the opinions expressed in the article and to come to their own conclusions.

CHAPTER 3: CRITICAL THINKING PROCESSES

Chapter 3 gives students tools to examine the ideas they are presenting or are presented with and to come to a considered judgment of their value. These skills are necessary for students to move beyond believing that whatever is published must be true to classifying ideas as fact or opinion, and finally to examining the evidence on which assertions rest, including their own opinions. As students approach these concepts, you might want to introduce them to the discussion of logical fallacies in Chapter 9, "Taking a Stand." You might also want to go over the various types of evidence described in Chapter 3.

To help students develop skills in recognizing the concepts presented in this chapter, select an essay from *A Writer's Reader* or bring to class copies of controversial articles and have students work in groups to identify kinds of appeal, types of evidence, and logical sequence, and to classify the ideas as fact or opinion.

Here's An Idea . . .

To introduce analysis, synthesis, and evaluation, bring to class a "Harper's Index" from *Harper's* magazine. Point out that the editors of the index have drawn together statistics from unrelated sources, and have students examine the page listing the sources. Then call their attention to the deliberate arrangement of the statistics in the index. Ask them why they think the editors list the statistics in this particular order. Suggest that the editors want readers to synthesize the statistics in a certain way. Ask what the purpose might be. What might the editors want readers to conclude? Have students play with other arrangements of the statistics, and ask them how these alternative arrangements could affect the conclusions readers might draw.

Recalling an Experience (Ch. 4, p. 55)

Helping students to write by recalling an experience is often easier and more moving than some of our other work as writing instructors. The raw material that students come up with might be incendiary and volatile, but it will certainly persuade you that instructors can help in the soul-making of their student writers. For personal and reflective writing, students are often quite comfortable writing from recall. For expository and analytical writing, they might be surprised at being asked to use recall as a writing strategy. For the research-paper assignment, students might be stymied. Yet as the authors point out, writing from recall is an important source for any type of student writing. Consider beginning this chapter by reading aloud for five minutes from a variety of sources to introduce students to the sound and the feeling of the language of recall. The grid on pages 371–83 identifies essays from *The Bedford Guide* that recall experiences.

Writing from recall is a good assignment to begin with because the chronological structure of narrative is easy for students to handle and can build their confidence as writers. However, a few students in your group who have writing anxiety or very low self-esteem might not respond well to writing from recall because they are extremely hesitant to reveal themselves, afraid to expose their innermost thoughts and feelings to others. Once these students feel safe and secure in the classroom environment, however, they usually enjoy writing from recall as much as other students do. After you create an atmosphere of support, encouragement, and constructive criticism, these students will open up and write well.

Some instructors hesitate to teach personal writing because of the difficult emotional or ethical issues it sometimes raises. If your first impulse is to avoid writing from recall altogether, talk with your colleagues or read about how to handle sensitive subjects should they arise. Two articles that address the difficulty of teaching personal writing by discussing the ways in which different instructors have handled it are "Ethical Issues Raised by Students' Personal Writing" by Dan Morgan (*College English* 60 [1998]: 318–25) and "Fault Lines in the Contact Zone" by Richard E. Miller (*College English* 56 [1994]: 389–408).

Chapter 4, "Recalling an Experience," contains the following activities:

- Responding to an Image (p. 55). Allow your students to use their imagination while examining these visual activity prompts. If necessary, have students free-associate responses to elements of each image. If they are given free rein for their own interpretations, they will most likely view analyzing these images as a rewarding way to begin thinking about writing in these modes.

  Ask your students what stories they think the pictures in the chapter-opening grid tell. Have them describe "snapshots" from their own memories that they could fit in the grid. What stories do recalling their "snapshots" evoke? Keep your students focused on how these images all relate to recalling experience.

- For E-Writers (p. 64). See page 73 of this manual for advice about how to use this feature.

> *Here's an Idea . . .*
>
> In response to the question about ads that send chills down the spine (p. 56), send your students off with the directive to note a print ad, a commercial, a billboard, or a bumper sticker that had that effect. Use the ads they describe as the basis of a class discussion and perhaps a brief writing assignment.

- For Peer Response (p. 69). See page 39 of this manual for advice about how to use this feature.
- For Group Learning (p. 67). See page 39 of this manual for advice about how to use this feature.

LEARNING FROM OTHER WRITERS

RUSSELL BAKER *The Art of Eating Spaghetti* (p. 56)

This essay shows students that times when we suddenly realize something has changed in our lives — moments of epiphany — can be good subjects for essays that use recall. Here Russell Baker remembers the pivotal moment in his life when he decided to become a writer. This essay can be doubly important to your students, because it dispels the notion that they are restricted to "proper" subjects for writing classes — a notion that turns many students away from writing.

To help students generate ideas for their own recall papers, have them write "Turning Points in My Life" at the top of a page and freewrite about the topic for fifteen minutes. Then, using Baker's memorable description of Mr. Fleagle as an example, ask students to write a brief character sketch of a person who was instrumental in one of the turning points they identify.

Questions to Start You Thinking (p. 59)

Meaning

1. The questions about Baker's reminiscence look at meaning as well as at style and quotations.

2. Baker relies on recall to create the connections between his present and his past. This use of memory links him as a professional writer to the student writers in your class.

As an in-class writing assignment, ask students first to describe some moment when they had a strong feeling (positive or negative) about writing and then to discuss the importance of that moment. Use this reflective writing in your first conferences with students. For more about conferences, see Chapter 2 of this manual.

3. This question can expand the perspective of student writers who will begin to recall similar experiences. Ask students to freewrite for ten or fifteen minutes in response to these two questions. Remind them that this is part of gathering information that they might use later in an essay. Respond to the questions yourself and read your responses to the class. Consider asking students to read their responses aloud as well. Collect, read, and comment on their responses, but do not grade them.

Writing Strategies

4. This question focuses students' attention on specific details and words in effective description. After studying how Baker uses diction, student writers can practice similar techniques. Ask them to form small groups and rewrite the description of Fleagle in paragraph 3, substituting some other adjective and adverb for *prim* and *primly*. Ask each group to invent three details that exemplify the adjective they chose and to select some other tag line to show Fleagle's "new" character.

Follow up by asking students to write two or three paragraphs describing some person from their past who, despite the students' first impressions, proved important. Ask them to imitate Baker's technique of repeating an adjective and adverb and to include three details and a characteristic statement.

5. This question asks students to consider the advantages of "showing" over "telling" when describing a character. Including an anecdote that demonstrates or embodies a character's personality makes a character sketch all the more effective. In this essay Baker's comic depiction of Mr. Fleagle passionately quoting Lady Macbeth before a class full of howling students amplifies our sense of Fleagle's excessive "primness."

To get students thinking about what would have been lost had Baker not included the Macbeth quotation, try reading the story aloud, skipping paragraphs 4 and 5. Without Baker's humorous example of Mr. Fleagle in action, the essay's last sentence, in which Baker ranks Mr. Fleagle "among the finest teachers in the school," might lose some of its comic impact.

For a journal entry or brief writing assignment, ask students to recall an occasion or situation that seems to capture the essence of someone they know or of themselves. Ask them to find a quotation to strengthen their anecdote and characterization.

6. Baker uses a chronological approach in this essay. To tell the story of Mr. Fleagle and his class, Baker must present the sequence of events clearly, ordered by time. This type of organization allows the audience to "relive" the experience. Remind students that a writer's purpose determines how he or she organizes ideas.

ROBERT G. SCHREINER   *What Is a Hunter?* (p. 59)

This essay illustrates that some writers use recall to define. Before assigning the essay, ask students to give their own definitions of *hunter* and *hunting*. After students have read the essay, ask them to compare their definitions with Schreiner's.

Questions to Start You Thinking (p. 62)

Meaning

1. Most students become aware of Schreiner's increasing uneasiness with his initial hunting experience by the third paragraph. Schreiner's skill with imagery and specific detail will affect many students viscerally. Prompt a discussion of how a writer can use careful observation and evidence from the senses by asking students how Schreiner made them "sick" (a frequent class comment in response to this essay).

2. This question should solicit diverse responses from your students. Ask them to imagine themselves expanding Schreiner's story into an account of the entire holiday. How would the grandfather and the cousin act in other situations? Encourage them to come up with a detailed biographical sketch of each character.

Here's an Idea . . .

Have students write a short paper to the author of "The Art of Eating Spaghetti" or "What Is a Hunter?" in which they explain their reaction to the essay of their choice. Be sure that they indicate why they liked or disliked the essay, what description is effective, what should have been developed more and what should have been cut, and any other comments they want to make.

3. Using Schreiner's essay as an example, point out that writing from recall encourages us to reflect on how past experiences have changed us. Ask students to brainstorm experiences that have changed them or brought them to a better understanding of themselves. Then ask them to write a journal entry in which they recount one of these experiences. Have them read the journal entries aloud either to the class or in their peer writing group.

Writing Strategies

4. Students often suggest that the best way to improve the essay would be to simply eliminate the first four sentences of the first paragraph. You might wish to point out how using a standard convention — such as a dictionary definition of a word — can make an otherwise stellar essay appear sophomoric. Invite students to think of alternative ways to introduce the essay. Then lead them to discuss which they prefer and why. Some students will note that the definition links to both the thesis and the title.

5. Suggest that students answer question 4 in small groups. Allow discussion time and then ask a spokesperson from each group to present the group's answer to promote discussion and evaluation of the essay. Some students will notice that the ending is powerful, without condemning the grandfather or the cousin, and that the word *silence* invites the audience to react subjectively. Encourage students to discuss their subjective reactions.

6. Schreiner uses more than one sense to involve his audience in this experience. He does not rely solely on sight but includes tactile and auditory "memories." Paragraph 5 furnishes graphic images. Students might shudder at these, but the images do vividly re-create the scene. Words and phrases that force the reader to see, hear, and feel include "spattered with splashes," "pink gobbets," "crimson blood," and "twitching." Point out that using "crimson blood" instead of *red* illustrates the effectiveness of precise descriptions. Encourage students to check a thesaurus when searching for the "right" word but to choose the words they find carefully. Too often students use inappropriate words when they do not understand the connotations.

7. Schreiner uses simple chronological order to organize his essay. In the first paragraph he introduces the topic of hunting, and in paragraph 3 he presents the initial major event of the hunting trip — watching his cousin kill the first jackrabbit. Details about the rabbit's death — its head "rocking from side to side," the "thin trickle of crimson [that] marred the gray sheen of the rabbit's pelt," the thump of the rabbit's head against the side of the pickup — bring the event to life for readers and hint at Schreiner's discomfort. Paragraphs 4–6 describe Schreiner's turn with the gun, the second major event. Reflecting on what he learned from the experience, Schreiner reveals his thesis in the essay's conclusion (para. 7): "I thought only of the incredible waste of life that the afternoon had been, and I realized that there was much more to being a hunter than knowing how to use a rifle."

LEARNING BY WRITING

The Assignment: Recalling a Personal Experience (p. 62)

This assignment works well as the first full-length essay in a composition course. Because it allows students to draw from what they already know, it builds their confidence as writers. Students can usually handle narrative writing fairly well, but emphasize that their purpose is to share the importance of an experience with readers, not just to retell what happened.

The authors caution students against choosing to write about an experience that is too subjective. This might be a good time to introduce your students to the value of using concrete sensory details. Explain that our five senses are the only way we have of experiencing our world, and we can make meaning only by taking in data through these senses and processing it. Tell them that if they describe to the reader exactly what they saw, heard, felt, smelled, and tasted, they can make their reader experience what they experienced and bring their writing to life. Then they can effectively bring the reader to understand their feelings about what they experienced. The phrase "Show, don't tell" is trite but useful. To help students choose a topic, brainstorm possible topics with them, using the board, and then discuss the feasibility of each.

Facing the Challenge (p. 63)

Again, in conferences and small-group work, encourage students to show, not just tell; empty assertions are often a major weakness of this type of writing. When students write "The sky was beautiful" or "The man was weird," challenge them to provide specific details that will reveal and prove the assertion. As they work in their peer-editing groups, encourage them to look for generalities and to ask one another questions that elicit specific details.

As a journal prompt, ask students to recall a vivid experience and describe it in candid detail, so as to appeal to as many senses as possible. Suggest that they consider an accident that they witnessed, a time when they were injured, a funeral, a happy occasion, an embarrassing or life-changing moment, a memorable party, or a bad or excellent meal. Ask volunteers to read their journal entries aloud.

Many students can find a main point for their essay by completing a starter sentence that focuses on the relevance of the experience: "The most important thing about my experience was . . ."; "My experience changed me by . . ."; "The way this experience shaped my life is. . . ." Have students use this starter sentence to freewrite about the meaning of their experience for ten or fifteen minutes. Then ask them to reframe their beginning sentence to express the importance of the experience and to use this as a working thesis statement.

Students will probably need some help in deciding which events should start and end their narrative and which could be excluded. If meeting an unusual person on a trip to Disney World changed a student's life, details about getting ready for the trip are probably irrelevant. Ask students to write their thesis at the top of their draft and to delete the details not directly related to it.

For more about providing support for underprepared students, see Chapter 4 of this manual.

Generating Ideas (p. 63)

Use the Discovery Checklist on pages 63–64 as an icebreaker early in the semester, or organize a class activity in which small groups swap tales and question one another about the details of their experiences. There are enough prompts here that each member of a small group can find one personal example to share, and often these insights grow into a piece of writing.

Here are several detailed suggestions for using some of the invention strategies that the authors cite.

Brainstorming (p. 63)   Surprisingly, many college students have not had practice brainstorming. To demonstrate this technique, write a topic in the center of a large chalkboard and ask students to call out whatever comes to mind without worrying about whether it makes sense. Choose a topic with which all students will be familiar — education, childhood, accidents, embarrassment, travel, jobs, family — so that every-one can participate.

Write down whatever the students call out. Now and then, stop and read aloud what you've written, repeating the topic again after six or seven words. More brain-storming will follow. After ten minutes of brainstorming, stop.

Next, ask students to identify patterns of associations. Using different colored chalk, circle each item in the pattern, and ask for a generalization about the pattern.

Here's an Idea . . .

Although journals are not discussed in this chapter, journal writing is a frequent source for recall, and journal assignments can prompt students to generate ideas. The following sequence of assignments will help students to begin to understand the value of journals. For more on keeping a journal, refer students to Chapter 16, "Strategies for Generating Ideas."

Day 1. Think back to a time when you broke a rule on purpose rather than accidentally. How old were you? Whose rule was it? Did you know what would happen if you broke the rule? How did you break the rule? Where? Why? Tell the story as you would tell it to a friend. Write in your journal for twenty minutes.

Day 2. Look back to what you wrote yesterday. Make a list of the visual images that you included in that entry. For the next twenty minutes, write in as much detail as possible about those images and any others that occur as you think back. How large? What texture? What color? What was next to the image you describe?

Day 3. Today focus on sound — or the lack of sound — in what you wrote on Day 1. Close your eyes and listen to what you recalled. What do you hear? In what pattern? For this entry, describe the sounds in the order that you heard them.

Day 4. Are there any smells or tactile feelings connected to what you have recalled? List any that you remember. Then put them into a sequence and conclude with a generalization about the overall smell or feel of the event.

Day 5. Go back to your initial entry. Choose a portion of it to develop fur-ther. Review your lists of sights, sounds, smells, and sensations, and choose some to make your revised piece of writing clearer and more vivid.

Erase the circles from one pattern to begin identifying another. Show students how the brainstorming pulled up more information and associations than they might have predicted and that it provides plenty of ideas with which to begin a writing assignment.

Follow up this exercise by asking students to spend ten minutes brainstorming a possible topic for their assignment. In class, quickly look over and comment on each student's list. Or ask each small group to make a list, and have one student read the list aloud. Direct students to Chapter 16, "Strategies for Generating Ideas," in their textbooks for more detailed information on brainstorming and other invention strategies.

Freewriting (p. 64)   To demonstrate freewriting to your students, choose a topic that is familiar to everyone and that stimulates interest in writing, and ask students to spend fifteen minutes writing about it in class. Tell them that if they have nothing to say about the topic, they should write "I have nothing to say about . . ." and keep their pens moving on the page for fifteen minutes. Afterward, ask students to talk about what happened while they were freewriting. Encourage those who started with "I have nothing to say" to report first. For the assignment on recalling an experience, your students will find freewriting an effective strategy to reflect on the meaning of the experience and to discover its importance. This strategy can therefore help them find a thesis for their essays. Have them write the phrase "This experience was important in my life because . . ." and then write on this topic for fifteen minutes.

Doodling (p. 64)   You can model this process by briefly describing an experience in your life and by using a chalkboard or marker board to sketch pictures that illustrate the experience. Then, add notes to illustrate main events, notable details, and so on. Ask students to think of an important experience in their lives and to spend a few minutes sketching or doodling to get ideas about it. If any students feel uncomfortable with this activity, suggest that they jot down notes or whatever else comes to mind.

Mapping Recollections (p. 64)   Mapping is another process you might want to model. Bring sheets of paper to class to record ideas. Then, mention an experience that all students will be able to recall, such as enrolling in school. Have them call out details they remember from the experience — people, statements, events, locations, and so on. Write down a different detail on each sheet of paper and tape it to a wall or board. Afterward, ask students to call out their ideas for grouping related details, for organizing details by importance, or for making other connections. Rearrange the sheets as they make suggestions.

A Reporter's Questions (p. 64)   Show how each of these questions can lead to further investigation by choosing an event and asking small groups of students to consider one question in relation to the event. For example, in response to "Who was involved?" students could list the people who were present and then further their investigation by describing what happened from the perspective of each person. Challenging students to move beyond their initial question will develop their critical thinking skills as well.

Ask each student to choose one of the reporter's questions and write about it in relation to the event. Consider having students interview one person outside of class about the event, checking that person's recollection against their own recollections and writing a short report on the results of the interview. Then ask the class to check the public experience of the event as reported in newspapers, magazines, and on television against their own recollections. Finally, have students write in class about the event, combining what they've learned from conversation or reading with their own memories. Collect, copy, and redistribute the pieces to all class members.

Here's an Idea . . .

Ask students to write a letter to Robert G. Schreiner about his essay "What Is a Hunter?" Then have them discuss in groups how they would feel and react if they received those comments about their own work. Are the suggestions specific enough to be helpful? Would any of the comments make them angry or defensive? How might the comments be phrased to make them more helpful or more palatable to the writer? These discussions will make students aware of how their comments need to be specific but supportive in order to be helpful. For more about collaborative learning, see Chapter 2 of this manual.

Sources of Support (p. 65)   Although their task is to write from recall, students will by this point have used the other writer's resources discussed in the textbook. As you work with students in conference on their drafts, point out how they've used the other resources. You might even ask the peer-editing groups to identify these as well.

Planning, Drafting, and Developing (p. 65)

Anxious writers might need a conference at this stage. Assist them by asking a reporter's questions about their thesis and jotting down their responses; then give them this information as a starting point. Constructing a time line of the experience they are recalling might be a useful way to develop their ideas.

Remind students that the purpose of this writing assignment is to explore how a pivotal experience affected their lives. Although moving chronologically through the experience is an obvious way to organize the essay, suggest that they think about organizing it in two parts: Use the first part to relate the incident or experience and the second to explain the meaning of what happened to them — expanding the main point or thesis.

If students are relying on only one sense in the first draft, ask them to make a separate list for each sense to build on what they have already developed.

Revising and Editing (p. 66)

This is a good time to introduce students to the process of evaluating their writing. Because this assignment is so personal, students often tend to include too much and then not want to cut anything. Through conferences, help them edit their material so that it is sharply focused; point out what seems unimportant and irrelevant. Because the order of events is so clearly etched in their memories, they sometimes tend to omit important transitions. Work with them to establish these missing connections.

Students will not automatically understand the need to proofread their writing. After you have pointed out problem areas or patterns of weakness in their drafts, have them clean up their essays. For specific editing recommendations, refer them to the "Quick Editing Guide" in their textbooks (p. A-25).

Other Assignments (p. 68)

Students might make journal entries on these topics. Afterward, break students into small groups and have them take turns reading parts of their entries if they feel comfortable doing so. Others should be required to ask at least three questions of the author about the experience. Also, the author should be able to answer the question "What has this experience meant to you?" This will give students practice with delving deeper into an experience to explore its significance — something that they will have to do in a full paper on the assignments.

APPLYING WHAT YOU LEARN (p. 69)

To show students how recall is used in different writing situations, particularly those outside the writing classroom, try the following:

1. For research assignments in other courses, ask students to begin a journal as soon as they've settled on one or two possible research topics. The journal should contain notes on their research activities. Suggest that they begin by writing for twenty minutes about what they recall about the topic or ideas related to the topic.

2. If you wish to introduce interviewing at this point in your course (the authors save it for Chapter 6), ask students to interview three authorities about a particular problem, such as privacy issues on the Internet. The students should determine what gives a person authority or expertise. To help students ask questions that will prompt recall about the problem, have them role-play an interview during class. Then have them write a report on their understanding of the people they interviewed.

3. Organize an oral-history project in which each student interviews an older person who has been successful in the career or profession the student wants to enter. Assign an essay in which students define the critical issues in their profession by incorporating what they learned from the people they interviewed.

MAKING CONNECTIONS

Recall is probably the major resource for writers in all professions and from all walks of life. Calling attention to how different writers use recall gives students more models for their own writing and encourages them to develop critical thinking skills, such as comparing and contrasting. The following writers use recall in their essays in *A Writer's Reader.*

Christy De'on Miller in "Give Me Five More Minutes" (p. 441) uses sensory detail to evoke the memory of her son, Lance Cpl. Aaron Austin, a marine killed in Iraq. Miller recalls the officers arriving with the terrible news and poignantly describes seeking to hold on to Aaron through his personal effects, finding comfort through the small memories of his life. Miller's essay explores how memory can sustain us in times of grief.

E. B. White in "Once More to the Lake" (p. 463) draws from his childhood memories of a lake in Maine as the basis for a comparison with his present observation of the same location. This essay can serve as a wonderful inspiration for students wanting to write about places they have revisited after years of being away — their old summer camps, neighborhoods, and so forth. Show them that they can use the same techniques that White uses.

Danzy Senna in "The Color of Love" (p. 458) uses recall to portray her relationship with her grandmother. Recounting an incident that illustrates her grandmother's prejudice, Senna — the daughter of a white mother and a black father — reveals both her anger toward her grandmother and her love for her.

Annie Dillard in an excerpt from *An American Childhood* (p. 577) recalls the triumph of discovering an amoeba with her microscope and the more important discovery that her independent quest was its own reward. Her childhood realization that learning was a "private passion" that did not require validation from her parents freed her for a life-long quest for knowledge for its own sake.

Carl T. Rowan in "Unforgettable Miss Bessie" (p. 580) uses memory to paint a vivid picture of his high school English teacher, a diminutive woman yet a "towering presence" in Rowan's memory. He recalls Miss Bessie's wisdom and courage as she gave Rowan and other students the educaton they needed to lift themselves out of a life of deprivation.

These writers look back over important events in their lives and interpret how the experiences have influenced them. As students read these essays, ask them to consider how each of the authors has used recall. For each essay, ask students to answer the As You Read questions on page 56.

RESOURCES FOR COLLEGE WRITERS

Your Assignment
Recalling an Experience, p. 62

Resources in Text
- Sample professional reading, p. 56
- Sample student reading, p. 59
- Facing the Challenge, p. 63
- Planning and developing the essay, p. 65
- Discovery and Revision checklists, pp. 63–64 and 67–68
- Editing Checklist, p. 68
- Uses of recall in real-world writing situations, pp. 69–70
- Peer review help, p. 69
- E-Writer help, p. 64

Resources on the Web Site
<bedfordstmartins.com/bedguide>
- Additional readings with activities
- "Ask the Draft Doctor" writing help
- Peer response forms
- Link to Exercise Central

Observing a Scene (Ch. 5, p. 71)

Many students surprise themselves when they turn to their senses for evidence. They often believe they have nothing to see, nothing to say, nothing to write about. They'll need your assistance to open their eyes and sharpen their senses. The writers in this chapter effectively draw on all five senses. As you discuss the two essays with students, stress the variety of sensory appeals and the diction the writers use to convey the impact on the senses to readers. Bring in passages from powerful writing from observation to read aloud to the class. The ending to "Dawn" in Gloria Naylor's *The Women of Brewster Place* (New York: Viking, 1982) works well as an example. The grid on pages 371–83 identifies essays from *The Bedford Guide* that use observation.

Encourage students to use journals to record observations. Bring in passages from the five-volume *Diary of Virginia Woolf* (New York: Harcourt, 1977, 1984). Or bring in samples of writings from daybooks, such as Donald M. Murray's. You might also want to share samples from your own journal. Examine how each writer uses evidence of the senses in the journal; follow up, if possible, with a demonstration of how one of the writers worked the journal or daybook entry into a fuller piece of writing.

Show slides of Claude Monet's paintings of haystacks or lily pads — the same scene but with different lighting or in a different season — to illustrate the impressionistic nature of subjective description. (Many college libraries have reproductions of paintings that they allow instructors to borrow; these might be more effective than small prints in art textbooks.) Following the discussion of Monet, ask students to revise two of their journal entries so that each one describes the environment from the same point of view but at a different time of day or night. Use several entries during a class period to demonstrate revising both for new perspectives and for specificity of observations. Ask students to assemble into groups to read their entries and to comment on detail, arrangement of details, sensory language, connotative shifts, and metaphoric patterns. Ask each group to select entries for presentation to the class.

Here's an Idea . . .

Plan a short field trip during a class period. Choose some nearby campus site. It doesn't need to be scenic, only accessible. Send students with notebooks in hand. Ask them to record sights, sounds, smells, tastes, and tactile feelings. When they return to the classroom, have each student contribute one detail and then classify each detail by sense on the board. When all of the observations are recorded, ask the students to close their eyes and use recall for five minutes. Ask them to write all of the additional details they now remember sensing. End the class early and send students back to the site to observe details that they might have overlooked.

Follow up, in or out of class, by assigning a short essay that objectively describes the site. Then assign a revision of the essay that subjectively describes the site. Or ask students to revise a description they've already written by rewriting it specifically for a reader with impaired vision. Most student writers rely too heavily on visual images; this exercise helps them to shape other images. It also makes them think more carefully about their readers.

Here's Another Idea . . .

Pass around three apples; then line them up in front of the class and ask students to write a paragraph or two describing them. You might want to suggest that they compare and contrast the apples. Have volunteers read their paragraphs to the class. Ask the class to decide which apple is being described. This activity will help students refine their observation skills to distinguish fine details. (Did anyone include smell?)

Chapter 5, "Observing a Scene," contains the following activities:

- Responding to an Image (p. 71). Allow your students to use their imagination while examining these visual activity prompts. If necessary, have students free-associate responses to elements of each image. If they are given free rein for their own interpretations, they will most likely view analyzing these images as a rewarding way to begin thinking about writing in these modes.

    Perhaps you have students who have gone bungee jumping and can viscerally respond to this image's perspective; they will be able to share their experience with the class. If not, students will definitely be able to put themselves in the position of both the jumper and the festival participants below.

- For E-Writers (p. 84). See page 73 of this manual for advice about how to use this feature.

- For Peer Response (p. 83). See page 39 of this manual for advice about how to use this feature.

- For Group Learning (p. 84). See page 39 of this manual for advice about how to use this feature.

LEARNING FROM OTHER WRITERS

ERIC LIU *The Chinatown Idea* (p. 73)

In this essay, Eric Liu's visit to Chinatown with his family turns out to be more than a simple shopping trip. Using a rich assortment of descriptive details, he creates a vivid impression not only of the sights, smells, and sounds of Chinatown but also of his inner feelings as he realizes that he is an outsider in the culture of his heritage.

Questions to Start You Thinking (p. 75)

Meaning

1. In paragraph 6, Liu reveals his family's purpose for visiting Chinatown: "We had come to this store, and to Chinatown itself, to replenish our supply of things Chinese: food and wares, and something else as well." Ask students what Liu means by "something else." Why can't his family stay in Chinatown long, even though they feel "fortified" by its "undiluted Chineseness"?

2. Have students reread paragraph 8, then ask them to list adjectives that describe how the family feels when they encounter Po-Po. Ask the class why the look in Po-Po's eyes shifted from "surprise" to "hurt." You might also discuss the guilt and

embarrassment conveyed by Liu's mother when she rationalizes why they did not let Po-Po know they would be in town — "we'd been uptown, had come to Chinatown on a whim, hadn't wanted to barge in on her unannounced" (para. 8).

3. Suggest that students freewrite to explore their interpretation of the final sentence and use these writings as a basis for class discussion. Do students think that Liu's shower symbolizes the discomfort he felt as an outsider in Chinatown? Is he washing away the shame over his family's encounter with Po-Po? Encourage the class to come up with a number of different interpretations, stressing that there is no single correct answer to this question.

Writing Strategies

4. For this question, you might consider having students complete a paragraph-by-paragraph analysis that identifies and evaluates Liu's use of sensory details. Which sense dominates his essay? How vividly do the details convey Liu's main impression? Ask students to compare and contrast their own mental image of Chinatown with the image that Liu presents.

5. The essay unfolds in chronological order, drawing readers into the scene along with Liu. This organizational pattern also allows readers to see the progression of Liu's reactions, from his initial wonder upon wading through the crowds on East Broadway to his exhaustion on the trip back to his suburban home. Within paragraphs (para. 5, for example), Liu often uses spatial organization, enabling readers to visualize places such as the Golden Gate market.

6. Students will likely view the encounter with Po-Po as the event that most clearly reveals that Liu considers himself to be a "tourist." Students might also point to a number of other minor events: for example, Liu cannot understand Cantonese (para. 2), has difficulty finding something to read in the bookstore (para. 4), and watches "with wonder" as a cashier totals their purchase with an abacus (para. 5).

MICHAEL COIL *Communications* (p. 75)

Michael Coil, a police officer and student, provides a behind-the-scenes perspective of a common scene from his workplace. His sensory details reveal both the physical and emotional atmosphere of the room where dispatchers wait for and react to emergency calls.

Questions to Start You Thinking (p. 77)

Meaning

1. Coil's observation begins with a description of the dispatch room's sights and sounds. At this point in the essay, the sounds are minimal: the hum from the computers' hard drives and a muted television (paras. 3–4). The only "real noise" is the dispatchers' conversation. When an emergency call comes in, however, the relative silence is broken (para. 6). The phone's ring is "loud, obnoxious, and ugly," the "air becomes thick and tense," and Coil can hear the caller screaming.

2. The word "hero" is used so frequently and in so many varied situations that students may not have a clear idea of how to define the term. Ask students to write a brief definition that describes some of the qualities they associate with a hero. As students consider why Coil describes dispatchers as heroes, ask them to refer to specifics within the essay. You might also ask the class why Coil added the phrase "modern-day" to the term. Is he implying that today's heroes differ from those in the past? In what ways?

3. Students may wonder why Coil, a police officer himself, is so shaken by the scene he witnesses in the dispatch room. He feels "helpless," powerless to assist the woman in distress, and he finds it difficult to unwind after the situation is resolved. Overall, Coil is impressed with the dispatchers' response to the call and with their ability to resume their casual conversation. He can't imagine being able to keep up that kind of work eight hours a day without feeling bitter. Do students conclude that he questions his own ability to handle a crisis so automatically and efficiently? However students respond, ask them to point to particulars in the essay that influenced their conclusions.

Writing Strategies

4. Coil's contrast of the dispatchers' behavior before and during the crisis call certainly creates a dramatic impression of the dispatch room. It also supports Coil's point that dispatchers are "modern-day heroes waiting to come to our rescue" (para. 8). By showing their friendly, relaxed conversation before and after the call, Coil illustrates their admirable — even heroic — ability to remain upbeat and energetic in the face of such a difficult job.

5. Consider having students work in pairs to respond to this question. While Coil appeals to the senses of sound and sight, he relies most heavily on auditory details. Ask students to find and discuss a paragraph that is particularly rich in sensory details. For example, in paragraph 6 alone, the phone's ring is "loud" and "obnoxious," the dispatcher's voice is "edgy," a voice "pushes out," and a chair "groans."

6. Ask students why they think Coil reserved the only dialogue for the caller. Students may note that it highlights the drama and personalizes the caller by giving her a voice. In contrast, Coil universalizes the heroes of his essay by not including dialogue from the dispatchers' conversation. The generalized portrayal of the employees makes it easier to extend Coil's description of them as heroes to all emergency dispatchers.

7. The first two paragraphs serve as Coil's introduction, with the thesis stated in the last sentence of paragraph 2. The contrasting major vantage points include outside the "unmarked brown wooden door" (paras. 1–2, 8) and inside the dispatch room (paras. 3–7). The final paragraph serves as the conclusion. Because of Coil's tight organization, students should have little trouble identifying these major parts of the essay and recognizing Coil's use of chronological order to arrange most of his observations (the atmosphere before, during, and after the emergency call). In his initial description of the dispatch room (paras. 2–4), Coil uses spatial organization.

LEARNING BY WRITING

The Assignment: Observing a Scene (p. 78)

Your students might need some advice about how to report a general impression of a scene or how to capture the "spirit" of a place. To encourage them to generate some insight from their observations, use your classroom as a laboratory. Ask pairs of students to observe the classroom carefully for two days, working together to describe the room and its occupants and then to record their general impressions. Ask each pair to formulate a thesis about their impressions. Write the thesis sentences on the chalkboard and discuss them with the entire class. This activity will help students learn to write in collaboration, and the writing they produce will give a sense of the writing community that is being established.

Facing the Challenge (p. 78)

It might be easier for students to understand the process of observing if you move through the initial stages for them, modeling the observing and writing behavior. Stand near a board and choose a spot to observe. Ask students to watch but not to interrupt and to remain quiet to allow any auditory stimuli to reach you. Write what you see, hear, smell, and touch as you look at the focal point. Write fast and attempt to use purely descriptive vocabulary. After five or ten minutes ask students to select the auditory vocabulary and the visual vocabulary. Remind them that if you had another board you could place the specific impressions in a list or column under "sound," "sight," and so on.

Compile a sampler of student observations about the classroom. Ask groups to determine whether the passages meet all of the assignment's criteria. This exercise prompts students to think about their role as students.

For more about providing support for underprepared students, see Chapter 4 of this manual.

Generating Ideas (p. 79)

Prewriting for this assignment could be in response to an event on campus — a dorm dinner, a large gathering at a biology test, a special performance by a national ballet group, a protest by student activists of some local, national, or international situation. Have the class brainstorm a list of campus occasions for which students gather. (For help, see the Discovery Checklist on page 79.) Break the class into groups and ask each group to attend an event from the list before the next class session. Then, in class, have the groups compare notes on what they observed. Students might have trouble settling on a main impression or insight and forming a thesis statement for this assignment. Ask each group to agree on two or three thesis sentences that give a general impression of the place and the people there or form a conclusion.

It is important to encourage students to make lists in preparation for this assignment. Ask each student to show you his or her list of observations during a three-minute in-class conference while the other students are moving from listing to drafting. Be ready to ask who, what, when, where, why, and how about each event. Many writers will approach the assignment with blinders on, even though the text encourages being open to observation. When you look at a list, help the writer determine if he or she has an abundance to write from.

Planning, Drafting, and Developing (p. 81)

The four patterns for organizing a series of observations, described in the diagram on on page 82, can be adapted to an in-class exercise. Take one of the lists generated from the field trip or from the class observation exercise. Either in small groups or in class discussion, have students organize the materials according to each pattern and discuss its effects. Then ask them to write individually one or two paragraphs in class in which they turn their lists or clusters into more structured pieces of writing. We recommend clustering — a technique students often find particularly helpful — for this activity. For more about clustering, refer students to "Grouping Your Ideas" (p. 322) in Chapter 17, "Strategies for Stating a Thesis and Planning."

Revising and Editing (p. 81)

Use the Revision Checklist on page 83 when students begin rewriting. Ask them to recommend additional questions for the checklist; often a writer struggling with an

assignment will have a concern that many in the class share but that no one has anticipated.

Other Assignments (p. 84)

Use these assignments as prompts for journal entries. Then ask writers for permission to distribute a sampler of entries for class discussion. Learning about alternative
perspectives helps students to develop critical awareness, and writing from observation
is an effective way to demonstrate these alternatives.

APPLYING WHAT YOU LEARN: SOME USES OF OBSERVING A SCENE (p. 85)

The authors make a strong argument for using observation as a resource for both
academic and real-life writing. Reinforce this discussion by asking your colleagues for
examples of successful writing assignments that direct their students to write from
observation. If your campus has a writing-across-the-curriculum program, contact some
instructors who are involved in it; they will probably have samples of student responses
to their assignments with specific comments on and evaluation of the use of observation. Psychology, sociology, and humanities instructors often make such assignments.

Ask students to review their required readings and look for examples of how professionals in other disciplines use writing from observation and to find passages from
other kinds of writing that rely on the senses. Organize small teams of two or three students and send them to the library and to their textbooks from other courses. Direct one
team to scan a local newspaper, another the *New York Times Magazine*, and another various travel books. Require one team to find accounts of lab or field experiments in a discipline with which at least one team member is familiar. Send students to books such as
Annie Dillard's *A Pilgrim at Tinker Creek* (New York: Harper, 1974), Sue Hubbell's *A
Country Year* (New York: Harper, 1986), Henry David Thoreau's *Walden* (1854), John
McPhee's *Coming into the Country* (New York: Farrar, 1977), or Stephen Jay Gould's *The
Flamingo's Smile* (New York: Norton, 1985). (You might arrange to put a variety of these
on library reserve.)

Have students generate a sampler of what they find, and use the passages for class
discussion. Ask students to identify and evaluate sensory images, to evaluate the precision of detail in the writers' observations, to describe the organization of details, and to
analyze the purpose of the observations in the context of the whole writing. By insisting
on a range of samples, you'll call attention to writing across the curriculum and discourage the stereotype that writing from the senses concerns only fiction writers.

MAKING CONNECTIONS

Observation is a major resource for writers, one that often goes hand in hand with
recall. Exposing students to the difference between a simple listing of observations and
an essay that effectively uses observation will increase their vision as writers and readers. The writers from *A Writer's Reader* listed here capture an audience by producing the
sights and sounds they observe, and they do so accurately and passionately.

Amy Tan in "Mother Tongue" (p. 445) uses the sense of hearing to observe the different kinds of English spoken in her family. She records exact wording, connecting
speech patterns to limitations for children growing up in homes in which English is a
second language.

Brent Staples in "Black Men and Public Space" (p. 479) uses observation to read the discomfort and fear in pedestrians he encounters when he walks at night. Staples, a black man, accounts for their reactions and recalls other, similar experiences and the awkward, humiliating consequences that followed. He discloses strategies he now uses to diffuse potentially dangerous situations that result from the fear he provokes in others simply because of the color of his skin.

Ruth La Ferla in "Latino Style Is So Cool. Oh, All Right: It's Hot" (p. 506) observes the Latino fashion scene. With meticulous detail, she describes characteristics of Latino style and how they reflect various facets of Hispanic culture. La Ferla's sensory details paint vivid pictures in the reader's mind and underscore the distinctive style that not only pervades the Latino community but increasingly infuses mainstream fashion.

As your students read these essays, they should consider the role that observation plays in them. For each essay, ask students to answer the As You Read Questions on page 72.

RESOURCES FOR COLLEGE WRITERS

Your Assignment
Observing a Scene, p. 78

Resources in the Text
- Sample professional reading, p. 73
- Sample student reading, p. 75
- Facing the Challenge, p. 78
- Planning and developing the essay, p. 81
- Discovery and Revision checklists, pp. 79 and 83
- Editing Checklist, p. 84
- Uses of observation in real-world writing situations, pp. 85–86
- Peer review help, p. 83
- E-Writer help, p. 84

Resources on the Web Site
<bedfordstmartins.com/bedguide>
- Additional readings with activities
- "Ask the Draft Doctor" writing help
- Peer response forms
- Link to Exercise Central

Interviewing a Subject (Ch. 6, p. 87)

Samuel Johnson, the eighteenth-century poet and scholar, often spoke of the need for the writer to have more "conversation" with the world. Although students might spontaneously and easily move into conversation with strangers on airplanes or at sports events, some will feel constrained by advice to explore conversation as a source for invention in writing. You will need to help students set up and conduct interviews, evaluate the materials garnered from interviews, and organize those materials to make the conversation and speakers take life.

Some of your students need to work on listening skills in order to develop beyond their cognitive egocentrism. Good listeners are better equipped to direct a conversation and to ask questions that elicit what they want to find out. In this chapter, the authors echo E. M. Forster with the corollary "How do I know what I think until I hear what I say?" They describe conversation as a resource through which writers often discover their own ideas as they speak them. Over and over in conferences, you'll see student writers light up with delight because they are realizing the purpose of a draft as they are talking about it. In class discussions, you'll see students surprise themselves with insights as they exclaim, "I didn't know I understood it until I said that."

The authors encourage writers to listen to other people with a "writer's ear," hearing not what they want or expect to hear but what the other person means to say. For many of your student writers, learning to listen as a writer will be a new activity. Remind them that you want them to develop their "writer's ear." One way to help them do this is to continue reading aloud at the beginning of class; choose pieces from your local newspaper, a favorite magazine, or perhaps a book you are reading. Have students read some of their favorite passages as well. One of our favorite examples of writing from conversation is Richard Selzer's "The Discus Thrower" from *Confessions of a Knife* (New York: Morrow, 1979). Also, the grid on pages 371–83 identifies essays from *The Bedford Guide* that draw on interviews.

Another way to help students develop better listening skills is to direct their attention to what is said in the classroom and what they hear. Emphasize the importance of using classroom conversation as a resource for writing by having students write a paragraph or two in class after a discussion of a reading. Ask them each to sum up the group perceptions or consensus about an interpretation for a student who is absent from class. Or introduce students to the terms *message* and *static* (or *figure* and *ground*) and ask them to write for five minutes describing the "message" each heard in the class. Then ask them to write for five minutes describing the static or noise — from their own interior monologue to the hiss of the radiator to a shout outside the classroom door — that competed for their attention. Have volunteers read aloud what they've written. Their answers might surprise you: Seldom do students learn what we want them to learn, and even more seldom do they agree on the most important thing they learned. As Patricia K. Cross suggests, such classroom-based research can help you to monitor what students are actually learning.

Because some students do not listen to their classmates during discussion but only to the "authority" — the teacher — draw attention to a particularly incisive or original statement by a class member. Tell the class to write either a direct quote or a paraphrase of what the student said. Then ask each student to read what he or she wrote and to determine with the original speaker whether he or she was clearly heard and appropriately quoted or paraphrased. Shifting the class dynamic from multiple student-teacher exchanges to student-student-teacher dialogue improves class discussion and increases students' confidence in peers as editors.

Chapter 6, "Interviewing a Subject," contains the following activities:

- Responding to an Image (p. 87). Allow your students to use their imagination while examining these visual activity prompts. If necessary, have students free-associate responses to elements of each image. If they are given free rein for their own interpretations, they will most likely view analyzing these images as a rewarding way to begin thinking about writing in these modes.

    Your students are likely to know at least one of the personalities in these photographs. Most will have seen Oprah Winfrey interviewing someone on her show; many will have seen Winfrey, Obama, Kwan, or Bono being interviewed. To help students think in terms of interviewing, assign them each to find an interview (written or televised) of one of these personalities. Ask students to write down the questions the interviewer asks that effectively reveal the personality and passions of the subject. What questions elicit what information? Which answers most thoroughly show the character of the celebrity? What do facial expression, voice tone, or body language contribute to the meaning of the words? If the interview is written, how has the interviewer included these details in his or her piece?

    Have students bring their notes to class and report on the interview. As a class, list the most effective questions and interview techniques. Discuss the differences the media — written or televised — make. Ask your students to suggest ways they might translate revealing visual details from a televised interview into writing, and jot some suggestions on the board.

- For Peer Response (pp. 97 and 100). See page 39 of this manual for advice about how to use this feature.

- For E-Writers (p. 98). See page 73 of this manual for advice about how to use this feature.

- For Group Learning (p. 101). See page 39 of this manual for advice about how to use this feature.

LEARNING FROM OTHER WRITERS

ELAINA RICHARDSON *Bono-Fire: U2's Brilliant Front Man Rocks Convention* (p. 88)

Most students will know who Bono is and may have seen or read interviews with him. However, they may not know some of the details of his life that Richardson presents in her essay. To give even further insight into Bono's humanitarian work, you might show a television profile of him, such as a 2006 feature from NBC News highlighting Bono's work in Ghana. If you have a classroom with an Internet connection and viewing screen, the video is available at <http://msnbc.msn.com/id/12940132>.

Questions to Start You Thinking (p. 91)

Meaning

1. Richardson points to several examples of Bono's "intensity" and the ways in which he has stepped out of the role of rock star to aid the world's poor. In para-

graph 1, she points to Bono's recent album, sold-out tour, and talks with influential world leaders, among other events and accomplishments. In paragraph 2, Richardson outlines Bono's goals for addressing poverty and HIV, and in paragraph 3, she describes how he has reached out to politicians and other key figures to achieve his goals. You might ask students to give their own definition of "rocker rebel" and to discuss how Bono, or other pop stars, live — or don't live — up to the definition.

2. In paragraph 2, Richardson describes Bono's goal of canceling the debt of poor nations while initiating trade reform and providing free HIV drugs to African nations. In paragraph 5, she lists the results: authorization of $435 million in debt relief from the U.S. Congress and discussions among world leaders about giving grants rather than loans to developing countries.

3. Richardson describes how Bono has changed from a purely angry artist (you might point to the description of him taunting fans in paragraph 3) to a respected activist who is able to reach out to world leaders — some with backgrounds and outlooks quite different from his own — to achieve his goals. Students might discuss why this evolution was important, even essential.

Writing Strategies

4. The background in paragraph 6 helps us understand how Bono came to be an activist. It gives the impression that he has always been sensitive to problems in the world, from his homeland of Ireland to Africa. Ask students if this background is adequate. What questions do they have about Bono that are not answered?

5. Students will easily pick up on Richardson's admiration and respect for Bono. She portrays him as an intense, charismatic rock star who has stood apart from most other pop artists by truly making a difference in the world. Ask students if they think that Richardson presents an unbiased picture of Bono or conveys her own opinion of him.

6. Ask students to determine Richardson's purpose. If her goal is to convey Bono's dynamic, passionate character, would paraphrasing be either sufficient or effective?

DAWN KORTZ *Listen* (p. 92)

Kortz, a former student at Dodge City Community College, interviews an old-timer about the history of Dodge City and concludes that it is important to take time to listen to stories. It might interest students to know that Kortz strengthened her essay by cutting the original version of approximately 1,900 words to 1,200 words.

Questions to Start You Thinking (p. 94)

Meaning

1. Kortz's title should cue students to her thesis. She mentions it at the end of paragraph 1 and again in her final paragraph. Ask students how significant stories are in a culture. What function, beyond entertainment, do they perform? Stories transmit culture; they teach us how to live; they hold up aspirations; and, as E. L. Doctorow says, they distribute the suffering so it can be borne. Your students may think of our literature as written, but here Kortz describes her appreciation of the oral tradition.

2. Ask students to find details in Kortz's essay that support their own impressions of Emmett Sherwood. What words imply Kortz's fondness for Emmett? You could

supplement this question by bringing to class an interview with a hostile tone and having students compare the two.

3. If students have trouble answering this question, ask them to consider the purpose of the interview. Is it to relate historical stories of Dodge City, or is it to reveal Emmett Sherwood? Where is Kortz's focus? Have students find historical details that Emmett relates and ask them why they think Kortz chose to include these details. Ask them how subjective Emmett's accounts might be. What might their subjectivity reveal about Emmett? To answer this question, call students' attention to Emmett's story of the waitresses in paragraph 4.

Writing Strategies

4. Emphasize to students that even though an assignment calls for them to rely on a particular resource such as interviewing, they will most often use other resources as well; here it is observation. Setting the scene is an effective way to open an essay. Kortz begins by putting us at the site of her conversation with Emmett. Ask students if they can picture themselves sitting in Mic-Leo's Café listening to Emmett. Call students' attention to paragraph 7, where Kortz returns to describing the café to close the interview.

5. Although Kortz describes Emmett's clothing and demeanor in paragraph 2, she skillfully interweaves details about him throughout her essay. Ask students to find places in which Kortz includes body language and facial expression to portray Emmett. Point out to them the small details, such as his eagerness, the "far-off look in his eyes" (para. 3), the "mischievous twinkle," his blush and dropped voice (para. 4), the reflective way he speaks (para. 5), his teasing smile (para. 6), and his stretching and the tilt of his head (para. 7). These details build to form a clearer picture of Kortz's subject.

6. The balance of direct quote and paraphrase can be worrisome for students, who want you to tell them exactly how much of each they should use. Kortz demonstrates an effective balance here. Ask students if Kortz uses enough direct quotation to give them a sense of Emmett's voice. Compare the material she quotes to the material she paraphrases, pointing out that Kortz has chosen to use Emmett's words where the sound of his voice is distinctive. Also ask students to note that Kortz often precedes or follows direct quotation with physical details that show Emmett's facial expression, body language, or the quality of his voice.

7. Kortz successfully selects and organizes her material in a way that conveys a clear dominant impression of her subject. Her introductory paragraph establishes the essay's first major emphasis — the "cozy, comfortable feeling" of the restaurant and the regulars who frequent it. The last sentence of this paragraph, her thesis, introduces Emmett Sherwood and reveals what she learned from him. In paragraphs 2 and 3, Kortz provides context for her subject as well as details that support the second major emphasis — the fact that Sherwood is clearly from "another generation" (para. 2). Paragraphs 4–6 then emphasize Sherwood's memories of the town, the Great Depression, and World War II. Kortz concludes by commenting on what she learned from Sherwood and how she hopes it will affect her (para. 8).

LEARNING BY WRITING

The Assignment: Interviewing (p. 94)

Caution your students against writing a paper about a roommate, a close friend, a boyfriend or girlfriend, or a close family member. They should select a subject whom they know only as an acquaintance. First-semester writers often have trouble fully reporting and describing what is familiar to them. In addition, students might not be aware of how much they respond to the nonverbal language cues of their roommates

> *Here's an Idea . . .*
>
> Ask students to find and bring to class three details about three different people. These should be what Donald Murray calls "details that reveal." Students tend to try to show their interviewee with a string of police-blotter adjectives. Instead, have them practice looking for a single detail that reveals the person: the teacher who quiets an unruly classroom with her own silence; the athlete crouched in the starting block who focuses all of her being on the track ahead; the grandmother whose eyes shine with tears as her tall grandson walks by in his graduation gown.

and close friends. Also, students tend to rely on recall rather than conversation to reveal a person so familiar to them. Insist that each writer arrange for an interview and not just recall a past conversation with their subject.

Facing the Challenge (p. 96)

It might be hard for student writers who have never formally interviewed someone to grasp how much material must be moved about, deleted, and condensed to shape a successful piece of writing from conversation. The model essays in this chapter are, of course, deceptively natural and free-flowing. Both essays move along smoothly and present the writer's voice clearly conversing with the reader as she reports and implicitly reflects on a conversation with a person whom we want to meet. The subject of each interview seems uninhibited and at ease. Shaping conversation from an interview into an essay like this will present a real challenge to most students. Richardson and Kortz have sifted through lengthy material, removed inconsequential remarks, and selected and rearranged pertinent information to support their purposes. Convince students that the more interview material they have, the easier their task will be when they begin this process.

Remind students that using a computer for writing and editing an interview can make the task less daunting. The For E-writers exercise in this chapter (p. 98) will help individual writers do this, but it can also be adapted for group work. Ask each student to print a copy of his or her interview and to have two or three peers review the transcripts and ask the questions suggested in the exercise. Also, ask students to hand in a copy of their transcripts along with their manuscripts and use this prewriting for "protocol analysis" when you and the writer meet to discuss how the essay originated and how effective it has become. Despite the caution from the authors about fair and accurate quotation, some writers will be as vague in writing down or even hearing quotations as they are in taking notes. Their transcripts will allow you to spot such problems with listening and recording skills. For more about providing support for underprepared students, see Chapter 4 of this manual.

Generating Ideas (p. 95)

Once again, journal assignments are particularly useful in generating ideas for this assignment. The Discovery Checklist on page 95 can be easily adapted into fifteen-minute journal entries. Suggest that students begin each entry with a list of people in each category and then write one statement for each person on the list. If, for example, a student has listed six people whose jobs or hobbies interest her, she could answer the question "Why?" with a follow-up statement for each. In a second journal assignment, students could report on an attempt to strike up an informal conversation with one candidate for the subject of the essay. A third entry could be a list of what the writer already knows or assumes about the candidate. Fourth could be the list of ten questions the writer might want to ask the candidate.

It's particularly useful for students to have a backup person to interview in case an interview can't be arranged because of schedules or the reluctance of the interviewee. Students should be aware that issues of privacy and confidentiality might arise in an interview.

Because many students are shy or even frightened about interviewing, we recommend a class activity in which they carefully observe a mock interview. Ask for one volunteer to interview three students during the next class period. The purpose of each interview is to discover what makes the interviewee unique and not just another student at Anonymous University. Ask all four to imagine campus settings in which interviewer and subject might run into each other and end up together for fifteen minutes owing to long registration lines, elevators that stop between floors in the library, and the like.

Ask one of the three student interviewees to role-play being aggressive, hostile, belligerent, obtuse, or impatient with the interviewer. Warn the interviewer that one of the persons will be difficult to interview. Have the class carefully observe the series of interviews. Follow up each interview by asking the interviewer, "What questions did you invent on the spot?" and "What did you learn that surprised you?" Ask the student interviewed, "What did you wish you had been asked?" and "Would you have asked any of these questions some other way?" Ask the class for their perceptions of what worked and what didn't with each interview.

You'll probably see that both the interviewer and the students interviewed become more comfortable and more efficient as the three interviews progress. In particular, you'll no doubt notice that the student interviewer revises the questions he or she asks, adds narrow questions and redirecting questions, and perhaps changes the sequence of questions. Comment on the importance of drafting and redrafting questions for interviews and the need to be a flexible interviewer, responding to the conversation rather than working through a fixed set of questions. By the end of the session, students should feel less hesitant about the research and interviewing for the writing assignment.

Although an exercise like this shows up most often in a speech or interpersonal communication course, as teachers of writing we are always teaching more about all of the communication skills than our course titles might imply. These exercises build more trust into the community of writers in your classroom. They also prompt students to think about their responsibility for shaping conversation, both in interviews and in class discussions.

Planning, Drafting, and Developing (p. 98)

After the mock interviews, ask students to write down everything that seemed memorable in each interview. Even though they haven't questioned the people interviewed, they have been listening. Collect their writings and return them the next day with a comment to each student about the quality of his or her listening.

Ask students to list the props that were important to each of the three interviews. Some students enter into role-playing seriously and come costumed and clearly acting a character. Others don't. Regardless, class members can imagine props for the campus setting. Have them decide which objects surrounding a person being interviewed can teach them more about that person.

Finally, ask students to use the questions about the insights they gained (p. 99) to write a short essay, individually or in small groups. The exercise simulates in the classroom the experience that each writer is asked to undergo in order to respond successfully to the chapter's major writing assignment. Don't underestimate how much guidance your students might need in using the interview as a resource.

Revising and Editing (p. 100)

The Revision Checklist on pages 101–02, along with the transcript, will focus writers' attention on specific use of the information they've compiled. Some of these questions can be incorporated into the For Peer Response exercise on page 100.

As peer readers and writers respond to each other's drafts, Clark Killion, an instructor at Dodge City Community College, uses a worksheet like the one on page 130 to get students to see how a given piece of writing balances different qualities, such as information about a topic versus information about a person, or paraphrased information versus quotations. The reader is asked to mark a dot where he or she thinks the paper falls between these two points on the continuum — for example, somewhere between "Paraphrase" on the left and "Quotations" on the right. If the paper has only one quotation and the rest of the subject's words are paraphrased, the dot will be far to the left on the line; if there are more quotations than paraphrased words, the dot will be closer to the right margin; if there is about the same amount of quoted words and paraphrased words, the mark will be in the middle. Then the peer reader writes a sentence or two below the continuum line about how the balance affects the draft — for example, "Because the writer has used almost all paraphrases, we hardly ever hear Mrs. Barkley's voice. If the writer used more of Mrs. Barkley's words, we would have a better idea of her personality." Finally, the reader suggests how the writer might develop a more balanced, insightful paper.

If you decide to use such a worksheet in your own classes, explain to students that the balance does not have to be in the middle to be most effective. A different kind of balance might show their subject better.

Other Assignments (p. 102)

Some of the alternatives offered here are based on oral history — an extremely rich resource that students should be aware of and should be encouraged to use. Demonstrate the cross-curricular nature of this writing resource by arranging for a historian, a folklorist, or a colleague whose research interest is oral history to explain the process to your class.

Allow students to choose from all of the assignments in this section. Some students might hesitate to work with the assignment on family oral history, thinking it too personal. Encourage a reluctant writer to incorporate information gathered from reading or surveys as well.

APPLYING WHAT YOU LEARN: SOME USES OF INTERVIEWING A SUBJECT (p. 103)

Ask students to describe their own experiences with using interviews as a resource for writing in other disciplines. Have them compare and contrast the focus of the questions asked in academic or professional interviews with those asked in popular magazines such as *People* or *Rolling Stone*. Also, ask students to report on the usefulness of good advising sessions; students who have had successful conversations with advisers assist their peers in seeking out academic support through advising.

MAKING CONNECTIONS

Conversation is a resource used in nonfiction to make an essay realistic and interesting, much in the way that dialogue is used in fiction. Students often hesitate to use actual conversations in their writing. Emphasize that if the experience or observation being written about includes a conversation, then the writer should not dismiss it or its possible impact on the audience. Encourage students to notice the different types of conversations in our society. The following writers use conversation in their essays in *A Writer's Reader*.

Amy Tan in "Mother Tongue" (p. 445) uses direct and indirect quotation to show us the contrast between the Standard English she learned in school and the expressive but less accepted English spoken by her Chinese American mother.

Ruth La Ferla in "Latino Style Is So Cool. Oh, All Right: It's Hot" (p. 506) interviews a number of Latino students as well as professors, journalists, and fashion designers to explore emerging Latino style. Ethic style has broad appeal, and sexy Latino style promises to be the next big trend, according to La Ferla's interviews. La Ferla's essay is a good example of how a writer can use other voices to explore and enliven a thesis.

Ask students to consider the role that interview plays in these essays. For each essay, ask them to answer the As You Read questions on page 88.

RESOURCES FOR COLLEGE WRITERS

Your Assignment
Interviewing a Subject, p. 94

Resources in the Text
- Sample professional reading, p. 88
- Sample student reading, p. 92
- Facing the Challenge, p. 96
- Planning and developing the essay, p. 98
- Discovery and Revision checklists, pp. 95 and 101–02
- Editing Checklist, p. 102
- Uses of interviewing in real-world writing situations, p. 103
- Peer review help, pp. 97 and 100
- E-Writer help, p. 98

Resources on the Web Site
<bedfordstmartins.com/bedguide>
- Additional readings with activities
- "Ask the Draft Doctor" writing help
- Peer response forms
- Link to Exercise Central

INTERVIEWING A SUBJECT

Writer _____

Reader _____

In each of the categories below, mark on the continuum line how you think this paper balances the two qualities listed. Then, below the line, write how the balance affects the paper. (Example: "Because the paper does little besides discuss a topic, we never really learn about the person being interviewed. What is it about HIM that makes the topic interesting?") Finally, suggest how the writer might change the balance. Do this even if you are satisfied with the writer's approach. (Example: By telling us more about the person you interviewed, we can begin to understand his viewpoint, and we can also begin to understand why it is a reasonable point of view.")

Information   Information
about the   _____   about the
topic   person

Objective   Subjective
information   information
about the   _____   about the
person   person

Description   What the
of the   _____   person
person   said

Paraphrase   Quotations
of his/her   _____   of his/her
words   words

Comparing and Contrasting (Ch. 7, p. 104)

Comparing and contrasting is a form of definition concerned with determining similarities and differences in classes of objects and concepts. Most writing courses emphasize comparing and contrasting because it is an essential vehicle for determining what something is or is not. When students write comparison-and-contrast essays, they frequently focus on differences between their subjects of comparison rather than on similarities. This is not always the most productive way to investigate a topic, because it downplays the defining characteristics among members of the same class. Although differences are important, be sure that students think also of similarities, particularly as they begin drafting.

You might refer students to writing that examines both similarities in and differences between subjects. The grid on pages 371–83 identifies essays from *The Bedford Guide* that compare and contrast effectively.

Chapter 7, "Comparing and Contrasting," contains the following activities:

- Responding to an Image (p. 104). Allow your students to use their imagination while examining these visual activity prompts. If necessary, have students free-associate responses to elements of each image. If they are given free rein for their own interpretations, they will most likely view analyzing these images as a rewarding way to begin thinking about writing in these modes.

  Ask students to recall striking contrasts they have encountered in their own home towns or where they have traveled. You might want to bring to class other photos demonstrating contrasts of various kinds, or direct students to bring in photos that show contrast. Ask students to account for differences in the photos and to look for any similarities. Point out that contrast sometimes contains irony, and that can provide an interesting angle for essays.

- For E-Writers (p. 113). See page 73 of this manual for advice about how to use this feature.

- For Peer Response (p. 116). See page 39 of this manual for advice about how to use this feature.

- For Group Learning (p. 117). See page 39 of this manual for advice about how to use this feature.

LEARNING FROM OTHER WRITERS

SUZANNE BRITT *Neat People vs. Sloppy People* (p. 105)

A frequent writer for newspapers and magazines, Suzanne Britt humorously contrasts the behaviors of neat and sloppy people. She attributes the contrast to a fundamental moral difference.

Here's an Idea . . .

Have students choose a subject and list the characteristics or qualities that it represents or suggests. Then ask them to list qualities that differ from those items on their first list. For example, if a student is examining the quality of honesty in a historical figure (perhaps Abraham Lincoln), ask him or her to compare this quality with the questionable honesty of another historical figure (perhaps Richard Nixon). Or students might compare, say, the characteristics of one building with another, pointing out something that is a little different in each. This exercise should stress developing a series of points and counterpoints.

Questions to Start You Thinking (p. 107)

Meaning

1. The last sentence of paragraph 1 suggests that Britt is partial to sloppy people. Ask students to find other specific places in the essay where she reveals her position. For instance, she describes neat people as "wasteful" (para. 10) and "insensitive" (para. 12), while she finds that sloppy people are full of good intentions (para. 3) and ambitious (para. 4).

2. Although students may find that they have characteristics of both groups, urge them to select the group with which they are most closely aligned. Then have them choose details from the essay that best describe them as well as the ones that don't apply. You might ask students to write an additional paragraph for the essay about the group to which they belong. Brainstorming in small groups will help students generate ideas for their paragraph.

3. Students may note that Britt aims to convince neat people to loosen up. Her primary purpose, however, is to entertain. Ask students to identify humorous examples in the essay. In the process of entertaining, however, Britt reveals some telling generalizations about the habits, demeanors, and philosophies of neat people and sloppy people.

Writing Strategies

4. Ask students whether Britt's blunt introduction works for this essay, which includes many other abrupt generalizations. Does her approach persuade readers to lay aside their preoccupations and enter the world set forth in the essay? (see "Writing an Opening" on page 340 of the text for more advice on writing openings). Consider asking students to create a different opening for the essay, perhaps using one of the techniques suggested in Chapter 18, "Strategies for Drafting."

5. Although students will likely point out the improbability of providing a full exploration in an essay of this length, ask them which details capture the essence of each personality type. Does Britt effectively relate those details to the underlying moral difference she mentions in paragraph 1? In addition, have students discuss whether her bias toward sloppy people prevents her from offering a full characterization of each personality.

6. Britt presents all of her observations on sloppy people, followed by her observations on neat people. Students should recognize this approach as the opposing pattern of organization, a simple organization that works particularly well since Britt's essay is short and her supporting points are not complex. You might ask students to rearrange the essay into the alternating pattern. Does it work? Why, or why not?

7. Students are likely to note that Britt uses an abrupt style throughout the essay, so the shift in paragraph 6 may not have caused any confusion. And the last sentence in paragraph 5 serves as a subtle transition: "A neat person would just bulldoze the desk." Ask students to come up with a more explicit transitional word or phrase.

8. Although Britt polarizes the two types of people, omitting any mention of similarities, students should recognize from her tongue-in-cheek descriptions and exaggerated generalizations that she is approaching her topic in a less-than-serious manner. The essay is successful because it is based on Britt's assumption that her readers are intelligent enough to recognize that such a profound contrast is unlikely. Had she believed that readers would accept her polarization in a literal way, her essay would not have its intended humorous effect.

9. You might begin by asking students for adjectives that describe Britt's tone. Encourage them to point to specific words, phrases, and examples that reveal her attitude toward the subject. Students will most likely consider the essay's humorous, light-hearted tone to be consistent with Britt's purpose.

TIM CHABOT   *Take Me Out to the Ball Game,
but Which One?* (p. 108)

Well-organized and filled with concrete details, Tim Chabot's essay compares and contrasts baseball with basketball to determine which sport should be considered America's favorite pastime. The idea that basketball might have eclipsed baseball in popularity should spur much class discussion. Try dividing the class into baseball and basketball fans and have them debate the issue, defending or attacking Chabot's argument.

Questions to Start You Thinking (p. 110)

Meaning

1. This question simply asks students to list the individual points of comparison and contrast, but as they list the points, students will start challenging them. For example, basketball fans might strongly disagree that baseball requires more mental skill than basketball (paras. 7–8). Others might take offense at the notion that basketball relies on "brute physical strength" (para. 7) — some might even interpret the term *brute* as racist, considering the high percentage of African Americans on NBA teams. Be prepared for a lively discussion and even a few antagonistic encounters. But try to defer the discussion until students have identified all of the similarities and differences in Chabot's essay and the way in which he arranges them. List the points on the board in the order that they occur in the essay. With this rough outline, students will see that Chabot spends more space on the differences. Emphasizing the differences serves the purpose of the essay — to show that basketball is threatening baseball's status as our national pastime.

2. This question is designed to stimulate students' critical thinking, to come up with similarities and differences for themselves. But be warned that the discussion of differences between baseball and basketball might degenerate into an argument about which is the better sport. Try to keep the class focused on the similarities and differences that Chabot did not mention.

3. This question draws attention to the purpose of Chabot's essay and thus shows the importance of having a point to comparing and contrasting. Chabot concludes that basketball is threatening baseball's claim as America's pastime. If basketball

widens its audience and baseball continues to be plagued by strikes, basketball will become America's favorite sport. Ask students how Chabot uses comparison and contrast to lead up to this conclusion. Which similarities and differences support this conclusion? For example, paragraph 4 states that basketball arenas create an "atmosphere that is urban and adult." Do students think this point adequately supports the conclusion that basketball needs to widen its audience? Why or why not? Chabot could have compared and contrasted these two sports in hundreds of ways, but a writer must select and limit his or her points of comparison and contrast. The essay's ultimate purpose is what determines which points are selected.

4. Some students will probably argue that football should be considered America's favorite sport, as it is the only other professional sport that rivals the popularity of baseball and basketball. Depending on the kind of response you get to this question, you might want to group students according to their preference for baseball, basketball, and football, and have them devise an argument for why that sport should be the official national sport. Have each group write a one-page proposal stating their reasons, read them to the class, and debate them.

Writing Strategies

5. Students might identify the thesis at the end of the essay, in paragraph 9, or as the last sentence in paragraph 1. This essay shows students that, for college-level writing, the thesis can be anywhere in the essay, as long as the essay is well-organized. Direct students' attention to the section "Stating and Using a Thesis" (p. 312) in Chapter 17, "Strategies for Stating a Thesis and Planning." In Chabot's essay, the process of comparing and contrasting basketball and baseball logically leads to the conclusion in the final paragraph.

6. Since Chabot argues in favor of basketball as the national pastime, ask students whether it is necessary for him to provide balanced support. Can he get away with developing one side more than the other? As students consider whether his support is sufficient, urge them not to let their own point of view on the subject interfere with their objectivity. Refer students to the first question on meaning, which asks them to identify the essay's points of comparison and contrast. With their responses to this question as a guide, ask students whether the points of comparison themselves as well as the support for each point are sufficient.

7. Make sure that students do not underestimate the importance of transitional devices in comparison-and-contrast essays. Have them identify each transitional device between paragraphs and between sentences within a paragraph. Phrases such as "in contrast" (para. 4) or "on the other hand" (para. 6) should be easy for students to spot. You might need to point out the importance of using a simple "but" or "also" as a transition. Carefully go over the section "Achieving Coherence" (p. 346) in Chapter 18, "Strategies for Drafting," for more about transitions.

8. Students should have little trouble identifying the first paragraph as the introduction and locating the points of Chabot's comparison and contrast: each sport's audience (para. 2), venues (para. 2), atmosphere (paras. 3–4), and pace (paras. 5–6). Chabot also contrasts the athleticism of baseball and basketball players (paras. 7–8). As discussed in the suggested answer for question 5, some students might mistake the last sentence in paragraph 1 for the thesis, but Chabot's well-organized essay logically leads to the conclusion/thesis statement in the final paragraph.

LEARNING BY WRITING

The Assignment: Comparing and Contrasting (p. 111)

Encourage students to choose a topic that they are in some way familiar with as well as interested in. Choosing a topic with inherent interest for your students will make getting started much easier and will fuel their enthusiasm during the development stages.

Facing the Challenge (p. 112)

Students often have problems determining the purpose of a comparison and contrast essay: Will it be primarily informative and explanatory or explicitly argumentative (or a combination of the two)? Remind them to always ask this question as they begin planning an essay. Also, students may have difficulty organizing comparison-and-contrast essays, so take advantage of any opportunity to discuss organization. By listing the points of comparison and contrast in the model essays in this chapter, students will begin to see how they are arranged.

Help students to determine the most effective organization for their essays by helping them:

- Choose a topic of manageable complexity.

- Make a preliminary list of comparative issues, including similarities and differences. This list can be used later for an outline.

- Decide whether to use an opposing or an alternating pattern of exposition.

For more about providing support for underprepared students, see Chapter 4 of this manual.

Generating Ideas (p. 111)

Although the Discovery Checklist on page 112 is an excellent resource for generating ideas, it is clearly not an exhaustive source of topics. Encourage students to think beyond the suggestions so as to expand their topic: For example, comparing holiday or family customs could be expanded to include customs of groups or even nations.

Consider assigning a group collaborative research and writing activity for this chapter. Working collaboratively will make the process of writing a comparison-and-contrast essay more concrete for students and might help them generate ideas for their own essays. Have the class collectively agree on a common topic and a clear purpose and then identify a number of important points for comparison and contrast. Divide the students into several groups, assigning at least one area of comparison and contrast to each group. Direct students to the library or another resource center and instruct them to rigorously investigate their assigned point(s) of comparison, making full use of the research strategies covered in the Quick Research Guide or *A Writer's Research Manual* (if your students' textbooks include this). Once the groups have collected their data, they should reconvene and collaboratively formulate their point-by-point arguments, deciding together which arguments are the most effective.

Or have groups of students choose a specific topic from a list of possible areas to investigate, such as leisure activities, social issues, educational issues, celebrities or historical figures, or commercial products. Have each group decide on the purpose of their comparison and contrast before they move on to identify differences and similarities.

For example, if students choose to argue for the superiority of one computer system over another, they might ask, What elements of the system are responsible for its popularity and effectiveness? Would students purchase the system based solely on what they know about it?

An alternative approach is to assign students to work in pairs. Each pair should decide the essay's focus. Once the topic and purpose have been determined, students can then individually pursue the development of specific points of comparison. After these points have been sufficiently drafted, have students pair up again to reshape the points. Together they should revise all points and arguments in accordance with the essay's overall purpose.

Planning, Drafting, and Developing (p. 114)

As suggested by the authors, encourage students to ask the classic journalistic questions: who, what, when, where, why, and how. These questions can be used to explore and develop nearly any subject.

The computer makes moving information around very easy, and students should be encouraged to take advantage of this capability in the early, exploratory stage of drafting their comparison-and-contrast essay. Ask them to use the computer to brainstorm a list of possible purposes for the topic they have chosen and as many issues of comparison and contrast as they can. Remind them to leave considerable space between entries to develop later. This technique is particularly effective on a computer because it allows students to identify seed ideas quickly, move them around as necessary, and develop them as more information becomes available.

Once students have clearly identified the purpose of the essay and have selected a number of comparative issues, ask them to arrange their essay to accommodate the most effective delivery — an opposing or an alternating pattern of exposition. After they have developed the comparative points, have them return to their introductory section on the essay's purpose and copy and paste it at the end. This move will allow them to amplify and revise their introduction to take into account the judgment they make in the essay.

Revising and Editing (p. 117)

The Revision Checklist on page 118 is a critical tool for ensuring that students have addressed the major issues in a comparison-and-contrast essay. Encourage them to use this checklist to make sure that they have (1) identified a clear purpose for the essay, (2) developed major similarities and differences to write about, (3) judiciously used evidence, and (4) arrived at a clear conclusion or judgment. Advise peer editors to ask, Does the essay have an introductory appeal that makes the reader want to continue reading? Is the pattern of exposition effective (opposing or alternating)? Is the essay tedious, falling into a boring, singsong pattern of development?

Other Assignments (p. 119)

Students are often comfortable comparing and contrasting because it offers them an opportunity to write about an extensive range of topics, from the personal to the cultural to the abstractly intellectual. Encourage students to investigate a wide range of possible topics by exploring some of these alternative assignments.

Some students might hesitate to work with assignments that seem too personal. If students are uncomfortable writing about personal experiences, encourage them to use their reading as a resource instead. Consider allowing them to choose from all of the assignments in this section.

APPLYING WHAT YOU LEARN: SOME USES OF COMPARING AND CONTRASTING (p. 120)

Learning to compare and contrast will serve your students well throughout their college life. Essay examinations, research projects, and investigative assignments across the disciplines commonly call for comparison and contrast. Ask students to bring to class examples of these assignments as they come across them in other courses.

MAKING CONNECTIONS

The following writers in *A Writer's Reader* compare and contrast to serve a number of purposes, including explanation, argument, and exploration. Ask students to choose any two essays to read out of class. When students return, have them write down a simple statement identifying the purpose(s) and major points of comparison for each essay, paying particular attention to whether the comparisons are effective. Take this opportunity to reiterate the importance of taking notes while reading.

Anjula Razdan in "What's Love Got to Do with It?" (p. 453) compares the institution of arranged marriage to online dating. Razdan asserts that because these institutions encourage rational deliberation in choosing a mate, they may lead to enduring love more often than relationships based on passionate impulse.

Danzy Senna in "The Color of Love" (p. 458) compares herself with her grandmother. Senna ultimately reveals her deep love for her grandmother, in spite of their sharply opposing values.

Judy Brady in "I Want a Wife" (p. 497) crafts a hard-hitting argument for gender equality simply by contrasting the household responsibilities assumed by each spouse. Brady's descriptions of the tasks performed by the wife so that her husband may be free to pursue his interests makes clear her implicit claim. Many students will recognize Brady's list as tasks their mothers have performed for them.

Tara Parker-Pope in "Custom-Made" (p. 502) contrasts iconic American-brand products with the peculiar products (at least to American tastes) that emerge after the companies have adapted these goods for specific global markets. She catalogs the accommodations that American companies make for both the palates and purchasing habits of their Asian and European customers.

James Poniewozik in "Why Reality TV Is Good for Us" (p. 520) examines the genre alongside dramas and sitcoms, showing why programs such as *Survivor* and *American Idol* are "the best thing to happen to television in several years."

Terry Golway in "A Nation of Idol-Worshipers" (p. 525) compares idols of the past with the celebrity idols of today. What has happened to our society, Golway asks, that so many take seriously the "fame and glamour" of entertainers rather than the substantive contributions of doctors, scientists, and firemen whose lives demonstrate "service and citizenship"?

Richard Rodriguez in "Public and Private Language" (p. 571) contrasts the use of English, his public language, with the Spanish his family spoke in the privacy of their home. He explores the impact of introducing English into his home and the effects on his family dynamic, concluding that while English opened to him the wider, public world, he lost something precious in his private world.

As your students read these essays and consider the roles that comparison and contrast play therein, ask them to answer the As You Read questions on page 105 for each essay.

RESOURCES FOR COLLEGE WRITERS

Your Assignment
Comparing and Contrasting, p. 111

Resources in the Text
- Sample professional reading, p. 105
- Sample student reading, p. 108
- Facing the Challenge, p. 112
- Planning and developing the essay, p. 114
- Discovery and Revision checklists, pp. 112 and 118
- Editing Checklist, p. 119
- Uses of comparison and contrast in real-world writing situations, p. 120
- Peer review help, p. 116
- E-Writer help, p. 113

Resources on the Web Site
<bedfordstmartins.com/bedguide>
- Additional readings with activities
- "Ask the Draft Doctor" writing help
- Peer response forms
- Link to Exercise Central

Explaining Causes and Effects (Ch. 8, p. 121)

A major change for first-year writers is moving from asking "What happened?" to "Why did it happen?" and "What will happen?" Cause-and-effect analysis is crucial for critical inquiry — in fact, much academic work requires it. It asks students to move back and forth from the concrete to the abstract, from the specific to the general, and to move among levels of abstraction. Students need to look back to analyze cause and to look forward to extrapolate effects. The authors acknowledge that this method of explaining is difficult but insist that it is a particularly empowering way of thinking and is critical to our growth as thinkers and as humane persons.

If you've been reading aloud at the beginning of class, don't stop now. Students need to be exposed to the language and logic of cause-and-effect analysis. Look for essays from a wide range of sources — for instance, newspapers and political or economic publications — to read to your class. You might refer students to writing that explores causes and effects. The grid on pages 371–83 identifies essays of this type from *The Bedford Guide.*

Chapter 8, "Explaining Causes and Effects," contains the following activities:

- Responding to an Image (p. 121). Allow your students to use their imagination while examining these visual activity prompts. If necessary, have students free-associate responses to elements of each image. If they are given free rein for their own interpretations, they will most likely view analyzing these images as a rewarding way to begin thinking about writing in these modes.

  The photo implies both causes and effects. Which ones can students identify? They might point to pollution — or, more specifically, greenhouse gases — as a cause of global warming (an effect). They might also point to industrial development as a cause of destruction of landscapes or of pollution (effects). How does the composition of the photo evoke feelings of threat or menace?

- For E-Writers (p. 135). See page 73 of this manual for advice about how to use this feature.

- For Peer Response (p. 136). See page 39 of this manual for advice about how to use this feature.

- For Group Learning (p. 137). See page 39 of this manual for advice about how to use this feature.

LEARNING FROM OTHER WRITERS

WILLIAM SEVERINI KOWINSKI   *Kids in the Mall: Growing Up Controlled* (p. 122)

William Severini Kowinski, an editor and writer for national newspapers and magazines, examines the economic and social impact of the growth of shopping malls in his book *The Malling of America.* In this excerpt, Kowinski examines the effects of "malling" on the teenagers who spend time working, shopping, and just hanging out in America's malls.

Questions to Start You Thinking (p. 126)

Meaning

1. Kowinski quotes a study commissioned by the International Council of Shopping Centers to explain what teens seek at the mall (para. 6). Ask students if they consider Kowinski's evidence credible. Encourage them to consider the purposes of the study and any possibility of bias. Although the concerns of the council differ from Kowinski's, their findings are still relevant to Kowinski's purposes. Point out that this is not always the case; students should consider purpose in evaluating a source. Ask them what other evidence Kowinski might have used. Many of your students may have been attracted to malls. Ask them if their experience supports the study's findings.

2. Many of your students are like the teens Kowinski describes: carefully engineered consumers. They are unaware of the forces that manipulate them to "choose" to devote their lives to material acquisition. Ask students to write down their goal in life. If they say "to be happy," ask them to define happiness. Ask them to list the five things they value most. Then ask them how they came to hold those values. Encourage them to look at long-term causal chains. Your students will think through this process more successfully if you ask them to freewrite about it for ten minutes.

3. Kowinski discusses the mall as a surrogate parent in paragraph 10. Refer students again to their own lists and the causes that shaped them and ask them to examine Karen Lansky's conclusions in light of their own experiences.

4. In paragraph 16, Kowinski finds that both the malls and suburban schools are "enclosed and controlled environments." Ask students if, based on their high school experiences, they agree or disagree with Kowinski. Do they find the movement toward more controlled environments that Kowinski describes (para. 17) positive or negative?

Writing Strategies

5. Students will need to consider long-term as well as immediate effects to determine whether the effects Kowinski describes are positive or negative. For example, in paragraphs 10 and 11, he describes the mall as a "structural mother" but one that "encourages passivity and consumption." Students may find it problematic that the mall rather than the family provides mothering for these teens. Similarly, the effect of acquiring the clothes-conscious skills that Kowinski describes in paragraph 7 may seem positive, but paragraph 8 follows with David Elkind's explanation of "the hurried child." Ask students to also examine both immediate and long-term effects of the jobs the mall provides. Again, ask them to consider the consumer mentality that Kowinski describes as they determine the value of this employment. Many of your students will find the sense of resignation at the end of Kowinski's essay disturbing. Ask them to describe what they think our society will be like in fifty years. Then ask them to analyze causes.

6. Have students work in groups to analyze each paragraph to answer this question.

7. Ask students to rewrite the essay's opening using one of the strategies for openings on pages 340–42 of *The Bedford Guide*. Ask them to share their new openings and decide which is most effective.

YUN YUNG CHOI　*Invisible Women* (p. 127)

Choi, a native of Korea, discusses how Confucianism has affected the lives of Korean women over the past few hundred years. She explains that this ideology distinguishes men as superior to women and thus has served as the basis for many kinds of discrimination and abuses of women over the centuries. Such debasement of women was not always a part of Korea's history, though, and in the early centuries of the Yi Dynasty women enjoyed relative equality and many of the same privileges as men. Despite the Korean government's efforts to improve sexual equality and individual freedoms in the past few decades, Choi notes, Korean society unfortunately still clings to the idea that men are superior to women.

Questions to Start You Thinking (p. 129)

Meaning

1. The effect Choi observes — the invisibility of women in Korean society — is attributed in paragraph 2 to the introduction and incorporation of Confucian ideology into the latter half of the Yi Dynasty. Choi quite clearly states the cause and links it to the subsequent effect.

2. Choi's discussion of the specific effects that the introduction of Confucianism had on women in Korea takes up a major portion of her essay (paras. 3–10). Ask students to go through each paragraph and find the changes Choi cites.

3. Choi's essay provides evidence that she has rethought some of the beliefs about women she absorbed as a child — that women are wives, and that the highest distinction a woman can achieve is to marry a president. She examines Korea's history and finds some of the causes responsible for the limited opportunities Korean women have had — namely, Confucianism — and discovers that prior to the introduction of this ideology, women in Korea were treated much better and had more equality with men. When asking students to consider what they think may have influenced the change in Choi's beliefs about women, remind them that Choi was a student at Harvard College at the time she wrote this essay. This rather lofty distinction has set her apart in many ways from most of the Korean women she describes, and perhaps this distance from her homeland has made her better able to examine some of the effects Confucianism has had on women in her country.

Writing Strategies

4. Point out that Choi's strategy here is to move from the particular to the general — a process known as *induction*. She uses an anecdote to establish a link between herself and her general topic, and she does so, we believe, quite successfully.

5. Choi compares the lack of rights and privileges women receive under Confucianism with the rights and privileges available to men in Korea. She also compares the status of women in the pre-Confucian Koryo and Yi dynasties with the status of women in the post-Confucian Yi Dynasty. Ask students to evaluate how effective Choi's essay would have been without these comparisons and contrasts. Can they think of another strategy by which she could have better made her point? If they were peer-editing her essay, what advice would they give her to improve it?

6. Choi clearly recognizes that readers may be unfamiliar with Korean culture. Perhaps most important, she provides contextual information about the history of Korean attitudes toward women. And she does not assume that readers understand current gender roles in Korea, either, so she offers examples of life for women both before and after Confucianism was adopted. She also defines the Korean

words she uses, such as *agnation* (para. 4), *anbang* (para. 5), and *chokpo* (para. 7). Ask students whether Choi gave them sufficient information to understand her culture. What else might she have done to address the needs of her readers?

7. This tightly organized essay clearly demonstrates the effects of Confucianism on Korean women. For an outline of Choi's introduction, thesis, major causes and effects, and conclusion, direct students to the heading "Planning, Drafting, and Developing" later in the chapter (p. 132).

LEARNING BY WRITING

The Assignment: Explaining Causes and Effects (p. 129)

Although your students have experience using the critical thinking skill required for this writing assignment, they might not realize it and might lack confidence in their ability to analyze causes and effects. In fact, this skill is universal, beginning in childhood with the question "Why?" — "Why is the sky blue, Mommy?" "Why can't I fly, Daddy?" Remind students that every day they ferret out explanations for what happens around them and the results of those events, trying to make sense of their lives, just as this assignment asks them to do.

One way to sequence this assignment with the assignments in the following chapters is to have students continue working with the same issue through this and subsequent chapters: "Taking a Stand" (p. 139), "Proposing a Solution" (p. 166), "Evaluating" (p. 183), and "Supporting a Position with Sources." (p. 199). Guide students to choose an issue they find interesting, and one that can be examined and written about for the assignments in each chapter. Hold conferences with them as they select an issue to be sure that they can adapt it for each assignment. For example, for the assignment in Chapter 10, students will need to identify a problem related to the issue for which they can propose a feasible solution. If your course contains a research component, the sequence of assignments can culminate in a more extensive research paper, and students can build their working bibliography and research archive as they progress through each assignment. Students can begin by generating an annotated bibliography of a cluster of readings discussing the causes and effects of their issue.

Next, students can write a paper evaluating the sources in their annotated bibliography, using Chapter 11, "Evaluating," the criteria for testing evidence in Chapter 3, "Critical Thinking Processes," and section C of the Quick Research Guide. If your students' books include *A Writer's Research Manual,* you might also want them to turn to Chapter 31, "Evaluating Sources." This assignment can be followed by the assignment in Chapter 8, in which students can discuss the causes and effects of the issue and incorporate source material from their bibliography. Following that, students can write sequenced papers about their issue, using the assignments in Chapter 9, "Taking a Stand" and Chapter 10, "Proposing a Solution." As they move through the assignments, they can continue to develop their working bibliographies and research archives.

Facing the Challenge (p. 132)

Effects are easier to demonstrate than causes. Working back and forth from causes to effects requires that writers be confident. In brief conferences, help students to decide whether they are ready to take on establishing causes or effects.

Expect that students will need more time for drafting, developing, and revising and that they will submit longer essays than they have previously. To help them focus and limit their essays, have them write the main point they want to make at the top of their working draft; then choose only causes or effects that have the strongest, most direct impact on their thesis.

Here's an Idea . . .

Organize four small groups and select four topics, such as the increasing costs of college tuition, the high salaries of professional athletes, the uses of cloning or stem cell research, and the political apathy of American voters. Ask Group 1 to spend half the period generating the causes of the increase in tuition costs and the effects of exorbitant salaries for professional athletes; Group 2, the causes of the use of cloning or stem cell research and the effects of apathy among voters; Group 3, the causes of professional athletes' salaries and the effects of the use of cloning or stem cell research; Group 4, the causes of apathy among voters and the effects of the increase in college tuition costs. Working with two topics and two analytical questions requires writers to flex some cognitive muscle. This is a cognitive skill highly valued in problem solving.

Have the group turn in lists of causes and effects. During the next class, give each group a list of causes for one problem and effects for another and ask them now to classify the causes and effects. Suggest categories such as short and long term, immediate and remote, most and least important, least and most unusual, and so on.

For more about providing support for underprepared students, see Chapter 4 of this manual.

Generating Ideas (p. 130)

Each kind of change cited in the Discovery Checklist on page 130 can unlock the gates of recall. Encourage students to freewrite or to brainstorm in response to several of the suggestions. The exercise of moving from the personal to the local to the national not only generates topics but also helps students to start asking about the connections between national change and personal experience. You can, of course, also move from the macrocosm to the microcosm in the brainstorming sessions. This shifting of perspectives will help students juggle several levels of thinking about cause and effect.

Students will also gain some flexibility in shifting perspectives as they wrestle with the variety of topics in the sequence of activities described in the Here's an Idea box above. More than likely, they will be surprised by the range and quality of ideas they are producing. Because they leave the class with many possible topics, with new directions in which to pursue ideas, and with controlling purposes for new essays, students will feel more confident about their ability to generate ideas for the topic they have settled on. Others will be better able to look at the list of causes or effects they have produced and feel more prepared to evaluate them.

Students sometimes make mistakes in identifying causal relationships. They identify a cause that, upon closer examination, did not actually cause what followed, or they identify an effect that did not actually result from what preceded it. In *The Literate Mind: Reading, Writing, Critical Thinking* (Kendall/Hunt, 1987), Thomas E. Porter explains how canons developed by nineteenth-century rhetorician John Stuart Mill can verify causal relationships. Have your students test their claims with these canons:

- **Canon of Agreement**: When the cause occurs, the effect must follow invariably. When the effect occurs, the cause must have preceded it.

- **Canon of Difference**: If the cause occurs and the effect does not follow, or if the effect occurs and the cause did not precede it, then the suspected cause is either not the cause or not the only cause.

- **Canon of Correlation**: In general, the intensity of the effect varies in relation to the intensity of the cause. (The greater the extent or impact of the cause, the greater the effect, and vice versa.)

Planning, Drafting, and Developing (p. 132)

If students have been successful in their use of prewriting strategies, they will have plenty of material to shape. Remind them that classification is a particularly useful way to analyze the causes and effects they now have at hand. Encourage them to be flexible in selecting materials and determining their significance.

Revising and Editing (p. 134)

Notice the range of questions in the Revision Checklist on page 135 and the For Peer Response exercise on page 136. All of the questions would be helpful during a workshop or peer-evaluation session. Plan to give the writers more time for revision of this assignment than you allotted for earlier assignments. The summary criteria of "thoughtful, searching, and reasonable" stated by the authors are useful to consider as you decide how to evaluate this assignment.

Other Assignments (p. 137)

These alternative assignments extend cause-and-effect thinking to broader, more diverse areas than the specific assignment for this chapter. These assignments require time to incubate, plan, and revise, so be flexible and give students who choose these assignments the necessary time.

APPLYING WHAT YOU LEARN: SOME USES OF EXPLAINING CAUSES AND EFFECTS (p. 137)

The applications cited here emphasize how important it is to master this habit of thought. Move students into a discussion of how cause and effect is used in the essays mentioned by the authors. Ask students to recall exam questions that asked for causal analysis. For help with identifying and answering exam questions, refer students to page 280 in Chapter 15, "Writing for Assessment."

MAKING CONNECTIONS

A writer's explanation of causes and effects is often interwoven with analyzing, taking a stand, investigating a problem, proposing a solution, and evaluating. The writers in *A Writer's Reader* listed here combine their resources by using cause and effect with other methods of development.

Anjula Razdan in "What's Love Got to Do with It?" (p. 453) explores the effect of arranged marriages and online dating services. Because these institutions encourage rational deliberation in choosing a mate, Razdan states, they may lead to enduring love more often than relationships based on passionate impulse.

Nancy Gibbs in "Free the Children" (p. 470) examines the effects of summertime freedom for schoolchildren. In a world of increasingly structured activities, Gibbs claims, children need summers to explore independence, try out new ideas and skills, and learn from experience.

Robert Jensen in "The High Cost of Manliness" (p. 475) takes a sobering look at the effects of society's definition of manliness. Jensen summarizes the commonly held perception that "a real man" should be competitive and aggressive, and then he argues that the effects of this view are "dangerous for women" and "toxic" for men themselves.

Stephen King in "Why We Crave Horror Movies" (p. 512) explains and defends horror movies by asserting that they "exercise" the "anticivilization emotions" in all of us (para. 11). He suggests that horror movies allow us to vicariously indulge our dark impulses, which, for most people, prevents them from being acted out in real life.

Steven Levy in an excerpt from *The Perfect Thing* (p. 540) examines the effects of the ubiquitous iPod on pedestrian interaction in New York. Levy concludes that the lack of communication attributed to the isolating effects of iPods has, in fact, been typical of New Yorkers all along.

Alex Koppelman in "MySpace or OurSpace?" (p. 546) looks at the unexpected consequences some teenagers face from posting on MySpace. As police and schools patrol MySpace in investigations, teenagers find themselves subject to school suspensions or police charges resulting from photos and information they thought was private. Koppelman goes beyond the immediate consequences to examine the chilling effects on how students perceive their First Amendment rights, citing evidence that teens' belief in their right to free speech has already been eroded.

Sherry Turkle in "How Computers Change the Way We Think" (p. 552) presents evidence that computer software and other such tools have affected students' cognitive processes. Among the results she sees are shifts in views on privacy and what constitutes the self. In addition, she notes that the speed of word processing and the brevity of PowerPoint programs have diminished habits of taking time to develop and fully articulate ideas.

Richard Rodriguez in "Public and Private Language" (p. 571) recounts his experience learning English as the son of Spanish-speaking Mexican American parents. Tracing both the positive and negative effects of his English-only schooling, Rodriguez conveys his complex stance on bilingual education, ultimately arguing against it.

As students read these essays, ask them to consider the role played by explanations of cause and effect. For each essay, have students answer the As You Read questions on page 122.

RESOURCES FOR COLLEGE WRITERS

Your Assignment
Explaining Causes and Effects, p. 129

Resources in the Text
- Sample professional reading, p. 122
- Sample student reading, p. 127
- Facing the Challenge, p. 132
- Planning and developing the essay, p. 132
- Discovery and Revision checklists, pp. 130 and 135
- Editing Checklist, p. 136
- Uses of explaining causes and effects in real-world writing situations, pp. 137–38
- Peer review help, p. 136
- E-Writer help, p. 135

Resources on the Web Site
<bedfordstmartins.com/bedguide>
- Additional readings with activities
- "Ask the Draft Doctor" writing help
- Peer response forms
- Link to Exercise Central

Taking a Stand (Ch. 9, p. 139)

Persuasive writing demands a great deal from writers. Not only are writers discovering and clarifying their opinions through combining several methods of thinking, but they are also attending to the perspective of the reader. Because persuasion is reader-centered discourse, writers must continually work with several cognitive and affective aims and strategies at once. Despite the difficulty of such writing, first-year students often suddenly spring to life as they work to state and defend an opinion or to propose a solution. Like other modes of discourse, it is a familiar process. Remind students that they already know much more about persuasion than they might realize.

Ideally, writing persuasion leads thinkers away from an egocentric perspective on the world. Long before students read the models in this chapter, they can be thinking about techniques of persuasion. Introduce them to the concept of "ethos"and show how it is an extension of "persona." Student writers need to think about shaping ethos both to persuade and to come to see themselves as thinkers with the authority and power to shape meaning. Help them become more analytical about the persuasion that assaults them daily, both to get past being manipulated by it and to come to understand how not to abuse appeals to logic or to emotions. Introduce them to the editorial page of the local newspaper by reading aloud from it so that they can hear the language of persuasion. You might also want to point students to argumentative readings in *The Bedford Guide;* see the grid on pages 371–83.

Raise students' consciousness about ads that bombard them daily in various media. Have them analyze ads and commercials to determine how real and trustworthy the "experts"are. Ask them to analyze political campaign statements and speeches by elected officials. Keep in mind that you are teaching them to "read" their world critically. Focus their attention on how each ad or commercial affects them. Ask them to talk about how an ad or political statement expresses an awareness of them as viewers, consumers, or voters. Ask them to classify those appeals to the viewer or reader that strike them as honest and trustworthy and those that seem manipulative. Then ask them to carry all of their understanding over into the writing process and into the several choices they must make as they shape their drafts.

Chapter 9, "Taking a Stand," contains the following activities:

- Responding to an Image (p. 139). Allow your students to use their imagination while examining these visual activity prompts. If necessary, have students free-associate responses to elements of each image. If they are given free rein for their own interpretations, they will most likely view analyzing these images as a rewarding way to begin thinking about writing in these modes.

    It should be easy for your students to identify with the photo that begins this chapter since it depicts a group of college students. Call your students' attention to details such as the age of the marchers and the writing on the T-shirt of the man on the right. Have them evaluate the importance of each word on the banner. Ask students whether, in their opinion, the stand these protestors are taking will have an impact. In recent years, student activism against exploitation of sweatshop workers has resulted in changes at some universities, such the decision to have college apparel come from only those suppliers who pay a living wage. Ask students to research other successes of student activism. What issues do they think are important to take a stand on? What is the most effective way to press for change?

Here's an Idea . . .

To demonstrate how persuasion works in advertising, give students the follow-ing assignment:

Analyze a television or radio commercial or a magazine or Internet ad and discuss the strategies the ad employs. If you use a radio, TV, or Internet ad or commercial, you will need to describe it; you can attach a magazine ad to your draft.

As you consider the strategies the ad uses, decide just what those strategies are supposed to make the consumer do. Consider the targeted audience. Then discuss your evaluation of the strategies. Are they effective? Do they reach the target audience? Do they persuade the audience?

- For E-Writers (p. 157). See page 73 of this manual for advice about how to use this feature.

- For Peer Response (p. 159). See page 39 of this manual for advice about how to use this feature.

- For Group Learning (p. 152). See page 39 of this manual for advice about how to use this feature.

LEARNING FROM OTHER WRITERS

SUZAN SHOWN HARJO *Last Rites for Indian Dead*
(p. 140)

Harjo takes a stand against allowing American Indian remains to be excavated in the name of archaeology, medicine, or fortune-hunting. As students read her essay, they should look for the different kinds of persuasive techniques Harjo uses. Her appeals to logic as well as emotions are effectively combined to make this essay convincing with-out being overbearing.

Questions to Start You Thinking (p. 143)

Meaning

1. The issue Harjo discusses is that people plunder the graves of American Indians looking for everything from valuable relics to intriguing curiosities. She shows the scope of the problem not by listing a number of recent incidents but by presenting readers with a chronology of atrocities committed while "collecting"such artifacts — starting with the Sand Creek massacre in the nineteenth century.

2. Harjo states her position in the second sentence of the essay: The laws now pro-tect the rights of those who plunder burial sites, while the laws should be protect-ing the rights of Native Americans and their ancestors. What does Harjo do to avoid alienating a reader who might disagree with her, given that she doesn't reserve stating her stand until later in the essay?

3. Harjo relies on the expert testimony of a physician and former surgeon general to support her claim that these remains serve no medical purpose. Do students

think Dr. Johnson's testimony is sufficient evidence to support this point, or does Harjo need more?

Writing Strategies

4. Based on the careful history she provides, Harjo seems to assume that her audience consists of non–Native Americans or those who know little about the problem she discusses. She does seem to feel that her audience will sympathize with the problem she presents and that if they are predisposed to disagree with her, they will still be able to be swayed by the emotional nature of the problem.

5. Harjo's evidence includes dates and careful figures tabulating the cost in Indian lives, the number of "artifacts" collected, and the prices such relics fetch on the market. She also relies on the testimony of experts in different fields — including a long-dead army officer, a current physician, and members of Congress who have supported legislation to protect Indian remains. Her attention to detail helps make this evidence highly convincing.

6. Harjo draws on her ethnicity to show how this problem is personal as well as communal. By making statements like "my own relatives' skulls are in the Smithsonian" (para. 2), Harjo forces a reader to recognize that this is not a purely scientific problem but one that touches real people's lives. Although a lawyer or an archaeologist, for example, would each have a specific professional position to add to the argument that Native American remains should be legally protected from disinterment, Harjo's ethnicity is especially suited to the angle she takes in this essay. Not only does she claim that these remains should be protected; she makes this claim on the grounds that it is personally insulting to force people to submit to having their ancestors' graves desecrated.

7. The opening sentence of her essay appeals to readers' emotions by suggesting that any American would be indignant about this kind of treatment to his or her relatives. At the end of paragraph 7, she relies on the reader to answer her questions with a clear sense that this is inexcusable excess. And her conclusion also depends on white Americans' guilt and sense of honor by asking them to think of family and help to rectify the "shameful past" (para. 15) of American Indian treatment. These appeals effectively enable readers to identify emotionally with the problem of ancestral respect regardless of their ethnic backgrounds.

8. This essay is both informative and quietly indignant. Harjo is not out to attack any particular person, but she is careful to make clear that she considers these practices atrocious. In describing graves as "desecrated" and collectors as "scavengers" (para. 5), as well as providing images of long-buried bones now "strewn about like litter" (para. 6), Harjo is strongly condemning both the practice of reopening graves and the people who find ways to justify this practice. Students should note that she lumps archaeological, medical, and biological efforts with "pseudoscientific" (para. 3) and mercenary ones in arguing that there is no reason to disturb graves. Are students convinced that all of these reasons are equally invalid?

SAM BENEN   *A Royal Mess* (p. 143)

In this essay, Sam Benen argues against online poker playing for college students. He discusses the scope of the phenomenon and enumerates the potential hazards to students, both financial and legal. Benen supports his argument with facts and personal observations, using both logical and emotional appeals.

Here's an Idea . . .

Have students create a two-column document on their computers. In the left column, have them type any passages from their sources (books, periodicals, and so forth) with which they take exception, or with which they especially agree, or will use as evidence. In the right column, have them type counter-claims, refutation, statements of agreement, or other comments. In effect, writers will be shaping dialogue on the screen. They will also have direct quotations at their fingertips to copy and paste into the text of their papers. Remind them to include source documentation when they type passages and to cite the sources when they use the material in their papers.

Questions to Start You Thinking (p. 146)

Meaning

1. Benen points to several hazards associated with online poker playing among students. In paragraph 2, he notes that there are no limits on how long people can play online poker or on how much money they can spend, potentially leading to significant losses. In paragraph 3, he suggests that students are set up to break the law by a major poker vendor's terms of use, which require players to be at least twenty-one and gambling in a state where this activity is legal. Finally, he notes that many underage players, unwilling to report gambling earnings to the IRS, defraud the agency. (In paragraph 7, he mentions in passing how addiction to online poker can harm students' grades and social life.) To answer question 1, students might find it helpful to highlight or check off the hazards as they read.

2. Benen discusses the reasons that students play online poker in paragraphs 4 and 5. These reasons include the fact that "seemingly everyone does so," and that the punishment is minimal. Further, despite efforts by banks to block online gambling transactions, students can easily get around these limits and access their money. Finally, some students can earn thousands of dollars through online poker playing. Students might discuss reasons for gambling beyond those mentioned by Benen.

3. In paragraph 1, Benen says that "reasonable people ought not to be alarmed by poker on TV and $20 games amongst friends." In paragraph 7, he says he "doesn't find any fault with students who keep up to a few hundred dollars in their poker account to play an occasional game." You might ask students whether they agree with the line Benen draws between gambling as a "harmless vice" and gambling as a serious problem.

Writing Strategies

4. Students should note that Benen uses both ethical and logical appeals throughout. In paragraphs 3 and 7, he discusses how common gambling practices lead students to break the law and evade income tax. Logically, he argues that the hazards of online poker playing are pervasive and serious. His support consists, apparently, of personal observations and experiences, as well as terms and conditions of sites, like <http://PartyPoker.com>, used in online gambling transactions. You might ask students whether the essay would have been strengthened by information from additional sources, such as national reports on student gambling, materials from organizations for compulsive gamblers, or personal interviews beyond the quotation from the anonymous student (para. 2).

5. Benen doesn't directly address the arguments of those who don't see student poker playing as a hazard, although he acknowledges that some gambling is fairly

Here's an Idea . . .

- Invite colleagues in for a panel or some point-counterpoint conversation on a widely controversial issue.
- Show in a videotape of a talk show in which participants express a variety of opinions.
- Alert students to any campus forum in which they can hear a range of opinions.
- Direct them to interview at least five students whom they do not know about a topic that might spark controversy.

harmless. Additionally, he points out one of the attractions of online poker: that some students can make thousands of dollars. Ask students if there are other views on gambling that they think Benen should have included.

6. Student responses to this question may vary widely. However, if Benen were writing for a parenting magazine, he might explore the hazards that online poker playing could pose to students' academic performance. He might also devote more discussion to gambling's potential financial consequences, such as financially strapped students having to borrow money from parents or others.

7. Benen organizes his reasons logically, linking them with clear transitions. Paragraph 1 serves as Benen's introduction, and his thesis statement is the final sentence of this paragraph. Each paragraph then explores a different hazard of online poker playing or explains why students continue to gamble despite the hazards. Benen concludes by reiterating his concern about the illegal nature of much of student poker playing and expresses displeasure that online casinos do not do background checks on players to curb illegal gambling.

LEARNING BY WRITING

The Assignment: Taking a Stand (p. 147)

Your students' task here is twofold. They must do more than set forth their opinion; they must also win the reader's respect for it. Covering types of evidence and kinds of appeals, this section extends the discussion from Chapter 3, "Critical Thinking Processes," in *A Writer's Guide*. You might want to refer students to this chapter for an overview of these terms and concepts.

Consider asking students to think about this assignment as a brief research paper. Otherwise, they might try to argue from only emotion or ethos and not challenge themselves to use critical thinking skills.

Facing the Challenge (p. 147)

To write successful persuasive papers, students need to choose a topic they feel strongly about. Encourage them to write about an issue in which they are invested. For a suggestion about how you might have students continue to write about the same issue in the sequential assignments described in Chapters 8–12, see page 142 of this manual.

Shy students might be hesitant to join a conversation in which opinions on a topic will vary widely. Use structured group discussions to help them develop a stand on their subjects. Spend a class session brainstorming and listing controversies that have aroused students' interest. This can be done individually or in groups. After about ten minutes, ask if anyone needs further explanation of any of the controversies. The explanations that students volunteer might already be shaped by an opinion; when you hear those, say, "OK, so your stand on that would be . . ." and write it on the board. Then check to see whether the discussion has generated at least two stands for most controversies. Ask each writer to choose one controversy and explore stands on it in ten minutes of freewriting.

Other students in your class will know right away what they want to write. These students might have difficulty listening carefully to an opinion opposed to theirs. Play devil's advocate with them, but insist that they restate your stand to your satisfaction before stating theirs or refuting yours. Be sure to call their attention to the authors' warning about providing plenty of evidence. Remind them that to be convincing, they must support their views with specific evidence. First, however, they must examine their own presuppositions to discover any bias in their position, or their process of selecting evidence may be tainted. For more about providing support to underprepared students, see Chapter 4 of this manual.

Generating Ideas (p. 148)

Recommend that students use the following headings from the textbook as a checklist when writing a persuasive paper.

Find an Issue (p. 148)   After some discussion and exploration of controversial subjects with the entire class, you need to give individual writers some help in selecting and narrowing a topic for writing. After students brainstorm and freewrite about possibilities, have pairs discuss their writing to determine if the writer wants to explore that topic or discard it. If a student decides to discard it, have him or her brainstorm a new list. Refer students to the third choice in "Other Assignments" (p. 164) for a list of possible topics.

Start with a Question and a Thesis (p. 148)   Have students state their topic in the form of a question and focus their energies on searching for evidence to support an answer to that question. Check each student's question to be sure it is expressed clearly, precisely, and succinctly and will lead to a strong paper.

Ask students to hand in clear statements of claim. Tell them immediately whether their statements can be argued within a short paper, whether they are clearly focused on one stand, and whether they are specific enough. Some students will have trouble narrowing and detailing their stand, so help them early in this stage.

Use Formal Reasoning to Refine Your Position (p. 149)   Ask students to try to break their statements of claim into a major statement, a minor statement, and a conclusion, as illustrated in the text. Then have them check the logic of the position, ensuring, for example, that the statement's conclusion always applies and that its major and minor statements are true.

Use Informal Toulmin Reasoning to Refine Your Position (p. 150)   Ask students to identify their claim, reason, warrant, and backing using the examples in the book. Can they identify any qualifications and exceptions to their claim? If so, how might they refine their argument? If you want to give students more information on the Toulmin method, you might refer them to Web sites such as Charles R. Swadley's Argumentation page (University of Oklahoma): <http://students.ou.edu/S/Charles.R.Swadley-1/argumentation.htm>. Students might also want to ask the "core questions" posed in the chart on page 153 of the text. Answering these questions will help them develop support for their position.

Select Evidence to Support Your Position (p. 152)   Students will have to make claims as they support their position. Some of them might find the terminology of claims to be daunting. Write the types of claims on the board and go through them. Remind students that they already use these types without knowing the terms. Ask students for more examples of each type to check for understanding.

Consider Your Audience as You Develop Your Claim (p. 154)   Remind your students that knowing their audience well will enable them to gauge the best and worst arguments to serve as evidence in their papers. Ask them to interpret what kind of audience to whom Benen is appealing and what evidence he uses to appeal to them.

Assemble Supporting Evidence (p. 154)   Explain to students that the greatest chunk of prewriting time will be spent in researching their topic using the resources in Part Two of *A Writer's Guide*. Encourage them to use the Discovery Checklist on page 152 to guide them in this process.

Caution students about statistics being subject to interpretation. Many first-year writers see statistics as absolutes and need to learn how to present them honestly and fairly. Encourage writers to make notes about the credentials of their experts as well as to watch carefully for fact and opinion in their experts' statements. Some students have difficulty assessing authority. Not only must they be convinced of their experts' credibility, but they must also convince the reader. Remind them that they will need to include the experts' credentials in their drafts.

Also remind students of the different types of evidence used most frequently; read parts of a case study, an example of statistics, and the testimony of an expert. ("The *Harper's* Index," published in every issue of *Harper's Magazine*, is one good source of statistics.) Listening to the different types of evidence available to them as writers challenges students to consider which would be most effective for their audience.

Record Evidence (p. 155)   Make sure in the beginning of the semester you make clear to students the value of taking and keeping accurate notes. Each student will have his or her own system, but you may want to go over some good methods of recording notes early in the semester. Point out the Works Cited page for Callahan's essay (p. 201 of Chapter 12) or Lamberth's essay (p. 205 of Chapter 12). Show students how to record their source information in MLA format. For more examples, refer them to the Quick Research Guide or to Chapter 34, "Documenting Sources," if their book contains *A Writer's Research Manual*.

Test and Select Evidence to Persuade Your Audience (p. 155)   After giving students a few days to settle on their topics and to think about them, divide your class into small groups. Each student should present his or her stand and supporting evidence to the group. Then have group members suggest other supporting evidence or arguments against the stand. Students should take notes on their peers' counterarguments and other evidence in order to consider them when they draft their papers.

As students amass evidence, recommend that they organize it on note cards or in a word-processing document — the way that many writers organize notes from research. It might help to establish a minimum requirement for evidence in their essays. Usually three pieces of evidence seem a sufficient number for student writers at this level. Anxious students might "pad" their essay with too much evidence. Explain to the class that this will not be persuasive.

Planning, Drafting, and Developing (p. 156)

The assignment suggests that writers have at least four parts of the classical defense: the statement of claim, the reasoned presentation of evidence, the reasoned analysis of opposed claim, and a formal and dramatic restatement of claim. Ask students to organize their note cards into these four categories and to write a short outline. They might need to see an informal outline sketched on the board. Also, suggest to students who resist outlining that they use a strategy such as clustering or mapping. (For more on outlining and clustering, refer students to Chapter 17 of their textbooks.) Check their outlines or plans to see if, at the level of major ideas, they have enough material to begin drafting. List any questions you would have as a person who might write the same persuasive essay or as an editor who is deciding whether the writing project should be encouraged. Underline any terms that demand early definition.

Look particularly closely at each writer's summary statement about opposing views. Assume the role of someone whose opinion contradicts the writer's; from your devil's-advocate position, list questions the writer needs to think about in paying attention to a friendly antagonist. Time spent evaluating during this prewriting period will save you and the writers time later.

Revising and Editing (p. 158)

Many writers have difficulty with this assignment because they still believe that anyone who holds a different view is necessarily a foe or just plain wrong. This attitude comes, of course, from dualistic thinking and from perceptions that the world is composed of absolutes. Persuasion asks writers to suspend that perspective and to admit that areas of difference exist. Writers must realize that a willingness to examine the differences, or gray areas, will lead them to a clearer understanding of their own ideas or even to new ideas. You will need to keep encouraging students to look at dissenting opinion not as a threat but as an aid to their reasoning. Remind them that when they contrast ideas they can more clearly appreciate the borders of each idea discussed.

Many schools have writing-center tutors who can read a student's persuasive essay specifically to see how fully and fairly the dissenting opinion and the writer's opinion are presented. If your college doesn't provide that service, have your students consult with peer editors in class and other students outside of class. Peer editors, of course, might give more reliable or specific advice about the balance of presentation and the force of the argument than the reader who comes to an essay cold, but the latter can help the writer see the general effect of his or her essay.

If there are no friendly antagonists to the specific opinion of a writer during a workshop or peer-editing session, you can role-play a friendly antagonist. By focusing your

Here's an Idea...

Have students create a word processor document with two columns. In the first column, have them brainstorm a list of questions that readers will have about their claims and warrants. Then have them cut and paste the questions in the order a reader might ask them. In column 2, have students draft answers to each question in order. Students can cut and paste column 2 into their essay draft, either copying it as a block of text, or moving sections to the most effective places.

attention on the summary or the acknowledgment of dissenting views, you can help writers with what might be the hardest part of the assignment. Even if you don't require peer response for all essay assignments, we recommend that you require it for this one. The cognitive task is harder than previous ones, so students need to be especially aware of their audience.

Another resource that we recommend is the Draft Doctor charts (p. 160 and elsewhere in the text), new to this edition of *The Bedford Guide*. These charts are designed to help students find and remedy weaknesses in their drafts. Allow your students a class period to work on their Taking a Stand drafts using the Draft Doctor for this chapter. Once they have been through this process, they will be more likely to use the Draft Doctors to revise later papers for this course or others.

Recognizing Logical Fallacies (p. 162)

Many students have never questioned the logic of statements — their own or those of others. The habit of scrutinizing reasoning requires practice. You serve your students well by taking time to help them identify and think about the effects of logical fallacies. Because good logic is valued so highly in college coursework —even if the faculty responding to it haven't identified it specifically in their evaluations — your students will be empowered once they know how to reflect on their thinking and their missteps in thinking.

Use the vocabulary the authors set down, but don't be discouraged if some students never match the label with the pattern. It is more important that they recognize that a problem with the logic exists. Once you and your students establish a vocabulary for talking about logic, you can use that vocabulary to comment on impasses in classroom discussion. Often, when class members notice that *ad hominem* ("to the person") arguments are being presented by proponents of one idea, they can then realize why they were frustrated by the "proofs." This is the kind of critical listening that skillful debating teams practice.

Other Assignments (p. 164)

1. Introduce persuasive writing with an in-class writing assignment that requires students to write a letter to an editor in response to an article in a local newspaper. Read several examples of letters as models for students. Have students read one another's letters to see that they have made clear their reasons for disagreeing or agreeing. Specify that the peer reader needs to understand the original view of the publication by seeing it restated in the letter. Many writers of letters to the editor (and writers of essay exams) just jump into their dissent without first establishing the context and the writing that provoked it. Finally, ask writers to revise, type their letters, and mail them.

2. This exercise provides good reinforcement for the understanding of types of claims (p. 152).

3. This assignment differs from the major writing assignment of the chapter only in that it offers a "menu." Some writers will be relieved to have a predetermined list of topics. Alert them to this alternative.

APPLYING WHAT YOU LEARN: SOME USES OF TAKING A STAND (p. 164)

Many college instructors ask for oral projects that include panels or debates on controversial issues. Ask your colleagues for typical assignments in which they ask students to state an opinion on a controversy and for recommendations of juniors and seniors who could serve as panelists and debaters in a classroom debate. Ask students to evaluate each panel according to the criteria of balance of opinions, definition of crucial terms, evidence, and clarity. Give that feedback to the panelists.

MAKING CONNECTIONS

Presenting one's position on an issue and giving the reasons and evidence supporting that position may be one of the most common uses of writing in our culture. The strength of the writing is enhanced by the author's commitment to the issue. The following writers take a stand in their essays in *A Writer's Reader*.

Anna Quindlen in "Evan's Two Moms" (p. 451) argues a controversial position: that gay marriage should be legalized. Quindlen presents a strong argument by balancing logical, emotional, and ethical appeal.

Nancy Gibbs in "Free the Children" (p. 470) takes a stand in defense of summer freedom for schoolchildren. Gibbs supports her claim that summers should be unstructured by remembering how her own unrestricted summers taught her self-reliance, allowed her to explore new skills and ideas, and fostered spiritual growth that sustained her through the long, focused months of school.

Barbara Ehrenreich in "Guys Just Want to Have Fun" (p. 482) argues that the corporate world's emphasis on "personality," "likability," and a "positive attitude" may allow men to advance farther in the working world than more diligent and skilled females. Ehrenreich anticipates objections to her argument, conceding that while "people skills" may reign, American employers will need high-achieving women to be successful.

Evelyn F. Murphy in "Why Not a Dollar?" (p. 488) argues that despite the Equal Pay Act of 1963 and Title VII of the Civil Rights Act, discrimination against women still exists in the workplace, with women continuing to earn less than men for doing the same work. Murphy contends that instead of closing, the gender wage gap has actually increased over the past fifty years.

Michael Abernethy in "Male Bashing on TV" (p. 515) speaks out against the increasingly negative portrayal of men on television. Abernethy cites numerous examples as well as expert testimony to argue that television's comic portrayal of men harms male self-esteem and undermines the feminist cause.

Terry Golway in "A Nation of Idol-Worshipers" (p. 525) takes a stand against the cult of celebrity that is so dominant in our society, arguing that we have lost sight of real "idols" who make substantive contributions to society rather than provide distractions.

William Zinsser in "The Right to Fail" (p. 567) argues that "dropping out is often a way of dropping in." He cites examples from history, literature, and other fields to support his unorthodox position.

As students read these essays, ask them to consider how each writer takes a stand. For each essay, have students answer the As You Read questions on page 140.

Here's an Idea . . .

Assign three students to each essay in "Making Connections" and ask them to take a stand that supports or challenges the writer's ideas. As a group, students must offer the class evidence for their challenge or support of the writer's thesis. Following each essay in A Writer's Reader are questions on content and strategy that might help the group in their reading.

RESOURCES FOR COLLEGE WRITERS

Your Assignment
Taking a Stand, p. 147

Resources in the Text
- Sample professional reading, p. 140
- Sample student reading, p. 143
- Facing the Challenge, p. 147
- Planning and developing the essay, p. 156
- Discovery and Revision checklists, pp. 152 and 159
- Editing Checklist, p. 162
- Uses of taking a stand in real-world writing situations, pp. 164–65
- Peer review help, p. 159
- E-Writer help, p. 157
- The Draft Doctor, p. 160

Resources on the Web Site
<bedfordstmartins.com/bedguide>
- Additional readings with activities
- "Ask the Draft Doctor" writing help
- Peer response forms
- Link to Exercise Central

Proposing a Solution (Ch. 10, p. 166)

We are rewarded for our skillful teaching of persuasion when we see students understand that they can do something about situations that bother them. All writing, of course, liberates the writer because he or she can name the world, shape the self, act against what oppresses. (Credit Paulo Freire with that idea.) But what happens more often in a classroom sequence on taking a stand and proposing a solution than during any other sequence of writing instruction is students saying that they feel empowered. At this point in the semester you can feel that the work you do with a writer makes a difference. Enjoy that.

The authors avoid the label "argument"; read other textbooks and you'll notice how other writers wrestle with defining the difference between persuasion and argument. We think *The Bedford Guide* makes an especially useful distinction between different kinds of persuasion: Proposing a solution is the logical and natural next step after taking a stand. The proposal builds on the experiences of student writers who have identified a problem and have advanced an opinion at variance with what readers know, admit, respect, and perhaps even share. For a suggestion about how students might build their skills by writing on the same issue through the sequence of assignments in Chapters 8-12, see page 142 of this manual.

With the proposal, student writers get to work from all of their resources, but particularly from imagination. Problem solving is one of the most complex cognitive processes; it is also one of the most satisfying because it comes to closure. Students can see that they have created something new and solid, and they even get a chance to see their ideas validated when other people nod to the proposal. It is crucial, then, that you provide those opportunities for readers to nod in response to your student writers.

Here's an Idea . . .

Use the following prompts to help students uncover some of the problems about which they have strong concerns.

1. What has made me angriest here at college has been _____.
2. Seeing _____ made me feel shame for the human race.
3. My life would have been much more pleasant this semester if the college had not _____.
4. My parents believe that _____ has to change.
5. The worst thing that happened to a friend at high school that could have been prevented was _____.
6. If I had the power to erase problems from my mother's/father's life, I would want to go back to her/his past and _____.
7. The biggest hassle for me in my hometown is _____.
8. Three things I would call "disgusting" are _____, _____, and _____.
9. Three things I would call "frustrating" are _____, _____, and _____.
10. My best friend says that America's biggest problem is _____, but I believe it is _____.

> *Here's an Idea . . .*
>
> Have students write a general heading: college, parents, work, dating, and so on. Then tell them to freewrite lies about the heading for ten minutes. Only lies can appear on the paper. Some will find the writing very slow; others will cover an entire page. This activity often generates an idea that becomes a thesis. It also encourages writers to view an idea differently.

When students receive positive feedback from a number of readers about the success of their proposal, they will be roused to independence as thinkers and writers. Also, refer students to models of proposals. The grid on pages 371–83 identifies such writings in *The Bedford Guide*.

Chapter 10, "Proposing a Solution," contains the following activities:

- Responding to an Image (p. 166). Allow your students to use their imagination while examining these visual activity prompts. If necessary, have students free-associate responses to elements of each image. If they are given free rein for their own interpretations, they will most likely view analyzing these images as a rewarding way to begin thinking about writing in these modes.

  Give your students the option to come up with a parody of a popular ad campaign that would help them propose a solution to a topic they would like to write a paper about.

- For E-Writers (p. 177). See page 73 of this manual for advice about how to use this feature.

- For Peer Response (p. 180). See page 39 of this manual for advice about how to use this feature.

- For Group Learning (p. 179). See page 39 of this manual for advice about how to use this feature.

LEARNING FROM OTHER WRITERS

WILBERT RIDEAU *Why Prisons Don't Work* (p. 168)

Rideau presents a somewhat unique point of view about prisons — that of a convicted murderer who has been imprisoned for more than thirty years. Discuss the ethical appeal of his position. How and why does his experience strengthen his argument? Encourage students to examine the evidence objectively to arrive at a sound evaluation of his proposal.

Questions to Start You Thinking (p. 169)

Meaning

1. You will get different reactions to this question. Much of the response will be based on how much credibility students think Rideau has (see question 8). Unconvinced students might argue that Rideau calls permanent incarceration ineffective only because he, as a criminal, does not want to be "permanently exiled." Convinced students might point to Rideau's evidence about Louisiana's crime rate

Here's an Idea . . .

To help students build ethos, ask each to write a "credo." Tell them to write as quickly as possible for fifteen minutes about what they believe. Have them start each sentence with either "I believe that . . ." or "I do not believe that . . . ." Then ask them to exchange their credos and have the readers write a description of the kind of person who holds those beliefs. If a peer identifies a strong humanist bias in a credo, the writer — who might or might not have categorized himself or herself as a humanist — could tap that tradition among like-minded thinkers to buttress his or her statements.

— the state with the highest lockup rate in the country still has one of the highest murder rates. Either way, encourage students to give specific reasons for why they are or are not convinced by Rideau's argument. The question points to a common debate: Is imprisonment a deterrent to potential criminals? Do we as a society focus on punishment or rehabilitation?

2. This question allows students to isolate Rideau's main points of argument. This might be a good time for the class to outline Rideau's essay on the board and discuss his reasoning. Students should see that Rideau falls firmly in the camp of rehabilitation and prevention as opposed to punishment. He says that prisons do not work because they are not an effective deterrent, simply a "response after the fact" (para. 3). Prisoners are held for too long, turning them into more hardened criminals (para. 4). He also argues that prisons do not do enough to rehabilitate prisoners (para. 5). Ask students if they can think of other reasons that prisons are ineffective or, if they disagree, to refute each of Rideau's points.

3. You can continue to flesh out the outline of Rideau's essay with this question. Most of Rideau's solutions are nothing new. Paragraph 7 focuses on the often-stated idea that education is the key to curbing crime. Ask students if Rideau is detailed enough in the solutions he offers in paragraph 7. Maybe they can offer more specific solutions in the area of prevention and education — detailed community programs or public school courses. Take this opportunity to urge students to provide well-developed and detailed solutions for their essays, nothing overly simplistic or general. ("We need more gun laws." Well, what kind? "We should ban television violence." Well, what violence? How? Why? Is censorship realistic?)

Rideau's proposal that prisons release older prisoners (paras. 4 and 5) is interesting. Make sure students notice this example of a writer coming up with insightful and innovative solutions to old, frequently discussed problems.

Writing Strategies

4. Before addressing this question, have students create a general list of society's justifications for the prison system. With those in mind, ask students to return to the essay. Remind them that Rideau's purpose is to prove that prisons do not work and to provide an alternative solution. To accomplish this purpose, he singles out various rationales behind the penal system and counters them. For example, he argues that prisons do not deter crime and do not rehabilitate because of the length of sentences and lack of education programs. While he acknowledges that prisons protect society by isolating "serial killers, serial rapists, professional hit men, and the like," he also contends that such cases are rare. Have students consult their original lists. Have they thought of a purpose for the penal system that Rideau does not cite? Would his solution be more palatable had he acknowledged and countered some other justifications for the prison system?

5. This question asks students to examine the very premise of a solution essay: Has the writer provided sufficient evidence to prove that there is a problem that needs a solution? The supporting evidence is probably the weakest link of Rideau's essay. To support his assertion that Louisiana's prison policy has not worked, he states one piece of evidence — that "Louisiana has the highest murder rate among states" (para. 3). He provides no source for this statement, no figures or statistics. What about the rate of crimes other than murder — robbery, assault, rape?

6. The evidence Rideau uses to support his solutions is more effective than his evidence for the problem (see question 5). For example, in paragraph 5, to support his proposal that older criminals should be released, Rideau cites specific evidence (murderers once working at Louisiana's governor's mansion) and experts (Warden John Whitley and penologists). But students probably will offer more evidence to make his argument more persuasive. For example, in paragraph 6, Rideau should provide an example of a prison rehabilitation program that has worked as evidence that educating criminals will end their criminal behavior.

7. Rideau cites Warden John Whitley and penologists (para. 5). Prisons and prison reform have been studied for years. Rideau easily could have cited more authorities to support his solutions. You might want to ask students to find some authorities themselves to back up Rideau's claims. Many first-year students take criminal justice classes. Ask them to draw from their lectures and texts in offering ways to strengthen Rideau's essay (or to disagree with it).

8. The credibility of the author is an interesting aspect of this essay. Students will disagree on this point. Does the fact that Rideau is a convicted criminal make him uniquely qualified to talk about the prison experience, or does his argument seem self-serving because of it? The mention of this fact in the first sentence suggests that Rideau considers that his status as a criminal makes him somewhat of an expert. But what has Rideau left out of his essay that could be attributed to his interests as a convicted criminal? Why doesn't he mention the victim of crime or the idea of appropriate punishment?

9. The circular pattern of the dog mirrors the circular logic of the prison system that Rideau outlines in the previous sentence. Students should note that progress does not occur in either situation: Just as the dog does not catch its tail, crime is not reduced. Do students find the ending to be appropriate or overly dramatic? Ask them how else Rideau might have ended the essay. What do they think about a one-sentence paragraph? Does it serve its purpose or does it violate a basic rule of paragraph development?

JOHN BARBIERI *Save Hydrogen for Later; Ethanol Power Is the Viable Option for Now* (p. 170)

John Barbieri argues that hydrogen is not a viable alternative to gasoline as a fuel, and he proposes ethanol as a more feasible option, backing up his claim by enumerating environmental and economic advantages of ethanol. Point out to students that Barbieri patterns much of his argument as comparison-contrast, contrasting the advantages of ethanol with those of hydrogen. Show students that in Chapter 19, "Strategies for Developing," the authors discuss comparison-contrast as a pattern of development (p. 366). Barbieri's proposal is a good example of how this pattern can be incorporated as a means of persuasion, not only used as a single pattern of development, as they discovered in Chapter 7.

Questions to Start You Thinking (p. 172)

Meaning

1. According to the author, the use of ethanol fuel would help reduce greenhouse-gas emissions (paras. 1 and 3) and dependence on foreign oil. Ask students whether Barbieri's proposal would have been enhanced by more background on these problems — for example, information about why greenhouse gases pose a serious environmental threat. Encourage knowledgeable students to share what they know about these problems.

2. As Barbieri explains in paragraph 2, ethanol is made by fermenting and distilling plant starch that has been converted into simple sugars. Because plants are the raw material, ethanol is a renewable energy source, unlike oil.

3. Barbieri clearly lays out the advantages of ethanol over gasoline and hydrogen in paragraphs 2 through 6, and he reiterates them in paragraph 7. The advantages include the fact that ethanol is a renewable energy source, produces less greenhouse gases than gasoline, could reduce dependence on foreign oil, is less of a source of pollution than hydrogen, is more easily stored and transported than hydrogen, and is less costly than hydrogen to implement as an alternative power source. If you teach in an agricultural state, your students may be aware of these benefits and others, such as higher sales of corn and other raw materials for ethanol. Encourage students to share what they know. Are there any disadvantages to ethanol not mentioned by Barbieri? (Some groups have claimed that the usage of fuel and fertilizers for growing the plant-based raw materials for ethanol offsets the benefits of this alternative fuel source.)

Writing Strategies

4. Have students identify the transitional words and phrases in each paragraph. They will see that Barbieri uses transitions both within paragraphs (e.g., "As a result" in paragraph 1, "Furthermore" in paragraph 3, and "Moreover" in paragraph 4) and between them. He uses the transitions "First," "Second," and "Third," to move clearly from one major advantage of ethanol to another.

5. You might ask students to highlight the evidence that Barbieri provides for each stated advantage of ethanol over gasoline and hydrogen fuel. They will see that his evidence is both statistical (e.g., the data about Brazil's reduced oil dependence in paragraph 3) and explanatory (e.g., the information about the storage and transportability of ethanol). However, students might identify ways in which Barbieri's proposal could be strengthened — for example, by including information about potential disadvantages of ethanol and why the advantages outweigh the drawbacks. Also, they may wonder why the author did not cite specific sources for the evidence and statistics that he provides. On a related point, you might note that while Barbieri is clearly very knowledgeable about his subject, he doesn't establish his qualifications for writing about the topic, making the citation of specific sources potentially more valuable.

6. Paragraph 7 provides a clear restatement of the points that Barbieri has made about the advantages of ethanol. However, some students may find it repetitive. You might have students discuss what an alternative conclusion might say or even rewrite the conclusion in small groups.

7. Barbieri's thesis appears toward the end of his introduction (paragraph 1), and the problems of greenhouse-gas emissions and dependence on foreign oil are stated in passing more than directly noted (in paras. 1 and 3). The solution to these problems — use of ethanol — is introduced in paragraph 1, and the reasons that this solution is more appealing than the alternatives are developed throughout the essay; see the response to question 3. The conclusion, paragraph 7, restates the

advantages of ethanol; see the response to question 6. In general, the essay is well organized, with transitions that lead clearly from one point to the next.

LEARNING BY WRITING

The Assignment: Proposing a Solution (p. 173)

Both of the models in this chapter have all of the parts of classical and formal argument. Check with your students to see if they can outline the problem, the clear formal statement of a solution, the reasoned presentation of evidence and appeals, the disqualification of alternative solutions, and a convincing recommendation of the proposed solution. As they write their own proposals, ask them to include these elements in their work.

Facing the Challenge (p. 174)

This assignment can overwhelm students if they settle on a complex problem and believe they must provide a detailed, workable solution for it. Reassure them that they don't have to solve the world's problems; a small solution to part of a problem is important and more realistic. Show them how to focus on a manageable part of the problem, detailing a solution for that part.

To make a successful proposal, a writer must first believe that a problem needs to be solved. Don't be surprised if some students tell you they don't feel strongly about any problem. You might need to organize a number of activities to provoke a response and opinion.

For more about providing support for underprepared students, see Chapter 4 of this manual.

Generating Ideas (p. 173)

To help students discover a problem that inspires them to want to think of a solution, bring in copies of the daily newspaper and news magazines and have small groups catalog the problems discussed and the frequency with which those problems come up. Then ask each group to write for fifteen minutes in response to the question "How does one of these problems threaten us now or in our future?" Collect the proposals and read them aloud. To promote analytical thinking about the problem, organize small groups to discuss short-term and long-term effects of one of the problems. Encourage each group to brainstorm as many solutions to the problem as possible.

Consider asking students to use a computer to freewrite about their solution or problem for ten minutes. Then they can examine the text on the screen, searching their writing for ideas that can be saved. Suggest that they cut and copy the writing on the screen to save what they consider valuable. Once they have these in a separate file, ask them to display the items and begin to work with the sequence of their information.

You can also use the Discovery Checklist on page 174 to prompt small-group discussion or brainstorming sessions as well as journal entries. Select one or two to focus on in class. (Improving the college system will always be popular with students because they do not usually feel they have a sounding board for their frustration with campus experiences.) Consider asking international students if any would be willing to talk about the personal, social, or political problems that exist in their culture or country. Or ask a colleague or a writer from the local newspaper to speak with students on a topic of concern to him or her.

Students will need to pay close attention to their audience early with this assignment. Remind them to use the list of questions on page 175 for help. After working with small groups and participating in class discussions, students should have developed an awareness of other students as their audience. Ask them, as writers, to consider the class as their primary audience rather than thinking about writing for only a single teacher. To reinforce the importance of audience, ask students to read their finished draft or revised rough draft to the class. By informing students of this before they begin to plan and shape their drafts, you place an important emphasis on considering the audience for this assignment.

Planning, Drafting, and Developing (p. 175)

When students begin to draft, have them respond in class to the following aspects of their topic. Ask them

- to list causes of their problem and effects of their proposal
- to describe the process of putting the proposal in place
- to compare and contrast the benefits of their solution with those of the solution most frequently offered
- to define any specialized terms in the solution
- to classify dissenting opinions with nonpejorative categories
- to divide their recommendations into personal, communal, and economic benefits

Although no one writer will need all of the material generated by these points, most will carry a good portion back to the draft they are shaping outside of class.

In brief conferences during in-class drafting, look at the disqualification or refutation section of your students' drafts. Many students have problems specifying the criteria that make their solutions the "best." Once they specify these criteria, they need to apply the same ones to the solutions they want to reject. Tell them what you see as the criteria they are using and whether they have applied each criterion to each of the solutions they want to disqualify. Even though this process sounds mechanical, writers need to systematically apply specific criteria to discover what thinking underlies their draft and then to highlight that reasoning in the draft.

Revising and Editing (p. 178)

By this point in the semester, students are wanting more from one another and might have already arranged informal conversations as follow-up to the workshops or to focus peer editing. The For Group Learning exercise on page 179 reinforces the community of writers only if you have firmly established the parameters of editing. Ask students to respond specifically to the writing. Comments such as "It was nice" or "It's good" do not offer writers the specific information they need to revise. Reactions should focus on specific parts of the essay: thesis, hook (the entry into the essay), appeal of the solution, and tone. If a point in the proposal seems unclear, a peer editor might ask, "What is the specific proposal you are offering?" This does not hurt or intimidate a writer. By writing lengthy comments first, the editor will be prepared for a specific and "collegial" conversation with the writer.

Suggest that students use the Revision Checklist on page 179 to write reflective pieces on their proposals. Have them submit their reflections with their essays, and then evaluate not only the manuscript but also the writers' willingness to reflect on their drafts and to revise.

Other Assignments (p. 180)

1. Have students rethink their Taking a Stand paper (Chapter 9) and cast it as problem solving. Even essays that seem only to be a defense of an opinion can lead to problem-solving discussion when you ask writers to think about what might happen if their opinion is not shared, say, by a national leader in a specific crisis.

2. An assignment to write a memo can be a valuable exercise because it forces students to narrow their description of the problem and their solution to a concise, focused piece of writing. Read aloud examples of memos proposing some change. Choose examples that are thorough, persuasive, and concise.

3. The descriptors here are loaded. Ask students to be careful to define their assumptions and beliefs about what makes something efficient, ethical, fair, or morally right. Expect that some responses will strike you as morally repugnant. Put aside your opinion in your assessment of the writing, just as you ask students to tolerate diversity of opinion in papers that persuade.

APPLYING WHAT YOU LEARN: SOME USES OF PROPOSING A SOLUTION (p. 181)

Advise students to investigate the example the authors cite about writing a proposal for a grade change. Ask students to collect any forms and guidelines for grade changes at your institution. Perhaps they can speak to another student who has filed a grievance. What were the results? Use an in-class drafting session and prompt the writers to recall "My learning experience that resulted in a grade that I did not earn." You can be a resource to students as they draft proposals.

MAKING CONNECTIONS

Each of the following readings from *A Writer's Reader* advances a solution to a serious problem. Remind students that the solutions they present in their essays must be practical and understood by most of their audience, as the proposals in these essays are. Clarity is imperative for this type of writing.

Robert Jensen in "The High Cost of Manliness" (p. 475) condemns our definition of masculinity as "dangerous for women" and "toxic" to men. Jensen argues that identifying as "masculine" such traits as aggressiveness and competitiveness forces men either to strive for control and dominance or to be branded as a "wimp," or worse, a "woman." He proposes that to meet the political and ecological challenges of the twenty-first century, we must stop defining what it means to be masculine or feminine and focus on defining what it means to be human.

Noel Perrin in "A Part-Time Marriage" (p. 494) proposes an alternative to traditional marriage. After experiencing the problems that come with divorce, he suggests a part-time marriage is a more practical solution to sustaining a relationship.

David Gelernter in "Computers Cannot Teach Children Basic Skills" (p. 536) examines the use of computers in American classrooms. He concedes that computers can benefit students by offering enrichment of basic instruction. However, Gelernter identifies weaknesses with educational software and explains how they exacerbate learning problems students already have. His solution is three-pronged: develop new, effective software; limit computer access to recreational periods; and never substitute computer instruction for student-teacher interaction.

As students read these essays, ask them to consider the role that proposals play therein. For each essay, ask students to answer the As You Read questions on page 167.

RESOURCES FOR COLLEGE WRITERS

Your Assignment
Proposing a Solution, p. 173

Resources in the Text
- Sample professional reading, p. 168
- Sample student reading, p. 170
- Facing the Challenge, p. 174
- Planning and developing the essay, p. 175
- Discovery and Revision checklists, pp. 174 and 179
- Editing Checklist, p. 180
- Uses of proposing a solution in real-world writing situations, p. 181
- Peer review help, p. 180
- E-Writer help, p. 177

Resources on the Web Site
<bedfordstmartins.com/bedguide>
- Additional readings with activities
- "Ask the Draft Doctor" writing help
- Peer response forms
- Link to Exercise Central

Evaluating (Ch. 11, p. 183)

This chapter challenges students to reflect on their processes of evaluating and to question, in particular, the assumptions or criteria that they use, almost unconsciously, when they make a judgment. Asking a student, "Why did you decide that this essay was inappropriate for a group of middle-school students?" or "How did you decide that this movie was R-rated?" focuses attention on the process of evaluating. Expect energetic discussion when students start to discover the intricacy of their judging. Also expect that you will need to point out to them when their essays aren't working because the criteria they are using might not be accessible to their readers. Continue reading aloud to your students from models of this type of writing so that they will begin to "hear" the style and content of written evaluation. The grid on pages 371–83 identifies essays from *The Bedford Guide* that use evaluation.

Chapter 11, "Evaluating," contains the following activities:

- Responding to an Image (p. 183). Allow your students to use their imagination while examining these visual activity prompts. If necessary, have students free-associate responses to elements of each image. If they are given free rein for their own interpretations, they will most likely view analyzing these images as a rewarding way to begin thinking about writing in these modes.

  Most of your students will have wrestled with some important decisions in the past year and will identify with the issue addressed in this image. Ask them how they go about making decisions. What sorts of criteria have they based their recent decisions on? Use the discussion to make them aware of the processes they engage in to evaluate their choices.

- For E-Writers (p. 195). See page 73 of this manual for advice about how to use this feature.

- For Peer Response (p. 194). See page 39 of this manual for advice about how to use this feature.

- For Group Learning (p. 191). See page 39 of this manual for advice about how to use this feature.

Here's an Idea . . .

Give students an idea of the role of choosing criteria in evaluation by bringing to class two or three bowls. Make sure the bowls are designed for different functions — for example, a cut-glass bowl, a crockery bowl, and a Tupperware bowl with a lid. Set the bowls before the class and ask students to write on a slip of paper which is the best bowl and why. Then ask each to read aloud his or her choice and explanation. This activity should lead to a discussion of the criteria that students use to make judgments and the necessity of setting criteria before they can defend a judgment.

LEARNING FROM OTHER WRITERS

SETH STEVENSON   *Wham! Bam! Buy a VW, Ma'am!* (p. 184)

Seth Stevenson evaluates a TV spot for Volkswagen that most of your students will have seen and will remember for the very reasons he sites as criteria for his judgment. Stevenson takes a balanced look at the ad, discussing its strengths and its weaknesses. He identifies the strong emotional appeal at work. You might want to show this spot or another one like it and ask students what appeals they see at work. Have them identify criteria they might use to evaluate the ad and come to some conclusion about its effectiveness.

Questions to Start You Thinking (p. 186)

Meaning

1. You might ask students how they react to the opening description of one Jetta ad and whether any of them have seen this spot. Why do they think some viewers might be surprised or shocked, and do they share that reaction? They might point out how the mundane beginning of the ad is interrupted by the violent crash, as well as the moment of uncertainty about what has happened to the passengers, as the picture fades to black.

2. Stevenson notes in paragraph 7 why claims about safety tend to appeal more to adults than to younger people: "Most parents are obsessively fixated on their kids' well-being, while most fancy-free young folks don't give safety much thought." Volkswagen's Kurt Schneider reports that the company was trying to find a way to make safety features appealing to 18- to 34-year-olds, the Jetta's target market. You might have students consider how the ad might have been scripted or filmed differently for an older audience.

3. As Stevenson writes in paragraph 9, he doesn't find safety claims appealing. How do students view such claims? Would they be more likely to buy a car because it is safe or because it is, say, stylish or fuel-efficient? In other words, would the Jetta ad motivate them as consumers, or is it merely an interesting bit of television?

Writing Strategies

4. In his thesis statement (in paragraph 2), Stevenson judges the Jetta ads as "pretty sharp," and he reinforces this judgment in his final paragraphs, in which he gives the ads a B grade. The criteria he sets out are execution (paras. 3–4) and concept — namely, the decision to focus the ads on safety (paras. 5–9). Given that *Slate.com* is a general-interest publication, do students think these criteria will appeal to Stevenson's audience? How might the criteria differ if the piece had been aimed at ad executives responsible for developing the next advertising campaign for Volkswagen?

5. Students might look at this question this way: Based on Stevenson's description and evaluation, is it clear why the ad is good enough to rate a B, but not good enough to rate an A? If students don't agree that the ad deserves a B, what information would they have needed to agree with Stevenson's rating?

6. The quotation from Kurt Schneider provides an important insight into why Volkswagen decided to make an appeal about safety to young consumers; this quotation adds credibility and depth to the piece. Ask students about other sources Stevenson might have included. For example, he might have quoted some young

people about the effectiveness or impact of the ads, asking them, for example, whether the safety campaign would influence them to buy a Jetta.

7. Stevenson's tone is fairly casual, even playful at times. (Notice "BLAM" in paragraph 1 and "Blah blah front-impact blah blah . . ." in paragraph 9.) He seems to regard advertising as a serious subject for analysis, but he doesn't take the Jetta campaign — or himself — too seriously, and it appears that he wants us to share this view. Ask students whether they find Stevenson's tone appealing or whether they would appreciate a more sober approach.

DENNIS O'NEIL   *Katrina Documentary Gives Voice to Survivors* (p. 187)

Dennis O'Neil takes a close look at Spike Lee's documentary *When the Levees Broke: A Requiem in Four Acts* and pronounces it an "ultimate victory." His analysis breaks the film into its four acts and includes examples on which he bases his judgment. You may want to show some scenes from Lee's film and ask your students to come to their own judgments of the documentary's effectiveness. Be sure that they identify the criteria they use to evaluate. Have them compare their evaluations with O'Neil's.

Questions to Start You Thinking (p. 189)

Meaning

1. As indicated by the quote at the start of paragraph 2, Lee made the movie because he believed that it was important to tell the story of Hurricane Katrina to people all over the world. For more insight into why Lee made the film, students might want to read an interview with him that appears on the HBO Web site for *When the Levees Broke*, at <http://hbo.com>.

2. According to O'Neil, Lee tells the stories of many Katrina survivors in their own words (see paragraphs 5–10). He also shows "harrowing and graphic images" of the disaster and its aftermath, such as the rusting roof of the Superdome and the heartbreaking return of survivors to the destroyed city.

3. In paragraph 11, O'Neil says that the ultimate victory of the documentary is that Lee "doesn't allow the silence [of the devastated city] to drown out the heart of New Orleans that still beats underneath it." You might discuss the generally hopeful note on which he ends the essay. Do students agree that there is some reason for optimism?

Writing Strategies

4. O'Neil's major criteria for judging Lee's film are sketched in paragraph 1. He is interested in how effectively the film humanizes ("cuts straight to the heart of") the Katrina tragedy and gives "voice" to the survivors. As O'Neil's first paragraph indicates, he judges the film to have succeeded on both counts. Throughout his discussion, he draws on the voices and describes how Lee shows the depth of the tragedy. You might take some time to discuss stated versus subtle or even implied criteria in evaluations. Would students have appreciated a more direct statement of criteria, or do they like the more subtle approach in this case? How might O'Neil have presented his criteria more directly or reiterated them as organizing principles?

5. Student opinions will vary here. Some may say that they would have liked to get more quotations from the film, while others might ask for more descriptions of scenes. Some students might want more quotations from Lee, while others might want perspectives from other film critics or social observers.

6. Again, student reactions will vary. Although some might argue that O'Neil should quote less and evaluate more, others may point out that quotations are essential given that O'Neil is writing about a documentary that emphasizes personal stories. Suggest to students that whenever they quote in a review or other evaluation, they should highlight quoted material in a bright color so that they can see quickly where they might need to balance quotations with their own observations.

7. The review is well organized, beginning with an introduction containing the thesis and the criteria for evaluation (para. 1). After providing a quotation from Lee and general background on the film, O'Neil pairs and discusses the four acts of the documentary, providing support for his judgment that the film effectively portrays the Katrina tragedy and "gives voice" to the Katrina victims. The conclusion consists of two paragraphs (11 and 12). You might point out how O'Neil ends with a quotation, this time Lee's voice. What effect does this quotation have on students? What do they think of the strategy of ending an evaluation in this way?

LEARNING BY WRITING

The Assignment: Writing an Evaluation (p. 190)

The assignment suggests that anything goes. If you agree that almost any subject choice can be evaluated successfully in the time given for this assignment, allow your experienced writers to choose a topic freely. Writers intimidated by the cognitive task, however, can choose a topic from the specific suggestions in "Other Assignments" (p. 196). If you prefer, limit students' subjects to the more traditional forms of media. For a suggestion about how students might evaluate the same topic they have addressed through the sequence of assignments in Chapters 8–12, see page 142 of this manual. Notice how the authors specify the twofold purpose for student writers: setting forth an assessment of the subject and convincing readers that the writer's judgment is reasonable. Keep these criteria in mind as you evaluate students' essays.

Some of your students might need a glossary to help them understand the vocabulary used in evaluating a written or filmed work. They can collaborate with you, either through class discussion or as a group project, to publish a glossary for distribution to class members. For definitions of literary terms, refer students to Chapter 13, "Responding to Literature." A few other useful terms are listed here, adapted from Elizabeth McMahan, Robert Funk, and Susan Day, *The Elements of Writing about Literature and Film* (New York: Longman, 1988), and M. H. Abrams, *Glossary of Literary Terms* (Stamford, CT: Thomson, 2004)). If students choose to evaluate food, music, or other subjects, have them work together to compile a glossary of terms relevant to their subjects.

archetype: A pattern on which things of a similar kind are based. It may also be a defining example of something.

flashback: A part of a story that interrupts a chronological order to relate past incidents.

frame: A single picture in a film (usually there are twenty-four frames in one second of film viewing time).

pan: A camera movement similar to that of a viewer moving his or her head to survey a scene from left to right or right to left.

tracking: The movement of a camera on wheels or tracks.

Facing the Challenge (p. 192)

Becoming aware of personal criteria is often difficult. Activities that direct writers to list criteria, to start questioning themselves to discover criteria, and to converse with others about criteria of judgment are critical for writers to become more sensitive and adept as evaluators. You might want to assign a comparison of readings in a reading journal to lead students into evaluation without being intimidated.

To help students discover the criteria they use unconsciously and also the need to make those criteria explicit for their audience, use the following exercise. Have them brainstorm a list of subjects for evaluation. Ask groups of students to select two subjects for evaluation. Pass around a basket with slips of paper with roles for individual group members on them: a prospective student, a state legislator, an architect, a disabled instructor, a new academic officer, and so on. Ask the group to determine the "quality"of their subjects and to discuss with one another how each of the persons involved might list and weight criteria for evaluation.

For more about providing support for underprepared students, see Chapter 4 of this manual.

Generating Ideas (p. 190)

Although students will be familiar with the subject matter for this writing assignment, they probably will not have developed the critical thinking skills required, nor

---

Here's an Idea . . .

A graduate instructor at Truman State University used comparison and contrast exercises with his class to lead them to the skills they would need to write a film review. He showed his class a lengthy sequence from the movie *2001: A Space Odyssey* about the computer HAL and an equally long sequence from the movie *Blade Runner* that focused on the android played by Rutger Hauer. He ended the class with a fifteen-minute writing session, asking students to compare their reaction to HAL with their reaction to the android.

During the next class, he asked students to share their reactions and made notes on the board about those reactions. He explained that he wanted the class to be able to state by the end of the period how each film had prompted their reactions. He asked students what characteristics made them call a film good or bad, requesting examples or clarifications of any characteristic that seemed vague. Whenever possible, he asked whether there was a specialized term for what a student had described; the class generated and discussed many film terms, such as *pacing, cutting, lighting,* and *voice-over.*

The instructor then asked small groups to discuss the use of three characteristics that established a perspective on the "humanity"of androids and directed them to systematically compare the use of each characteristic in 2001 with that in *Blade Runner.* After twenty minutes of discussion, groups could make many generalizations about how the films had worked. Both large-group discussion and small-group work included serious analysis, leaps to interpretations, and statements like "Yes, that was skillful use of background music, but what really made the movie make sense was . . ." The instructor then assigned students to evaluate what the films reflected about humanizing technology.

will they be familiar with the critical ideas they need to complete the work satisfactorily. Before you send students out to work on their own, you might want to model the process of generating ideas for an evaluation essay.

Brainstorm on the board the characteristics that students look for in a restaurant (you might include cafés and fast-food establishments). From this list, ask students to work in small groups to distill these characteristics and state the criteria by which they evaluate a restaurant. Next, make a brainstorming list of local restaurants. Ask each student to select one of these restaurants and in a journal entry evaluate it according to the criteria his or her group set forth. Finally, have the peer groups reconvene and share their restaurant evaluations. Follow up with a class discussion of what students learned about evaluation and criteria from this activity.

Have students use the Discovery Checklist on page 193 as a basis for self-assessment. Ask them to explain (1) how they have used recall or other resources to back up a judgment, (2) what criteria they are aware of using in an evaluation, (3) where they might use comparing and contrasting to evaluate further, and (4) how they have succeeded at distinguishing the subject from the rest of its general class ("inclusion-exclusion" or Aristotelian definition). Then ask them to assess the strongest and weakest parts of the evaluation and to set one goal for revision. Have them turn in their assessment with their essay.

Planning, Drafting, and Developing (p. 193)

This assignment requires high-level critical thinking skills, so recursive planning, drafting, and developing will be very important. Give students plenty of time to work and rework through these stages. Help them to break the writing process into small chunks and to develop a schedule for completing the work by the deadline. Schedule plenty of time in and out of class to work with students on plans and drafts.

When planning, ask students to compose a statement of purpose, a thesis statement, and the criteria for evaluation. Remind them that any or all of these might change as they think more deeply about the topic and draft their ideas. Ask students to draft a purpose statement for their project. Discuss with them how it will provide guidance for writing.

As students work on organizing their essays, emphasize that because they are trying to inform readers of their evaluation of the chosen topic, they should probably state the thesis sentence early in the essay. Ask them to analyze Stevenson's and O'Neil's organization by outlining each of these essays. Is the organization of each effective? Encourage students to try different patterns of order for their own essays. Do they intend to provide general information about the topic first and then apply the criteria? Or do they think that organizing by the criteria will work better? How are they going to order the criteria — possibly from least important to most important? If they are working on a computer, this shifting will be easy. When writers can easily move points around and ask, almost mechanically, "How do these two look the same?" and "Where do these differ?," they will often discover relationships that are both new and incisive.

Outlining point by point will also help writers to make connections. Shaping subject by subject allows writers to bypass the synthesizing activity that produces insights and new ideas. If students have failed to make an evaluation when comparing subjects, look first to see if the problem lies in the way they've shaped the draft.

As you go over drafts in conference with students, alert them to the appropriate use of specific details. Although this assignment is not a descriptive or a narrative essay,

Here's an Idea . . .

Ask each student to bring to class his or her response to an exam question that required evaluating (perhaps from a history test calling for assessment of the social climate during the McCarthy era, or from a philosophy quiz asking each student to compare and contrast Plato and Aristotle). Then have each student analyze the effectiveness of his or her answer in terms of what he or she has learned about evaluative writing in this chapter, and suggest how the response could be improved.

specific evidence — examples and details — is necessary to show and convince readers of the validity of the position the writer has taken. Also encourage students to rewrite dry, dull introductions and conclusions.

Revising and Editing (p. 194)

At this point, encourage students to avoid sweeping positive or negative generalizations. Suggest that a peer editor play devil's advocate and defend whatever parts of the subject a writer has found fault with. This activity often leads the writer to consider whether his or her fault finding was extreme, imprecisely explained, or too generally described.

Several of the items in the Revision Checklist on page 195 can be incorporated into the For Peer Response exercise (p. 194). It's often easier for peer editors than writers to identify an unbalanced discussion of the subject or to circle judgments that are too strident or too general. Expect these workshop sessions to take more time than sessions focused on a less complex task. Either form smaller groups or suggest that the writing group carry the discussion over to some out-of-class locale. Students enjoy the workshop format and often feel that they gain more from face-to-face communication than from receiving written evaluations. Remind writers that they need to jot down the helpful comments and suggestions for additional reasons and criteria.

The For E-Writers activity on page 195 will help students to assess their writing for specific factual evidence and help them to avoid one of the major pitfalls of college writing — supporting opinion with opinion. As they look at the correlation between their judgments and evidence, they can also check to be sure that they have inserted suitable transitions at the appropriate spots. Also remind them to check correct punctuation and the spelling of books, television shows, or movies.

Other Assignments (p. 196)

1. You serve your students well when you teach them how to evaluate their own education. The authors suggest several important criteria for course evaluation. Ask students to brainstorm the behaviors of teachers whom they call excellent and those whom they do not recommend. As you would anticipate, they will have a wide range of criteria for good teaching, and some criteria will clearly reflect how much responsibility students take for their education. This assignment could easily benefit from imagination if students define the "ideal" circumstances for a course to help a first-year student enter the academic community.

   As an instructor, you need to caution students to use pseudonyms for teachers whom they evaluate in either a general or specific way during class discussion. We guarantee that once students realize that evaluation of a course is an appropriate and safe topic in your writing classroom, they will start sharing experiences, observations, visions, and analyses quite enthusiastically.

Remind students that evaluating gives them control over their education that parroting never allows. Encourage them to write full evaluations and explain where they need specific examples, illustrations, or details.

2. Although the assignment clearly suggests criteria that are literary, don't be surprised if some writers generate criteria that are personal and response-oriented. Novice readers and writers of literature typically begin with and fall back on their reactions about relevance to their lives, subjects that make them comfortable or uncomfortable to read about, and memories or associations triggered by some of the reading. If students have difficulty evaluating what they read, hold a conference with individual writers to discuss critical reading skills and to lead them through the questions for analyzing literature (see Chapter 13, "Responding to Literature"). Have the writers keep paper at hand — or sit at the computer in your office — and jot down the insights that come up.

3. Parts of this assignment could lead to publication. After students have read their rough drafts, ask them to type and mail them to specific critics of their local newspaper. This might also encourage students to notice the different and strategic locations of these columns. Students might also submit their reviews to the campus newspaper. Encourage students' writing by emphasizing their role as consumers. They can influence the success of a business or the marketing of magazines and textbooks, but first they must use critical thinking in their evaluations.

APPLYING WHAT YOU LEARN: SOME USES OF EVALUATING (p. 197)

Have students bring to class study questions or exam questions from other courses that ask them to evaluate. Suggest that they ask other instructors what criteria they use in evaluating books or artifacts in their fields. Recommend that they talk to someone in their chosen career fields about the role that evaluation plays on the job.

MAKING CONNECTIONS

People often judge quickly, with opinions based on assumptions or cultural bias. In these essays from *A Writer's Reader*, each writer has used evidence in his or her evaluation. Solid evidence separates opinion from the informed critique and creates a strong, dynamic piece of writing. Students might notice this distinction quickly, as they move through the questions at the end of each essay.

Stephen King in "Why We Crave Horror Movies" (p. 512) examines the value of horror movies in terms of our mental health. He argues that they "exercise" the "anti-civilization emotions" in all of us and suggests that horror movies allow us to vicariously indulge our dark impulses, which, for most people, prevents such impulses from being acted out in real life.

Michael Abernethy in "Male Bashing on TV" (p. 515) evaluates the comic portrayal of men on television. He concludes that "male bashing" is a more serious problem than many would think.

James Poniewozik in "Why Reality TV Is Good for Us" (p. 520) defends reality television against critics who attack its morality. Examining the reasons for its success, Poniewozik holds that the genre is "the best thing to happen to television in several years."

Steven Levy in an excerpt from *The Perfect Thing* (p. 540) evaluates the impact of the iPod on the social fabric of Manhattan. In examining the lack of social interaction that forms his criteria, Levy admits that the disconnectedness blamed on iPod use was typical of New Yorkers long before the onset of wires and ear buds.

William Zinsser in "The Right to Fail" (p. 567) questions the narrow criteria by which we judge students as failures, claiming that "the right to fail is one of the few freedoms that this country does not grant its citizens." Zinsser makes a case for the "dissenters and dreamers," providing examples of dropouts who have gone on to great success. Failure, Zinsser claims, can be a learning experience, and fear of it stifles creativity. Defining success only in traditional ways unfairly condemns young adults who seek fulfillment through nontraditional paths that often benefit society.

As students read these essays, ask them to consider the role that evaluation plays therein. For each essay, ask students to answer the As You Read questions on page 184.

RESOURCES FOR COLLEGE WRITERS

Your Assignment
Evaluating, p. 190

Resources in the Text
- Sample professional reading, p. 184
- Sample student reading, p. 187
- Facing the Challenge, p. 192
- Planning and developing the essay, p. 193
- Discovery and Revision checklists, pp. 193 and 195
- Editing Checklist, p. 196
- Uses of evaluating in real-world writing situations, pp. 197–98
- Peer review help, p. 194
- E-Writer help, p. 195

Resources on the Web Site
<bedfordstmartins.com/bedguide>
- Additional readings with activities
- "Ask the Draft Doctor" writing help
- Peer response forms
- Link to Exercise Central

Supporting a Position with Sources
(Ch. 12, p. 199)

This chapter prepares students for one of the most common assignments in college: taking a position based on reading and thoughtfully examining a subject, and supporting this position with evidence from the reading. The cognitive tasks involved demand the full range of critical thinking skills discussed in Chapter 3 of *The Bedford Guide*: analysis, synthesis, and evaluation. This assignment also demands that students move beyond dualistic and multiplistic thinking to relativistic thinking. (See Chapter 3 of this manual for more information on cognitive development.) Preceding chapters of *The Bedford Guide* have prepared students to analyze causes and effects, to take a stand and support it, to identify problems and imagine ways to fix them, and to come to sound judgments. They will use all these skills as they enter the academic exchange of ideas on their subject and take a position on it.

Some students will approach this assignment with enthusiasm; others will be anxious that they have nothing to contribute to what may be a long-standing academic discussion. You can ease anxiety by explaining that each of us brings different experiences and perspectives to any discussion, and since the culmination of our experiences and knowledge is unique, so will the conclusions we draw from reading and thinking about a subject. Remind students that writing is an act of discovery, and they will discover their own unique ideas as they write and respond to their reading.

Students can benefit from reading different examples of writing that takes a position based on sources. The grid on pages 371–83 refers students to several such examples in *The Bedford Guide*.

Chapter 12, "Supporting a Position with Sources," contains the following activities:

- Responding to an Image (p. 199). Allow your students to use their imagination while examining these visual activity prompts. If necessary, have students free-associate responses to elements of each image. If they are given free rein for their own interpretations, they will most likely view analyzing these images as a rewarding way to begin thinking about writing in these modes.

  It is likely that some of your students have confined themselves to searching for evidence on the Internet or in computer databases. Discuss other avenues for finding evidence as shown in the collage at the start of Chapter 12. Ask students to identify subjects that might be productively explored using these other avenues. Encourage them to venture beyond familiar and convenient avenues of inquiry.

- For E-Writers (p. 226). See page 73 of this manual for advice about how to use this feature.

- For Peer Response (p. 227). See page 39 of this manual for advice about how to use this feature.

- For Group Learning (p. 213). See page 39 of this manual for advice about how to use this feature.

LEARNING FROM OTHER WRITERS

DAVID CALLAHAN *A Question of Character* (p. 201)

David Callahan takes a position on the shifting goals of Americans, maintaining that the population in general and young people in particular increasingly equate happiness with wealth. Callahan supports his claims with a variety of evidence, documented in MLA style. As students analyze this essay, remind them that Callahan is modeling the techniques they will use to state and support their positions.

Questions to Start You Thinking (p. 204)

Meaning

1. Callahan's position, expressed in his thesis in paragraph 1, is that over the past two decades, Americans have increasingly associated happiness with financial and material gain. This position is sure to generate class discussion, with some students agreeing strongly with Callahan and others expressing quite different views. Take some time to discuss the central premise and encourage students to share their views.

2. Callahan is especially concerned about young people, particularly those of college age. As he notes in paragraph 4, a shift toward materialism among college students began in the mid-1970s, and he argues that financial and material gain remains a primary goal among today's students. Later in the piece, Callahan describes a rise in consumerism among young Americans. Ask students why Callahan is concerned with young people in particular.

3. Callahan refers to behavior in which consumers, not wanting to appear less prosperous or successful than others, try to buy the same amount and quality of goods as their peers. He argues that more and more Americans compare themselves not with their true financial equals but with "reference groups" who make a lot more money. Ask students if they are familiar with this behavior. They will probably be able to give a variety of examples based on their experiences from high school, from their neighborhoods, and so on.

4. Direct students to the annotations of the essay, noting where he introduces the points about goal shifts in the general population (para. 1) and goal shifts among young people (para. 3). Also, ask them to consider the evidence for these points, which lead effectively to the conclusion presented in paragraph 10. There, Callahan writes, "A majority of Americans consistently report that they don't have enough income to live the life they want." Would students give a similar report of their income relative to their goals?

Writing Strategies

5. Point out the Works Cited list on p. 204. This list includes three books, two periodicals, and a report from a research institute — a range of sources. Help students see the different ways in which Callahan has drawn on the sources, by summarizing, paraphrasing, and quoting directly. Do they think that he has backed his position adequately? Also, ask students what types of evidence might be missing from Callahan's essay. For example, might interviews with students have shed more light on their values and goals?

6. This question provides a good opportunity to talk about how, in the work of experienced writers, the author's voice tends to dominate as he or she uses sources in the service of a position. Often, this means that experienced writers use fewer

direct quotations than less experienced or less confident writers. However, well-chosen direct quotations certainly lend life and depth to writing. If students would prefer to see more quotations in Callahan's piece, ask where do they think they would be most effective?

7. Callahan's tone is serious and respectful, and it is appropriate given his purpose of informing readers about what he sees as a serious issue. His concern about Americans' obsession with money and possessions comes through clearly. In paragraph 6, Callahan notes, "As making money moved front and center, young people stopped caring about other things." And he concludes his essay by saying that Americans have crossed the line between "a healthy desire to get ahead and a relentless struggle to keep up." Can students imagine how Callahan's tone or style might differ if he were writing for, say, a student humor magazine?

8. Students may notice that Callahan uses longer paragraphs than are standard in newspaper articles, and he includes full source citations, unlike typical news articles. Ask students why they think these differences exist, noting the need of newspapers to convey information briefly. You might also note that the narrower column width of newspapers means that paragraphs tend to be shorter. Students might also notice that Callahan's vocabulary tends to be more sophisticated than that in newspapers, which must appeal to readers with widely varying reading skills.

MELISSA LAMBERTH   *Overworked!* (p. 205)

Melissa Lamberth cites a variety of sources to support her position that Americans are overworked. To underscore the seriousness of her position, she describes several negative effects of overwork. To respond to possible objections to her position, she debunks the notion that less time in the workplace would result in lower productivity, or that stress management programs can adequately address the problems resulting from overwork.

Questions to Start You Thinking (p. 208)

Meaning

1. As Lamberth states in her first paragraph, she believes that employees need to have shorter workdays or more time off to be safer, happier, and more productive. Ask students whether they agree that excessive work hours are in fact a problem for them, their friends, and their family members. Encourage students to share stories of their own work situations.

2. Lamberth points to several problems associated with overwork, including lack of time for family and leisure, risk of accidents while driving and operating other machinery, and reduced job performance. Ask students if they can point to problems not mentioned by Lamberth. Additionally, you might broaden the discussion by asking students about the potential benefits of hard work. Are there cases in which the benefits might exceed the disadvantages?

3. Lamberth believes that employers should play a major role in improving the lives of overburdened workers. She suggests that they take such measures as making overtime optional, hiring workers to take on extra work (or giving the work to other employees), and giving workers more time off. Ask students whether, as Lamberth suggests, much of the burden of reducing worker stress should rest with employers. Do they find her suggestions to be practical? You might also ask whether any students have either run or managed a business. Such students might have interesting perspectives to share.

Writing Strategies

4. Lamberth uses varied sources to support her position — a press release, two online articles, a textbook essay, and a book — and she effectively balances source information with her own observations. Students might suggest other types of sources Lamberth could have included. For instance, business groups, such as the U.S. Chamber of Commerce, might provide more of the employer's perspective.

5. Lamberth considers opposing views in paragraphs 7 and 8; these paragraphs provide good models for making counter-claims in response to such views. In paragraph 7, she addresses employers' concern that hiring temporary workers to relieve overburdened employees would not be cost-effective. She counters this claim by asserting that rested employees are more productive employees. In paragraph 8, she dismisses stress- and time-management programs as impractical responses by employers to overwork among employees.

6. Students' views about Lamberth's use of exclamation points will vary. This punctuation shows her enthusiasm for her topic, but some may find these marks overdone or inappropriate for a college essay. Explain that sentences ending in exclamation points can read like shouting, so this punctuation is best used sparingly. If your students are using the version of *The Bedford Guide* with the Handbook, you might refer them to section 20d.

7. Lamberth's thesis is the last sentence of her introduction (para. 1). After presenting her thesis, she provides historical background on the problem of overwork. She then discusses the reasons why overwork is a problem and proposes what could be done about it. All the while, Lamberth cites sources that back her position. She concludes by reiterating her position and the benefits of reduced workloads for both employers and employees.

LEARNING BY WRITING

The Assignment: Supporting a Position with Sources (p. 208)

Don't assume your students will come to this assignment with careful, analytical reading skills. The truth is that most of our students have never acquired the habit of reading. Many do not read beyond what is required of them for a class and have not developed critical reading skills. The advice and strategies in Chapter 2 of *The Bedford Guide*, "Reading Processes," is a good place to start if you detect weaknesses in this area. Ask students to work through the five steps on page 104 of this manual as they analyze the cluster of readings from which they are developing a position. To write based on these readings, students must have a sound grasp of each writer's ideas and how he or she supports them. This exercise will provide them with that understanding.

Students will practice a variety of skills with this assignment: analyzing readings, assimilating the information with their own ideas to arrive at a position, stating a thesis, supporting the thesis with source materials, integrating those source materials into their drafts, and documenting the sources correctly. A cluster of readings from *A Writer's Reader* works well for teaching these skills. As an alternative, you might want to assign a specific group of readings you've selected and placed on reserve in your library, located on the Internet, or copied for your class. Be sure to supply an appropriate number of selections for students to analyze and draw from in the amount of time you've allowed for the assignment. Sources should include all the information students will need for their Works Cited entries.

If your objectives include having students locate information on a topic, you will need to help them find and narrow a topic and identify an appropriate number of readings from the kinds of sources you want them to use. Give them specific directions about the kinds of sources you will allow. For example, if you want students to use only sources from certain databases to which your library subscribes, give them a list of acceptable databases. Discuss the different types of periodicals they might use. Tell them if they are restricted to journals or if they may use articles from newspapers or popular magazines. The sources they use will affect the level of discourse in their papers, and you will need to determine the level of source material they can handle. Chapter 30, "Finding Sources in the Library, on the Internet, and in the Field" (in *A Writer's Research Manual*) shows students how to locate different types of sources.

If your course includes a research paper, you may want to use this assignment as preparation for incorporating and documenting sources, or you may want to teach this chapter with some of the chapters in *A Writer's Research Manual,* if your textbook includes that. If it doesn't, direct students to the Quick Research Guide for help.

Facing the Challenge (p. 211)

Students frequently lose their own voices when working with sources. Many lack the confidence to express their own ideas strongly amid the ideas of writers they consider much more knowledgeable than they. Others have not fully formed their own ideas and wind up over-relying on the voices of their sources. One way to help students find their own voice is to have them write a first draft without their sources. Allow class time for drafting so that students do not lose confidence and refer to their sources before they have shaped and fully articulated their own ideas. If students have access to word processors or laptops to write their drafts, they can insert source material easily in their next draft. Emphasize that evidence should be used only to support and explain the students' own ideas. During revision, they can incorporate material from their reading in appropriate places, launching, capturing, and citing source information as explained in the text. As students insert source material, they can recast sentences to make the draft flow smoothly. You might want to direct them to strategies for achieving coherence in Chapter 18 (p. 346).

Generating Ideas (p. 209)

Encourage students to look for sources that express a variety of views on their topic. This is a good time to discuss the reliability of sources and how to determine which are acceptable for academic writing. If students are choosing their own cluster of readings, hold individual conferences to check their selections. You can do this quickly

---

Here's an Idea ...

Suggest that students keep an annotated bibliography of all their college readings — not just the ones for this assignment — on the computer. Working with a word-processing program makes it easy to move information around. Have students describe their reactions to each reading. In addition, they can practice summarizing by writing a short paragraph or two covering the reading's content. They should include their evaluations of the ideas in their annotations, as well as author credentials and publication details for in-text citations and documentation of sources. Building a bibliography in a computer file trains students to read critically and document correctly. They can add to their file throughout their college careers and use it as a resource for writing.

while other students analyze their readings in class. Set up an outside appointment for those students whose choices present problems. Make sure that they understand the ideas presented in their sources and are moving toward a position of their own. Encourage students to keep a reading journal in which they respond to the readings and record new ideas that occur to them. They can mine their journals for ideas as they devise a thesis and develop their positions.

Ask students to submit copies of their reading notes or journal entries with their drafts. These copies will give you information about how students are using their reading. Look for notes that are too general or that only list facts without coming to any conclusions.

Planning, Drafting, and Developing (p. 213)

Many of your students will struggle with finding a thesis for their position papers. Ask them to complete the following statements:

- "The topic and/or main idea of my readings was . . ."
- "The biggest point of disagreement among the authors was . . ."
- "I agree that . . . "
- "I disagree that . . ."
- "My idea about this is . . ."
- "I think that . . ."

Completing statements such as these can help students sort out their own ideas from the ideas in their sources. Ask students to imagine that they are in a room with the authors of their readings and they are discussing the topic, each holding forth with his or her own ideas. What do the students imagine themselves interjecting? How would their part of the conversation go? Tell them that their part of the conversation should be their unique voice that comes through in the paper.

Don't assume that your students are already skilled at quoting, paraphrasing, and summarizing. Set aside class time to practice these skills. Choose an essay from *A Writer's Reader* or an essay from another source and break students into small groups. Ask them to paraphrase specific passages, to summarize a section of the essay, and to choose three memorable quotations. The groups can exchange and critique each other's work, or you can show the work of each group on an overhead projector for the class to critique. Have them use the directions for quoting (p. 214), paraphrasing (p. 218), and summarizing (p. 220) to check their work. Then have them write a correct Works Cited entry for the piece.

Revising and Editing (p. 223)

The Development Checklist (p. 222) will call your students' attention to problems with source material they have incorporated into their drafts. The Draft Doctor on page 228, new to this edition, addresses the most common problems we find when students work with sources. It will offer students invaluable help with handling sources: deciding how to use them most effectively, incorporating them into the draft, citing them in the text, and listing them at the end of the paper. Direct your students to work through their drafts using The Draft Doctor. Finally, remind students to use the Revision Checklist on page 227 to examine their drafts more broadly for potential problems.

Other Assignments (p. 231)

1. Students often find the idea of writing for an Internet audience more intriguing than writing for the usual audience for college papers. If you need help with the technological aspects of this assignment, consider creating a joint assignment with a colleague in the computer department. Or have students mock up pages using word-processing software.

2. This assignment will focus students on judging the value of sources in academic exchanges. Direct their attention to the criteria for evidence in Chapter 3 (p. 39), as well as Chapter 11, "Evaluating."

3. Encourage students to choose an event connected to their major or another field of interest. You can encourage them to explore primary sources, such as first-hand accounts of historic events, by restricting the time period you allow them to choose from.

APPLYING WHAT YOU LEARN: SOME USES OF POSITION PAPERS SUPPORTED BY SOURCES (p. 231)

Ask students to bring in assignments from other courses that require them to read from a variety of sources and support a position. Consider inviting a panel of former students to talk to your class about experiences they have had gathering information to support a position in college, at work, or in their communities.

MAKING CONNECTIONS

Barbara Ehrenreich in "Guys Just Want to Have Fun" (p. 482) takes the position that college men, unfairly, may gain more marketable skills playing poker and partying than their female counterparts do studying. She draws on books, newspaper articles, and interviews to support her position that corporations look for qualities such as "personality" and "likability" in prospective employees.

Evelyn F. Murphy in "Why Not a Dollar?" (p. 488) presents solid support from a number of credible sources for her position that women's wages lag behind men's for one reason: discrimination. She systematically eliminates other explanations, providing facts and statistics from government sources, which she documents at the end of her essay. Although Murphy does not use MLA-style documentation, her essay is a sound example of drawing from sources and documenting them to support a position.

Ruth La Ferla in "Latino Style Is So Cool. Oh, All Right: It's Hot" (p. 506) relies on interviews to support her position that Latino influence in fashion is the hottest new trend. La Ferla lends credibility to her claim by quoting a wide variety of sources: young Latinos who display their cultural heritage in their dress, fashion and Latino magazine editors, leading apparel makers, designers, a fashion photographer, and a Fordham sociology professor and author of a book on Latino images in the media.

James Poniewozik in "Why Reality TV Is Good for Us" (p. 520) draws on a number of reality TV shows as sources backing his position that reality TV is good for both producers and audiences. Poniewozik analyzes the shows to support his claim.

David Gelernter in "Computers Cannot Teach Children Basic Skills" (p. 536) asserts that computers in classrooms are not the boon to learning they are touted as, basing his conclusions on an analysis of educational software. To the contrary, he argues, most software is a detriment to children's education and must be completely redesigned.

Alex Koppelman in "MySpace or OurSpace?" (p. 546) uses interviews and print sources to explore how the Internet site MySpace is being used as an investigative tool by schools and police departments. Koppelman concludes that students' First Amendment rights are at stake and that the impingement on their privacy erodes their belief in "the fundamental values of free expression that we as a nation supposedly hold dear."

As students read these essays, ask them to consider the role that evaluation plays therein. For each essay, ask students to answer the As You Read questions on page 200.

RESOURCES FOR COLLEGE WRITERS

Your Assignment
Supporting a Position with Sources, p. 208

Resources in the Text
- Sample professional reading, p. 201
- Sample student reading, p. 205
- Facing the Challenge, p. 211
- Planning and developing the essay, p. 213
- Discovery and Development checklists, p. 212 and 222
- Revision and Editing checklists, p. 227 and p. 231
- The Draft Doctor, p. 228
- Uses of supporting a position with sources in real-world writing situations, p. 231
- Peer review help, p. 227
- E-Writer help, p. 226

Resources on the Web Site
<bedfordstmartins.com/bedguide>
- Additional readings with activities
- "Ask the Draft Doctor" writing help
- Peer response forms
- Link to Exercise Central

Special Writing Situations

Responding to Literature (Ch. 13, p. 235)

This chapter could be the only introduction to literature that many of your students encounter in college. Assigning literature in your composition course fosters students' critical reading skills as well as their ability to write with different audiences and purposes in mind. Students must learn a complex method of analysis in order to interpret literature. Chapter 13 provides students with the information and structure they need to begin this kind of writing. Often students assume that they have experience writing critically about literature, but after some discussion you will probably discover that their past writing consisted mostly of opinion papers. As a result, students will need to be both challenged to think more critically about the literature they read and encouraged to feel more confident about their role as critic.

Chapter 13, "Responding to Literature," contains this activity:

- For Peer Response (p. 254). See page 39 of this manual for advice about how to use this feature.

LITERARY ANALYSIS

Learning from Other Writers (p. 236)

Students are often ensnared by the short story "The Lottery." Before they read this tale of horror by Shirley Jackson, remind them that an insightful analysis depends in part on their knowledge of the material — the story, various contexts shaping the tale, and specific elements in the writing being examined. Undergraduates often enter a college classroom with at least one prior reading of this short story in high school. Encourage them to reevaluate elements of the story that they might not have noticed in their first reading.

Read the following quotation from Shirley Jackson to your students before they read the story. After "The Lottery" was published in *The New Yorker*, many people wrote to Jackson, and their letters shocked her. She said,

> Curiously there are three main themes which dominate the letters of that first summer — three themes which might be identified as bewilderment, speculation, and plain old-fashioned abuse. In the years since then . . . the tenor of letters I receive has changed. I am addressed more politely, as a rule, and the letters largely confine themselves to questions like What does this story mean? The general tone of the

---

Here's an Idea . . .

Before students read the story, hand them blank slips of paper (except one, which is marked) as they enter the room. Tell them that one slip is not blank and that the person who has it will be the winner. Ask that person to wait to reveal him or herself until after the class has read "The Lottery."

early letters, however, was a kind of wide-eyed, shocked innocence. People at first were not so much concerned with what the story meant; what they wanted to know was where these lotteries were held, and whether they could go there and watch.

– Come Along with Me (1968)

SHIRLEY JACKSON   *The Lottery* (p. 237)

Published in 1948, this story has become a classic in American short-fiction anthologies. Students will appreciate the many skillful twists Jackson uses. After its conclusion, you might need to dispel students' assumptions about the type of person who could create this plot. Tell them that Jackson lived with her husband and four children in a small Vermont town, where, in her own words, she spent a good portion of her time "washing and dressing the children, cooking, washing dishes and clothes, and mending."

Questions to Start You Thinking (p. 243)

Meaning

1. Students often flip through pages in the story and look for a specific location. Ask them why a writer would allow these two important details to remain unknown. Suggest that they analyze the impact of omitting the chronological time while including details about the season and the activities that begin the story.

2. Take students through the story in parts. Ask them if they see any memorable characters or conversations in the beginning of "The Lottery." Move them into an examination of the "drawing" process and then to the ending. Write their responses to these parts of the story on the chalkboard and ask them to compare their qualifications of the most memorable characters in each part.

3. This question should create animated discussion. Allow all students to respond. Their answers will move the class into an effective analysis of question 5. Some students will understand the ending of the story only after discussion. Explain that they should not be ashamed. Shirley Jackson skillfully constructed the plot to be ambiguous.

Writing Strategies

4. Your students might reside in a state that has a lottery. Ask them to list the components of state lotteries that are comparable to the lottery in the story. As you write these on the board, ask students to examine the possible motives for creating a state lottery. Are any of the reasons similar to those that led to the creation of the village's lottery?

5. This question is crucial to a precise analysis of the story. You might want to ask students to form groups and answer it collaboratively. Instruct each group to discuss the story and then to furnish one response to the question.

6. To encourage a longer and more detailed response to the question, use it as a journal prompt. Have students freewrite for five or ten minutes in class, or write their response as a homework assignment.

JONATHAN BURNS   *The Hidden Truth: An Analysis of Shirley Jackson's "The Lottery"*
(p. 246)

Questions to Start You Thinking (p. 247)

Meaning

1. The first thing students should do in analyzing an essay on literature is to iden-tify the thesis. Stress that a clear, sound thesis should organize the essay, determine what evidence students select from the story, and keep them from slipping into summary (see question 4). Burns's thesis is the final sentence of paragraph 1. Show students how well the thesis statement provides an organizational pattern for his essay (first characterization, then symbolism, then description) and keeps him focused on supporting the thesis instead of retelling the story. Encourage students to follow this model in their essays.

2. Students should recognize that the thesis statement roughly outlines the major points Burns will make. He will discuss the "unsuspicious characterizations, unob-trusive symbolism, and ambiguous descriptions" (para. 1) that make the ending so surprising. The essay demonstrates the importance of using specific evidence from the story to support the thesis. Ask students which specific elements Burns uses to demonstrate the story's "unsuspicious characterization." Ask the same for "unob-trusive symbolism" and "ambiguous descriptions." Have students write a formal outline for Burns's essay, indicating his major points and specific evidence for each.

Writing Strategies

3. This question anticipates the error students most frequently make when begin-ning a literary analysis: They often rely on a summary or book-report formula from their past academic work. Read aloud to them the inside of a book jacket or the summary on the cover of a paperback and remind them that these do not constitute analysis. Point out the difference between Burns's writing and the material you have just read: Literary analysis presents readers with a critical evaluation rather than a plot summary.

4. Burns's essay provides a good example of literary analysis that focuses on tech-nique, whereas most first-year college writers address theme. Take time to distin-guish between theme and technique. Write the column headings theme and tech-nique on the board. Brainstorm a list of topics about "The Lottery" or another short story and place them in the appropriate category. For example, "Jackson's treat-ment of death" applies to theme, but "Jackson's use of foreshadowing" addresses technique.

5. The introduction of this essay is delightful. It proves to many students that a lit-erary analysis is not boring or pedantic. The initial sentence "hooks" readers and entices them to read further. Burns clearly states his thesis after capturing the atten-tion of his audience.

6. As critics, students can examine the structure for this essay. Ask them to explain why they have supported either the present structure or challenged it with an alter-native.

7. Students will realize that they are in effect analyzing an analysis. Suggest that this is what you do as an instructor and ask them to assume that perspective in answering this question. Many might find the conclusion somber and ominous. Ask them to suggest how they would maintain the power of this conclusion with a

different tone. For those students who believe the conclusion is effective, ask them to defend their response.

8. This question anticipates the most difficult parts of literary analysis for first-year college writers: organization and coherence. Be sure students notice how Burns allows his thesis to determine the order in which he makes his points, instead of following the chronology of the plot — a major mistake many first-year writers make. Ask students to point to specific sentences and phrases that reinforce the cohesiveness of Burns's essay. Emphasize the importance of transitions.

Analyzing the Elements of Literature: A Glossary of Terms (pp. 248–49)

Remind students that they need to use these terms in their written literary analyses. Spend time with them on the terms before they begin their papers; understanding how these terms are used in literary analysis will increase students' confidence in producing their own analyses. Ask students to read the list of terms and then to notice where and how Burns uses them in his paper.

Students who understand a single component of literature, such as plot, character, or setting, can construct a thesis about one of these elements. The additional information that we include here on specific types of plots might also help students to generate ideas for an essay. Of the many variations of plot structure, we describe three basic types: the planned plot, the Chekhovian plot, and the slice-of-life plot. You might want to copy the illustrations on the next page as a handout for your class.

The planned or highly structured plot was perfected by Edgar Allan Poe, Henry James, and other American short-story writers of the nineteenth century. It is also the structure that Shakespeare uses in his five-act plays. The planned plot contains six elements — exposition, incentive moment, conflicts, complications, climax, and resolution — each fully developed and easily discernible. At the beginning of the story, the exposition or background information — the setting, mood, main characters, and initial situation — is clearly set forth. Then the incentive moment occurs: This is the event that begins to change the initial situation. Next the conflicts, both external and internal, are set forth. Then the complications — events that complicate the conflicts — are narrated, and the central or major conflict becomes clear. This conflict leads through the complications to the climax, an event that is a direct result of the central conflict. The climax is the point at which the ending becomes inevitable. Finally, the resolution (which is not the same thing as a solution) of the central conflict occurs, and the story concludes. At the ending a state of equilibrium is restored, but the situation is different from that at the beginning of the story. Thus the plot is a well-rounded whole, with each part interrelated with the others and each part a logical cause-and-effect result of the preceding parts.

The Chekhovian plot, developed by its namesake, Anton Chekhov, was extensively used and modified by twentieth-century writers such as Ernest Hemingway, John Steinbeck, and Shirley Jackson. Chekhov's typical plot includes the first five parts of the planned plot structure but no resolution. It ends on a peak of intensity at the climax, and nothing is resolved, no equilibrium restored. This approach has been popular with modern writers because of the prevailing attitude that many conflicts cannot be resolved and that many problems have no solution.

The slice-of-life plot was developed as impressionistic authors (similar to impressionistic painters) endeavored to capture a moment in time, rather than attempting to offer solutions to life's problems. Most of these stories begin in medias res (in the middle of the action), progress through conflicts and complications, and end at the climax.

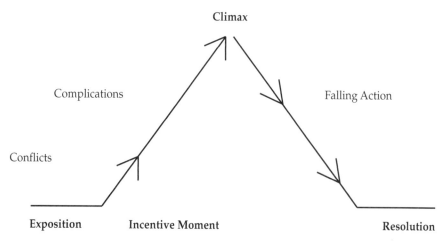

THE PLANNED PLOT

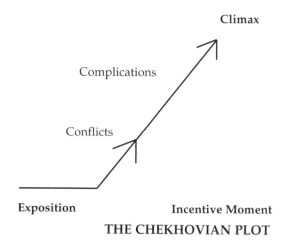

THE CHEKHOVIAN PLOT

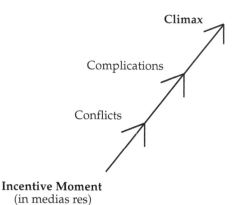

THE SLICE-OF-LIFE PLOT

Irwin Shaw, Stephen Crane, O. Henry, Shirley Jackson, and Kate Chopin often use this kind of plot.

LEARNING BY WRITING

The Assignment: Analyzing a Literary Work (p. 250)

Removing the anxiety that often precedes this assignment is as important as learning the literary terms for analysis. Group work and class discussion show students that they have valid and evocative ideas that will serve them well in this assignment. Continue to remind students that one need not be a professional critic to effectively analyze literature. Student writers often produce quite impressive (and sometimes even brilliant) analyses. These essays are often the result of a student passionately pursuing an idea that strikes him or her as significant on a first reading. Encourage students to trust their instincts in these matters.

If students keep reading journals in response to the literature they read, they might find that they already have the beginning of a thesis when they are called on to write analysis. Journal entries can be especially helpful early in the study of literature to help students focus on pieces they want to spend more time studying and perhaps writing about. In reading-response journals, students jot down their thoughts about what they have read immediately after completing the reading. Have they had similar experiences? Does the protagonist remind them of someone they know? Does anything in the story, perhaps the way it ends, make them angry? Puzzled?

When students begin this type of journal, they tend to write a synopsis of the story, to attempt a thumbnail character sketch, or to analyze symbols. Check their early entries to guide them away from the kind of writing that was often required of them in past classes.

Find a Subject (p. 250)

Reading broadly will help students find a subject. Advise them to read short stories from as many genres as possible, perhaps starting with a mystery, followed by a science fiction story. Traditional American realistic fiction (Hemingway, Fitzgerald, Crane, and Wharton, to name a few authors) is also a good place to start. Give students advice about where to find a variety of stories. Many read only when required, so they might find this assignment daunting. The more your students read, the more comfortable they will become with literature and the analysis of it. After they have found a story in which they have significant interest, ask them to record their three most striking reactions to it. A passionate positive or negative reaction to a piece of literature will usually produce a strong basis for an analysis.

Generate Ideas (p. 250)

Have students form groups with those who have selected the same literary text for analysis. Ask them to respond to the questions in the Discovery Checklist appropriate for their selection (pp. 251–53). These checklists will help students to see how many choices they have in constructing a thesis. As students discuss and argue the merits of the piece, they will generate both ideas and enthusiasm. Tell them to take notes during the discussion, especially on comments that they think will help them write their analyses.

After the groups have responded to the checklists for twenty minutes, ask each student to record two thesis statements for a literary analysis. Then ask students to read their theses aloud to allow the class to hear as many thesis statements as possible.

Remind students that sharing ideas is invaluable; if two of them choose to write about symbolism in "The Lottery," they can offer each other meaningful advice, and their essays can still be quite different. Encourage students to commit to a thesis before they leave the class.

Consider Your Audience (p. 253)

Tell your students to keep these two questions in mind as they plan their essay: What does my audience already know? What do I need to tell them? Students writing about a work unfamiliar to their classmates will have to provide more information about the work. If you allow students to write about works the class has not studied, be prepared to spend at least one class period working on synopsis and summary.

Identify Your Support and Develop Your Main Idea or Thesis (pp. 253–54)

As students comb their reading work for support for their main idea, their thesis will come into sharper focus. Ask them to follow the model in their textbook (pp. 253–54), refining their thesis statement by making each word more specific and explaining it in more detail. Check their statements as they work and encourage them to keep refining it if necessary. Their papers will be much easier to write and support if their thesis statement is specific.

Introduce Your Essay (p. 254)

In reviewing the importance of an introduction and a conclusion, present students with a brief list of some ways in which they can begin an essay: question, quotation, proverb, exclamation. Constantly reinforce the importance of intriguing the audience with the first sentence — what journalists refer to as "a good lead" — and presenting the thesis clearly, as Jonathan Burns does.

Support Your Interpretation (p. 255)

While you meet briefly with students individually, give them the day in class to look for quotations that support their ideas and to work on their drafts. Ask to read their thesis statements and any other writing they've done up to this point to support their idea. Use these brief conferences to help students discover additional evidence and alternative uses of evidence. Establish a deadline for completion of the rough draft if you have not done so already.

Conclude Your Essay (p. 255)

Remind students that a powerful essay should not merely wind down. If a conclusion simply recounts the thesis verbatim, the writer has failed to develop his or her ideas. Encourage students to leave readers with an emotional or intellectual "punch." For more ideas on introductions and conclusions, refer students to Chapter 18, "Strategies for Drafting."

Revise and Edit (pp. 255–56)

Have students revise their drafts based on the suggestions in the Revision Checklist on page 255 in order to focus their attention on the content and structure of their draft. Encourage them to read their essay aloud to themselves, listening for the strongest and weakest sections. Point out the additional information in the textbook on the format for a literary analysis. The quotations students select to support their theses should appear in the rough draft; do not allow students to refer indirectly to quotations. They must select the most powerful support for their thesis. Remind them that they should show their evidence, not talk about it or around it.

A Note on Documenting Sources

Emphasizing the importance of documenting sources is critical. Far too many students enter colleges and universities with little understanding of proper documentation, and their composition classes are usually their first opportunity to learn it. The Quick Research Guide provides an overview of documentation, and Chapter 34 treats documentation in more detail. Your students should read this chapter thoroughly if their textbooks include *A Writer's Research Manual*. Demonstrate the following skills in class to ensure that students understand how

- to paraphrase and quote, and to distinguish between the two (See also Chapter 12.)
- to create an explanatory endnote
- to document sources properly in the text of their essay
- to create an informative list of works cited

For essays about literature, the proper method of documentation is the MLA style, so spend class time demonstrating it. Make an effort to create exercises for your students (short sample bibliographies, for example) to give them practice with the accepted principles of formal documentation.

STRATEGIES FOR WRITING ABOUT LITERATURE: SYNOPSIS AND PARAPHRASE

Learning from Other Writers: Synopsis (p. 256)

This skill is essential for student writers. Emphasize that a clear synopsis will not only assist in establishing the chronology of a story or novel but will also challenge the skill of any writer to determine what to leave out of the information presented. Students might be asked to compose a synopsis in writing for other disciplines as well. Assignments in business and in other college courses often require a summary because a summary encapsulates necessary information.

In reading the synopsis of "The Lottery" after the critical analysis of the same work, students can readily apprehend the differences in content and form. Reiterate the distinction that the authors make between synopsis and paraphrase: A synopsis condenses information; a paraphrase retells or restates information for clarity and is not primarily concerned with length. One student remembers the difference by using the word "squeeze, as in extract only the best," to refer to a synopsis.

JONATHAN BURNS   *A Synopsis of "The Lottery"* (p. 257)

Emphasize that a synopsis is a summary of what happens in the work. As the authors point out, it describes the first level of meaning — the literal level. Students should not think of the synopsis as an interpretation but rather as a tightly constructed statement of what the author has said. One important benefit of writing a synopsis is that it encourages students to become intimate with the plot and characters of a story.

Jonathan Burns's summary of "The Lottery" pays careful attention to date, setting, primary characters, and plot. Although he necessarily leaves out material, emphasize to your students that he leaves out nothing that is essential to the plot or the impact of the story. Remind students that the synopsis is not a substitute for the story but a distillation of it, reducing it to its minimum number of important elements.

Questions to Start You Thinking (p. 258)

Meaning

1. Most students will not have difficulty understanding Jackson's story. Ask those who "didn't get it" the first time if Burns's synopsis was useful to them. What did he explain that managed to clarify meaning for them?

2. A synopsis does not at all re-create the experience of reading a short story: It packs all the necessary facts about the plot but lacks the style and flair that the writer uses to make the story enjoyable. Emphasize again to your students how important a synopsis is in helping them to understand long, complex works.

3. Your students will have little difficulty responding to this question: Most agree that Burns's synopsis demonstrates no knowledge of "hidden meaning" embedded in the tale. Some might notice an assumption that Burns makes about the story's ending, though. The last line in Jackson's story indicates that the townspeople were "upon her," referring of course to the protesting Tessie. The story leaves it at that. Burns, however, says in the last line of his synopsis that "they stoned her." This statement is technically incorrect, as Jackson does not explicitly state whether Tessie is stoned to death, even though most readers assume she was.

Writing Strategies

4–6. Most of the class will agree that Burns's chronology is in order, and that he retells the tale accurately and clearly (except for his last assumption about the fate of Mrs. Hutchinson). Ask the class to work in small groups or with a partner to critique Burns's synopsis. Have students jot down what they would add to or delete from Burns's synopsis to improve it, and then have them share their critique with the class.

7. Remind students that a synopsis should always be objective. The purpose, again, is to condense the information presented in the story and restate it for clarity — in other words, getting the facts straight and in chronological order.

When writing literary analysis, many students have difficulty devoting enough time to analysis on their first attempt and spend most of their essay giving a synopsis or plot summary instead. Point out that Burns's literary analysis incorporates an account of facts and details from the story into his interpretation of what the story means. When we assign literary analyses, we recommend that students devote no more than one-fourth to one-third of an essay (if that) to plot summary, and we ask them to be sure to devote the bulk of their essay to a discussion of what they think the story means.

LEARNING BY WRITING: SYNOPSIS

The Assignment: Writing a Synopsis of a Story by Kate Chopin (p. 258)

The assignment asks students to construct a synopsis of this story. They should be able to present this synopsis effectively in two hundred to three hundred words. Ask them to follow a specific process when whittling down their writing:

1. Read carefully and highlight the important ideas and elements.

2. Write the rough draft and read for clarity and coherence.

3. Eliminate and organize information.

4. Make a word count.

5. Read aloud and revise the draft as you read.

6. Read the story again.

7. Reread the draft and determine if it is ready to be finalized.

8. Proofread carefully.

KATE CHOPIN *The Story of an Hour* (p. 259)

Students are often intrigued by the powerful irony in this short story. Before they read this tale of reversal by Kate Chopin, remind them that an insightful analysis depends in part on their knowledge of the material — the story, the various contexts shaping the tale, and the specific elements in the writing being examined. Encourage students to think about Chopin's view of women and relationships from her nineteenth-century perspective. Ask them to reevaluate elements to which they might have been indifferent in their first reading. In particular, ask them what they make of the themes of suffocation and freedom that are so prominent in Chopin's writing. Also, ask them about the story's irony: What does it mean when the dead are alive and the living are dead? How do students feel at the end of the story? What are their attitudes toward Louise and Brently? Do they feel sympathy, relief, confusion? What overall themes, movements, and ideas do they see?

Writing a Paraphrase of a Poem (p. 261)

Although students might have worked with paraphrase in their research assignments, they will learn more about their ability to analyze by incorporating paraphrase into their evaluation process. Often students respond to poetry with a cacophony of moans and complaints. Paraphrasing poetry reconditions this initial response and allows them to decode the poem's language before they analyze and evaluate it.

OTHER ASSIGNMENTS FOR WRITING ABOUT LITERATURE (p. 261)

1. This assignment provides students with the opportunity to analyze their favorite type of literature and increases the probability for success in producing a literary analysis.

2. Students might find this task to be the most difficult format for a literary analysis. Confer with them in choosing this assignment and assess the viability of their thesis. Have they selected two characters, or two symbols, or two plots? Ask them to test their choice by listing the similarities and then listing the differences. If both lists are equally long, strong, and parallel, then they should be able to create a comparison-and-contrast essay without frustration. Also rehearse the two basic structures of a comparison-and-contrast essay: alternating and opposing. If necessary, refer students to Chapter 7 of the textbook for additional explanation of these structures.

3. This assignment corresponds with the preceding discussion, "Writing a Paraphrase of a Poem" (p. 261). Paraphrasing can force students to engage with the language of poetry and demystify a genre that some students find daunting.

4. The personal connection to the content of the poem "The Road Not Taken" will energize students' writing. Suggest that once they begin their essays, they attempt to write poetry of their own. If they have already written some poetry, encourage them to revise and reexamine their poems after analyzing the writing of Frost.

5. Students like Robinson's poems because they find them accessible. This assignment asks students to connect literary analysis to personal experience. Most students can easily identify an experience in which their perception of someone turned out to be different from what they expected and can then link that insight to "Richard Cory."

6. This assignment will appeal to many students. We ask that the students working on it produce a collaborative analysis. They can select a song, television program, or movie and work together on all stages of the writing process to produce an effective analysis. The ESL students in your class might profit from joining a group and working collaboratively on such a topic.

Writing in the Workplace (Ch. 14, p. 263)

When students leave your course, they should be prepared for a variety of writing environments. Many, however, do not know the proper language and structure for a business letter. The ability to correctly construct a memo, a letter of complaint, or a résumé will add to students' confidence. If they have written a business letter in the workplace, then suggest that they experiment with another format in this chapter. Students can refer to these models throughout the semester, with or without your assistance. Don't be surprised if your students pay closer attention to these kinds of writing. They appreciate knowing the pragmatic applications of what they have learned in composition.

Chapter 14, "Writing in the Workplace," does not contain boxes with specific suggestions for peer response, group learning, or e-writing activities. For more about incorporating these into your course, see pages 39 and 73 of this manual.

GUIDELINES FOR WRITING IN THE WORKPLACE (p. 263)

Business writing includes a variety of forms and purposes and must always carefully consider audience and context if it is to be successful. Emphasize the range of writing activities that business professionals engage in — from simple memoranda to detailed financial reports, executive reports, feasibility studies, and proposals. Whatever the kind or form of the writing, however, it must accomplish the following:

- clearly state its purpose
- understand its audience
- use an appropriate tone
- present its information in a straightforward manner

Remind your students that more than two thousand years ago, Aristotle taught that clarity is the most important virtue of style — a lesson well worth remembering today.

Know Your Purpose (p. 264)

Encourage students to strive for a firm and clear statement of purpose before they begin drafting. Have them ask themselves, "What do I want this piece of writing to do? What do I need to say to accomplish it?" Most business writing serves one or both of the following purposes: to provide information and to attempt to persuade. An end-of-the-year report to shareholders is an example of the former; a proposal designed to solicit a contract represents the latter. Business writing occasionally serves to explore, such as in feasibility studies that attempt to determine whether something is possible, but exploratory business writing is relatively rare.

Keep Your Audience in Mind (p. 264)

Understanding one's audience is critical in business writing because each audience has its own requirements for successful writing. Tell your students that understanding an audience is closely related to understanding the purpose of the writing. If the purpose is to persuade, students need to know what appeals (especially logical arguments) will work effectively with their readers. If the purpose is to inform, students must make

---

Here's an Idea . . .

To give students practice writing formal e-mail correspondence, ask each peer group to create a company and assign positions to each member of the group. Allow them to spend twenty minutes in class coming up with (1) their company's goals, (2) three things the company does well, and (3) three obstacles to the company's success. Have the CEO of each company report on these things to the class, and advise all employees to take notes.

Next, ask students to write two different kinds of formal e-mail correspondence, using what they've discovered about the companies. One e-mail should be internal, to a colleague, and the other external, to an employee in another company. Allow writers to decide whether their e-mail will take the form of a memorandum, a letter, or a résumé and what their purposes will be.

---

judgments about the audience's level of knowledge. Emphasize to students the importance of a writer's relationship to his or her audience; if writers do not understand their audience, they cannot achieve their purpose.

Use an Appropriate Tone (p. 265)

A writer's tone indicates to the reader of a business communication what the writer thinks of him or her. Emphasize that the tone must be appropriately formal and rarely jocular or chatty. Although the tone should never be condescending or pompous, it should always be polite and restrained. Courtesy is axiomatic to business writing. Even letters of complaint should be respectful of the reader.

Present Information Carefully (p. 265)

Encourage students to write in such a manner that sentences and paragraphs quickly yield their meaning. Readers should be able to skim through the writing and quickly distill key ideas and information. Students should be particularly careful to present accurate information and to identify important elements early on with clear topic sentences. There is no place in good business writing for unnecessary amplification or even brief digression: The text should be as succinct and concise as possible.

BUSINESS LETTERS (p. 266)

The format of a business letter is illustrated on text page 267. Remind students that a flush left/block paragraph is an appropriate business format.

Consider having students write a business letter. Suggest that this exercise be a letter of complaint or inquiry. Have them use peer editors in the classroom to proofread the final rough draft. If students are in the computer lab, they can print out their first draft or work at the computer together. You might need to remind students that the final typed business letter should contain no errors. Their complaints or applications might be ignored or discarded because of poor mechanics. Tell students that letters that result in a written response from the recipient will receive an A on the assignment. If this assignment occurs late in the semester, you might want to require only that they mail their letters to receive an A.

MEMORANDA (p. 270)

Memorandum writing is usually foreign to undergraduate students. You might want to suggest that students draft a memo to someone in the class. Reinforce the structure and specify that a memo must present a message in very few words.

E-MAIL (p. 270)

E-mail has become a common vehicle for business correspondence, and your students should be familiar with it. Although e-mail sometimes conveys a feeling of informality because of its ease and speed of transmission, electronically transmitted documents can be quite formal. Students should remember that e-mail in the business world is usually expected to conform to standard formal writing practices, many of which we have just addressed. Your students should be no less careful in their electronic writing than in traditional forms of writing. In particular, they should be concerned with knowing their audience, writing toward a purpose, and being concise, precise, and appropriate. Have your students work on their e-mail habits by writing a series of half-page and one-page messages that parallel the writing assignments for business writing (résumés and letters of application and complaint).

RÉSUMÉS AND APPLICATION LETTERS (p. 272)

Several students might have drafted a résumé already; they could bring in the most recent version to share with their group. Most of your students will need to practice this skill. Ask them to sketch out the rough draft of an emphatic résumé during a class period. Remind them to emphasize their talents and skills. This exercise also reinforces for novice writers the importance of mechanics and format. For help with layout and headings, refer them to Chapter 21, "Strategies for Designing Your Document." Suggest that students peruse the want ads, choose a job in a field that interests them, and compose a letter applying for the job. If some students have already composed a real letter of application, suggest that they bring the letter to class for writing groups to assess.

Writing for Assessment (Ch. 15, p. 277)

Your students need the information in this chapter! It focuses on pragmatic strategies to succeed in a writing environment that they will be sure to encounter in their college careers. Many students, out of anxiety or inexperience, fail to read carefully and to understand exam questions. Many "clutch" and fail to use the writing processes they have been practicing all semester. Even with limited time, writers can use the processes of discovering, developing, and revising ideas to demonstrate the quality of their thinking about what they are learning. Try to sequence this chapter into your syllabus by midterm, when most students will be asked to write on demand. If you asked students to write a timed essay during the first week of your course, use this chapter to build on those efforts. The strategies for writing essay exams are skills that students can use immediately and successfully.

Chapter 15, "Writing for Assessment," includes this activity:

- For Group Learning (p. 285). See page 39 of this manual for advice about how to use this feature.

ESSAY EXAMINATIONS (p. 277)

We suggest that you not waste much energy lamenting the fact that writing on demand does not allow writers enough time and space to produce their best and fullest writing. Instead, focus on helping them demonstrate competency in such writing situations. Students tend to demonstrate the same strengths and weaknesses they have in writing situations over which they have more control. And certainly the opportunity to bring knowledge alive rather than subject it to a multiple-choice evaluation fosters active learning.

Why do instructors use essay exams even though they take considerable time to assess? We think most teachers appreciate the pragmatic and cognitive results of an essay exam. Most courses incorporate multiple forms of measurement, but essays remain a reliable structure of evaluation that requires critical thinking and proficiency

---

Here's an Idea . . .

To help students answer specific questions, put short-answer and essay-exam questions on an overhead transparency or handouts. Have students do the following:

- Underline the key words.
- Identify the number of parts the answer will require.
- Determine the information they must provide in each part.

For example, if the exam reads, "The medieval world revolved around the manor, the castle, and the church. Discuss the role each institution played in the medieval world," students should underline the words *medieval, manor, castle, church, discuss,* and *each* and identify that the answer will have three parts: (1) Discuss the role of the manor, (2) discuss the role of the castle, (3) discuss the role of the church in the medieval world.

---

in equal measure. Essay exams assess both whether students have acquired knowledge and if students are synthesizing the new ideas they have been exposed to in a course.

In some states students might be required by law to take a competency test that includes an essay. This exam is often a pass/fail test at the second-year level.

Learning from Another Writer (p. 278)

Questions to Start You Thinking (p. 279)

Meaning

1. The main idea is clearly in the first sentence of Cohn's exam answer: "Research on infants is probably the best way to demonstrate that some factors in perceptual organization are innate." Point out how this sentence rephrases the exam question and uses key words from that question. Also draw students' attention to how the structure of each paragraph includes a different research finding and to how the key word research is repeated in each paragraph.

2. This question asks students to read the essay from the instructor's perspective. Such an activity helps students develop self-assessing skills.

Writing Strategies

3. Have students list the instances of concrete and specific answers. Show them similar instances in other samples of student exams.

4. If any students answer yes to this question, you've got a good opportunity to talk about "bluffing" in exams. Many students, in fact, end exam essays with such

---

Here's an Idea . . .

Have groups of students create an essay exam. This exercise will give students the opportunity to practice their critical reading skills by preparing questions for an essay exam on readings. Ask class members to vote on a selection of readings from *The Bedford Guide* that could form a unit. Next, discuss the information they want to assess and the different criteria for the questions students will create. The groups should vary the type of questions they produce on their exam, using the guidelines in the textbook, and look carefully at each type of question to decide the criteria for evaluating it. Be sure to limit the number of questions students will write — four seems to work well in a short period of time.

After your students have constructed their questions, collect them and read them aloud, or you might want to have the groups give one another the exams. Students might answer all questions, choose just one question to answer, or come up with consensus answers. If you ask them to select only one of the questions to answer, also ask them to explain why they have selected the question they did. You might discover the type of question that most appeals to students and why they feel confident in answering it.

Return the exams and answers to the originators and ask each group to assess the responses with a letter grade. Caution students that this is not an opportunity for retaliation but an experience that can increase their chance for success in essay examinations. Finally, distinguish among the levels of competence (the A, B, C exams). Use the sampler of responses that you have read aloud or that groups have answered together to show how a competent (C) paper meets the criteria and how a B or an A paper exceeds them.

claims — more from lack of confidence in the writing than from attempts to put something over on instructors. Some of those students even write apologetic or hesitant conclusions such as "What I think I showed here is that there are innate features . . ." or "I hope I have made it clear to you that there are innate features. . . ." Such conclusions, of course, could weaken what might otherwise be clear and assertive writing. Talk with your students about revisions that enhance and weaken an essay.

Generating Ideas (p. 279)

Some instructors try to teach students to follow exam directions carefully by giving a pop quiz, such as "You can earn up to 50 points extra credit with this quiz or you can lose up to 10 points credit. First, read all the directions carefully. Then do exactly what they tell you." And half the class might have started doing all the silly things each question directed them to do, discovering at some point that other students were sitting quietly and smirking because they had already read all the way through the directions to the last statement, which said, "Now ignore everything you have just read, sign your name, and sit quietly until your colleagues finish their exam." Those who didn't read ahead probably never again will forget to first read all of the exam questions carefully. The authors' advice that students resist the temptation to start scribbling (p. 279) is crucial. Do whatever you need to do to make your students hear and follow it.

Understanding assessment and evaluation removes much of the anxiety for students and enables instructors to create a valid measure of knowledge and proficiency. Discuss with students the list of directive words on page 279. Advise them to read each exam question and to underscore any directive words. Remind them that directions such as "three examples," "causes and effects," "in all the literature we discussed this month," and "choose four readings" are exactly the directions that instructors expect them to follow and that will be part of the criteria of evaluation. Have them underscore such terms.

Try using a very simple exercise that combines several directive words and asks students to suggest what information they would supply in an exam. For example, ask them how they would respond to the following directions: "Evaluate why snakes produce a fear response," "Describe the fear response elicited by snakes in humans," "Trace the development of the fear of snakes," and "Contrast the fear response to snakes and to lizards." We believe that this exercise is especially important to first- and second-year writers because they often lack the experience to discriminate among tasks.

Planning for Typical Exam Questions (p. 280)

Bring in additional examples of exam questions to give students the chance to practice the kind of thinking they will need to do while prewriting for in-class essay exams. Or bring in provocative quotations and have impromptu writing sessions in which students respond to the quotations. Try this wake-up exercise to prompt discussion. Tell students, "Discuss your reaction to and thoughts about the following statement . . . ," and then ask them to write for five minutes. In-class exercises allow you to observe how students respond to "short answers" and to report back to them about their test-taking skills.

Drafting: The Only Version (p. 282)

The advice here is clear and practical. Perhaps one of the most valuable strategies you can impart to students is how to organize their time for an essay examination. Ask them for the systems they've used up to this point — what has worked and what has not. Remind them that they must divide their time quickly and effectively at the begin-

---

Here's an Idea . . .

Ask your students to write a letter to you about their "postexam evaluations" of their graded responses to the group essay exam. Ask them to use the Essay Exam Checklist (p. 284) for the prewriting and then to tell you what they discovered about their performance. In their final paragraph, they should report two resolutions they have made to help them on the next on-demand writing situation they encounter.

---

ning of the exam and not rely on verbal warnings. Many students have stated that they spend too much time on the first few questions and run out of time at the end. ESL students might need particular reinforcement and repetition for planning strategy at this stage. Help all students relax by letting them know that instructors do not expect perfection in timed writings.

Remind your students to make their essays clear and smooth for the instructor. Advise them to double-space their answers so that they can go back and insert material or write above lines they have crossed out.

Revising: Rereading and Proofing (p. 283)

We have observed many students in on-demand writing situations and can testify that many finish early. We are always surprised when those students don't take the extra minutes to read back over their responses and revise. Assuming that students have prepared carefully for the essay exam, they can use the rewriting opportunity to dramatically improve their responses. Often, they'll see that they left out one example when the assignment specified three. Or they'll realize that they haven't defined all the terms required. At the content level, the students need to use any time left to check for competence.

In addition, because their responses are read against one another for content and for overall impression of the quality of their thinking, students need to use questions like those in the Essay Exam Checklist (p. 284) that evaluate performance and that can lead to important revisions.

Ask students to talk about any revisions they made that they thought were important to their success with the exam. Share your observations with them. Encourage them to learn to pace themselves in on-demand writing situations. Often the test administrators will write the time remaining on the board.

Here's an Idea . . .

Bring to class a number of essay test questions. (Ask colleagues in other fields to supply some.) Have students practice thesis statements for their papers by turning an interrogative sentence into a declarative sentence that states the thesis, or by restating an imperative sentence as a thesis sentence. Explain to students that by restating the question in this way, they will be sure to answer exactly the question that was asked rather than making the mistake of just writing about the topic in question.

Here's an Idea . . .

Write one topic on the board. Then give the class five minutes to decide on a slant and to write a thesis and a scratch outline of the major points they will develop in their writing. Have each student read his or her thesis and major points to the class. Respond to each major point, commenting briefly on whether it is on topic, adequately limited, and clearly expressed as a logical sub-point of the thesis. Limit your comments to two minutes or less if possible. From this activity students will see the variety that is available in responses to only one prompt and thus will feel freer to make the topic their own.

The For Group Learning activity in this chapter (p. 285) will also help students to see the variety of answers for any one question. Even if the question calls for a factual answer, one individual will answer the question differently from another. Help students to build confidence to respond to the prompt honestly and not try to impress the instructor with a formulaic response or with a lot of hot air.

Observe and take notes about the rewriting behaviors of your students during essay exams. Compile a folder with these notes and past essays. Ask your colleagues for samples of completed essays that represent all points on a grading scale. Keep these as a current and accessible source of material to use when advising students on the strategies for this type of writing.

SHORT-ANSWER EXAMINATIONS (p. 284)

You'll notice that we recommend using many of the Questions to Start You Thinking as warm-up exercises; these could just as easily be adapted to practice short-answer exams. Have students trade their answers and evaluate them after a discussion of what minimally constitutes a short answer. Ask them to spend ten minutes revising the short answers for which they did not receive full credit and then to write a short self-assessment letter about goals they will set for taking their next short-answer exams.

TIMED WRITINGS (p. 284)

Consider simulating this experience to assist your students in preparing for their exams in other courses. Many of your students' courses in the humanities, the social sciences, philosophy, and literature will routinely use in-class essay exams. Another reason to require in-class writing in your course is that practice in this type of written evaluation helps students strengthen their skills in critical reading and critical writing.

If your college uses any wide-scale assessment for placement, exemption, proficiency, or graduation competency, students should have experiences similar to those they will undergo during those assessments. Is this practice "teaching to the test"? Of course it is. But if the assessment calls for a writing sample — and we all agree that only a direct measure of actual student writing is appropriate — do not hesitate to help students prepare for it. Among other things, such a simulation can help demystify the writing exam.

Again, observe the in-class writing strategies of your students and report back to them. Bring in photocopies of student essays (without names) and ask students to evaluate them — either holistically or using primary-trait scoring — and establish a range of least to most successful responses. For more about these types of assessment, see Chapter 6 of this manual.

If you don't use a grading system comparable to the college- or state-mandated assessments, you might want to duplicate and explain the scale for timed writings. This information will assist students in their understanding of the evaluation and connect it to the timed writings in your classroom. Again show students how you apply criteria of evaluation and give them a sampler of student responses that range from least to most successful. Then ask them to use the Essay Exam Checklist on page 284 to write a letter evaluating their performance as in-class essay writers.

As you discuss topics for in-class writing assignments with students, review the essay-exam questions discussed in the section that begins on page 280. Remind them that they will have only one topic for a timed writing and will usually be expected to develop it more fully than they would if they were answering several questions on an essay exam. Also remind them that the purpose of an in-class writing assignment is to see how well they write, whereas the purpose of an essay exam is to see how much they know. Bring in some topics that you and your colleagues have used, and ask students to explain how they would respond to each prompt.

Finally, allow students to use the in-class essay as a first draft. Ask them to revise the essay. Help them to generate a peer-evaluation checklist and set up a workshop or peer-editing session. Have them submit all drafts and peer advice. In your final comments to the writer, focus on how effectively he or she revised from in-class draft to final submission. In our classes, students are required to submit one revised timed writing among the essays in their portfolio. Usually students will have written three timed writings, including the diagnostic essay, before portfolios are assembled.

WRITING FOR PORTFOLIO ASSESSMENT (p. 286)

With the growing emphasis on institutional assessment, portfolio assessment is becoming more and more widespread. At some point, your students will probably be required to produce a portfolio. Advise them to pay close attention to the directions they are given and not to rely on what they have done in the past. Requirements will vary from instructor to instructor, course to course, and institution to institution, and a great deal rides on successfully meeting those requirements. Explain that portfolio assessment has big advantages: It provides the opportunity to revise, to implement all of the strategies that students have learned, and to present their best writing for a grade. For more about using portfolios in composition courses, see Chapter 6 of this manual.

Consider asking students to write reflective pieces on at least some of the essays they write. This will give them a context for their presentation portfolio piece, and it will give you a chance to provide feedback on their revision process. Encourage them to use the Discovery Checklist on page 289 as a starting point in their response. Guide them to look at specific strengths and weaknesses in each essay and help them devise strategies that they might use to revise the weak areas. The more they reflect on their own writing, the more they will improve.

Caution students that dressing up their presentation portfolios is no substitute for putting forth their best writing effort. No matter how nice their portfolios look, the writing must speak for itself. Also, we can't emphasize enough the need for students to back up their writing. Countless times we have seen students despondent because a file or document that contained all of their portfolio writing was destroyed on their computer's hard drive or CD. A flash drive or zip disk is a good investment.

A Writer's Strategies

Strategies for Generating Ideas
(Ch. 16, p. 294)

Some instructors choose to begin their course by teaching Part Four of *A Writer's Guide*, while others encourage their students to dip into these chapters throughout the term, as needed. However you decide to use this part of the book, be sure to spend some time with your students on Chapter 16. Few students have had past opportunity to focus on this important first step in the writing process: that of discovering a subject. This chapter not only provides specific techniques for finding ideas, but it also gives students advice about the importance of taking the time to get ready to write.

Chapter 16, "Strategies for Generating Ideas," contains the following activities:

- For Group Learning (p. 297). See page 39 of this manual for advice about how to use this feature.

- For E-Writers (pp. 299 and 307). See page 73 of this manual for advice about how to use this feature.

FINDING IDEAS (p. 294)

Most students enter college believing they have little to write about and even less that is worth saying. One of the most important things they can learn in a composition course is how to search their minds and to use other resources to find a topic and ideas to support it. In this section the authors provide detailed suggestions to help students get over this hurdle. Here we've also included a description of an additional device, the tagmemic grid, which our students have found useful for generating ideas and material to begin their drafts. Take class time to allow students to practice each of the discovery techniques.

Building from Your Assignment (p. 294)

Students often plunge into writing without a clear understanding of the assignment. Refer to the steps on page 296 each time you assign writing. Having a clear and specific understanding of the task will allow students to focus inventive processes in the right direction and help them avoid a false start that might frustrate and discourage them.

Brainstorming (p. 296)

We can't overstate how useful this technique is in generating ideas for writing, for class discussions, and for solutions to personal problems. Tell your students that brainstorming, like most invention strategies, is more than a way to begin; it can be equally profitable to the writer who is redrafting and to group members who come to an impasse in problem-solving. The more students understand about how each person approaches a topic differently, the more relaxed and productive they will be about brainstorming ideas they can use in their writing. Don't assume that all of your students enter college practiced in this skill.

Here's an Idea . . .

Have students list everything on which they consider themselves to be experts. Most will not believe they have any area of expertise, so ask them how many are experts on making excuses to parents? On programming a cell phone or DVD player? On finding information on the Web? On decorating a dorm room? On caring for a younger sibling? They will get the idea and soon generate a lengthy list. In the process, they will discover that they do have something to say.

The For E-Writers tip on "invisible writing" (p. 299) is especially effective for brainstorming. Because students can't see what they are writing, they are freed from concern about grammar, spelling, and punctuation errors. This strategy is particularly helpful for students with high writing anxiety and even writer's block. Before students start this activity, assure them that you will not go through the writing and mark the things that are "wrong."

Freewriting (p. 298)

Ask students to freewrite for ten minutes in class and then to tell you what happened. Most skeptical writers are astounded by how difficult it is just to write "nothing to write about" over and over. It seems that the mind shifts into gear and comes up with something to shape into meaning. But that "something" is not arbitrary; it is often an insight or realization that the writer feels compelled to explore. Ten minutes of freewriting might be more writing than some writing-anxious students have ever produced in one sitting. Consider asking students to freewrite on a computer. The speed of word processing makes it a good tool for freewriting. Also, students who experience serious physical difficulties with cursive writing can write more easily on a computer.

It's helpful to compile a repertoire for directed and nondirected freewriting activities for your students. Here are a few methods:

- Read aloud your own poetry and the poetry of other writers at the beginning of class. Before reading the poetry aloud, instruct your students to write anything that comes into their minds — as Peter Elbow calls it, "first thoughts." Give students five to ten minutes of class time to freewrite a response.

- Read aloud to students for the first three or four minutes of each class a provocative newspaper article or essay. Ask students to freewrite in response to the content.

- Use the statistics found in "The *Harper's* Index" as a prompt for freewriting. Students will find it entertaining as well as informative to peruse these numbers compiled in the monthly magazine.

- Introduce persuasive writing by asking students to freewrite about what makes them angry. When they finish, they will be fired up and move eagerly into the assignment.

- Introduce causal analysis by asking students to observe a painting or photograph of people for a few minutes and then to freewrite until you ask them to stop. Then have them read over what they have written and speculate about what might have caused them to write part of the passage. Continue by asking them to freewrite about what happened the day before the scene depicted in the image, what happened in the first ten minutes after, what happened in the three years leading up to what the image depicted, and what might happen a week after the depiction.

Doodling or Sketching (p. 299)

Using doodling as a writing resource will be a novel idea for most students. This strategy will emphasize the notion that ideas for writing can come from anywhere, and they should use whatever strategies work best for them. Use doodling to spur a discussion of other possible invention strategies. Encourage your students to give free rein to their imaginations.

Mapping (p. 301)

Like doodling, mapping is a good strategy for visual learners. Additionally, it taps into students' spatial creativity. You might bring packages of sticky notes to class so that students can practice the type of mapping shown in the figure on p. 302 of the text. Model the process to get them started.

Imagining (p. 302)

Discuss with your students the writing of Alvin Toffler and John Naisbitt and the impact their ideas have had on thinking in our society. Ask them to bring in other articles or essays that imagine futuristic scenarios that might result from present-day practices.

Imagining a reader's point of view is crucial to successful writing. For many of your students, considering other possible perspectives is difficult because of egocentric thinking. Hold conferences with them about the specific reader they have imagined for their essay and the assumptions they have generated about what the reader knows and feels (see the Quick Start suggestion on p. 302).

Asking a Reporter's Questions (p. 303)

It's important that writers use this discovery device for each writing assignment during the course. Reading about a process differs radically from experiencing it, and students will not believe how productive these invention strategies can be until you ask them to practice them. Even though this pattern of questioning comes naturally to many problem-solvers, some students need practice so that it becomes habitual and feels natural.

These questions can also become the method for successful peer editing. Ask students to reformulate general remarks to be more constructive. Remarks like "That introduction was too boring" or "That thesis didn't sound right" usually provoke a defensive response from a writer. Show students that using a reporter's question to shape a criticism, such as "Why did you include the list of details in the introduction?" or "What was your thesis?" directs the writer to the part of his or her essay that needs revision. While this skill does take practice, it works well with student writers.

Seeking Motives (p. 305)

The authors explain that using Burke's pentad is similar to asking a reporter's questions but differs in that Burke's pentad focuses on motivations for an act. Using this systematic questioning, students can generate an amazing amount of detailed information with which to develop their topic.

Here's an Idea . . .

Bring in ads from one issue of a weekly news magazine. First ask the class to identify the assumption about consumer values that underlies each ad, and then make a list of all the assumptions. Ask students to challenge each assumption by reversing the statement. If the class identified the assumption "Americans value speed," a reversal would be "Americans value a slow, steady pace."

Next, have the class challenge an assumption by qualifying it with *some* and *others:* "Some Americans — particularly those who live in a megalopolis — want subways to whisk them four miles to work in three minutes flat. Others — including the residents of Mayberry, RFD — want to check out the new grass as they amble to the office." Have students write several variations. Comparing and contrasting is one way to generate new ideas from old facts.

Bring to class some articles from newspapers or weekly news magazines such as *Time* or *Newsweek.* On the board, make a column for each pentad component (actor, agency, and so on). Then recall details of an event described in an article and fill in the columns with relevant information. Next break the class into groups and distribute the articles, asking the students to compile more details for each component. Have the groups report back the additions to each column as you record them on the board. Finally, ask students to generate additional information by combining components, and record the results. Be prepared to cover the board.

This exercise produces a surprising amount of information, and students will readily see the potential for developing their own ideas with Burke's pentad. Requiring them to submit pentad information with drafts will allow you to point out where they might use other information to develop their ideas more fully.

Keeping a Journal (p. 306)

Every first-year writing course should include some kind of daily writing. Ask students to spend at least fifteen minutes a day writing in a journal or on a computer (have them print the text). For some students, that will be more time than they've ever spent writing.

Requiring students to keep journals will lead many to reclaim writing as a way of talking to the self and as a way of soul-making. Many will find journal writing valuable enough that they will continue to write in a journal long after you require it. Daily practice, with flexible topics, will free up writers and help to demystify the act of writing. Suggest some specific topics but leave a few entries per week up to the writer. Comment tactfully on the kinds of writing that you expect — not just a "daily record" but something that shows the writers actively involved in some personal or critical way with the activities within and around them. If need be, ask students to rethink and revise daily records.

Journal writing also provides opportunities for metacognition as well as personal expression. We recommend a shift to or the introduction of a reading journal to encourage students to see themselves as critical readers and to improve their reading and evaluating skills. Remind them that they can review their journal entries when they are generating topics for assignments or need to provide additional evidence for a claim. Show them examples of Virginia Woolf's diary, which she clearly uses as a place to freewrite, to record conversations and reflect on them, to try out ideas, or to imagine an alternative to what she's observed and analyzed. Both novices and veterans in an academic community need ways to process what is happening within and around them. Try keeping a journal at the same time about what is happening as you teach writers. At the end of the semester you can evaluate what has been successful and what has not and use these logs to change your course syllabus.

Do not grade journals; instead, respond with comments that tell the writers you are "listening." In particular, point out ideas that could be developed into longer writings and patterns of feelings or ideas that suggest topics the writers could tap for writing assignments. Establish a dialogue with students through their journals. Encourage them to select two or three entries from the journal that they can work into a connected sequence of writing and submit for evaluation as a series.

Some instructors choose not to collect journals at all during the semester. We believe that you should create a system that works for you, but bear in mind that a journal is a writer's tool, a record and a source for ideas, a place for self-evaluation and analysis. If a student chooses to ignore the value and benefit of writing daily in a notebook or journal, he or she will learn the natural consequences. We write daily, and our students know this; we share any and all tidbits we find about journal and response writing.

Consider introducing students to the following perspectives on journal writing. In *A Writer Teaches Writing* (Boston: Houghton, 1984), Donald M. Murray calls his log or journal a "daybook":

> I am able to make use of fragments of time because my tools, first and foremost my daybook, are with me at all times. . . .
> I use an eight-by-ten-inch notebook because it fits in the outside pocket of the case I sling over my shoulder. I use a spiral book because it can easily be bent back and made to fit my lap or whatever surface. . . .
> If you decide to try a daybook or log, remember that it does not contain finished writing. It can be a place for writing a draft, but my book at least has all sorts of other writing that doesn't even look like writing. Everyone's daybook will change and evolve as the writer changes and evolves. . . .
> The spirit of play should never be lost. It is central to the conception of this book. What I am trying to do in this book is to explore for myself and for you —in that order — the writing process and a way of teaching that will make that process available to my students. This is such a serious business, it must not be taken too seriously. (68, 69–70)

Professor Ann Berthoff asks students to keep a double-entry journal for their research process. On the left side of the page the student logs notes about readings, observations about the material, interpretations of research data, and revisions of the research question. On the right side of the page, after looking again at each entry and reflecting on it, he or she writes any new perceptions or clarifications or revisions of the entry that might go into the essay. A double-entry journal can be fairly easily accommodated by word processing. Some programs have a split-screen feature, and most programs have a column feature. Berthoff encourages students also to observe and write about their process of research and reflection. This kind of journal leads students to reflect on their reflecting.

The Tagmemic Grid

This additional invention strategy, not covered in the textbook, is particularly useful for comparing and contrasting and for asking questions in order to clarify definitions. The tagmemic grid, a heuristic developed by Richard E. Young, Alton L. Becker, and Kenneth L. Pike in *Rhetoric: Discovery and Change* (New York: Harcourt, 1970), can galvanize classes who work together with this exercise. If you decide to experiment with it, set aside several class periods.

Basically, the rhetoricians who developed the tagmemic grid assume that we discover and generate new ideas by combining and recombining units of "qualification." As we look at a topic, we see more and different things each time we shift our perspective. Young, Becker, and Pike borrow the descriptors *particle, wave,* and *field* from physicists to describe a systematic process of shifting perspective. They also introduce three major questions for writers to ask after each shift. The result is a nine-part matrix of materials.

When they work with this grid, students find that they have generated large chunks of material to refine further in their shaping of a thesis, to use for developing their hunches, to provide support for generalizations, and to lead them as they think through a topic. From the abundance of perspectives, facts, half-ideas, guesses, observations, intuitions, and descriptions generated by the grid's systematic questioning, students move easily into drafting an essay. It is one of the most "aerobic" prewriting strategies we know of; students will comment on how hard they thought and will appreciate the quantity of writing they produced.

Begin with the vocabulary: A *particle* perspective breaks down a topic into all the parts that it comprises. A *wave* perspective looks for the interrelationship of several particles as they create a continuum of meaning. A *field* perspective describes the larger range or area of relationships into which the topic meshes. Shifting among these perspectives is like using a zoom lens to focus in and out.

Because student writers often leap across levels of abstraction when they are drafting and don't consciously know what high-speed intuiting and thinking happened during the leap, this technique is particularly useful in helping them to discover and to develop the interstices. Readers need the interstices. Most writers reviewing their work are still so caught up in creating it that they don't notice the gaps in the writing that have been left by the leaps across levels of abstraction.

For each of the perspectives, Young, Becker, and Pike recommend asking questions about contrast, variance, and distribution: "How does this contrast with others in its class?" "How much can this vary and still be itself?" and "How is this distributed within its class?"

What follows is a model of how to organize a grid on a board. The second diagram is a grid that one of Shirley Morahan's composition classes generated over two days of prewriting for an assignment to write about a campus issue on which students had an opinion. The topic is familiar enough: inadequate campus parking. When you lead students through these questions, you model for them a behavior of constantly asking questions to generate ideas and to clarify the relationships of ideas. As with brainstorming, stop now and then and read aloud what you've written on the board. Ideas come as frequently from arbitrary juxtaposition as from logical association.

SAMPLE TAGMEMIC GRID

	CONTRAST How does it differ from others in its class?	VARIATION How much can it change and still be itself?	DISTRIBUTION How is it distributed within a system?
PARTICLE (Static)			
WAVE (Dynamic)			
FIELD (System)			

COMPLETED TAGMEMIC GRID

	CONTRAST How is it unique?	VARIATION How much can it change and still be itself?	DISTRIBUTION How does it fit within a system?
PARTICLE	Parking 80 percent around dorms; 20 percent by classroom buildings. No meters. Fines enforced only for students. Unpaved gravel lots. Potholes. Crowded by 9 a.m. Unlike UMSL, no visitor parking. Many small lots; no parking garage. No protection from the elements. Unclear markings. Lack of specialized parking. Poorly lit. 200 spaces short of cars registered.	Build garages in the 20 percent of lots near classroom buildings. Pave lots over summer with fees generated by meters. More complex registration with more options. Meters for visitors and prime-time class hours. Put in underground parking in 20 percent of lots. If more costly, still problematic. More bureaucracy with more options? Safer lots with more lighting.	Integration of parking with services unusual on campuses. Scanty parking typical of state universities? Lack of specialized parking more frequent in less crowded campuses. Bad roads typical of public institutions.
WAVE (Inadequate facilities)	Affects more students than inadequacies of cashiers. Less solvable during academic year. Physical inadequacy more than academic. For commuters, more delays, stress, violence. For residents, not a daily hassle. Unevenness of opportunity. Bad administrative planning, such as lack of classrooms, unconcern for people who should be served.	Shift in student perception of university. New mission of university requires decrease of inadequacy. Planning can consider future effects. Increase in students' happiness; bring in more students. Good parking = close-to-perfect campus personality. Other campus facilities still inadequate; keeps reputation. Keeps students happier longer. Source of stress becomes academic inadequacies?	Transportation and parking perennial student problems. More of a problem in rural and small college towns? Physical facilities always low priority with campus planners? Same bad planning shown over and over on other campuses. Typical example of administrators' indifference to students.
FIELD (Inefficiency of campuses nationwide)	Less modern than urban campuses. Typical of state-funded universities. Minimal student input into planning. Little application of business theory. Result of rapid growth of school in 1970s. Complicated by shift from in loco parentis. Less "ecological."	Life becomes easier; school becomes nationally known. Sell "parking model" to other campuses; new revenue. Improved academic environment; increased learning. Makes it twenty-first-century campus. Shows others how to use good planning.	Part of unnecessary stress of American life. Miniature of parking problems in many crowded areas. Bad conditions like highway and bridge systems. Lack of specialization part of American individualism? Injustice of picking on poorest members familiar nationwide. Part of grimy contemporary quality of life.

Contrast (First Vertical Grid)

Particle What are the essential characteristics of this "particle" that distinguishes it from others in its class? What makes it unique in its class?

What are the essential characteristics of your campus parking lot that might not appear on another campus? How are these the characteristics of this particular campus parking lot and not of any parking lot?

Wave How do the several particles organized here in a wave differ from others of their class? What makes this process different from other processes like it?

How would the organization of handicapped spaces and of faculty, student, and staff spaces differ from organization of spaces in a commercial parking lot or (to change the class) differ from organization of building space?

Field How do the several waves working together as a system differ in their functioning from some other systems of their class?

How would the hierarchical privileges regarding parking lots and libraries at an educational institution differ in policy from those of health-care and in municipal institutions?

Variation (Second Vertical Grid)

Particle How much can these essential characteristics vary or change with the subject still remaining in its class?

Could a parking lot operated commercially by students still be considered "campus parking"? Could spaces be "first come, first served" and the lot still satisfy the needs of campus parking?

Wave How much could this process vary and the subject still be itself?

How much could the organization of spaces change from academic rank having privilege to choice spaces for nonpolluting vehicles and for carpooling vehicles without widespread complaints about the parking area not serving the "campus"?

Field How much could the several waves change in the way they work together as a system with the subject remaining itself?

How much could the campus parking policy of state institutions be redesigned for health and aesthetic concerns without legislative criticism of misuse of funds tagged for "campus parking"? How much could the university banish hierarchy of privilege in campus parking and retain it in library privileges and remain the "same friendly campus"?

Distribution (Third Vertical Grid)

Particle How are the essential characteristics and their variations distributed in a larger context?

To what extent are the problems of the campus parking lot representative of similar problems in long-term planning by the institution? How much does the lack of handicapped access to campus parking mirror the lack of handicapped access to the institution's buildings and grounds overall?

Wave How are the waves, the organizations of processes, distributed in a larger context?

Is a "rank-has-privileges" parking policy a typical American pattern? How frequently is "faculty first" demonstrated in American universities?

Field   How is the system distributed in a larger context of systems?

How much is the rigidity demonstrated in administrative responses to faculty and student complaints about poor campus planning, as evidenced by the parking situation, a function of any bureaucracy? How frequently in American urban areas would redesign for health and aesthetic concerns override cost-analysis concerns?

As Morahan's class moved down the perspective and across the heuristic, the questions became more detailed at the same time that they required a more analytical response. A wide variety of questions occurs, and a wide variety of connections is made. If you use the tagmemic grid with your students, you need to be able to ask those narrowing and restating questions that follow the basic question for each category. As you do that, you show students the need to ask the right questions in order to come to new insights.

Encourage students to go off and practice asking these questions systematically. Don't be discouraged if on their own their materials are not as numerous and their insights not as startling as during the synergy of the class session. Many students have never been shown how to think through a topic; they will have to practice before they feel confident and competent with the mental habit of inquiry. Even if your writers come up with scanty grids, incorporate the basic questions from the three perspectives in your comments about writing whenever appropriate. Remind writers that systematic questioning will almost always lead them in some new direction or generate some new materials.

GETTING READY (p. 308)

We call it "pencil sharpening": all those ways people have developed to put off starting a draft. The desk needs to be organized. Oh, and the right music must be playing. We suspect you have your own methods of pencil sharpening and that some kind of inventing and incubating occurs even as you fiddle around with the environment in which you will start to write. Talking about these predrafting behaviors can reassure writers about how natural and human their own drafting behavior might be. Share your pencil-sharpening techniques with students, and tell them about some of the bizarre rituals of professional writers or your friends.

Strategies for Stating a Thesis and Planning
(Ch. 17, p. 310)

Instruction on planning an essay accompanies the main assignment for each chapter in *A Writer's Guide*, along with advice on developing a thesis to guide a paper. However, students might at times find that they need more help preparing to write or that they need to focus on the structure of their essay in order to revise it. Refer these students to Chapter 17 of their textbooks for more information about stating and using a thesis and organizing their ideas.

Chapter 17, "Strategies for Stating a Thesis and Planning," contains the following activities:

- For Group Learning (p. 313). See page 39 of this manual for advice about how to use this feature.
- For E-Writers (p. 325). See page 73 of this manual for advice about how to use this feature.

SHAPING YOUR TOPIC FOR YOUR PURPOSE AND YOUR AUDIENCE (p. 310)

It is crucial that students identify their purpose and audience before they begin to write. This knowledge will help them make decisions about both the information to include and the structure to follow. Ask them to work through the activity on page 312 using the writing task on which they are embarking. Have them write the audience and the purpose at the top of the page when they begin planning. The constant reminder will help them stay focused as they build their writing.

STATING AND USING A THESIS (p. 312)

Even though most writers benefit from thinking more carefully about stating a thesis and using it explicitly or implicitly to organize their writing, some will latch on to this as the only strategy for shaping a draft. The authors discourage this habit by emphasizing that a writer arrives at a thesis in multiple and unpredictable ways, tapping many resources.

Many students have trouble grasping the difference between the topic and the thesis. Have students work through their ideas using the questions in the chart on page 315. Then direct them to the Draft Doctor on page 320. This tool, new to the eighth edi-

---

Here's an Idea . . .

Have students select one essay from their portfolios and highlight the thesis statement. If it is implicit, ask them to write it at the top of the first page. Then have them exchange papers with a classmate who will evaluate the thesis using the four suggestions for writing a thesis on pages 316–17. Have the pairs discuss their evaluations with each other and offer suggestions for strengthening the thesis statements or cite reasons that they are sufficiently strong. Follow up by having each student report to the class what he or she will do to revise the thesis.

> *Here's an Idea...*
>
> To help students refine their thesis statement, have them rewrite it, eliminating all of the "to be" verbs (*is, are, am, was, were*). You may want to have students work in groups, helping each other to find ways to recast the sentences. In eliminating "to be" verbs, students are forced to provide more specific information. A precise thesis statement will guide students' choices about information they should include or exclude as they write.

tion, will be invaluable in helping students shape their ideas into a workable thesis statement and then refine it. Time spent crafting a clear working thesis will eliminate problems that are much more difficult to remedy later. Often writers come to know exactly what they want to say only by writing about it first. Remind students that they will find the Draft Doctor equally useful when drafting and revising.

Direct students to complete the activity on page 314 and ask peer readers to apply the four suggestions about stating a thesis on pages 316–17 to the theses that students generate. If any need revision, the peer readers should make suggestions by rewriting them. Such revisions will show the writers specific examples of how the originals might work better.

Or ask each group to collaborate and state a thesis for each group of details. Tell students to write down the best statement once they have agreed on it. Collect the theses for each group and ask the class to identify which theses fit the criteria for effective thesis statements.

Encourage students to examine how the authors in *A Writer's Reader* use thesis statements. Assure them that imitating the style or organization of an essay they admire is an effective way to improve their own writing. If students liked the way an author organized an essay or presented a thesis, encourage them to try a similar technique in their own essays.

Unlike most essays that students are accustomed to reading, the thesis in Anna Quindlen's "Evan's Two Moms" (p. 451) and Evelyn F. Murphy's "Why Not a Dollar?" (p. 488) appear at the end of the piece, for lasting impact. Michael Abernethy in "Male Bashing on TV" (p. 515) places his thesis well into the body of the essay (par. 9), so you might use this essay to discuss the benefits and problems of stating the thesis after it has been developed and supported. Robert Jensen in "The High Cost of Manliness" (p. 475) places his thesis statement at the beginning and restates it at the end. Ask students what would be lost or gained if he delayed his thesis, stating it only at the end.

In E. B. White's "Once More to the Lake" (p. 463), students will have some difficulty articulating the implied thesis. Once the class has agreed on a thesis statement that fits the essay, have students discuss what each essay would gain or lose if White had included an explicit thesis statement. Where would it be placed?

ORGANIZING YOUR IDEAS (p. 319)

Organizing is one of the most important yet most dreaded parts of the writing process. Students must understand that a clear order of ideas is necessary for an effective paper. Remind them, too, that organizing is recursive and that it changes throughout the entire drafting and revising stages. Nevertheless, some attention to organization

---

Here's an Idea . . .

To help students with planning, Kay Berg of Sinclair Community College
requires her students to attach a cover sheet to their drafts using the acronym
STAMP. Before they draft, students must name the *subject* of their essay, the *the-sis*, the *audience*, the *methods* of development they plan to use, and their *purpose*
for writing.

---

early in the process will pay off for a student writer. The chart on p. 322 can serve as a
great introduction for students.

Grouping Your Ideas (p. 322)

Each of these strategies can be demonstrated in class. Follow up a vigorous brain-storming session with the suggestion that students step back a moment and decide how
to link items that you've scrawled all over the board. Students will find several ways to
do this, so have several colors of chalk or markers on hand. Focus on one item and have
students turn the clustering into an outline for an essay.

After completing the activity on clustering, students often comment that they can
understand the organization of ideas from this model more clearly than from others.
Many incorporate this strategy into the organization of each essay in the course. Several
students become very hierarchical and construct an intricate cluster that approximates
the structure of an atom. The most important result, however, remains the students' dis-covery of a strategy that works for them.

Outlining (p. 325)

Your students will be required to write outlines in other courses. Professors will ask
for outlined material, and they will expect formal outlines with both MLA and APA

Here's an Idea . . .

Suggest that your students try the following alternative ways of organizing
their drafts (adapted from Donald M. Murray's *Write to Learn,* 1990).

- Ask students to brainstorm a list of everything they might want to include in
  their paper. Have them divide a page into three columns labeled "Beginning,"
  "Middle," and "End" and place each idea for their paper in the appropriate
  column.

- Have them cut their paper into separate paragraphs to play with the order.
  Students can also do this with the cut-and-paste feature of word-processing
  software.

- Ask students to imagine the questions a reader might ask and to respond to
  them in the order that he or she would ask them.

- Have students draw a flowchart with arrows. Which ideas flow into which?

---

research papers. You do your students a disservice by not requiring them to practice this skill. Find ways to use outlines in your course. During conferences, stop and work with students to scratch out an informal outline of where an essay seems to be headed; ask students to write an outline in class as they begin drafting an essay; and encourage them to find out whether their word-processing program has an outline function and to try using it.

Give your class time to complete the outlining activities in this chapter with their peer groups. As you move around the room, you will hear students discussing the best way to structure information and deliberating over which category belongs under a general heading. This collaboration will reinforce the text and your instruction.

The sentence outline is useful both for guidance in a longer drafting of an essay and for self-assessment in the revising of a paper. To focus students' attention on the questions they need to ask themselves about relationships of part to part, use the two handouts that follow, or find your own highly specific sentence outline from a student research paper and scramble the sentences. Have groups of students re-arrange them into a complete outline. There will, of course, be several logical and appropriate organizations of the material — a point that we always emphasize to students when we discuss organization. This discovery can point students to ways they might revise drafts as well.

Here's an Idea . . .

As you cover various writing skills and strategies throughout the course, have students pull drafts from their portfolios and practice what they've just learned. This activity will reinforce the new skills, show students the practical nature of what they are learning, and demonstrate the ongoing process of revision.

Introduction

Sexism refers to those attitudes and actions that relegate women to a secondary and inferior status in society.

Sexism is found in health textbooks.

Sexism occurs in the illustrations.

Sexism occurs in the narrative.

Sexism is present in children's literature. It is destructive and restrictive, and for these reasons I feel it is important to examine sexism, its effects, and the efforts being put forth to end it.

Vukelich, McCarty, and Nanis conducted a study.

Sexism has definite destructive effects on children.

Sexism is found in children's pleasure-reading literature.

Picture books are sexist.

Stewig and Knipfel conducted a study.

Little progress has been made to end sexism in picture books.

Studies have been undertaken to explore sexism in children's picture books.

Nursery rhymes are sexist.

Fairy tales are sexist.

Award-winning books are sexist.

Caldecott Medal winners have been found to be sexist.

Sexism is found in mathematics textbooks.

Newbery Award winners have been found to be sexist.

Sexism occurs in elementary-school textbooks.

Children formulate their self-images through sexist literature.

Restrictive adult role models presented in children's literature are unhealthy.

Sexism has psychological effects on people.

Sexism is particularly prevalent in math word problems.

Sexism is found in social studies textbooks.

Sexism occurs in the illustrations.

Organizations have been formed to study sexism.

Sexism occurs in the narrative.

Basal readers are sexist.

Lists of nonsexist books and guidelines for determining sexism have been published.

Sexism occurs in the illustrations.

Sexism occurs in the narrative.

Few changes have been made over a ten-year period.

New nonsexist books are being written.

Sexism occurs in the illustrations.

Some efforts are being made to combat sexism in children's literature.

People must become aware of the problem of sexism.

Teachers can do much to fight sexism in their classes.

Conclusion

I. Introduction

    A. Sexism refers to those attitudes and actions that relegate women to a secondary and inferior status in society.

    B. Sexism is present in children's literature. It is destructive and restrictive, and for these reasons I feel it is important to examine sexism, its effects, and the efforts being put forth to end it.

II. Sexism is found in children's pleasure-reading literature.

    A. Picture books are sexist.

        1. Studies have been undertaken to explore sexism in children's picture books.

            a. Vukelich, McCarty, and Nanis conducted a study.

            b. Stewig and Knipfel conducted a study.

        2. Little progress has been made to end sexism in picture books.

    B. Award-winning books are sexist.

        1. Caldecott Medal winners have been found to be sexist.

        2. Newbery Award winners have been found to be sexist.

    C. Nursery rhymes are sexist.

    D. Fairy tales are sexist.

III. Sexism occurs in elementary-school textbooks.

    A. Sexism is found in mathematics textbooks.

        1. Sexism is particularly prevalent in math word problems.

        2. Sexism occurs in the illustrations.

    B. Sexism is found in health textbooks.

        1. Sexism occurs in the illustrations.

        2. Sexism occurs in the narrative.

    C. Sexism is found in social studies textbooks.

        1. Sexism occurs in the illustrations.

        2. Sexism occurs in the narrative.

    D. Basal readers are sexist.

        1. Sexism occurs in the illustrations.

        2. Sexism occurs in the narrative.

        3. Few changes have been made over a ten-year period.

IV. Sexism has definite destructive effects on children.

    A. Children formulate their self-image through sexist literature.

    B. Restrictive adult role models presented in children's literature are unhealthy.

    C. Sexism has psychological effects on people.

V. Some efforts are being made to combat sexism in children's literature.

    A. Organizations have been formed to study sexism.

    B. People must become aware of the problem of sexism.

    C. Lists of nonsexist books and guidelines for determining sexism have been published.

    D. Teachers can do much to fight sexism in their classes.

    E. New nonsexist books are being written.

VI. Conclusion

Strategies for Drafting (Ch. 18, p. 334)

Although advice about how to draft an essay accompanies the main assignment for each chapter in *A Writer's Guide*, students might find at times that they need more help at this stage of the process or when revising requires them to draft new material. Refer these students to Chapter 18 in their textbooks for more advice about shaping and revising paragraphs with topic sentences, as well as about introductions, conclusions, and transitions.

Chapter 18, "Strategies for Drafting," contains the following activity:

- For E-Writers (p. 335). See page 73 of this manual for advice about how to use this feature.

MAKING A START ENJOYABLE (p. 334)

Ask your students early in the semester about the ways in which they put off starting and then actually start to write. List these reasons on the board and note how they fall into categories like those the authors present in this chapter. Suggest that students read this list of "getting started" techniques and write a journal entry or two about the ones that they use or decide to try.

RESTARTING (p. 335)

At the beginning of your course, write the French word *essayer* on the board and explain that it means "to try." When writers create an essay, they try to describe, observe, recall, and persuade, and usually in combination. Explain that the structure of an essay, with a central or main idea supported by paragraphs containing examples, details, conversations, and images, has been evolving over a period of approximately four hundred years in the Romance languages. Read students the following description of French writer Michel Montaigne's publications as a way to reassure them that the form has relied historically on the importance of revision: "The first two volumes of his *Essays* were published in 1580; in 1586–88, he thoroughly revised and expanded the earlier volumes and wrote a third one. Even after the publication of the edition of 1588, he continued to revise and expand the *Essays* through marginal annotations during the last four years of his life" (Wilkie and Hurt, *Literature of the Western World* [Englewood Cliffs, N.J.: Prentice, 1997]). Ask students to describe their restarting techniques in self-assessment writing or in journal entries that focus on their work as writers.

Here's an Idea . . .

Generate discussion about the variety of ways in which writers make and use paragraphs by giving your class an essay that you have typed as one block without paragraph indentation. Ask each small group to agree about what parts of the essay constitute paragraphs and what reasons they have for setting off each part. Compare the reports from each group in a class discussion. There will be a great deal of agreement and some justified variance of opinion.

PARAGRAPHING (p. 336)

Paragraphing is one way of inventing. Some students write a controlling or topic sentence and then generate supporting materials. Other writers jump right in and stop later to read over what they've written in order to shape new paragraphs or to reshape old ones. So although the authors introduce paragraphing as a strategy for shaping a draft, take seriously their explanation that each strategy presented here can be used at any time in the writing process.

USING TOPIC SENTENCES (p. 337)

To increase student awareness of and skill with writing topic sentences, use the "cloze" procedure. Take published paragraphs and remove the topic sentence. Ask students to work in groups to construct one. Then reverse the procedure, giving students a topic sentence and indicating that there should be three levels of abstraction in the sentences that follow. Ask students to generate additional sentences —they choose how many — that would incorporate three levels of abstraction. (We have adapted this exercise from Francis Christensen's discussion of generative rhetoric in *Notes toward a New Rhetoric* [New York: Harper, 1967]).

For examples of how professional writers use topic sentences, refer your students to *A Writer's Reader*. Pick one or two essays from those the class has already read and have students locate the topic sentence in each paragraph. How does each topic sentence relate to the essay's thesis? Why might the author have chosen to place the topic sentence where it is? Have students rewrite one or two paragraphs with the topic sentence in a different location. Students enjoy and gain confidence from tinkering with the work of a professional writer.

WRITING AN OPENING (p. 340)

Even as the authors discuss shaping introductions, their advice can also be applied to the redrafting and rewriting process. Many writers feel stymied by beginnings. Encourage them to put down anything and keep writing until something takes shape. Then they can write the introduction.

The value of collaboration cannot be minimized. Ask students to move into their groups and to work through the activity on openings and conclusions (pp. 344–46). Discuss their evaluations of the best and worst openings and conclusions. Reinforce the need to begin and end with power. A *lead*, the term used in journalism for the first sentence of a story, can seduce or bore the reader. Rehearse the many options from which students can choose for an effective lead in their writing. You might want to add others to the list: a startling statistic, an effective quotation, background on the topic, a description of the scene. Ask students to think of some others.

Have students select an essay they are working on and identify the kind of opening they have used. Then have them choose two other kinds of openings suggested in the text and redraft the opening of their essay with each one. Either in class or in peer groups, discuss which opening works best and why.

Professional writers use the same kinds of openings discussed in this chapter. Ask students to look at some of the openings in *A Writer's Reader*. Brent Staples in "Black Men and Public Space" (p. 479) begins with a story. Sherry Turkle in "How Computers Change the Way We Think" (p. 552) introduces the subject and comments on it. Michael Abernethy in "Male Bashing on TV" (p. 515) opens with a warning. Stephen King in

Here's an Idea . . .

Assign students to bring to class three great openings and three great conclusions. Show them on an overhead projector (along with some of your favorites). Have the class identify the kinds of openings or conclusions they are. Ask students to share what they like about them. Ask them which kinds would be effective on their own essays.

"Why We Crave Horror Movies" (p. 512) begins by expressing a dramatic opinion. What effect do these openings have on the reader? Does the opening "hook" them? What tone does the opening create? How is it tied to the thesis? Have students find examples of different kinds of openings. Ask them to suggest other kinds of openings mentioned in the text that might be effective for the essay.

WRITING A CONCLUSION (p. 343)

Your students might notice that the same devices that make good openings also work well as conclusions. Encourage them to play with both openings and closings; emphasize playfulness.

Have your students select an essay they are working on and write three alternative conclusions. Suggest that they use a different kind each time. Have them share their alternatives with the class or with peer group members and discuss their advantages and disadvantages. Particularly focus on any shifts of meaning that — right or wrong — accompanied the redrafting of the concluding paragraphs.

Ask peer editors to suggest alternative conclusions or even to write one alternative conclusion to the essays they are working with. As they work through the exercises in the text, remind students that many essays simply stop — as if someone has fallen off the page. Tell students to end with a punch; these words will be the last ones heard by the audience.

Have students look at conclusions in *A Writer's Reader.* Judy Brady in "I Want a Wife" (p. 497) ends with a pithy statement. Robert Jensen in "The High Cost of Manliness" (p. 475) restates his thesis. Ask students to identify the kinds of conclusions the authors have used and to suggest other kinds of conclusions that might be effective. Ask them what feeling the conclusion leaves with the reader. What tone does it create? How does it support the thesis? Does it reiterate it or provide an example for it?

ACHIEVING COHERENCE (p. 346)

Students often express concern about the flow of their essays without having a sound idea of what that term means or how to achieve it. Encourage them to think of transitions as bridges between ideas, linking them together, or as stepping stones that lead from one thought to another. The authors offer a practical catalog of transitional devices. Reinforce it by directing students' attention to the transitions used in the essays in the text. Take some time in your analysis of readings to focus on how the writer helps them as readers to "cross over to the writer's perspective." Be sure to have peer editors look closely at the transitions in essays so that the writers can think again (when they revise) about the connections between parts. The activity on page 349 will make writers aware of transitions they have used and encourage them to consider how they might add or change transitions as they revise.

One of the best ways for students to learn to write coherent essays is to examine other writers' use of transitions. Select one or two of the essays in *A Writer's Reader* and have students identify all of the transitional markers. E. B. White in "Once More to the Lake" (p. 463) uses transitions denoting place or direction, whereas Danzy Senna in "The Color of Love" (p. 458) uses transitions denoting time. Stephen King in "Why We Crave Horror Movies" (p. 512) uses clear transitional words and sentences, repetition, and pronouns throughout his essay. Have students look for transitional paragraphs. What is the purpose of each one? What do they contribute to the flow of the writing? What ideas do they provide bridges between? Have students look at one of their own essays. Do the authors in *A Writer's Reader* use transitional devices that would work well in the students' essays?

Strategies for Developing (Ch. 19, p. 350)

Although advice about how to develop an essay accompanies the main assignment for each chapter in *A Writer's Guide*, students might find that at times they need more help developing their ideas or revising their essays to support their generalizations. Refer these students to Chapter 19 for more advice about using examples, details, division and classification, process analysis, comparison and contrast, and causal analysis to develop and support the ideas in their essays.

Chapter 19, "Strategies for Developing," does not contain boxes with specific suggestions for peer response, group learning, or e-writer activities. For more about incorporating these into your course, see pages 39 and 73 of this manual.

GIVING EXAMPLES (p. 351)

Underdeveloped writing is a primary weakness of first-year writers. While they're usually capable of drafting impressive generalizations, they often omit details that the reader must fill in. Emphasize that providing support is the writer's responsibility.

Ask groups of students to provide examples for a series of generalizations that you have culled directly from student writing. Have them brainstorm a list of examples for each generalization. Our students find the ladder of abstraction exercises useful for this activity. Join one of the groups and participate as a novice writer.

Have your students find essays in *A Writer's Reader* that demonstrate using examples. Judy Brady in "I Want a Wife" (p. 497) layers examples of tasks a wife performs to make her point. Michael Abernethy in "Male Bashing on TV" (p. 515) gives examples of TV shows that depict men as incompetent, selfish, and lazy. William Zinsser in "The Right to Fail" (p. 567) presents examples of men and women who have achieved great success through nontraditional avenues, and Nancy Gibbs in "Free the Children" (p. 470) gives examples of free summer moments that help shape children. Have students look at one or two of their own essays and mark examples they have used in them. Do the examples the authors provide in *A Writer's Reader* give students new ideas for examples they might use or suggest places in their essays that might need to be developed further?

Here's an Idea...

Ask students to select a draft from their portfolios and find an example that they have used in it. In the margin have them draw a ladder of abstraction (p. 352 in Chapter 19). Beginning with the words from their draft, direct them to refine the example, making each level more specific. Students should move at least two levels.

PROVIDING DETAILS (p. 353)

The writing by Mother Jones gives specific details and a list of facts or examples. Guy Garcia hits the reader with a barrage of statistical details to make a point. The use of statistics and objective details imbues an essay with a strength equal to that of pure description.

Ask groups to write a collaborative paragraph after they have accumulated the details for one of the subjects listed in the activity on page 355. Remind them that you will be collecting these paragraphs and reading them aloud and that each group member shares the writing responsibility in this assignment.

Have students find essays in *A Writer's Reader* in which details provide a clear image. E. B. White in "Once More to the Lake" (p. 463) uses details to describe his childhood sense of the lake. Tamara Draut in "What's a Diploma Worth, Anyway?" (p. 561) uses statistics to demonstrate the eroding financial future for college graduates. What senses do the details appeal to? What details have students provided in their own essays? Have them mark passages in which they have used details and brainstorm other kinds of details they might use to give the reader a clearer image.

DEFINING (p. 356)

To illustrate that writers must define terms so that the reader clearly understands what they mean, ask students to write down the age of someone who is old —only one age. Then ask them to write down the age of a young person. Going around the room, have each of them reveal the ages they've written and point out the wide range of differences in the class's definition of "old" and "young." This exercise provides another opportunity for you to stress the importance of writers putting themselves in the reader's shoes, not assuming the reader knows what the writer means.

Assign the activity in this section as an out-of-class assignment. In class, ask students to form groups and exchange definitions.

Students can find professional models of definition in *A Writer's Reader.* Judy Brady in "I Want a Wife" (p. 497) uses an extended definition. Robert Jensen in "The High Cost of Manliness" (p. 475) first establishes society's definition of a "real man" before proceeding to persuade the reader the definition has harmful effects. Have students find other essays in *A Writer's Reader* in which the author has defined a term. Ask them why the author chose to provide the definition in that instance. Can they find places in which a definition is not provided but would have been helpful? Have them identify places in their own essays in which adding a definition might be helpful.

REASONING INDUCTIVELY AND DEDUCTIVELY (p. 357)

Inductive and deductive reasoning are fundamental supporting patterns for writing. Students will grasp the necessity of supporting a statement with examples or details, but they often need practice in finding the most effective way to present their reasoning. When they draft or revise, encourage them to try both patterns, first moving from particulars to their general conclusion and then ordering their draft in the opposite way, stating the main point first, followed by examples, details, or similar instances. By comparing the effectiveness of the two different arrangements, students can determine the best presentation for their reasoning. Reinforce the notion that professional writers look for the most effective way to present their reasoning by having students do the activity on page 359. The checklist on page 359 will help students check the accuracy of their reasoning.

Students will find examples of both kinds of reasoning in *A Writer's Reader*. Michael Abernethy in "Male Bashing on TV" (p. 515) uses inductive reasoning when he begins by describing a number of TV programs and ads that depict men as lazy and incompetent and then comes to the general conclusion that negative images of men unfairly dominate television programming. William Zinsser in "The Right to Fail" (p. 567) makes a general statement and then demonstrates his thesis by applying it to men and women whose unconventional paths resulted in important contributions to society.

ANALYZING A SUBJECT (p. 360)

Because analyzing can be challenging for students, you might want to work through an activity like the one on pages 361–62 of the text. Write a subject on the board (like "college") and suggest a purpose for analyzing the subject (such as "to analyze the benefits and challenges of a college education"). Then write general categories for analysis (such as "benefits" and "challenges") on the board and ask students to call out examples for each category.

Later in the class or as homework, ask students to write a brief essay analyzing the subject covered in class, drawing on the collaboratively developed examples and adding any others that come to mind. (For brief essays like this, students should focus on a limited subject such as "three benefits of college.") After they've completed the writing, have them exchange papers with a partner for peer review. Reviewers should share their thoughts about the effectiveness of the analysis by answering questions like the following:

- Is the purpose of the analysis clear?
- Is the main point clearly stated? (The statement of the main idea may include the purpose.)
- Are the supporting points well developed and clearly related to the purpose?

The Bedford Guide includes several models of analysis that students might want to consult, such as Stephen King's "Why We Crave Horror Movies" (p. 512) or Sherry Turkle's "How Computers Change the Way We Think" (p. 552).

ANALYZING A PROCESS (p. 362)

Many students will be eager to try process analysis as a strategy for developing their essays because giving directions and following instructions are such familiar activities. Remind students that, in order to be effective, they must analyze the process carefully and sequence the steps clearly.

Ask students to find examples of process analysis in *A Writer's Reader*. Susan Brady Konig in "They've Got to Be Carefully Taught" (p. 564) traces the process of teaching young children multiculturalism, and Annie Dillard in an excerpt from *An American Childhood* (p. 577) retraces the steps to her childhood discovery that learning is valuable in and of itself.

DIVIDING AND CLASSIFYING (p. 364)

We recommend that you have students complete activities that demonstrate division and classification. Dividing and classifying helps literal thinkers ease into abstractions. Novice writers overwhelmed by information and facts from all of their classes find these strategies to be useful for both sorting out the material and making connections across the disciplines by identifying categories that apply to every learning experience. In addition to the exercise presented in the text, here are two division and classification exercises that work well:

- Introduce division and classification by having students wear T-shirts to class. Ask each student to model his or her T-shirt, and then have the students arrange the T-shirts into classes. Some will be obvious: concert shirts, political-message shirts, designer shirts. Encourage students to also invent new classifications of shirts. Then direct them to write a short essay from the stance of an anthropologist drawing conclusions about the Composition I natives from the evidence of their T-shirts. During the next class, have students form workshop groups, read the essays, and make specific revision suggestions. Finally, select three or four final drafts to evaluate in class.

- For a classroom exercise designed to foster higher-order thinking, photocopy police reports of the weekly homicides from a city newspaper. Organize the class into small groups and ask each to read all of the reports and to form some conclusions about what the data might indicate. Each report specifies the name, age, address, and occupation of the murder victim; the location of the murder; the time of the murder; the weapon used; and the conditions, motive(s), and case status. From the mass of information, students look for common features and try to group sets of features.

The entire campus is filled with raw data that students can analyze through division and classification: behaviors at sporting events, bumper stickers on cars in parking lots, the ways students select seats in classrooms. Encourage student writers to observe the data and classify them with the purpose of coming to understand some new truth about human psychology or some characteristics of campus life. Help students see that

Here's an Idea . . .

To teach process analysis, bring containers of blocks, Tinker Toys, LEGO bricks, or packets of collage materials to class. Number each container. Have students choose a partner, take one container for the pair, and build an object with the toys or form a collage with the art materials. They must use only the materials from their container. When they are finished, tell them to write a process-analysis essay with directions for assembling the product. Because of time constraints, they will probably need to take notes and write their essay outside of class. At the end of the class period, they must disassemble their product and return the pieces to the container. Direct them to number their essay with the container's number and to bring the completed draft to the next class.

During the next class, redistribute the containers and the essays with the corresponding numbers. Make sure no one receives his or her own essay. Ask the students to read the essays and assemble the products according to the directions. When the partners have assembled the products as well as they can, ask the writers to view the finished product to see if it is exactly the same as the one they built and described. Have students discuss where the writers were on target and where they veered off. What information was missing that would have been helpful? What information made the process clear? Confusing? You might want to provide a sheet for readers to evaluate writers' process analysis.

they can use these methods of thinking not only to bring order to what might have intimidated them but also to discover some new ideas in what had seemed "obvious."

Ask students to look for division and classification in *A Writer's Reader*. Ruth La Ferla in "Latino Style Is So Cool. Oh All Right: It's Hot" (p. 506) classifies elements of Latino fashion. Terry Golway in "A Nation of Idol-Worshipers" (p. 525) divides idols into two categories: fantasy and reality.

COMPARING AND CONTRASTING (p. 366)

Students often enter an undergraduate composition course with little practical information on how to write a comparison-and-contrast essay. As a result, they produce a draft that reads like a "stew," with similarities and differences erratically thrown into paragraphs. If you clearly explain the opposing and alternating plans of organizing information, students will be able to see the differences.

When students begin to write a comparison-and-contrast essay, insist that they construct lists immediately after they decide on a thesis. Have them record similarities in one list and differences in the other. Then have them examine the lists; if the lists are not equal in strength and length, ask them to reevaluate their choice of writing topic or the content of their lists.

Use the tagmemic grid on page 209 of this manual with paragraphs as well as with entire essays. Because students are working with one part of a larger essay, they might find materials in the essay to include in a paragraph developed by comparing and contrasting. This focused writing exercise will also foster students' critical reading skills. For more help with comparing and contrasting, refer students to Chapter 7 of their textbooks.

For examples of comparing and contrasting in *A Writer's Reader*, refer students to Richard Rodriguez's "Public and Private Language" (p. 571) or Anjula Razdan's "What's Love Got to Do with It?" (p. 453).

IDENTIFYING CAUSES AND EFFECTS (p. 369)

This strategy is especially useful for challenging students' biases and assumptions. Before students do the exercise in the textbook, ask them to brainstorm a list of contemporary problems, to choose one, and then attempt to establish its cause and effect. What kind of evidence would writers need to provide in order to establish the relationships that students claim? Refer students to page 162 in Chapter 9 of *A Writer's Guide* and ask them if any of the relationships they've identified rely on a logical fallacy. For more about explaining causes and effects, refer students to Chapter 8 of their textbooks.

Students will find excellent examples of a professional's use of cause and effect in *A Writer's Reader*. Stephen King's "Why We Crave Horror Movies" (p. 512) is a favorite essay with students, and his notion that horror movies act as a safety valve for our darker impulses justifies the fascination that many students have with the genre. Sherry Turkle in "How Computers Change the Way We Think" (p. 552) describes fundamental changes in students' thinking habits since the advent of certain computational technologies. Noel Perrin in "A Part-Time Marriage" (p. 494) explores the damaging effects of too much intimacy in a marriage. In "Why Not a Dollar?" (p. 488) Evelyn F. Murphy identifies discrimination as the cause of the gender wage gap. Ask students to explain why these authors' explanations seem feasible. What makes a cause-and-effect argument successful? Why?

Strategies for Revising and Editing
(Ch. 20, p. 371)

Because your students will be dipping into Chapter 20 at various points during the semester, take some time when you first discuss revising to comment on this chapter's organization. The authors begin with a focus on rethinking the paper and work their way around to other activities (such as "cutting and whittling"), which, of course, affect ideas but are not as likely to keep them from being communicated. Remind students that the Quick Editing Guide at the end of their textbook also provides advice about editing and proofreading.

Chapter 20, "Strategies for Revising and Editing," contains these activities:

- For E-Writers (pp. 376, 378, and 386). See page 73 of this manual for advice about how to use this feature.

- For Group Learning (p. 387). See page 39 of this manual for advice about how to use this feature.

RE-VIEWING AND REVISING (p. 372)

Many of your students will at first rely on passive rather than active learning. Even if you write careful descriptive and evaluative comments on their drafts, these students will want to "fix" whatever you diagnose as "wrong" and will most likely think that "revising" means proofreading and editing. They prefer to practice surface rather than deep revision. Your challenge is to lead them into the practice of revising deeply.

You will need to show students that revision is a multistage and recursive process. Emphasize the authors' three specific points for revision — purpose, audience, and structure — to make this complex process more manageable. Just as any aspect of writing is easier if broken into parts, revision will be more productive if students focus on each of these three points separately. From the beginning, encourage peer readers to focus first on meaning, then on form and structure, and then — only when the preceding elements are satisfactory — on editing. When peer editors base their responses on the hierarchy of "macro revision" and "micro revision," they will learn to use it in their own revision as well.

Here's an Idea . . .

Some students compile sound support for their thesis, but their organization is a jumble, showing no logical order. Have them highlight each main idea with a different color highlighter. Then have them go through the essay highlighting each detail, example, or piece of evidence with the color that corresponds to the idea it supports. This process will help students see where each piece of information should be placed. They can use the cut-and-paste feature on their computer programs to move the information into a logical arrangement. Caution them that they will still need to use transitions to connect the information and make the text flow smoothly.

Here's an Idea . . .

To help students see the dynamic arrangement of information in an essay, have them put their information in boxes. Draw a box around each part of the essay. The size of the box should represent the importance of the idea. For example, the paragraph with the thesis statement might be a 4-by-5-inch box, while the opening paragraph is a 3-by-3-inch box. If the most important point is in the conclusion, it might be the largest box. Students must then decide what impact they want the information in each box to have — how to arrange the boxes. Do they want to emphasize the largest box by putting it first? Do they want a dynamic arrangement leading up to the largest box? Have them play with the arrangement, deciding what order is most effective.

Turn the Revision Checklists in this chapter into posters for dorm rooms and writing centers or into handouts to attach to drafts. Ideally, students who practice surface revision will learn to internalize these questions during the semester. In class, have students select a draft they are working on and read through it considering only purpose and making revisions based on the checklist on page 373. They should write their thesis statement at the top of the draft and use it to focus their revision. When they finish this revision, have them begin the process again, reading only for audience, using the checklist on page 374; finally, they should repeat the process by reading only for structure and support, using the checklist on page 375.

Devote at least a week of your course to revision workshops. Schedule these during the week before students turn in their portfolios for the final grade. Allow students to meet with you and with one another during these classes. Students who need additional help with mechanics can move between the classroom and the writing lab.

We have found that the handout on page 233 helps our students significantly improve the structure of their drafts. To prepare for the revision workshop, we direct students to create a copy of one of their essays on the word processor, then to position the cursor in front of each sentence in the essay and hit Return, making a list of the sentences. We then have them double space between each paragraph and print the document to bring to the next class.

During the revision workshop, we show the handout on an overhead projector. Using the draft that students have prepared, we move through the handout with them step by step. Your students will discover that they can see strengths and weaknesses in

---

Here's an Idea . . .

Have students exchange essays or work with one of their own. Write this question on the board: "Does the reader finish each sentence with more information than when she or he started?" Have students read slowly and methodically through the writing to answer the question. Readers should underline any sentence that does not add information and return the essay to the writer. Writers must then decide the purpose, if any, that each underlined sentence serves and whether they should delete it. Either as a class or in groups, have students discuss their choices.

a new way with their reformatted documents. Remind them to use the handout to revise their other essays. Seeing sentences in a list can also help them edit more carefully.

We cannot overemphasize the importance of conferences at the revision stage. Although conferences can be time-consuming, the more of them we have, the better we are at focusing on the skills students need to develop. Because the revision stage is one of the most difficult, both students and instructors benefit from conferences in order to confirm that students are using their energies in the most productive ways possible.

Roy Peter Clark of the Poynter Institute of Media Studies is one of the masters of the writing conference. His advice in the following exchange illustrates one method you can use in conferences to give students control of their writing by asking questions that push them into revision:

> Andy read his essay aloud to the group of journalism professors and editors gathered together for a week's discussion of the writing process. I asked if anyone could help Andy improve his work in one minute. A fine editor used his minute to make suggestions on how it could be reorganized and improved. Then it was my turn: "Andy, what do you think of the story?"
> "It's OK, I guess. It's a first draft, so I know it needs some work." "What did you have in mind?" "Maybe I should work on the lead?" "What part of the writing was your favorite part?" "I guess the part near the end when I describe the stained-glass windows." "What would happen if you moved this part?"
> – *Free to Write* (1987)

For more advice about conducting conferences with your students and working with peer editors, see Chapter 2 of this manual.

REVISING FOR EMPHASIS, CONCISENESS, AND CLARITY (p. 376)

Students revise on two levels: content and mechanics. The terms used by the authors — *macro revision* and *micro revision* — are useful. The more difficult task is revising for content. Often students do not want to change their writing, and they try to avoid critiquing the writing once the first draft is completed. Emphasize that they are working on rough drafts — "sloppy copy," as Roy Peter Clark calls it —and work with them to understand what is powerful in the language they create.

Reinforce the authors' advice about stating first or last (p. 378) by asking students to play with writing alternatives. If their drafts are on a disk, it is easy enough for them to print out the text. Then they can go back and look at where they stressed what mattered most. If they placed the important idea first, ask them now to create a new file in which they rearrange their materials to lead up to a conclusion that stresses what matters most (and, of course, vice versa). This might mean rewriting the entire essay and shifting it from a deductive to an inductive pattern of organization, or it might mean simply reworking the introduction and the conclusion. Ask students for a printout of each alternative revision. Compare and contrast both versions and describe to students how each affects you as a reader.

Students often confuse effective repetition with repetition of unproved generalizations and redundant word choice. Prepare a sampler of student writing to help them distinguish repetition that deadens their prose from repetition that quickens it. In class discussion, ask students to defend or refute the use of repetition in each writing.

REVISING FOR STRUCTURE

1. Write your thesis statement (real or implied) at the top of a separate sheet of paper, or cut and paste (or write) it at the top of a new computer file.

2. Go through the body of your essay and find the topic sentence of each paragraph. List the sentences on the sheet of paper or cut and paste them in the computer file, leaving adequate space between to include the remaining sentences in the paragraph. If the paragraph does not have a topic sentence, write one for it.

3. List or cut and paste each sentence in the paragraph under the topic sentence.

   (Note for word processors: Put the cursor in front of each sentence and hit Return. Double-space between paragraphs. After you've cut and pasted the topic sentence from each paragraph, put it in boldface.)

PARAGRAPHS

4. Does each topic sentence add information about the thesis? Mark any that do not. Do you need to eliminate this paragraph? Should you show its connection to the thesis?

5. Do you need to change the order of the paragraphs to make ideas flow better? Do you need to add transitions within or between paragraphs?

SENTENCES

6. Look at each sentence in the first paragraph. Mark any sentences that do not support the topic sentence. Do you need to move them to a different paragraph? Do you need to create a new paragraph with a new topic sentence? Do you need to eliminate any sentences altogether?

7. Cross out any sentence that does not add new information.

8. Find sentences that do not clearly connect to your thesis. Do you need to change or add to the writing to make the connection clear?

9. Look at sentence order. Do ideas flow? Do you need to move any sentences?

   (Repeat steps 6 through 9 for each paragraph.)

10. Is there a paragraph that is thin (not many sentences)? What is its purpose? What information do you need to add?

The section on cutting and whittling (pp. 379–81) contains the voices of real writers who love words and the careful crafting of them. There's something inspirational about the section that is sure to light up some of your writers, but there will be others whose acquaintance with words is still very formal and hesitant. Those writers who believe they have performed epic deeds by turning out two hundred words will be nonplussed by the authors' discussion of the joy of revising from a "paunchy" two hundred words to a "svelte" one hundred and fifty.

At least once in the semester, use a class period only for cutting and whittling. While the students work on their manuscript, go around the room reading their revisions and answering questions like "Does this sound OK?" As an experienced reader and writer, you have a greater appreciation for and understanding of stylistic choices, and you need to be available as a resource.

Expect to have trouble guiding some writers into cutting and whittling. Curiously, many students are more willing to let you help them examine the quality of their ideas and their thinking than the quality of their style. You might want to teach those writers to revise for wordiness by using examples of long-winded, overcomplicated style in other writing than by citing such passages in their own. The authors provide some fine examples and tell you where to find more. Students may also go to their textbooks, to the *Congressional Record,* to official memoranda, to college catalogs, and to legal documents to find examples of style that often intentionally obfuscate meaning. While George Orwell's essay "Politics and the English Language" would be useful, don't overlook the annual *Time* essays on the state of the language or William Safire's columns in the *New York Times Magazine.* And if you are really brave, bring in a chunk of your own writing and ask students to suggest where you might cut and whittle. Although you might be nervous at first, you will likely receive clear and accurate questions that help you produce a stronger draft.

You could also give students an anonymous piece of student writing — something from a previous semester or another class or even from your own undergraduate days — that you've typed on a disk. Have them copy that chunk onto their flash drive or disk and ask them to reduce the "paunchiness" by 25 percent. This exercise requires students to use a computer for the kind of revising that you expect for all of their writing. In

---

Here's an Idea . . .

Many students can aurally identify errors in their writing that they may miss when they read. Have students bring to class two copies of their drafts. Have them form pairs and give them these directions:

As your partner reads your draft to you, follow on your own copy, placing a colored stick-on dot beside each place in the manuscript that sounds wrong to you. Readers, you must be sure to read the draft exactly as the writer has written it. When the reader has finished reading your draft aloud, go back through your copy and check the places you've identified with dots to determine what the problem is. Then correct the problem, placing a different colored dot beside errors you've fixed, so you know what you have corrected and what still needs attention. You can ask your partner or the instructor for help in places where you are unable to identify the problem.

addition, as the authors point out, many word-processing programs have grammar and style checkers that let writers create a dictionary or a glossary of items that the program checks and brings to their attention. For example, students who realize that they have a penchant for certain windy words and phrases could add those to their style-checking program and get extra practice correcting them when the program finds them.

EDITING AND PROOFREADING (p. 384)

This section defines the importance of proofreading and furnishes instructors and students with strategies that actually work to improve the mechanics of a piece of writing. Our personal favorites are the tips to read the essay backwards to discover the mechanical errors and to ask students to read the essay aloud. Students frequently are surprised to hear something that they did not intend to place in the essay or that is incorrect.

The Editing Checklist on page 386 corresponds to the sections in the Quick Editing Guide at the end of the textbook. Although this guide is mentioned in the text, take time to show it to your students if you haven't already done so. The students most likely to ignore the text might be the ones who will need this useful information the most.

Although you have probably already developed a system for marking mechanical errors, we offer the following suggestions. Using any color other than red, place a checkmark in the margin next to the line in which the error or errors appear. For ESL students, place the checkmark directly over the word. Instead of identifying for the writer the kind of error made, ask him or her to find the error, discover what type it is, and then correct it. If your students cannot figure out what type of error it is, ask them to talk to you about it during a conference.

When you respond to a group of rough drafts, collect and type a list of common errors. Copy the mistakes as they appear. Record entire sentences if they indicate a common error, such as fused or run-on sentences. When you return the rough drafts, ask students to form groups, and give each group a list of the errors. Have them correct the errors and identify the type of mistakes that have been made. Afterward, collect the lists and discuss the mistakes and corrections.

Answer to Activity: Editing and Proofreading (p. 388)

Robert Frost, one of the most popular American poets, ~~He~~ was born in San Francisco in 1874, and died in Boston in 1963. His family moved to new England when his father died in 1885. There he completed high school and attended college but never graduated. Poverty and problems filled his life. He worked in a wool mill, on a newspaper, and at various odd jobs. Because of ill health he settled on a farm and began to teach school to support his wife and children. Throughout his life he dedicated himself to writing poetry. By 1915 he was in demand for public readings and speaking engagements. He was awarded the Pulitzer Prize for poetry four times — in 1924, 1931, 1937, and 1943. The popularity of his poetry rests in his use of common themes and images. Everyone can relate to his universal poems, such as "Birches" and "Stopping by Woods on a Snowy Evening." Students read his poetry in school from seventh grade through graduate school, so almost everyone recognizes lines from his best-loved poems. America is proud of its son, the home-spun poet Robert Frost.

Strategies for Designing Your Document
(Ch. 21, p. 389)

Because your students will be dealing with document design in any writing task they undertake, whether it be in their college courses or in the workplace, it will benefit them if you teach Chapter 21 early in the semester. It is critical that you introduce students to your college writing center or computer lab. This resource is as vital to them as the college library. Arrange for an orientation with the lab director, and provide an opportunity for hands-on experience as students work through the strategies in this chapter.

Many of your students will be familiar with word-processing programs, but you will need to give extra attention to those who are inexperienced with a computer. A hands-on introduction to the lab can do much to dispel these students' anxiety. Make clear to your students any requirements you have for formatting the papers they will write for you. If they meet your expectations, you can then focus on their writing without the distraction of weird fonts or inappropriate headings. Many professors are sticklers about the formatting of papers for their classes, so learning to follow expressed formatting requirements is important for your students' success.

How students perceive themselves as writers is another factor in their success. While there is no substitute for sound writing, clean document design can bolster students' perception of themselves as writers. The professional appearance of a word-processed document can give students more confidence. Because of the ease of revision, students revise more frequently and more extensively when writing on a computer. With the freedom to write, back up, go ahead, stop, loop back, and experiment, drafts become less costly and students become more willing to take risks and change approaches. Novice writers often have low self-esteem, and once they become computer-literate their writing and revisions increase in quality and quantity.

If you have long been an advocate of using the computer for writing, you will probably have creative strategies to supplement the authors' advice. For more information on using the computer for teaching writing, see Chapter 5 of this manual.

Chapter 21, "Strategies for Designing Your Document," contains this activity:

- For E-Writers (pp. 393, 400, 401, and 413). See page 73 of this manual for advice about how to use this feature.

UNDERSTANDING FOUR BASIC PRINCIPLES OF DOCUMENT DESIGN (p. 392)

The four basic principles listed by the authors are the same rhetorical strategies used for writing: understanding the audience and determining how one can achieve the purpose for communicating with it. Once students understand that, they can move on to considering the best document design.

Have students use the Discovery Checklist on page 392 to get information about the audience and their expectations. The illustrations of *USA Today* and the *Wall Street Journal* (Figure 21.1) demonstrate the different expectations of each publication's audience. Bring to class *Vogue, Sports Illustrated,* a professional journal, and *Popular Mechanics.* Discuss audience differences and expectations. Then ask students who the audience might be for their writing in different tasks. Discuss the audiences' different

Here's an Idea . . .

Bring to class three novels: a best-selling novel for adults, a novel for young readers, and a children's book for preschoolers — perhaps a Caldecott winner. Ask students which one they would expect if someone gave them a novel to read over the summer. Which would be appropriate for their three-year-old niece? Which novel would they give to a young person in elementary or middle school? What would be the result of giving the young person one of the other books? Look at the books' covers. What makes each attractive to a specific audience? When students open the books, what differences do they see? What features make the design more appropriate for one audience than another? What purpose do students think the author or publisher had in mind?

expectations, including the specific formatting required by professors in different disciplines. Ask colleagues for examples of papers formatted according to their requirements and show these to your students. Discuss with them cover sheets and identifiers, font size and type, use of headings and other such divisions, headers and footers, and documentation styles.

Each audience that students consider will have a different set of constraints. Brainstorm several different audiences and discuss what some of their constraints might be. Just as it is imperative that students never lose sight of their purpose when they write, they must keep that purpose in mind when they make design decisions.

CREATING AN EFFECTIVE DESIGN
FOR YOUR DOCUMENT (p. 396)

Have students look at several different fonts when you take them to the computer lab for orientation. Even if you are specific in your requirements, they may have freer rein in other classes, and this is a good opportunity to emphasize audience consideration. They may need to see that some fonts are more difficult to read than others. Remind them that their instructors will be reading twenty to eighty papers in one sitting. Warn them that instructors will not be fooled if students try to hide insufficient length with large fonts or lack of substance with fancy fonts.

Unless your students have some background in journalism or art, they will probably never have considered white space a commodity. Call their attention to the white space in the integrated and displayed lists (p. 401). What will the audience expect in the students' documents? What will be most effective for their purpose?

Students will find that features such as displayed lists and headings are used extensively in the workplace and the community. Ask them to bring examples and discuss the reasons for using such features in each case. Call their attention to academic disciplines that use these features in formatting papers.

Spend some time working with students on parallel phrasing. They need to be competent with this skill in all aspects of their writing, from outlining to the parallel words and phrases connected by conjunctions that they will use in writing essays.

Here's an Idea . . .

Format a student essay, with the name blanked out, in several different font sizes and styles. Bring copies to class and ask students to evaluate them for ease of reading, aesthetic appeal, and appropriateness for the assignment. Ask them how they think a professor might react to each of the versions and why. Comparing document designs in this way will demonstrate to students how their instructor might view a draft with excessively large type or increased margins or with novelty typefaces. It will also emphasize the importance of following appropriate conventions of document design for papers they submit.

USING VISUALS TO REINFORCE YOUR CONTENT (p. 410)

If your computer skills don't extend to the importing of graphics, don't despair. Your purpose here is to teach students when graphics are appropriate and how writers should integrate and credit graphics in the overall design of their document.

If you want to show students how to import graphics or create graphs and charts with a computer program, you will need to make arrangements either to demonstrate in your classroom or, better yet, to provide a hands-on demonstration in your computer lab. The lab director and assistants may be able to help by training either you or your class. Many of your students will have learned these techniques in their computer classes or on their own if they have interest in designing Web sites, and you may be able to set up a peer training session in your computer lab. If you decide to do this, allot one class period to train students to create tables and graphs and to import a graphic, and another to allow them to practice these skills.

Strategies for Understanding Visual Representations (Ch. 22, p. 418)

Students will immediately recognize the relevance of Chapter 22 to their daily lives. Ours is a society deluged with visual imagery at every turn. The power to manipulate with visuals is constantly exploited by marketers in a capitalistic society and by those others whose aim is to shape public opinion. Visual imagery lends itself to the rapidity with which we must ingest information. In a highly competitive world, the right image can capture our attention and dispense carefully packed information in seconds. Our students spend much more time reading visual images than they spend reading written text, and it is imperative that they be armed with strategies to interpret what they see.

The authors mention several kinds of visual representations in addition to advertisements. Ask students to bring to class one of these other types of visual representations and comment on its effects. Take this opportunity to connect your composition course with courses in art, design, or mass communication. Point out that the same analysis of visual representations takes place in these fields.

Chapter 22, "Strategies for Understanding Visual Representations," does not contain boxes with specific suggestions for peer response, group learning, or e-writer activities. For more about incorporating these into your course, see pages 39 and 73 of this manual.

USING STRATEGIES FOR VISUAL ANALYSIS (p. 419)

If you have students write about visual representations, require them to include a copy of the image they analyze when presenting their essay to peer groups or submitting it to you for comments. You won't be able to assess the quality of analysis without seeing the image yourself.

Encourage students to refer to the figure on p. 422 so that they can apply the three levels of visual analysis as they examine visual representations.

Here's an Idea . . .

Scale is the relative size of an object in a visual representation. The cues we use to judge scale are (1) the relative size of other objects around the image and (2) distance, which we must judge by layers on a flat surface. In visual representations, the third dimension, depth, is only an illusion. We have no way of knowing the size of the Volkswagen from the Figure 22.6 photograph. Ask students to imagine an image of a house as tall as the Volkswagen's bumper situated slightly behind the image of the car, or draw this image on the board. How far from the car do they judge the house to be? Then ask them to imagine or draw the same image placed slightly in front of the car, covering a portion of the car's fender. How does this change their perception of the size of the Volkswagen?

LEVEL ONE: SEEING THE BIG PICTURE (p. 420)

After students work through an analysis of the image in the text (p. 422), have them practice these strategies on images you bring to class or other images in the book, or ask them to bring in images they have found to be puzzling. Advertisements work well for this exercise, but don't neglect other types of visual representations. Encourage students' interest in the fine arts by asking them to analyze images of paintings and photographs as well. Good, thought-provoking examples of these open each chapter in Part Two, "A Writer's Situations," and in *A Writer's Reader*. Your library may have other prints available, and your art department probably has a library of slides. The authors work with still images in the text, but don't forget the imagery students see on MTV, on VH1, or in television commercials. They need to consider these images critically. Bring to class a tape of a television commercial and ask them to apply to it the visual analysis skills they are developing.

LEVEL TWO: OBSERVING THE CHARACTERISTICS OF AN IMAGE (p. 421)

Here students are working on a literal level with the photograph in the text. Take them through the analysis the authors provide; then have them analyze the images in the text, some images you bring to class, or images you have asked them to bring. It is important that they practice these skills before moving on to interpretation.

LEVEL THREE: INTERPRETING THE MEANING OF AN IMAGE (p. 429)

Take this opportunity to discuss connotation as well as denotation. Use the words *red* or *flag* as examples of connotative language, and ask students what other images come to mind with the literal images of a hue or a flag. How might a visual image connote more than its literal elements? Ask students if they think a visual image can be more or less richly connotative than language.

When you analyze images, the students' work will be more productive if, rather than having them work individually, you put them into groups or have them work as a class. Students' analyses will be influenced by their cultural background and their life experiences, so they will often interpret an image differently from the way a classmate does. The variety of viewpoints will enlighten and enrich your discussion.

Refer students to the logical fallacies the authors discuss in Chapter 9 (pp. 162–63). How might these fallacies apply to the use of imagery and language in the ads discussed in their textbook? The car ads, for example, suggest snob appeal, a kind of bandwagon argument. The Oldsmobile ad (Figure 22.7) implies that Oldsmobile owners are superior to other car owners. The Volkswagen ad (Figure 22.6) also uses snob appeal in a reverse kind of way. Those who own Volkswagens spurn the usual trappings of consumerism for a purer lifestyle. Have students examine the visual components without looking at the language. Can visual image alone contain logical fallacies? How? Which ones? Ask students to analyze other advertisements for logical fallacies.

When you discuss signs and symbols, return to the Volkswagen ad. Bring to class an even more current Volkswagen ad, or ask students to describe the ads for Volkswagen they have seen on television. How has the focus of the ads changed?

Here's an Idea . . .

Bring to class some controversial magazine ads such as those for Abercrombie and Fitch or Benetton. *Vanity Fair* magazine ads or ads from foreign magazines are good sources. Direct students to closely examine the advertisement and consider the following questions:

- What does the ad claim?
- What elements make it effective or ineffective? (Consider colors, objects, text, setting, and characters.)
- Who is the target audience? How do the ad's details relate to the probable audience?
- What, if any, message does the ad send?
- Would you buy the product based on this advertisement?

Then direct students to formulate an argument about the strategies the ad uses to appeal to consumers. Have them develop an outline based on that thesis and draft a short paper.

Students will find an image at the beginning of each chapter of *A Writer's Reader* (pp. 440, 474, 501, 529, and 560). Divide your class into groups and have each group analyze one of the images and report back to the class. Students might use the "Responding to an Image" prompt accompanying each visual to guide their analysis.

CHAPTER 8

Teaching *A Writer's Reader*

While the essays in *A Writer's Guide* provide students with examples of the kind of writing the chapters' assignments require, the selections in *A Writer's Reader* attempt to do more. Arranged thematically, these pieces engage students in topics that are important to their lives and offer a variety of suggestions for writing, from reflective personal essays to critical analysis and research.

Few composition instructors would dispute the importance of the connection between reading and writing. For the most part, writing-as-process pedagogy contends that one activity nourishes the other: Writers must learn to read their own work critically, and reading critically is a kind of rewriting — by discovering new ideas, questioning them in relation to one's own, and synthesizing them into a new understanding. In the case of first-year composition students, this process is essential. Reading not only inspires novice writers to consider viewpoints and ways of thinking beyond their own, but it also establishes and validates their role in a community of writers. Covering "A Process of Reading" in Chapter 2 of *A Writer's Guide* will help students understand the reading process and enhance their critical reading skills.

This section of Practical Suggestions introduces you to the features in *A Writer's Reader* that foster students' critical reading and writing skills, and it offers advice about teaching each chapter in the reader, with summaries of the selections, answers to the questions about the selections, ideas for starting class discussion, and follow-up questions to take your conversation even further.

USING *A WRITER'S READER* TO TEACH CRITICAL READING

The authors have included in *A Writer's Reader* essays and prompts designed for students with a wide range of reading skills. Even underprepared students, some of whom might have difficulty reading for comprehension, can make some progress toward learning to read more critically. Encourage these students to spend time thinking about the As You Read question at the beginning of each selection and to pay attention to the vocabulary glosses throughout *A Writer's Reader.*

Encourage all of your students to read the Expanding Vocabulary question and to look up the words in the question before they read a selection. Remind students that you, too, look up unfamiliar words as you read an essay or article. Emphasize that it is their responsibility as active readers to investigate terms or phrases they do not know. Stress the importance of understanding the meaning of a word in its context and of considering both its denotation and connotation. Ask students to log new words and phrases in their journals as they read each essay. Whenever possible, have them work in groups to respond to the textbook's questions and to arrive at definitions of new words and phrases.

Journals might be the single most important tool for teaching your students to speak back to and interrogate what they read. Have students read pages 23–24 on keeping a reading journal, and require them to keep a response journal for all of their readings during the course. Use the journal prompts in *A Writer's Reader* to introduce students to the reflective process of keeping a journal, and as the term progresses, move students into using their journals for more critical responses to their reading.

Before assigning students a particular selection from *A Writer's Reader*, spend class time preparing them to answer the Reading Critically questions following the selection. These questions focus on critical thinking strategies covered in Chapter 3 of *A Writer's Guide*, and most first-year students will be encountering for the first time the kind of critical thinking that these questions require. As often as possible, have groups of students test a writer's evidence and identify the kind of appeals he or she is using. Working through these points with peers will encourage students to ask the same questions of their own arguments. For more about teaching students to read critically, see pages 102–04 of this manual.

The following features in *A Writer's Reader* provide students with the opportunity to practice essential critical reading skills: namely, evaluating and synthesizing a range of sources, from the Internet to political rhetoric to academic research.

Responding to an Image

These visual activities are designed to act as stimuli to get students thinking about whatever topic they're trying to tackle, and to do so right away. Each image has been hand-selected to directly correspond with the material in the first two parts of the book. Use these visual activities as an icebreaker, or even as potential paper topics. For more on this type of material, turn to Chapter 22 in *The Bedford Guide,* "Strategies for Understanding Visual Representations" (p. 418).

Web Search

The second page of each chapter in *A Writer's Reader* contains an Internet activity. If you know nothing about the Web and are wondering how you'll ever guide students through it, don't despair. Most of your students will already be at home in cyberspace, and these experts are usually happy to help the novices. The first time you assign a Web Search activity, pair students in the know with beginners. Exploring together will increase the comfort level for students who are just learning how to surf. Caution the experienced students not to do everything themselves, and encourage novices to take notes they can refer to later.

Whenever you assign an Internet activity, remind students that they must spend time evaluating the reliability of information they find on the Web. Advise them to note the publisher and its purpose for publishing on the Web. If your students' textbooks include *A Writer's Research Manual,* refer them to Chapter 31 for more on evaluating sources. Section B of The Quick Research Guide, included in all versions of the text, also offers advice on selecting Internet sources and a checklist to guide students to reliable information. Also take the opportunity to discuss students' experiences surfing the Internet. What kind of useful information are they finding there? What role, if any, do they think the Internet will play in their lives?

For more information about using computers and the Internet in your course, see Chapter 5 of this manual.

Paired Essays

The last two essays in each chapter of *A Writer's Reader* are paired essays, indicated as such in the table of contents. These essays address the same issue from differing viewpoints or offer slightly different takes on the same subject. As a pair, they give students an opportunity to practice comparing and contrasting different sources. Remind students that there are many other points of comparison between the essays besides the ones raised in the textbook. Encourage students to make their own comparisons between both the content of the essays and the writing strategies that the authors use. Have students brainstorm in their journals or as an in-class writing activity to come up with as many connections between the essays as they can. Even the most absurd comparisons might raise relevant discussion or writing topics.

Emphasize the range of thought on the issues the pairs set up as a way of highlighting the need to learn critical thinking skills such as evaluation. Consider bringing in additional viewpoints to expand discussion of the paired essays. First have students brainstorm a list of viewpoints other than those represented by the authors. Where would readers be most likely to encounter these different ideas? Ask students to look for and bring in essays and articles that complicate the discussion set up by the pair. Students might find connections among other essays in the same chapter or bring in perspectives from more current sources, such as newspapers or online magazines.

CHAPTER 23: FAMILIES (p. 440)

The essays in Chapter 23, "Families," explore what it means to be a family. They range widely in their views and presentations: Christy De'on Miller struggles to come to terms with her marine son's death in Iraq; Amy Tan offers a poignant glimpse of how her Chinese immigrant mother's imperfect English has influenced Tan's writing; and Anna Quindlen takes a stand on the rights of gay couples to legal and binding marriages. In an interesting exploration of arranged marriage, Anjula Razdan compares the tradition to online dating, and Danzy Senna, a biracial writer, comes to terms with her white grandmother's racial prejudice. In this chapter's paired essays, E. B. White dramatizes a father's realization that his own childhood is being displaced by his son's, and Nancy Gibbs remembers the freedom of her childhood summers and wishes the same for her own daughters. Although both authors reflect on childhood summers, their different purposes result in very different focuses. While Gibbs aims to persuade readers that it is important for children to have freedom to explore, White reflects on the inevitable passage of life from one generation to the next.

Students might wonder how the concept of "family" can be interpreted in so many different ways. Tell them that the essays in this chapter might require them to reconsider their own assumptions about what constitutes a family. Ask them to come up with their own definitions of "family" during five minutes of freewriting. Join them by writing your own definition and reading it aloud to encourage volunteers to share their responses to the class. Discuss the answers the class has produced. Consider bringing a dictionary to class and reading aloud its definition of family as a frame of reference.

Responding to an Image (p. 440)

Allow your students to use their imagination while examining these visual activity prompts. If necessary, have students free-associate answers to elements of each image. If they are given free rein for their own interpretations, they will most likely view analyzing these images as a rewarding way to begin thinking about writing in these modes.

Encourage your students to bring in some of their own family photographs and perhaps to write an essay based on their photographs. How do the photographs accurately or inaccurately reflect the nature of their family relationships and experiences? Be sure to remind students that these photographs just as often hide information about their subject as they reveal such information.

Web Search (p. 441)

Have students print out and bring to class what they find during this activity as a way to begin the discussion about families. Ask them if they were surprised by what they found, if the information met their expectations, and what they were unable to find. You might want to ask students to bring family photos related to the ones they find in the archives. Students are interested in their genealogy, and most will offer stories about their own families. Encourage students to tell a variety of stories by reminding them that there are many different definitions of "family" in this chapter. For more about using this activity, see page 244 of this manual.

CHRISTY DE'ON MILLER   *Give Me Five More Minutes* (p. 441)

Miller writes of the death of her son, a marine killed in 2004 in Iraq. In a lengthy narrative opening, she relates how she received the news of his death and some events that followed. Beginning in paragraph 12, she lovingly recalls her son, her memories tinged with grief, by describing the various objects she uses to help recover his memory. She ends, somewhat surprisingly, by communicating her lack of animosity for her son's killer, whom she forgives because of her hope to spend eternity with God and her son. You might ask students how they respond to Miller's conclusion.

As You Read (p. 441)

Students should recognize the wide range of objects that help Miller recall her son's memory: his watch, with its two alarms set to go off five minutes apart (which gives the essay its title); things he has chewed on, like pen caps and his dog tags; tape recordings of his voice; a pair of house shoes in which lingers the smell of his feet. What she misses particularly are things that would conjure his scent — his childhood blanket, long since discarded, as well as the personal effects laundered by the military before their return to her.

Pop Quiz

1. How, specifically, was Miller's son killed?

2. What are Miller's feelings about the Iraqi insurgent who killed her son?

Questions to Start You Thinking (p. 444)

1. *Considering Meaning.* The reference to the title comes in paragraph 12, but students will likely recognize that Miller herself would cherish "five more minutes" with her son, even though this point is not made explicitly in the essay. This second meaning gives the title a great sense of poignancy.

2. *Identifying Writing Strategies.* You might ask students to think about why Miller chose to open her essay with the particular narration of how she learned of her son's death in combat. How else might she have begun? What would be different if she had opened by relating, say, her son's funeral or the story of his decision to join the Marines in the first place? They should see that the focus of the essay is her grief, and this is the story of the moment her grief began.

3. *Reading Critically.* Ask students to brainstorm individually in writing, jotting down words they would use to describe the personal attitude Miller presents in the essay. Then have them share what they have come up with. The overall sense is one of loss and sadness, though feelings of deep affection and pride for her son come through as well. The sense of love that infuses the essay keeps any shred of bitterness at bay.

4. *Expanding Vocabulary.* You might take a moment to have students come up with their own definitions of eternity. Then share with them dictionary definitions you bring to class. Miller uses the word figuratively in paragraph 2 — the same way you might say you waited an eternity to see the doctor. In paragraphs 19 and 20, she uses the word quite literally, although in its most religious sense of achieving life eternal and the eternity that the Christian God represents.

5. *Making Connections.* You could begin discussing this connection by asking students what, in their experience, are the similarities and differences in the relation-

ships that mothers and fathers have with their sons. What evidence can they point to in the Miller and White essays to support their observations? It is interesting to note that Miller's memories take a very different form from those of White, who conflates memories of his own childhood with the present-day experiences of his son. Finally, a close analysis of each writer's conclusion shows a stark contrast: White feels "the chill of death," while Miller is certain of being reunited with her son for eternity.

Journal Prompts (p. 444)

1. Stress to students that the memories prompted by smells are not always happy ones — for every pleasant memory prompted by the aroma of a favorite childhood dish bubbling on the stove, there are unhappy memories prompted, say, by the antiseptic smell of a hospital room. Students might choose to write in their journals about one of each.

2. Students could certainly use Miller's essay as a jumping-off point for this journal writing because her grief as the mother of a dead child comes through so palpably. Ask them to consider as they write why grief over the death of a child might be especially difficult.

Suggestions for Writing (p. 444)

1. Have students start with individual brainstorming to come up with lists of important people in their lives whom they've lost to death or in some other way. Depending on the age of most of the students in your class, these may range from grandparents who have died to close friends who are no longer in their lives. After they have chosen a subject and as they plan and draft their essays, suggest that they make sure, like Miller, to depict their feelings about the loss as fully as possible.

2. This topic, the war in Iraq, is probably better left to individual writers rather than to classroom discussion, where it might spark unproductive controversy. Suggest that students who choose this topic access an online time line of the conflict in Iraq so that they that can think about their responses to the war as it has progressed. Arab-American students may have especially interesting viewpoints to offer here.

AMY TAN   *Mother Tongue* (p. 445)

In "Mother Tongue," novelist Amy Tan uses cause and effect to explore the differences between the "family talk" English that she uses with her mother and the correct English that she uses to address everyone outside of the family. Tan offers a touching glimpse, using her mother's experience, of how speakers of "broken" English are treated in American society. More specifically, she addresses some of the stereotypes that the American education system has applied to Asian American students and recounts her rebellion against them.

As You Read (p. 445)

Tan speaks of the embarrassment and shame at parents' imperfect English felt by many children growing up in non-English-speaking homes. Some of your students might have experienced this themselves. Tan goes on to speculate that these children's lower scores on the language portion of achievement and placement tests give a false picture of their aptitudes and limit what fields their teachers encourage them to pursue, thus reducing the range of possibilities that these students imagine for themselves.

Pop Quiz

1. What is the tool of the author's trade?

2. What terms does Tan use to characterize her mother's English?

Questions to Start You Thinking (p. 450)

1. *Considering Meaning.* This question will help students consider various patterns of discourse and tone. Tan's essay illustrates the problems that can result for people who have a hard time switching from private discourse patterns to public or standard ones. How many discourse communities do your students belong to? Are they conscious of a need to use different "Englishes" in different groups?

2. *Identifying Writing Strategies.* Tan's use of quotes from her mother's speech allows us to share in her family's private language — to see and, if we read it aloud, hear it. Ask students to consider the audience for which Tan is writing.

3. *Reading Critically.* To facilitate a discussion of audience, have students discuss how they would write about a particular incident for a variety of different audiences. For example, how would they write about their relationship with their mother in a letter to a friend, in a school psychology paper on parenting, or in a letter nominating her for an award? Once students have a sense of how audience affects a writer's choices, ask them what constraints Tan faces in different situations.

4. *Expanding Vocabulary.* Ask students if they have come to similar conclusions about people who speak "limited" English. Have they ever done what Tan describes salespeople and clerks as having done to her mother — ignoring or pretending not to understand her — when they encountered people who spoke imperfect English? Lead students to discuss some of the assumptions that society tends to make about people whose language or way of expressing themselves varies from the norm.

5. *Making Connections.* For this question, you might have students create a diagram that highlights similarities and differences as well as causes and effects. Begin by asking them to make a quick list of the points of comparison and contrast in Tan's and Rodriguez's experiences. You might direct students to the Venn Diagram Home Page at <http://venndiagram.com>, where they can use the "Create-a-Venn" tool to organize their list. With their diagrams in front of them, ask students to go a step further to present the effects of each similarity or difference, using arrows to link each effect to its cause. Discuss how similar experiences might have different effects.

Journal Prompts (p. 450)

1. This journal prompt offers students the opportunity to demonstrate their analytical skills. Have they ever been in situations where they used incorrect English? Ask them to write about it in their journals and discuss their experiences with the class.

2. Most students will be able to share an experience that involves "translating" language or fashion to their parents, regardless of their cultural backgrounds. Ask them to recall certain words or phrases that they have had to translate for their parents, or certain trends in clothing or accessories that their families didn't understand.

Suggestions for Writing (p. 450)

1. Suggest to your students that they take special care to bring their language to life by writing the speech exactly as they hear and remember it. To get your stu-

dents started, read some examples from writers such as William Faulkner and Zora Neale Hurston who use regional dialects in their work.

2. This assignment ties in nicely with Chapter 6, "Interviewing a Subject," and offers an excellent opportunity for students to practice interviewing skills. Before students begin this assignment, have them brainstorm in groups about what questions should be asked of each interview subject.

ANNA QUINDLEN   *Evan's Two Moms* (p. 451)

Quindlen, a nationally syndicated columnist and Pulitzer Prize winner, takes a stand in this essay on the rights of gay men and lesbians to legal and binding marriage. Quindlen's argument cites some of the basic legal and economic benefits that are denied to homosexual couples — benefits that married heterosexual couples are automatically entitled to and take for granted. Essays of this kind can really polarize some classes, so be sure to remind students to avoid logical fallacies and emotional attacks while discussing this topic.

As You Read (p. 451)

Quindlen supports the need to legalize homosexual marriage by naming specific rights denied to gay partners without the protection of legal marriage: economic benefits such as health insurance coverage, joint tax returns, and Social Security survivor's benefits. She mentions legally entitling these survivors to shared personal property and, more important, protecting their right to care for a dying or disabled partner whose family disapproves of the relationship.

Pop Quiz

1. Name at least one advantage marriage offers that is denied to same-sex couples.

2. What was the case of *Loving v. Virginia* about?

Questions to Start You Thinking (p. 453)

1. *Considering Meaning.* Quindlen makes it clear that without the protection of legal marriage, gay partners are vulnerable to society's prejudices. Ask students to consider whether her appeal to "love and commitment" (para. 10) is a persuasive argument for extending the right to marry to same-sex partners. Once you have students go over the main points, ask if they have read or heard about anything in the media lately that addresses the issue of gay and lesbian rights. What are some of the justifications for the suspension of or advocacy for these rights? Why are heterosexuals entitled to certain rights that are denied to homosexuals?

2. *Identifying Writing Strategies.* This question about the comparison of gay marriage and interracial marriage might generate a heated debate among students, so try to steer them away from attacking one another and urge them instead to concentrate on critiquing one another's ideas. Discuss some of the reasons that miscegenation was forbidden by those who created our legal system in the first place. Then ask students whether they can make any connections between the basis for that discrimination and the discrimination against gay men and lesbians that Quindlen discusses in her essay.

3. *Reading Critically.* Quindlen relies largely on emotional appeals in her essay, although she also uses logical appeal as well. Ask students to identify her emotionally charged language (and stylistic devices, such as her use of fragments in

the first paragraph) and to describe its effect on them. Even the title couches the issue in emotional terms. Do students think that Quindlen strikes the right balance between these two kinds of appeal? Why or why not?

4. *Expanding Vocabulary.* Ask students what they think of when they consider the word *marriage.* Do their definitions differ dramatically from the way Quindlen would define it? You might also ask them to consider the following questions: What constitutes a "good" marriage? What are the basic requirements for any marriage? Do marriages always include children? By extension, you could ask them what constitutes a family. Do their definitions of *family* and *marriage* differ from those of their parents? How many "families" do they belong to, according to their various definitions?

Bring in several dictionaries and have students compare their various definitions of the word *marriage.* Are the definitions equally accurate or adequate?

5. *Making Connections.* Once students have recounted some examples of discrimination directed toward gay and lesbian families in Quindlen's essay and Asian American families in Tan's essay, ask them to consider some of the forces, such as the law and the media, that have shaped and continue to perpetuate discrimination against minority groups. Ask groups of students to research specific instances of discrimination and report on them to the class.

Journal Prompts (p. 453)

1. Have students write their own description of marriage. Then read them the dictionary definition and ask them to think of as many arguments as they can to defend their definition, writing them down in their journal. A good follow-up for this exercise would be to have students defend their definitions of *marriage* in small peer groups.

2. Have students share their responses to this prompt with the class. After they have said what their ideal parents would be like, ask them if they think it would be possible for them to live up to their description of ideal parents if they become parents themselves.

Suggestions for Writing (p. 453)

1. To get students motivated for this topic, have them come up with as many different definitions for the word *family* as they can. What are the key ingredients that bind a family together: love, blood, the law? Based on their definitions of family, ask them to consider how many different types of "families" they belong to. Which one has the most significance for them? Why?

2. Brainstorming as a class would be a good way to begin this writing assignment. Make a list on the board of the advantages and disadvantages of this type of family. Ask students to support their choices, and enlist the help of other students to examine what assumptions inform these choices.

ANJULA RAZDAN   *What's Love Got to Do with It?* (p. 453)

A child of parents who marriage was arranged, Razdan explores how reality television and online dating services are introducing the tradition of arranged marriages to twenty-first-century Western culture. Although she presents evidence supporting arranged marriages, Razdan also defends the Western romantic ideal. Students who have grown up in a culture where arranged marriages are rare should be intrigued by the essay's title and content.

As You Read (p. 454)

Some students might initially scoff at the idea of arranged marriages, describing them as a thing of the past. Others might think that arranged marriages occur only in non-Western societies. This essay, then, may jolt students into considering the benefits of such an arrangement. Razdan quotes experts who assert that arranged marriages succeed because they are based on compatibility and logic — not passion and physical attraction, to which they attribute the failure of many marriages. Do students think that passion and physical attraction fuel a marriage or lead to its deterioration?

Pop Quiz

1. Why were arranged marriages common in Europe before the nineteenth century?

2. According to the experts Razdan quotes, why are arranged marriages more likely to result in "enduring love" than traditional Western relationships?

Questions to Start You Thinking (p. 457)

1. *Considering Meaning.* Begin by asking students how and why they use cyberspace. Do any of the advantages of online shopping, researching, and communicating also apply to online dating? Is it easier to find a suitable spouse online than through traditional means? Is it safer? More economical? To further the discussion, direct students to paragraphs 13–15, where one of Razdan's sources explains that because "online interaction tends to downplay proximity, physical attraction, and face-to-face interaction, people are more likely to . . . attain a higher level of psychological and emotional intimacy than if they dated right away or hopped in the sack." Do students agree that this is a benefit of online dating?

2. *Identifying Writing Strategies.* Students might list differences regarding infidelity, finances, and "growing apart" as reasons for the high divorce rate. Ask them to dig deeper, however, to speculate on a deeper cause. You might direct students to paragraph 7, where Razdan presents the modern Western bases for choosing a mate — proximity and physical attraction. End the discussion by having the class evaluate Razdan's cause-and-effect analysis.

3. *Reading Critically.* Ask students to define the terms *relevant, credible,* and *sufficient.* What makes statistics credible? What makes a quotation relevant? Divide students into groups and ask them to find and evaluate several different types of evidence in the essay. Students might wonder why Razdan didn't draw more heavily on personal observation for support, especially since she begins her essay by referring to her parents' arranged marriage. Could she have used first-hand observations to further illuminate her case? Generally, is first-hand experience as reliable as other types of evidence? Is it as credible?

4. *Expanding Vocabulary.* Suggest that students begin by looking up the dictionary definition of *love.* Does the definition successfully capture the meaning of this abstract term? How can a writer make the intangible concrete? To explore these questions, ask students to finish the sentence, "Real love is . . ." Have them share their definitions with the class and then decide on a definition that Razdan could have used in her essay.

5. *Making Connections.* Both essays acknowledge that divorce is common in today's society. The statistics Razdan presents and the experts she quotes underscore that

the typical Western approach to marriage is not always successful. Noel Perrin takes a different approach, drawing on personal experience to show that marriage is a flawed institution. Encourage students to discuss whether Perrin's divorce could have been prevented if his marriage had been arranged. How might Razdan react to Perrin's solution of a "part-time marriage"?

Journal Prompts (p. 458)

1. Students will probably be familiar with the writing style of personal ads, but bring in some examples from a newspaper or a Web site, and provide students with a maximum word count and a list of common abbreviations. After students write their own personals, have them work in groups to analyze the content and form of their ads. For example, how many mentioned physical appearance? How many said they were looking for a "soul mate"? Have groups write a short summary of their findings, reporting on what the writing style of an ad seems to suggest about the writer's personality.

2. To generate interest in this prompt, ask students to brainstorm examples that illustrate and perpetuate the romantic ideal of "love at first sight." Encourage them to draw upon literature, movies, music, and television.

Suggestions for Writing (p. 458)

1. Razdan's essay contains a number of possibilities for personalized writing topics. Have the class brainstorm a list of ideas that could serve as springboards for writing. You might suggest that students write for *Utne* magazine as Razdan does, encouraging them to keep their audience in mind as they select their topic, generate and arrange ideas, and draft their essay. Students may want to visit Utne's Web site at <http://utne.com> to familiarize themselves with the magazine's audience.

2. Many students will view arranged marriage as an anomaly. Additionally, their knowledge of the topic is probably limited, so they will benefit from some research. If students are inexperienced researchers, you might ask each student to find one article and then pool the class's findings. Guide students to select evidence that, like Razdan's, is credible, relevant, and sufficient. Chapter 9, "Taking a Stand," will guide students in composing their argument.

DANZY SENNA   *The Color of Love* (p. 458)

Tensions between generations of a family are so common that students should relate to the conflicting emotions that Senna expresses in this essay. As she relates her tenuous relationship with her grandmother, Senna effectively combines description and dialogue to recall her experience for readers.

As You Read (p. 458)

Growing up, Senna struggles to understand her grandmother's racist views, which are particularly hurtful given Senna's biracial heritage. Ask students how it can be possible to love and to dislike someone at the same time.

Pop Quiz

1. What country was Senna's grandmother from?

2. What incident sparked the main confrontation between Senna and her grandmother?

Questions to Start You Thinking (p. 462)

1. *Considering Meaning.* Have students trace the essay's opening paragraph, creating a two-column list of similarities and differences. Then ask them to continue filling in the columns with examples and details from the remainder of the essay, specifically from paragraphs 3–7. Encourage students to discuss which differences created the most conflict, and why.

2. *Identifing Writing Strategies.* From paragraph 2, where the grandmother is sitting at a fancy dinner table in the prime of her life, to the last paragraph, where the grandmother lies critically ill, Senna incorporates telling details and examples that vividly convey her grandmother's personality to readers. Ask students what main point Senna's details convey. In groups, have students select a key passage and explain how its details and examples directly contribute to their impression of the grandmother and to the essay's thesis.

3. *Reading Critically.* Students usually have an easier time highlighting details and examples (see question 2 above) than they have describing tone. Point out that examples reveal the author's attitude toward his or her topic and audience. With that in mind, students can brainstorm adjectives that describe the tone and point to specific details that contributed to their choice of adjective. Students might comment that although Senna is frustrated with her grandmother's limited views, she nevertheless grew to understand her and — of course — to love her. Would they label the tone as nostalgic?

4. *Expanding Vocabulary.* The description of the grandmother in paragraphs 27–31 shows her to be far from "indestructible" as the family gathers to await her death. What makes someone "immortal" in a figurative sense? Students might mention that writers, actors, musicians, and artists are immortalized by the works they create. What about people who do not leave behind material legacies?

5. *Making Connections.* To help answer this question, students might first write a dialogue between Senna and the child of a married gay couple. You might also ask students if bans against gay marriage will be as unthinkable in thirty years as bans against interracial marriage are now. If not, why not?

Journal Prompts (p. 463)

1. To reveal how ubiquitous verbal abuse is, consider showing a tape of a typical television sitcom in which insults and put-downs are often the foundation of the comedy. Ask students whether sarcasm can be considered abusive. With a clear idea of what constitutes verbal abuse, students should be better able to respond to this prompt.

2. Before students respond to this prompt, have them review paragraph 18 (where the grandmother responds to Senna's criticism), scan the remainder of the essay, and reflect on whether the grandmother has changed. Remind students that their interpretation will affect how they respond to this assignment. Then have students share their sentences with the class. Students should be ready to defend their response by pointing to specific passages in the essay and explaining their interpretation.

Suggestions for Writing (p. 463)

1. Freewriting is an ideal technique for exploring this topic. Have students exchange their freewriting with a peer who will read it with a reporter's questions in mind (the five W's and an H; see page 303 of *The Bedford Guide*). This initial feedback should help students as they focus their ideas and develop them into a first draft.

2. To introduce this assignment, have students bring in a newspaper or news magazine. As a class, brainstorm examples of prejudice from articles in these publications. Students can also offer examples from personal experience or observation. Once you have a good-sized list on the board, work with students to identify causes of the prejudice. Students might mention age, upbringing, and lack of education or exposure. Chapter 8, "Explaining Causes and Effects," and Chapter 10, "Proposing a Solution," will help students organize and develop their essay.

E. B. WHITE   *Once More to the Lake* (p. 463)

In this essay, White juxtaposes memories of childhood vacations at a Maine lake with the story of a later visit to the same spot in the company of his son. His combination of recall and observation weaves a vivid pattern and finally surprises the reader into a recognition of the cyclical nature of human existence and the inevitability of death.

As You Read (p. 464)

Throughout the essay, White emphasizes the blurring of the boundaries between his adult self and his memory of himself as a boy, and also between himself and his son, that he feels during the summer at the lake. Students will find that his perception finally crystallizes only at the end of the essay, when he realizes the cycle will complete itself in death.

Pop Quiz

1. What new sound at the lake provides a reminder that many years have passed since White had last visited the lake?

2. What sight makes White suddenly think of death?

Questions to Start You Thinking (p. 469)

1. *Considering Meaning.* It might be helpful to have students make lists of comparisons and contrasts. What aspects of the lake and summers there does White include in his description? What does he seem to have left out? Can students think of a reason for this omission? Ask them what their own images of the lake are.

2. *Identifying Writing Strategies.* To encourage a variety of responses, have students identify four images that White uses to evoke a different sense. For instance, the smell of the lumber in the bedroom (para. 2), the feel of the damp moss in the bait can (para. 5), the sight of the dragonflies at the tip of the fishing rods (para. 5), and the sound of the outboard motors on the lake (para. 10). You might want to organize students into small groups for this question. Ask them to share with one another the details that were the most memorable for them, and why.

3. *Reading Critically.* Students will have little trouble pointing out the things that have stayed the same and the things that have changed since White was a child at the lake. To move such a list into a discussion of tone, ask them to look carefully at the details and images White uses to describe these changes and consistencies. How does his word choice create feelings or impressions for the reader? Where do students see White being nostalgic? Where is he pragmatic?

4. *Expanding Vocabulary.* Ask the class to supply alternative words and phrases that would be more appropriate to the "voice" of a child. For example, *hellgrammite*

could be described as "a fly egg," and *undulating* might become "moving" or "shaking." This substitution can lead to a discussion of the need for writers to use language that is in line with the "voices" they select.

Definitions

primeval: wild, primitive, unexplored since the dawn of time

transposition: changing or exchanging places

hellgrammite: fishing bait; the larva of a fly

undulating: rolling smoothly

cultist: one committed to the beliefs of a marginal group (usually religious)

petulant: grumpy, pouting

5. *Making Connections.* Remind students that good writers use concrete detail to make their recollections come alive for readers (as discussed in Chapter 4) and that description and dialogue are two effective vehicles for conveying detail. Have students work in groups to identify a strong descriptive passage in White's essay, listing the details that contribute to its impact. Next, have them read an excerpt of dialogue from Senna's essay. How does dialogue bring the event to life? Consider asking students to turn the dialogue into a narrative passage. Share the passages with the class, discussing whether something is lost in the translation. What factors might influence a writer's decision to use either dialogue or description?

Journal Prompts (p. 469)

1. Encourage students to use a variety of senses to describe this place. In addition to a physical description, have them include other details that describe the smell(s) of the place, the sounds one hears there, and the different textures that can be seen and touched there.

2. White compares the thunderstorm to a dramatic performance in paragraph 12. Have students brainstorm in small groups to discuss which metaphors or similes would work best for their descriptions of the natural events they have witnessed. Creative sessions of this kind often lead to wonderfully inspired essays.

Suggestions for Writing (p. 469)

1. Stress to students the importance of using sensory detail to discuss the place they remember from childhood. Their recollected smells, tastes, sights, sounds, and touch all form the basis for a contrast of memory with contemporary reality. Have them use White's essay as a model for structuring their own essays.

2. Ask groups of students to discuss their views on how nostalgia influences our interpretation of the past. In addition, they might discuss whether a bad memory functions in the same way that nostalgia does. Which is more vivid?

NANCY GIBBS   *Free the Children* (p. 470)

Gibbs, a columnist, editor, and mother, writes passionately about allowing children to savor the freedom that summer brings. She asserts that parents who give their children freedom give them the opportunity to explore, make choices, skin a knee or two, and ultimately grow. She acknowledges the difficulty parents might have in giving up control and supervision but determines that doing so is necessary. This essay presents a great opportunity for students to discuss their own summer experiences. Older students may have insight into what Gibbs is writing about as they, too, might have had summertime adventures similar to the ones Gibbs remembers. Younger students may have had overscheduled summers filled with various types of camps. Hearing what both groups of students have to say should create a lively discussion.

As You Read (p. 470)

Before asking students to respond, have them complete the Quick Start activity that asks them to freewrite about their own childhood summers. Ask them to share the type of activities that they were involved in and then to compare those to the suggestions Gibbs makes. Point out the simplicity of her suggestions: "ice cream . . . before dinner"(paragraph 5) and "build[ing] a fort" (paragraph 6). Have students discuss the value, both short and long term, of such activities. Ask students if Gibbs hints or directly states their value. You might also highlight the title of this essay, which may have made students initially think that the essay would have a "political" thrust. What type of thrust, if any, does it have? Social? Educational?

Pop Quiz

 1. Why are children's summers so clogged with activities?

 2. Why are children kept inside during the summer?

Questions to Start You Thinking (p. 472)

1. *Considering Meaning.* Before having students respond, ask them to reread the first sentence of paragraph 3, in which Gibbs states "I want summer not to count because what happens as a result counts for so much" and the first sentence of paragraph 5, where she states "That's because summer should be a season of grace — not of excuses but of exceptions." Have students locate other paragraphs where Gibbs, either directly or indirectly, presents benefits.

2. *Identifying Writing Strategies.* Point out that in paragraph 6, Gibbs begins to discuss what needs to happen in order for children to be able to experience, savor, and grow from unscheduled, unsupervised summers. She mentions the need for re-education and in paragraph 7 mentions the importance of "nerve." Her use of a specific personal experience involving the temporary disappearance of her daughter shows that she understands the parental fear associated with freedom. She lived through this fear, yet continues to allow her children freedom, illustrating how important the idea of a "free" summer is. She learned firsthand that letting go takes nerve, but the end results are worth it. Point out that personal examples add to the writer's credibility.

3. *Reading Critically.* Reinforce the concept of audience here. Before students answer this question, ask them to reread the section in the text regarding "Purpose and Audience" (pp. 14–18) and consider some of the key questions regarding audience. The introduction to the reading includes the fact that Gibbs originally wrote the essay for *Time*. Ask students to hypothesize about the readers' various demographic characteristics — age, for example — and then to make a connection between those characteristics and Gibbs's lack of evidence. Is specific evidence necessary, or would readers relate to Gibbs's point because of their own experiences?

4. *Expanding Vocabulary.* Students may need to ponder this question for a while. Ask them in what context they hear the word *rehearsal* and have them come up with a definition. Can we rehearse for life? For example, can submitting assignments on time, working on a team project, or presenting a speech to a class be considered

rehearsing for the tasks required in future jobs? In what way is a carefree summer a rehearsal, and for what? If students consider the type of activities that go on during rehearsals (mistakes, for instance), they might have an easier time understanding the significance of rehearsal in relation to Gibbs's writing purpose and main point.

5. *Making Connections.* Students, no doubt, will reveal their own educational experiences as they answer this question. Ask them to discuss ways in which freedom is integral to education. Then have them recall their middle school, junior high, or high school years. Would learning have been possible in an unstructured classroom? For a more directed discussion, suggest that students, either individually or as a class, research the philosophy behind Montessori schools. In what ways is the philosophy different from or similar to that of most public schools? How do they imagine Gibbs and Konig feel about the Montessori philosophy?

Link to the Paired Essay (p. 472)

In paragraph 7, Gibbs acknowledges that summer is a "precious time to be together as a family." From that statement, students should surmise that Gibbs would approve of the time White spends with his son. The nostalgic tone of White's essay illustrates how important it was for him to spend time with his son, and how "those summers had been infinitely precious and worth saving." Suggest that students write a brief postcard from Gibbs to White and from White to a parent of one of today's overscheduled children. What would each say? What tone would they use?

Journal Prompts (p. 472)

1. Your students' ages and their own past experiences and observations will influence how they respond to this question. What is the daily life children — say, in grammar school — like today? What are their daily activities and chores? Once students consider these questions, ask them to comment about the lack of downtime and the resulting stress.

2. Students can do a quick reflection here to determine the level of supervision in their lives. Those who are parents will have an easier time answering this question. Specifically, working parents might feel that Gibbs diminishes the benefits of parental supervision. Given many of the growing problems in today's society (drugs, child abduction, computer misuse and overuse), is Gibbs naïve in her belief that children should be unsupervised? Ask students to share their responses and examples with the class. They might begin with the common expression (and one most children hate to hear) "When I was young. . . ."

Suggestions for Writing (p. 473)

1. Ah, summer! Sometimes those summer vacations all blend together, but sometimes one summer is particularly memorable. Students can brainstorm, or you can share some of those times caught on film: *Summer of '42, Grease* (summer love), *Stand by Me, Parent Trap, Sisterhood of the Traveling Pants,* and so many more. Each of these films captures a significant summer experience. Have students reflect on their own summers to identify a particular experience — perhaps one involving a vacation, a job, a camp, or another important place or circumstance. Once they have described their experience, they can decide on the role supervision played in it and where in the essay they might comment on the necessity of oversight.

2. The ideal summer break will vary depending upon the audience students select. "Ideal" might not be the same for an audience of working parents as it is for those who do not work. In that case, students will need to temper "ideal" for a realistic audience. After students brainstorm activities and events, have them classify them

and perhaps even connect them to a level of supervision. Students will then be ready to write a draft. As they write, remind them to provide specific details to enliven and illustrate their points.

CHAPTER 24: MEN AND WOMEN (p. 474)

Chapter 24, "Men and Women," is likely to be one of the students' favorites; everyone, no matter what his or her circumstances, is affected by gender roles and their demands, and this chapter offers a variety of perspectives on gender stereotyping, expectations, and biases. Robert Jensen is alarmed by the way society defines manliness, and Brent Staples reveals what it means to be a black man in a society that fears black men. In humorous pieces, Barbara Ehrenreich asserts that college boys get points for partying, and Dave Barry pokes fun at male-bashing stereotypes. Next, Evelyn F. Murphy takes on gender-based salary inequities. Finally, the paired essays in this chapter address marriage: Noel Perrin wryly describes the benefits of a new type of marriage, and Judy Brady weighs in with a satirical tribute to the role of wives.

Ask students to react to the content of each essay in their reading journal and to use these responses when they are called on to add their own voice to the debate. Encourage them also to keep a record of their experiences with gender preconceptions. How do students' surroundings contribute to their identity as a man or woman? Are these definitions at odds with their self-images?

Responding to an Image (p. 474)

Allow your students to use their imagination while examining these visual activity prompts. If necessary, have students free-associate answers to elements of each image. If they are given free rein for their own interpretations, they will most likely view analyzing these images as a rewarding way to begin thinking about writing in these modes.

Encourage students to consider the body positions and seating arrangement of the man and woman in this photograph. How do nonverbal cues contribute to the photograph's message? What might be the source of the tension or conflict apparent in the photo? Ask the class whether nonverbal communication differs by gender.

Web Search (p. 475)

The range of gender-specific Web sites is remarkable in itself. For example, students might be surprised to discover how many Web sites are devoted to men's rights or women's health. Encourage students to examine why differences exist. Are the Internet publishers correct in grouping sources this way? Are such stereotypes harmful? Why, or why not?

Ask students to identify the kinds of information they find on these sites: Are there articles, images, chat rooms? Why might these forums be particularly suited to addressing gender issues?

For more about using this activity, see page 244 in this manual.

ROBERT JENSEN   *The High Cost of Manliness* (p. 475)

In his essay, Jensen acknowledges the common and limited notion of what it means to be a man in today's society. He argues that associating men with "strength, aggression, and competitiveness" has negative effects for men, women, and society in general. To frame his position, he begins and ends his essay with a call to eliminate the stereotypical concept of masculinity. Students will probably not be surprised by the traditional definition of masculinity, and their experiences, regardless of gender, can illuminate the discussion of Jensen's conclusions.

As You Read (p. 475)

Before students read this selection about how society's definition of masculinity is damaging to both men and women, ask them to provide their own definition of masculinity. After students read the essay, ask them to share their definitions and to identify similarities and differences between their definitions and what Jensen considers the "dominant conception of masculinity" in our society today. What Jensen thinks about the conception should be readily apparent; however, what students think may not be, and their opinions could lead to a lively and maybe even divided class discussion.

Pop Quiz

1. According to Jensen, who endorses the idea that men are "naturally competitive and aggressive" (paragraph 4)?

2. Jensen admits that our behavior is influenced by our DNA, but are there other influences?

Questions to Start You Thinking (p. 478)

1. *Considering Meaning*. Direct students to paragraph 4, where Jensen summarizes the dominant conception of masculinity. In class discussion, call on students to list effects of this common conception. Students can find these effects beginning in paragraph 6 and extending through paragraph 16. In paragraph 16, students might be surprised by Jensen's assertion that there are "political and ecological challenges that can't be met with this old model of what it means to be a man." Ask them to comment on this point. Do they think that Jensen is exaggerating or just carrying his argument to a natural conclusion?

2. *Identifying Writing Strategies*. Jensen's use of comparison is most obvious in paragraph 10, where he mentions obvious physical differences. In this paragraph, he also mentions that men and women are similar. However, he doesn't specifically state how. Does he need to? Ask students how men and women are similar. Do they agree that current conceptions of masculinity have masked similarities?

3. *Reading Critically*. Evidence is essential for writers to reach valid conclusions and for readers to understand and accept those conclusions. Have students comb the essay to highlight Jensen's evidence. Can they differentiate facts from assertions, specifics from generalizations? What do they think of paragraph 13 where Jensen discusses 9/11?

4. *Expanding Vocabulary*. Jensen notes that this "recurring intellectual fad" once went by the name of "evolutionary psychology" and earlier by "sociobiology." Do these terms seem like mumbo jumbo, or does such terminology give credence to conclusions reached by psychologists and sociologists? Is this fad of evolutionary psychology simply a new take (or a new phrase) on the age-old belief that men and women behave differently because they are "fundamentally different" (paragraph 12)?

5. *Making Connections*. It might be interesting to begin a discussion of Jensen's and Ehrenreich's observations by first looking at the end of their essays, both written around the same time. Jensen states that men need to strive to be humans first.

Ehrenreich contends that we need "Americans, of whatever gender" to compete in the global market. Students might point out that the underlying assumption is that both genders matter because of the contributions they can make. Students most likely will recognize that the bulk of Jensen's essay is devoted to the negative effects of society's stereotypical image of what it means to be male. He directly calls for erasing or replacing such images. What does Ehrenreich call for? You also might ask students to consider some related questions: How does Ehrenreich's use of humor affect her message or the impact of her message? Is she stereotyping? If so, is it creating problems? Or is she stereotyping because of the problems she has observed? Ask students how gender affects each writer's take on the topic. For an additional assignment, consider having students write to Ehrenreich as they imagine Jensen might after he read her essay.

Journal Prompts (p. 478)

1. Over the years, students will have heard a number of insulting expressions hurled at men by other men as well as by women: "You run like a girl," "That's a girlie shirt," "Stop acting like a girl." Ask students to add to this list and then to reflect on how these phrases are meant to insult men. Are such phrases ever acceptable? Are they damaging? If so, to whom?

2. Jensen devotes a large part of his essay to discussing the negative effects of a limited view of masculinity. In his last paragraph, he presents the ultimate negative effect — the demise of our planet itself. Ask students to theorize how a particular view of masculinity could be related to the demise of the planet. Can they establish a cause-effect relationship or a specific chain of events?

Suggestions for Writing (p. 478)

1. Refer students to Chapter 19 of the text to review different strategies for developing a point. Students might define "human strength" by using examples, by giving details, by creating a definition, or by dividing and classifying. Have students determine which strategy or combination of strategies will best help them accomplish their purpose.

2. Point out where in the essay Jensen acknowledges biological factors, and lead a discussion as to why he makes this point and why he has placed it in the middle of his essay. This assignment lends itself well to group brainstorming. To prepare students for this essay, divide the class into different groups and assign them some aspect of popular culture, education, sports, or children's toys. Within that given area, students can generate a list of social forces and discuss the effects of our society's messages about what it means to be male or female. To most students, the Barbie doll might jump out as the most obvious stereotypical toy, but there are other possibilities. Also, students might consider how music videos can contribute to stereotypes. Give students the option of individually developing the group's assigned topic or finding their own.

BRENT STAPLES   *Black Men and Public Space* (p. 479)

In an essay drawn exclusively from personal experience, journalist Staples reveals the effect — first startling but later predictable — that he has had on pedestrians as he walks through the city late at night. His plentiful and detailed examples clearly show that the fear and flight reactions he receives are neither isolated nor ignorable. While Staples comes to understand the rationale for the behavior, he remains unnerved by it and, therefore, modifies his own behavior to prevent further similar reactions.

As You Read (p. 479)

Students will readily understand from the author's examples how people respond to his presence. Underlying their behavior is one cause — he is a black man who has been stereotyped or typecast. Why did it take Staples so long to identify the cause?

Pop Quiz

1. What does Staples mean by the phrase "language of fear"?

2. Why does Staples decide to repress his rage rather than act upon it?

Questions to Start You Thinking (p. 481)

1. *Considering Meaning.* Before students answer these questions, ask them to reflect upon how strangers respond to Staples. Do they consider the strangers' behavior out of the ordinary, expected, preventable? Then have students determine the misconceptions by pointing out where they are directly stated or implied within the essay. In paragraph 2, Staples uses the phrase "unwieldy inheritance." What do students make of this phrase?

2. *Identifying Writing Strategies.* The bulk of this essay is devoted to examples that reveal the effects Staples has on others. In paragraphs 11 and 12, he seeks to reduce those effects by modifying his own behavior. For example, in paragraph 11, he states that he has changed the way he moves around others: giving "wide berth" and being "calm and extremely congenial." However, in paragraph 12, he mentions that he announces his presence to others around him and at the same time lessens tension by humming melodies from popular classical songs. He summarizes the rationale for this technique with the ending sentence "It is my equivalent of the cowbell that hikers wear when they know they are in bear country." Have students discuss whether this analogy effectively captures Staples's point.

3. *Reading Critically.* Have students verbalize Staples's purpose for writing this essay. Is it to inform or persuade? Suggest that they look at the explanations for the three types of appeal (pp. 40–42) and identify where in the essay Staples uses them. For instance, students might mention the emotional impact, both on Staples and on them, of the example in the first paragraph. They might also consider how, overall, the examples make an ethical appeal as they reveal Staples's credibility. At the same time, he makes a logical appeal through clear and relevant examples. Objectivity is partially achieved with a large number of examples showing that the reactions he has received are neither isolated nor infrequent. He underscores this point by stating general truths that he has come to learn: "Such episodes are not uncommon. Black men trade tales like this all the time."

4. *Expanding Vocabulary.* Suggest that students look at each word within the context of the sentence and read the sentence aloud. Consider reversing the posed question for them: Why shouldn't Staples use formal language in this essay? After all, his intended readers are educated, he is educated, and his vocabulary reinforces who he is (a respected journalist), as opposed to whom others perceive him to be because of his race.

5. *Making Connections.* Undoubtedly, students will point out that both Senna and Staples are victims of prejudice of their "unwieldy heritage," as Staples puts it. However, Staples is victimized by strangers whereas Senna feels the sting of her grandmother's prejudice. Which is worse? In which situation is prejudice more difficult to counter?

Journal Prompts (p. 482)

1. Students' first response will likely be no. They might refer to this essay, to Senna's, or to their own experiences, observations, and readings to point out negative effects of stereotyping: racial profiling, hate crimes, discrimination. On the other hand, some students might identify situations where stereotyping is necessary or useful. Ask them to share these instances with the class. To generate class discussion, have students listen to a particular radio station or watch a music video. In order to find entertainers who would be of interest to intended audiences, do music or TV executives need to stereotype? Was Staples stereotyping when he decided to "whistle melodies from Beethoven and Vivaldi" (paragraph 12)?

2. Allow students to write their responses privately. Ask them to revisit Staples's first paragraph and note his use of specific details. Challenge them to include details to develop their response to the situation. Have students reread their responses, paying particular attention to their own reaction, and have them comment on the appropriateness of their response. Remind them that the lack of a response (i.e., ignoring a situation) is also a type of reaction.

Suggestions for Writing (p. 482)

1. Some students might have difficulty imagining that they can be feared for who they are. They may have an easier time with this topic if it's expanded to include being misjudged because of prejudice or stereotypes. Help students create a list of topics by exploring different possibilities on the board, having them chime in as ideas occur to them. For example, have students think about the various roles they play in life (athlete, honor student), their own interests and hobbies (computers, skateboarding), and their outward appearance (race, clothing). Once students have a topic in mind, advise them to develop their chosen experience with well-selected and -developed examples. As Staples does, students can end their essays with a solution, either one they implemented or one they wish they had.

2. To assist in their analysis, have students comb Staples's essay to identify causes of stereotyping. They might also consider Jensen's essay and his point about social conditioning. For additional information, students can conduct outside research. Given that the topic of racial stereotyping is broad, students may be overwhelmed with their search results and need help in sifting through the information they find. Also, point out that students can determine causes based on examples, as their research will produce plenty of these.

BARBARA EHRENREICH   *Guys Just Want to Have Fun* (p. 482)

Ehrenreich's essay blends personal experience with research to question the current trend in the business world to reward even academic-underachieving males with jobs, while women still tend to remain undervalued in the workplace, despite a higher graduation rate. By comparing existing hiring practices, including personality tests, with those of the past, Ehrenreich reaches an intriguing (but perhaps unpopular) conclusion about the relationship between gender roles and employment opportunities.

As You Read (p. 482)

Evident from the title of this essay (a twist on Cyndi Lauper's 1983 hit song "Girls Just Want to Have Fun") to the last sentence, Ehrenreich uses a light-hearted approach to reveal a serious problem — the perceived connection between many males' low academic scores and their rise in the workplace, in direct contrast to women's relatively higher scores and surprisingly low employment and advancement rates. Have students discuss the function of humor in the essay. Does it advance, illuminate, or obscure Ehrenreich's point? Would her essay be more or less effective if she didn't couch her point with humor and occasional sarcasm?

Pop Quiz

1. According to the *Washington Post* article, why was a woman not hired for a customer-care job despite the fact that she passed a skills test?
2. What negatively affects a résumé?

Questions to Start You Thinking (p. 484)

1. *Considering Meaning.* This essay probably will bring out some strong reactions, most likely from male students, who could feel as if they are being bashed. (See "Male Bashing on TV" p. 515.) Promote objectivity when discussing this essay's content. Ask students to create their own list of traits of, and differences between, male and female college students so that they will be more prepared to discuss their position on the differences that Ehrenreich states. Are today's male students all "slackers" (paragraph 3)? In paragraph 4, she directly states that "literacy," "numeracy," and "high GPAs" have been replaced by the more desirable and immeasurable qualities of "personality" and "attitude." Ask students to scan the essay to determine which gender she believes is associated with these desirable traits. Then ask them where she makes this point and what evidence she offers to support it.

2. *Identifying Writing Strategies.* Ehrenreich's premise is essentially based on cause and effect. For example, during her college career in the 1960s, she noted that men got most of the jobs; therefore, she assumed that enrolling and achieving in the same difficult courses that men did would result in her getting a job. She reasoned that high-achieving women in the academic world would become high-achieving women in the corporate world. However, her research and personal experiences as an undercover journalist disclosed a different outcome. Either her initial cause-and-effect reasoning was faulty or other intervening factors developed. Was there a shift in the corporate culture, as she contends, or is there another possible cause? For this discussion, students can refer to the text's "Revision Checklist" for cause and effect (p. 135). Students can also refer to "Recognizing Logical Fallacies" (pp. 162–63) to determine whether Ehrenreich's reasoning is sound.

3. *Reading Critically.* Ask students to reread the first sentence of the last paragraph to analyze not only what Ehrenreich's says but also how she says it. Are gender-segregated classrooms really her solution? Discuss with students the impact of tone on a message.

4. *Expanding Vocabulary.* Provide students with a definition of *patriarchy* and ask them to come up with examples of a patriarchal society. Challenge students to then provide their own definition of *matriarchy* and to determine if shifting from one to another is likely. They can then decide if Ehrenreich is using the term in a *hopeful* more than in a literal way.

5. *Making Connections.* After reading "Why Not a Dollar?" students will be able to identify the one reason Murphy gives for the wage gap. Would Ehrenreich concur? Is discrimination the absolute factor behind the change in the corporate climate?

Journal Prompts (p. 485)

1. Allow students to freewrite about their college experiences thus far and ask them to comment about general gender differences as well as specific ones, such as study habits. Do students see differences? If so, what do they attribute them to — gender or other factors?

2. Students can gain a better understanding of what qualities they think are important by writing a generic job description. Share with them some sample job descriptions so they will have a basic format to follow. Students can share their descriptions with the class to see if common characteristics exist. You might compare those with qualifications included on various Web sites, such as Quintcareers.com, <http://quintcareers.com/job_skills_values.htm>, or JobWeb.com, <http://job web.com/joboutlook/2007/student2.htm>. Students can also conduct their own Web searches. Whether or not these qualities are gender-related can be the focus of class discussion.

Suggestions for Writing (p. 485)

1. Students can use a part-time job, full-time job, or volunteer work as the basis for this essay assignment. Once students have selected a particular job, have them list what actions and traits were valued and how they knew what was valued. For instance, they might refer to raises, evaluations, compliments, or supervisory assignments.

2. Some students may have come from a gender-segregated school. Ask those who have to share their experiences. Did they feel that such an environment helped them to advance? If so, in what way — scholastically, personally, socially? Were there drawbacks? Were adjustments necessary as students moved from gender-segregated schools into non-segregated ones? If students were not in a gender-segregated classroom, do they wish they were? Students can conduct a Web search by using such terms as "gender segregated classroom" or "single sex education." Point out that students should seek balanced research. Many sites are sponsored by particular organizations or groups that may be biased, advocating one position for their own gain. Although students may decide to take a stand on just one side of this issue, they will benefit from looking at both sides. Decide whether students should select a specific audience (maybe even Ehrenreich herself) or a general audience. Having a designated audience may help them arrange their points and select convincing research.

DAVE BARRY   *From Now On, Let Women Kill Their Own Spiders* (p. 485)

Many of your students may be familiar with Dave Barry from reading his widely syndicated newspaper column or one of his books. Barry's voice makes this piece unique and provides an opportunity to discuss voice in addition to purpose and satire.

As You Read (p. 485)

The essay raises the issue of male-bashing and of stereotypes. It should generate a lively discussion, as many male students will have been stung by such remarks. Ask students to consider why women might engage in male-bashing when they know such blanket statements are inaccurate and unfair. Is there a male equivalent for denigrating females? What are the effects of such language use?

Pop Quiz

1. According to Barry, what is the commonly held, negative stereotype expressed in the letter he received from Susie Walker?

2. Name the two inventions, thought of by men, that Barry says will make life better for all people everywhere.

Questions to Start You Thinking (p. 487)

1. *Considering Meaning.* Barry engages in hyperbole to satirize the war between the sexes, specifically the use of stereotypes. In paragraph 2, Barry refers to a commonly held male stereotype and retaliates with several female stereotypes in the following paragraph. Although Barry couches his discussion in humor, ask students if they believe him when he says in paragraph 5 that his point is serious. Do they find humor an effective way to approach this subject?

2. *Identifying Writing Strategies.* Barry asks rhetorical questions in paragraphs 3, 4, and 6. Ask students to work in groups to locate questions and to list the evidence Barry uses to support his answers. Students will have no trouble concluding that Barry's use of wildly exaggerated and unfounded evidence adds to the satirical tone of his essay. Students will also note that Barry's rhetorical questions allow him to make generalizations about women while insisting that he will not respond in kind (para. 3).

3. *Reading Critically.* The silliness of Barry's generalizations about women — their obsessions with new shoes, Leonardo DiCaprio, their appearance, and moisturizer — correspond to the equally ridiculous stereotypes of men.

4. *Expanding Vocabulary.* Students might have fun describing their own ideas of a utopian future. What would make life perfect? Ask them to brainstorm characteristics of a utopian community. Then ask them to follow Barry's example and insert some humor.

5. *Making Connections.* While Brady, too, uses satire, her tone is different from Barry's. Explain to students that tone is the writer's attitude toward the subject or the audience. Then ask students to account for the differences in the tone of the two essays. In what ways is Brady's voice different from Barry's? Which piece do students feel is the more effective use of satire? Why?

Journal Prompts (p. 487)

1. Generating ideas for this prompt will work well as a class exercise. Ask one student to record responses on the board as the class brainstorms inventions. Students could develop their list into an essay either as individuals or as a collaborative effort. If you decide to have them collaborate, it might work better to have them assemble into smaller groups.

2. For this prompt, students will need to record relevant remarks from the conversation. Encourage them to report clues about the intentions of the participants by analyzing their voices and body language. Ask them to move beyond immediate effects and consider long-range effects on the participants, the subjects, and society in general.

Suggestions for Writing (p. 488)

1. Most of your students can readily draw from their own experiences for this assignment. Many will have been judged by gender or ethnic stereotyping. Ask them to consider how they differed from those expectations, and what resulted from the prejudging. They should be able to form a general conclusion based on their experiences and observations.

2. Writers like Barry make using humor seem deceptively simple. This assignment will give your students a chance to stretch and experiment with voice. Those who find it difficult to make humor work for them will gain new appreciation of the skills of writers who do it well.

EVELYN F. MURPHY   *Why Not a Dollar?* (p. 488)

Murphy relies on her strong economic background to reveal that the wage gap between men and women is widening, despite the fact that women are catching up to men in "education, experience, and capital," which are the standard reasons given for the gap. Her conclusion, while simply stated, has ramifications for all.

As You Read (p. 488)

The prevalence of statistics in this lengthy essay may overwhelm some students. To reinforce that the statistics serve a purpose, have students highlight or underline the statistics in the essay (or in a select number of paragraphs) and ask them to point out what those statistics support. Mention that Murphy's essay is largely a response to the 23-cent gender gap cited by statisticians. By using statistics, she is, in a sense, fighting fire with fire. Additionally, the numbers make her findings and comparisons immediately apparent.

Pop Quiz

1. What do most Americans believe about the wage gap between men and women?

2. According to Murphy, during what period was the gap at its widest?

Questions to Start You Thinking (p. 493)

1. *Considering Meaning.* Murphy's data is impressive, and she organizes it logically to make her ideas understandable. Direct students to paragraph 4, where she casts doubt on the argument given for the wage gap in 1965. Ask students to explain what Murphy means by the "merit gap." By using statistics collected from 1965–1990, she shows that the gap has not disappeared, despite the fact that women have caught up on merit.

2. *Identifying Writing Strategies.* During a first reading of the essay, students may not have noticed italicized words and phrases in the essay. Have them reread the essay and identify the italicized words and phrases. Ask for a few volunteers to read aloud the sentence where these words and phrases appear. Their classmates can hear Murphy's voice, and will be better able to respond to the question about tone, as they hear her sarcasm, outrage, irony, and so on.

3. *Reading Critically.* Before students can evaluate how convincing her explanation is, they first must be able to state what her explanation is. They will find this explanation stated in one word — *discrimination* — in the last paragraph. In this cause-and-effect essay, Murphy provides evidence to discount the given cause (merit) for the gap, and seeing no other logical (economical, educational, social) cause, determines that the only possible explanation is discrimination. Encourage students to review the essay and to discuss Murphy's findings. Is her cause-and-effect argument a sound one? Has she considered and discounted other possible causes for the gap? Suggest that students refer to the questions about causes in the text's "Revision Checklist" for cause and effect (p. 135) and apply them to Murphy's essay.

4. *Expanding Vocabulary.* Students' age will determine how familiar they are with the term "male chauvinist." If you have access to a computer in class, visit some dictionary sites to find the origin of the word *chauvinist* and trace how it was used in the 1960s and 1970s, predominately by women's liberation groups, as a slur against males. (You may also point out that the phrase was often completed as "male chauvinist pig.") Lead the class in a discussion as to why the term is associated with that era. If students think that the term is used less today, ask them to explain why. What is different today that might account for the infrequent use of that phrase?

5. *Making Connections.* Ask students if Tamara Draut, "What's a Diploma Worth, Anyway?", and Murphy are making the same point or if they are merely writing about the same topic area (wages). Draut's position is that wages are declining for both males and females with bachelor's degrees. Murphy's point is that women's wages are not keeping up with men's. If wages are indeed declining, as Draut contends, are men's and women's wages declining at the same rate? Does Draut differentiate men's earnings from women's, or does she group them together? After considering these questions and their responses to them, students can consider whether Draut's statistics affect Murphy's argument and, if so, to what extent.

Journal Prompts (p. 493)

1. To get students to think about their position on this issue, consider posing the question from Murphy's essay that is repeated in the Quick Start on page 488 of the Instructor's Annotated Edition: "What should women be earning today compared with men?" Then have students respond to the following questions in their journal. If a man and a woman were applying for the same job and have the same education, experience, and so on, should they be hired at the same salary and given equal raises? Why, or why not?

2. Many students seek a college degree because they have been influenced by successful men and women. Give students some time to list some women they consider to be successful. Based on their list, have women achieved equality with men? Does the answer remain the same if they consider other women in the community, government, medicine, and so on?

Suggestions for Writing (p. 493)

1. Murphy devotes twenty-two paragraphs to explaining the problem and countering the traditionally accepted reason for it by offering new statistical evidence. She devotes one paragraph (paragraph 23) consisting of one sentence to revealing the cause. She does not explain what discrimination is or specifically label the type of discrimination. Given her topic, students can infer that she is referring to gender discrimination. Since discrimination can come in many forms, ask students to create a working definition for their essay and to use this definition to help make and develop their point. In this essay students can write about discrimination against different groups, or they might also focus on one particular group. Remind students to enrich and enliven their essays by offering details and examples. If they do outside research and collect statistics, suggest that they interpret such statistics for their readers, as Murphy does in paragraph 15.

2. As a class, explore various topics related to the workplace. Students can then select one of these topics, determine their stance, and then compose their thesis. Students can also conduct a general search in <http://yahoo.com> or in <http://google.com> by using the term "workplace" or "workplace" plus "controversies" or "issues." Since students will essentially be writing an argumentative essay, underscore the importance of stating a position and developing it logically and fully with solid evidence culled from credible sources. (You might refer stu-

dents to both Chapters 9 and 12 of the text.) While Murphy relies primarily on statistics in her essay, encourage students to select evidence that will help them to best develop their position.

NOEL PERRIN   *A Part-Time Marriage* (p. 494)

Perrin, an essayist and professor, offers what might seem like a blueprint for the modern American marriage. Ask the class to go over Perrin's cause-and-effect argument carefully; you might want to divide it into premises and conclusions and analyze it in depth.

As You Read (p. 494)

Students will note that Perrin identifies one primary problem with marriage: People with medium to low levels of intimacy cannot sustain a seven-day-a-week relationship. They enter a marriage with unrealistic expectations of the meaning of closeness. But society provides no theory of a less than full-time arrangement, dooming their relationships.

Pop Quiz

1. How, according to Perrin, do American couples achieve a part-time marriage?

2. Name one cause Perrin cites for the increase in divorce rates.

Questions to Start You Thinking (p. 496)

1. *Considering Meaning.* The effect of divorce on Perrin is evident in his tone, which seems to be a combination of disbelief and resignation. Ask students if they perceive other emotions in his writing. Suggest that they locate one section that supports their answer. How enthusiastic is his commitment to the idea of "part-time marriage"? In this discussion, students are sure to comment on his reaction of going to books, something a teacher might be more likely than others to do. How might Perrin's profession influence his attitudes?

2. *Identifying Writing Strategies.* Perrin's solution has become a reality in many students' homes. Ask students if they believe this solution offers a greater promise of success.

3. *Reading Critically.* Students should have no trouble recognizing how Perrin's vividly imagined postdivorce scenario makes his proposal seem feasible and even desirable. Ask students to specify what kept their interest as they read Perrin's essay. Would any of them have preferred a more fact-based, statistical presentation for this essay? Why? Be sure to encourage them to consider the issue of audience for this essay. How did his audience affect the way Perrin chose to convey his message?

4. *Expanding Vocabulary.* Allow students freedom to respond to this question; they might inject a few opinions about teachers as a group and lead the class into an animated discussion.

Definitions

straight-arrow: conservative and upstanding

pillar of the community: someone who is dependable, reliable, and actively involved

dominant: overriding, governing

self-contempt: hatred of oneself

de facto: actual; in fact if not in theory

glucose tolerance test: a medical test to determine how high blood sugar levels can go

5. *Making Connections.* Ask students to consider couples they are familiar with in order to answer these questions. How might a "part-time marriage" resolve some of the tensions that Barry comically portrays?

Link to the Paired Essay (p. 496)

Students might role-play Perrin's and Brady's stances to try to answer these questions. Break students into small groups to come up with dialogues between the two authors. Students can use the insights as the basis of individual essays.

Journal Prompts (p. 497)

1. This question is a perennial favorite of students. As an opening exercise, ask them to write about which marriage they favor. Then ask them to share their journal entries with the class.

2. Encourage students to take a humorous or sarcastic approach to this assignment if they do not seem interested in doing the assignment as it stands. Tell them that as long as they are specific about the rules for such marriages, anything goes.

Suggestions for Writing (p. 497)

1. Every student will have considerable knowledge of the consequences of divorce. To help contextualize students' personal experiences with divorce, furnish them with a statistic or two. Bring in the current figures on divorce for people under age thirty or on the number of families that still have two biological parents living in the home. Hearing these statistics can shock students into a greater readiness to address the topic in their writing.

2. Warm up students by asking them to give examples of alternative designs of marriage that exist in American culture. (Remind them that this is not the place to be overjudgmental.) Brainstorming with the class will produce several different models to assist students in the development of their own theses. One of our personal favorites is a news story from Nevada in which a disc jockey challenged the marriage laws of the state by marrying a duck during his radio program. The marriage was quickly annulled, but it seemed to prove a point — and he definitely took a stand.

JUDY BRADY   *I Want a Wife* (p. 497)

Brady's satiric definition of a housewife always provokes highly charged responses from male and female readers. Remind students that the essay was written in 1971, and ask them how social roles have (and haven't) changed since then. Instruct students to pay attention to how Brady incorporates analysis and observation into the structure of her essay while taking a stand on the inequitable division of domestic labor.

As You Read (p. 497)

Your students will see that wives, in Brady's view, tend to all the menial responsibilities of marriage: housekeeping, child-rearing, and the details of social commitments. In this arrangement, having a wife would relieve one of these chores and allow one to move through life unfettered, while having a husband would only mean assuming these responsibilities for another person as well as oneself.

Pop Quiz

1. What physical and sexual needs "should," according to Brady, be met by a wife?

2. Why should everyone want a wife, according to Brady?

Questions to Start You Thinking (p. 499)

1. *Considering Meaning.* Brady presents a functional definition of the traditional American housewife. You might want to underscore her assumption that a wife is equal to the sum of her duties. How is that assumption, in itself, an attack on social expectations? It might be difficult for students to articulate their understanding of Brady's satiric intent. Ask them to analyze her language carefully. How do we know that she does not mean her words exactly as written?

2. *Identifying Writing Strategies.* By carefully detailing the daily routine of housewives, Brady incorporates observation into her essay. Ask students which of the listed duties would not be part of a contemporary list.

3. *Reading Critically.* Some of your students might be put off by Brady's tone or might fail to see the humor in her essay. It is important that you remind them that Brady wrote this essay around 1971, when many women were beginning to rethink their roles as wives and mothers. It might be helpful to ask students to imagine themselves as their mothers or grandmothers when formulating a response to this question.

4. *Expanding Vocabulary.* Brady's straightforward language is an essential part of her satiric purpose. She wants her thesis to intrigue the audience; it cannot accomplish that end as effectively if it is obscured by pedantic or esoteric terms. Her sarcastic phrases add to her satiric assault.

5. *Making Connections.* Students will have divergent views about this question that may fall along gender lines. Discuss these views and how Murphy might consider any arguments about *traditional* roles beside the point.

Link to the Paired Essay (p. 499)

Perrin devotes much of his essay to a hypothetical marriage in which a separated couple have come to a reasonably comfortable accommodation. You might ask students whether Brady would find this accommodation realistic given gender roles in marriage. Have times truly changed since Brady wrote her piece?

Journal Prompts (p. 499)

1. This prompt would work well as a fifteen-minute writing assignment at the beginning of the class period. Ask students to share their versions of the ideal mate with the class. How closely do their ideal mates resemble Brady's hypothetical perfect wife?

2. Encourage your students to really let their imaginations run wild for this assignment. They might find it helpful to brainstorm in small groups before beginning this project. Group members should help one another cite as many stereotypes as possible for each role.

Suggestions for Writing (p. 500)

1. For this assignment, stress that providing clear examples and definitions is of paramount importance. Ask students to give specific examples of their expecta-

tions and to define what they perceive as the "social norm" before they explain how their expectations differ from it. To assist students in evaluating their parents' marriage, you might ask them to list what they feel are the positive and negative attributes of their parents' relationship and have them use this list to develop their discussion.

2. It might be worthwhile to brainstorm as a class before beginning this assignment. Ask students to discuss television representations of housewives from thirty or forty years ago. Many of them will be familiar with reruns of *The Brady Bunch, Bewitched, All in the Family, The Flintstones,* and other shows. Do the wives depicted on these programs resemble the dutiful creature Brady conjures up in her essay? Talking about the roles of husbands and wives on these programs will give students a sense of how the ideal housewife was depicted back then, and will give them a basis for their comparison with wives in the twenty-first century.

CHAPTER 25: POPULAR CULTURE (p. 501)

Remind students that "popular" culture not only expresses social values but also helps to shape those values. Too often, students' critical skills come to a screeching halt as they turn on the television or computer or settle into a movie. It is vital, however, that the constant barrage of information from our media universe be subjected to critical analysis and inquiry. Help students to develop their media literacy by assigning readings and writing activities, such as the ones in this chapter, that require them to focus critical attention on various forms of popular culture.

The essays in this chapter discuss issues raised by television, film, and fashion industries. Tara Parker-Pope examines the adaptation of iconic American products for global markets, and Ruth La Ferla touts Latino style as the next hot fashion trend. Stephen King argues that horror films serve a purpose by allowing us to vicariously express our antisocial urges safely, and Michael Abernethy criticizes the increasingly negative portrayal of men in commercials and television sitcoms. The paired essays in this chapter present opposing views the of the now ubiquitous genre of reality television. James Poniewozik defends the genre from its many critics, whereas Terry Golway laments what *American Idol* reveals about our shifting cultural values.

By the time most of us have reached adolescence, we have become experts and sophisticates in the field of entertainment. Students' familiarity with the subjects at hand might help them to be more adventurous as critics. Encourage some experimentation: Let them write like the experts they are.

Assign students to keep a daily log of news, blogs, or magazines they read, music they listen to, and television programs, films, or videos they see. How often do they run across the kinds of images and messages this chapter discusses? How are their reactions different from and similar to those of the writers who appear in this textbook? Has their work in this chapter — and in the course as a whole — changed the way they perceive popular culture?

Responding to an Image (p. 501)

Allow your students to use their imagination while examining these visual activity prompts. If necessary, have students free-associate answers to elements of each image. If they are given free rein for their own interpretations, they will most likely view analyzing these images as a rewarding way to begin thinking about writing in these modes.

Ask students about the general purposes of comic strips. Someone will probably mention that comics often have a more complex intention than simply eliciting laughter. Does this comic strip effectively accomplish the writer/artist's purpose? Consider having students evaluate it using the rubric on the *ReadWriteThink* organization's Web site at <http://readwritethink.org/lesson_images/lesson223/comic-strip-only.pdf>. As a follow-up activity, students can create their own comic strips that comment on advertising or some other aspect of popular culture. Suggest that students who prefer not to draw create their strips using clip art. Have the class exchange comic strips and evaluate them using the criteria in the rubric.

Web Search (p. 502)

Since this assignment demands close scrutiny, ask students to print their selected ads (in color, if possible) and bring them to class. Direct students to "Facing the Challenge" on page 112 of *The Bedford Guide* to reinforce the point that comparison and contrast must serve a purpose. That is, students' essays must ultimately convey a clear and compelling main idea about their selected ads or about advertising in general. To help students determine their thesis, have the class brainstorm to decide on points of comparison and contrast such as the use of images, text, color, product placement, positioning, font style, and so on. As students begin to organize their information, they may find the alternating pattern of comparison and contrast to be the easiest way to frame their points (see pages 114–16 of *The Bedford Guide*). It might also be helpful for students to investigate the decade associated with their ad. For more about using this activity, see page 244 of this manual.

TARA PARKER-POPE   *Custom-Made* (p. 502)

Parker-Pope, a *Wall Street Journal* reporter, offers plentiful examples to illustrate how a product can be tailored to the specific tastes and needs of a given locale. By including manufacturers' successful and unsuccessful attempts of to market a product globally, she underscores the importance of knowing the preferences of the target market. While students may be surprised at some of the food combinations, such as ice cream with a sweet corn topping, Parker-Pope helps them to understand the economic reasons for custom-marketing products for worldwide appeal.

As You Read (p. 502)

Parker-Pope's examples make this essay fun to read. One way to introduce this reading is to create a simple matching quiz that includes food products on one side and countries on the other. Before reading the essay, ask students to match one to the other. Have them find the answers as they read. Lead a class discussion about their correct answers and their assumptions about the people and tastes in a given country.

Pop Quiz

1. What mistake did U.S. auto manufacturers make when they introduced their products to Japan?

2. How did Ben and Jerry's involve British consumers in attempts to market ice cream?

Questions to Start You Thinking (p. 505)

1. *Considering Meaning.* Show different advertisements for the same product. You might use print ads or go to YouTube, at <http://youtube.com>, enter a product or company name, such as Gap, and look for videos of different commercials. Discuss how the product or brand is marketed to consumers of different ages. Students will easily identify how a product is advertised to appeal to a particular audience. Students can then relate this idea to selling a product internationally. In paragraph 6, Parker-Pope mentions exploiting economies of scale and "making . . . products appeal to local tastes." These practices boost sales, as evidenced by the "300 million packages of Cheetos" (paragraph 17) sold when the product was adapted for Chinese consumers.

2. *Identifying Writing Strategies.* The examples serve Parker-Pope's purpose because they prove her point about the importance of adapting to markets. Students' favorite examples will be determined by their own cultural tastes and experiences. What might seem unusual to one student (pizza with salmon) might not seem so strange to another.

3. *Reading Critically.* Ask students to identify where quotations appear in the essay, noting both the source and the source's accompanying credentials, before they respond to this question about the effectiveness of the quotations. The quotations provide insight into companies' decision-making processes, their struggles, and their need to adapt.

4. *Expanding Vocabulary.* Students should recognize the phrase "custom-made" as referring to creating something (often clothing) for an individual customer. Given the thrust of the essay, they should also understand that it relates to the word *custom,* as in *tradition,* and relates to creating something (such as cars, food, Pampers) based on the customs of those in a particular region or country.

5. *Making Connections.* Poll students to see if they have seen examples of advertisements that have been tailored for the Latino community. Suggest that they consider the actors or the ethnicity of those featured in the ad, the fashions, the location, the music, and so on. Challenge students by giving them a product and having them create an ad based on the Latino characteristics included in La Ferla's essay.

Journal Prompts (p. 506)

1. This "yuck" or "yum" response allows students to reflect on their own tastes that may or may not be associated with their heritage, upbringing, and so on. Students can share their responses and reasons in a class discussion.

2. While students can respond to this prompt individually, it might be fun to use it for a group activity. You might bring in a product for each group, give each group a country, and then ask how the product might be adapted for the given country. Another option is to bring in one product and give each group a different country for which the product should be marketed. Have groups share their ideas and explain why they marketed the product the way they did. Depending on the country, students may need some time to study the country to learn about its people, traditions, food, and so on.

Suggestions for Writing (p. 506)

1. During a class brainstorming session, have students list competitive products (Coke versus Pepsi, for example) and have them bring in print ads for these products. Or they can visit YouTube, at <http://youtube.com>, and enter the product names followed by "ad" or "commercial." They can then collect details about the ads to use in their comparison-and-contrast essay. Remind students to collect the same type of information for each product, such as music used, personality or tal-

ent used, type of ad, and so on. They can then determine what type of comparison-and-contrast pattern (opposing or alternating) to use to arrange their details. If this essay is their first using comparison-and-contrast, suggest that they plan and review their organizational pattern with you, referring to Chapter 7 of the text as needed.

2. This activity is a good opportunity for field research, and students will enjoy doing some of their own product comparisons outside of the classroom. Suggest that they bring a notepad so that they can keep notes, perhaps making a chart to compare, say, the fit, stylishness, and price of jeans. In their writing, they should make sure to provide plenty of examples to make it clear how well various products meet, or don't meet, their criteria.

RUTH LA FERLA *Latino Style Is Cool. Oh, All Right: It's Hot* (p. 506)

La Ferla, a fashion editor and writer, explores the influence of the growing Hispanic population on today's fashions. Her examples and quotations reveal not only the extent of the popularity of what has come to be known as Latino style but why Latinos and non-Latinos are adopting the style. She discovers that Latinos are acknowledging and celebrating their heritage through their fashion, while non-Latinos are intrigued by what they consider to be the sexy, glamorous Latino image.

As You Read (p. 507)

La Ferla's essay investigates the extent of and reasons for the current appeal of Latino style. Before students read the essay, ask them to describe what they consider to be key characteristics of Latino fashions. When they have finished reading, have them compare their listed characteristics with those La Ferla includes. Are they similar? On what did students base their characteristics: television, peers, music videos? Ask them how they felt about completing this exercise. Did they feel uncomfortable stereotyping?

Pop Quiz

1. What apparel makers are marketing Latino fashion?

2. Why are non-Latinos attracted to the Latino style?

Questions to Start You Thinking (p. 511)

1. *Considering Meaning.* Ask students to skim the essay to look not only for the reasons but also for the source of those reasons: La Ferla herself, a student, a professor, and so on. Have students discuss whether each gives a similar reason. Are students influenced more by one particular source than another? Why?

2. *Identifying Writing Strategies.* If students respond appropriately to "Considering Meaning," then they have essentially identified the reason for (cause of) Latinos' adopting the styles associated with their traditional culture. Based on their reading, students will most likely point out the effects of this trend on the fashions of both Latinos and non-Latinos. Students can discuss the extent of the effects as well as the effectiveness of this cause-and-effect strategy based on La Ferla's writing purpose — to define Latino style and explain how and why it is being embraced by Latinos and the fashion industry.

3. *Reading Critically.* Students can review their answers to "Considering Meaning" if they identified quotations for some of the reasons for the appeal of Latino style. However, La Ferla includes quotations for other purposes, too: to describe, to disagree, and so on. Have students skim the essay for those types of quotations as well. As students evaluate the quotations, they might conclude that the wide range of quotations (mostly positive) correlates to the wide appeal of the Latino style.

4. *Expanding Vocabulary.* Students can use a dictionary or define the words within the sentence's context. Which words are most suggestive of the Latino style as students have come to understand it from reading this essay? What is the relationship between these words and the phrase "visual shorthand" used in paragraph 8?

5. *Making Connections.* Hold a class discussion on the value of celebrating a heritage. Students can point to specific examples within this essay and their own lives to support their response. Have students summarize Konig's position on the issue. Is she stating that there is anything wrong with a child's identifying with his or her heritage? Also, how might Staples respond to the idea of asserting, visually or otherwise, his or her heritage?

Journal Prompts (p. 511)

1. Considering that some students, like Konig's own daughter, may not have a direct or strong connection to their heritage, you may want to have students freewrite privately. As students reflect on the contribution of their cultural or ethnic heritage to their personal style, point out that they should consider subtle as well as obvious manifestations: colors or patterns of clothing and even a chosen lack of style.

2. Have students describe what they are wearing from head to toe. Ask them to consider why they have worn those particular clothes. Perhaps they made their selection based on the weather, their activities for the day, how tired they were when they got dressed, and so on. Then ask them to explain why (and even where) they bought those clothes. What do they think the clothes say about them?

Suggestions for Writing (p. 511)

1. The key words in this assignment are "Take some time." Challenge students to do just that, explaining that this essay demands that they select compelling details that make a subject come alive for readers. (See Facing the Challenge for Chapter 5, p. 78). Keeping a record of what they see is also essential to being able to classify the styles. Suggest that students use a consistent method of taking and arranging their notes. "Record Your Observations" (p. 79) may be helpful.

2. No doubt students have seen examples of how our society is adapting to the booming Hispanic population. For instance, Home Depot, a major home improvement store, now has all of its aisle signs in both English and Spanish. Phone menus are given in both English and Spanish, as are driving tests and tests for receiving General Educational Development (GED) credentials. Students can brainstorm other examples as well. In terms of what has caused the increase of the Hispanic population, students may need to conduct some research. One article on CNN.com (<http://cnn.com/2006/US/05/10/hispanics/index.html>) provides some insight as to why Hispanics are the largest minority and lists the accompanying economic and political effects of the growth in this population. Students can use this article as a springboard for their research.

STEPHEN KING   *Why We Crave Horror Movies* (p. 512)

Stephen King's essay explains and defends our fascination with horror movies by arguing that they "exercise" the "anticivilization emotions" in all of us (para. 11). He suggests that watching horror movies allows people to vicariously indulge their dark impulses, which, for most, prevents them from being acted out in real life. King's essay is an excellent example of a close analysis of a concept.

As You Read (p. 512)

King names several reasons we like horror movies — to prove that we are not afraid, to reinforce the feeling that we are normal, and to have fun. Students will need to go a bit further with this last reason, to King's claim that we all harbor the darkest of urges and that horror movies provide safety valves that allow us to vent our most uncivilized feelings.

Pop Quiz

1. According to King, what emotions are accepted in civilized society?

2. What do the "hungry alligators" represent to King?

Questions to Start You Thinking (p. 514)

1. *Considering Meaning.* Ask students to cite some specific examples of King's humor. Possible responses include the opening line claiming that we are all "mentally ill," the reference in paragraph 8 to picking one's nose, the reference to the "rotten little puke of a sister" in paragraph 10, and calling Jack the Ripper an "amateur-night surgeon" in paragraph 8. Point out to students that King's humor is an example of what we call "black" or "dark" comedy. Ask them how his use of black humor is similar to the argument he is making about horror movies — that as civilized people, we feel somewhat uncomfortable about being entertained by murder and mayhem, but at some level it satisfies a need.

2. *Identifying Writing Strategies.* King uses analysis in paragraphs 3–5 as he methodically ticks off the reasons we crave horror movies. He then develops his analysis by qualifying and explaining his reasoning. Ask students to quickly outline King's essay in class in order to illustrate the organization of his analysis.

3. *Reading Critically.* This question addresses King's appeal to his readers. He basically accuses his audience of harboring dark impulses, even calling us "mentally ill" (para. 1), but he tones down this accusation by including himself as one of the mentally ill. Have students imagine what the essay would be like if King did not temper his use of the accusatory "you" with the inclusive "we." Ask students whether they would have resisted his argument or have been offended if he did not include himself. This discussion will make students consider how they address their audience in their own essays. Direct their attention to Chapter 9, "Taking a Stand," which discusses ways in which writers should consider and respect the reader.

4. *Expanding Vocabulary.* Students might have problems understanding why King calls horror movies "innately conservative." Paragraph 4 suggests that no matter how ugly things might seem on the screen, they are not as bad as the horrors that exist in real life. Ask students to give examples of some real-life horrors. Are fictional horrors less severe and, therefore, more conservative than real-life horrors? King's statement also implies that despite the murder and mayhem, most horror

movies end by punishing evil and restoring order. Furthermore, by purging us of our "anticivilization emotions" — our anarchistic, revolutionary impulses — horror movies help to maintain the established order of things.

Definitions

innately: having a natural tendency toward

revolutionary: bringing about or constituting radical change

5. *Making Connections.* Students may initially note that these two genres are quite different and, therefore, could not possibly share the same purpose. To get the discussion rolling, ask the class to identify some similarities in viewers' reactions to both genres. You might also begin by listing on the board King's reasons for the popularity of horror movies, then asking students to find similar points in Poniewozik's essay. Students might note where Poniewozik states that reality television "provokes" and "offends" so that people "sit up and pay attention" (para. 11). They might also point to paragraph 15, which asserts that reality shows give "polite society" a "wedgie."

Journal Prompts (p. 514)

1. Ask students to classify which sick jokes evoke particular reactions. Are some kinds more acceptable than others? Why, or why not?

2. Have students come up with a list of "base instincts" (such as anger, hatred, and violence) that they think need to be safely "exercised." In arguing that horror movies fulfill our need to express dark impulses, King implies that ignoring or suppressing these feelings can be dangerous. Ask students whether they agree or disagree.

Suggestions for Writing (p. 515)

1. Emphasize that students' essays should refer to specific movies but have them limit their selections to two or three examples. First-year writers often try to include too many examples, which can lead to disorganization, underdeveloped ideas, and superficial analysis. Many have difficulty with organization. To help guide your students, we suggest this type of organization: (1) introduction, (2) thorough definition of the genre, (3) examples of movies that are characteristic of the genre, (4) explanation of why this genre is interesting and satisfying.

2. The idea that "the horror film has become a modern version of the public lynching" (para. 6) suggests that people have always needed to act out their "anticivilization emotions" in some kind of public way. To help students better understand the question, try restating it with a different example: Are horror movies a modern version of the bloody coliseum games in ancient Rome? Have horror movies simply provided a safer outlet for natural impulses we have needed to express for centuries?

MICHAEL ABERNETHY *Male Bashing on TV* (p. 515)

Abernethy takes offense at television's portrayals of incompetent, uninvolved, and unintelligent men. By including a myriad of examples from commercials and sitcoms, Abernethy provides evidence of this one-dimensional portrayal. He then offers research to support his assertion that the pervasiveness of this stereotyping has negative implications for viewers, especially young boys.

As You Read (p. 515)

Ask students whether they agree that male bashing on television is a serious problem. To what extent do they think the comic antics of male television characters can have a detrimental effect on boys' "self-image, self-concept, and personal aspirations" (para. 15)?

Pop Quiz

1. How are male characters in television comedies different today than they were years ago?

2. How did J. C. Penney respond to criticism of their commercial that featured an incompetent father?

Questions to Start You Thinking (p. 519)

1. *Considering Meaning.* Suggest that students respond to this question by brainstorming about what generates poor comedy. Ask students which television sitcoms they dislike, and why. Then have them consider successful sitcoms, either past or present. Do those shows have the comedic attributes of "creative writing" and "imaginative characterizations" that, according to Abernethy, form the basis for good comedy?

2. *Identifying Writing Strategies.* To underscore the seriousness of the problem, Abernethy first establishes its pervasiveness, citing examples from current advertisements and television sitcoms. He uses contrast when he juxtaposes today's degrading male characterizations with those from the past. He also traces the positive effects of the women's movement on the portrayal of female characters and contrasts their elevation with the current depiction of their male counterparts. Point out to students how these strategies work to support Abernethy's main strategy, argument.

3. *Reading Critically.* Students will recognize Abernethy's examples from current television shows and commercials, but they might not be as familiar with examples such as *Alice* or *Amos 'N Andy*. Does this affect the impact of his examples? Ask students whether male bashing is considered less problematic because it occurs mostly in comedies and commercials as opposed to dramas. Do students associate comedy with fiction? If so, how might that account for the fact that people may find the issue trivial?

4. *Reading Critically.* If Ward Cleaver can be considered the quintessential intelligent male sitcom character and Al Bundy his complete opposite, then who is in between? Do sitcom writers sometimes poke fun even at seemingly intelligent male characters? Consider the stereotypical absent-minded professor. Ask students to reshape one of the characters mentioned in the selection according to standards that Abernethy would accept. What would this character be like? Would he still be funny?

5. *Making Connections.* Students may note that Barry uses satire and outrageous generalizations about women to make the point that male bashers are just as much off the mark. Barry, however, doesn't suggest that the problem is very serious; in fact, he uses these stereotypes to generate laughter. Students will thus probably conclude that Barry would disagree with Abernethy's statement about good comedy. The class might be amused by the fact that a number of years ago a television sitcom called *Dave's World* was based on Barry's books —and, yes, Barry was often one of the bumbling male characters that Abernethy criticizes.

Journal Prompts (p. 519)

1. Although this question is about the portrayal of men and women on television, students might also consider whether turnabout is fair play in other arenas. For example, is it fair for a woman to receive special consideration when applying for a job in a male-dominated field?

2. Ask students whether they prefer physical comedy, such as that used by the Three Stooges, or verbal bantering, the backbone of *Frasier*. Ask them to jot down their favorite comic movies or television programs. Do they see any similar traits that will help them with their definition?

Suggestions for Writing (p. 519)

1. Class discussion is an ideal way for students to generate ideas for this essay. Divide students into groups that support Abernethy and groups that think that he is overreacting. Each group can brainstorm additional examples or conduct research to help them support their positions.

2. Have students work in pairs for this assignment, with one student examining a men's magazine and the other looking at a women's magazine. Students can share their findings with each other and then with the class. In what ways, if any, do their findings relate to Abernethy's claim that males are portrayed negatively in television sitcoms and advertising?

JAMES PONIEWOZIK   *Why Reality TV Is Good for Us* (p. 520)

Although he acknowledges their lack of reality and questions some of their ethics, Poniewozik provides insight into the popularity of reality television shows, ultimately defending the genre. Using examples from both reality television and traditional network fare, he reveals that reality television owes its success to its shocking nature, ability to create a community of viewers, carefully chosen participants, and unexpected results. Students may have their own reasons for watching or not watching reality television, and these may be worth discussing before assigning this reading.

As You Read (p. 520)

Ask students which reality television characters they respect, and discuss the characters' positive qualities. In the course of the discussion, students might debate whether they consider the personalities to be fictional characters or real people. What is the difference? Suggest that students look at the end of Poniewozik's essay, where he writes about resilient participants who search for the American dream.

Pop Quiz

1. How have recent nonreality shows (sitcoms and dramas) contributed to the popularity of reality television?

2. Who is Lady Tiger?

Questions to Start You Thinking (p. 524)

1. *Considering Meaning. The Apprentice*, which had participants compete for a job running one of Donald Trump's businesses, was the number one show on NBC in the spring of 2004. Consider showing an episode in class and asking students to hypothesize about the show's success. Do their reasons correspond to Poniewozik's? Paragraphs 11, 15, and 17 contain some of Poniewozik's reasons for believing that "reality TV is good for us." Ask students if they can identify the reasons and discuss whether they agree with them.

2. *Identifying Writing Strategies.* Have students scan the essay for Poniewozik's criteria. For example, he believes that television shows should leave viewers feeling "part of a communal experience" (para. 9). In paragraph 11, he says that television should "rattle viewers' cages." Perhaps the most controversial criterion is that television should challenge traditional beliefs and ideas or, as he puts it, give the audience a "wedgie" (para. 15). When he applies these same criteria to traditional network situation comedies and dramas, they fall short.

3. *Reading Critically.* At the outset of his essay, Poniewozik concedes that many aspects of reality television are neither real nor defendable. Do students think that the placement of this concession is wise? Can they think of any instances where delaying opposing arguments might be more effective? Mention that in the body of the essay Poniewozik mainly focuses on one major point of opposition (the moral case against reality television), refuting it with numerous examples as well as testimony from network executives.

4. *Expanding Vocabulary.* In criticizing the character development of current dramas, Poniewozik refers to *CSI Miami* and *Law and Order*. Discuss with students some of the characters in these shows. Do they find them formulaic (the tough guy, the sassy and attractive woman, the lab nerd)? Do reality television participants break this mold, or are they beginning to resemble each other as well?

5. *Making Connections.* Do students believe that these shows are modern-day televised versions of arranged marriages? Suggest that students explore this idea in a written comparison-and-contrast response by considering such issues as who determines the "pool" of candidates, what monetary awards are involved, and what outside forces influence mate selection.

Link to the Paired Essay (p. 524)

Both Poniewozik's and Golway's essays seem to be aimed at a general, yet reasonably well-informed, audience. The pieces aim to persuade readers, but they express quite different views. Ask students to articulate these views and highlight support for them in each essay. This strategy can help them determine which argument is more convincing.

Journal Prompts (p. 525)

1. Invite students to explore and voice their opinion about reality television in a letter to the editor (the essay first appeared in *Time* magazine).

2. Judging from the turnouts for auditions, many Americans dream of being a participant in a reality television show. Tell students that an estimated seventy thousand people auditioned for *American Idol 2*. Invite students who would like to be a participant to write a letter to the producers beginning with the words "Please consider me a candidate for . . ." If they have no interest in being on a show, ask them to write a letter that explains their lack of interest.

Suggestions for Writing (p. 525)

1. This assignment challenges students to tap into their creative and persuasive talents. To write convincingly, students will need to understand their audience, provide enough information to explain their show's intent and basic format, and highlight reasons that it will be successful. You might refer students to Chapter 21, "Strategies for Designing Your Document." Discuss how headings and other elements of design may make their essay more enticing for their readers and also easier to navigate.

2. Creating a class-generated list of reality television shows and evaluation criteria will give students a solid start on this assignment. As they research the topic and compose their drafts, remind students to apply the criteria to the show they are evaluating and to include specific examples to support their conclusion about whether the show meets or does not meet the established criteria for success.

TERRY GOLWAY   *A Nation of Idol-Worshipers* (p. 525)

Primarily by using the reality TV show *America Idol* as an example, freelance writer Golway expresses his disappointment that Americans adulate celebrities or would-be celebrities more than they do real-life heroes. He fears that such worship reflects a growing trend toward superficial values and aspirations.

As You Read (p. 525)

Journalist Golway asserts that Americans of all ages are unduly and inappropriately influenced by media-made idols. Based on what they read, ask students if they think Golway's main purpose is to vent, inform, or to persuade. Have them refer to specific examples in the essay, and to elements such as tone, to support their answer.

Pop Quiz

1. Who, according to Golway, is worthy of being an American idol?

2. What is the purpose of paragraph 10?

Questions to Start You Thinking (p. 527)

1. *Considering Meaning.* Use headlines from magazines, newspapers, and television news shows to reinforce Golway's point about Americans' interest in the lives of celebrities. Golway is concerned that many adults and children obsess over celebrities while ignoring the important achievements of more obscure figures. Highlight specifics in the essay that point to the negative effects of such misplaced worship. Students might mention the superficial need for fame (paragraph 4), misplaced aspirations (paragraph 8), the waste of "time, money, and energy" (paragraph 11), and the continuation of the cycle of idol worship (paragraph 14). Direct students to the end of the essay if they have difficulty pinpointing what Golway believes society should value instead.

2. *Identifying Writing Strategies.* These questions address the concept of audience. Golway, a distinguished journalist, understands that he is writing to an educated audience and that every position has two sides. Therefore, he acknowledges that it is okay for people to spend a few "frivolous moments watching a silly show just for fun" (paragraph 9). He adds that even he has followed the exploits of a celebrity golfer. He then acknowledges that revering people for their celebrity status is noth-

ing new. Using the word "Still" (paragraph 11), he signals the shift back to his argument.

3. *Reading Critically.* Ratings for *American Idol* and other shows like it would have been easy for Golway to find. Therefore, his omission is intentional. Given the glut of exposure celebrities receive (See "Considering Meaning" activity), Golway most likely thought that such information was unnecessary. You might bring up this point as students share their responses to question 3.

4. *Expanding Vocabulary.* Narcissism is defined as "self-absorption, egotism, vanity." Students can discuss ways in which shows like *American Idol, America's Top Model,* and *Dancing with the Stars* encourage narcissism. However, be prepared for some students to give examples of shows like *Extreme Makeover: Home Edition* that refute Golway's contention.

5. *Making Connections.* Ask students to find common denominators between the views expressed by both writers. Students might state that there is an emphasis on packaging people, reflecting society's superficial nature.

Link to the Paired Essay (p. 528)

Certainly students will acknowledge that any writer is influenced by his or her experiences and perceptions. These factors determine perspective, purpose, and choice of details. Students can reach their own conclusions as they find similarities/differences in the two essays. Admittedly, Golway has not watched many episodes of *American Idol,* and he also limits his essay to talent shows. On the other hand, as a TV critic, Poniewozik watches a great deal of television and, while he doesn't always have positive comments about reality TV shows in general, he does find that *American Idol* is better in some ways than other shows. Specifically, he notes in paragraph 19 that viewers can learn from shows like *American Idol;* elsewhere (paragraph 12, for example), he states that often reality shows are :"filling in for duds." Such a statement suggests that he doesn't advocate a steady diet of such television fare.

Journal Prompts (p. 528)

1. A novel way for students to comment on their attitudes toward the show is to have them fill in the blanks of 1-800-_ _ _ - _ _ _ _ , which parodies the phone number call-in system of talent contest shows like *American Idol.* They could create 1-800-NOT-AFAN or 1-800-YOU-ROCK.

2. Students may or may not have seen an episode of American Idol; after all Golway hadn't seen one until 2006. Episodes can be rented or seen on YouTube (<http://youtube.com>) by typing in "American Idol" as the search term. A quick view of a contestant or another part of the show can get students in the right frame of mind to answer this question about the popularity of such shows.

Suggestions for Writing (p. 528)

1. To enable students to respond to this question about reality television and what it says about American viewers, bring in a current issue of *TV Guide* or another type of television magazine. On the board list different reality television shows broadcast during a given week. Students can contribute to this list, pointing out the type of show, reasons for its appeal, and what it says about its viewers and our society. Students will have an easier time writing this essay if they, like Golway, limit themselves to a few shows in the same category. Another option is to counter Golway's position by discussing a show (or shows) that presents a positive image of society, giving us worthy idols.

2. Before students research, lead them in a class discussion about the characteristics that may be associated with a highly rated program. For example, they might consider genre, actors, time of broadcast, and so on. Have students add to this list. Research should produce plenty of data, so encourage students to create some type of graphic organizer or chart to help them collect and arrange their data. Students can create their own, or the class can generate one for all to use.

CHAPTER 26: E-TECHNOLOGY (p. 529)

Students wake up to music on their iPods, check their e-mail, text-message with friends, and update their MySpace pages with their latest photos — often all before heading to class. It is undeniable that technology has infiltrated their lives, affecting how, when, where, and to whom they communicate. This chapter presents a range of readings that encourage students to reflect on the role of technology in their personal, social, and academic lives. A *Harvard Magazine* essay discusses why and how blogging is being used at Harvard Law School. Computer scientist and critic David Gelernter questions the ability of educational software to teach children even basic skills. On the lighter side, Steven Levy writes about the ubiquitous iPod and its critics. Author Merrill Markoe pokes fun at online personality quizzes. In the paired essays, Alex Koppelman tackles the complex privacy issues associated with social-networking sites like MySpace, and psychologist and sociologist Sherry Turkle ends the chapter with a provocative essay about how computer technologies influence the way we think.

Students can read, reflect on, and react to these readings in their journals, or given the nature of the chapter, you might consider creating a wiki for your class. Students may have used Wikipedia for school work but may be unaware of how a wiki works. A wiki is a Web site that allows users to add, edit, or remove content. The benefit of a wiki is that it fosters collaboration among its users, making it ideal for classroom use. Free wiki sites exist where instructors can create an account for their class and limit it to only registered students, who gain access through a password. PB wiki (<http://pbwiki .com>) claims that using its site to create a Web-based wiki is as easy as making a "peanut butter and jelly sandwich." A special section for educators provides examples of how a wiki is used in elementary through college classrooms. Another wiki, Wetpaint (<http://wetpaint.com>), claims to combine "the best elements of wikis, blogs, and social networks." Should you decide to create a wiki, you can limit access to those in your class.

Responding to an Image (p. 529)

Allow your students to use their imagination while examining these visual activity prompts. If necessary, have students free-associate responses to elements of each image. If they are given free rein for their own interpretations, they will most likely view analyzing these images as a rewarding way to begin thinking about writing in these modes.

As students view this image, ask them to separate the foreground from the background. Have them locate the dominant figures in the foreground, the man and the woman. Ask them to describe the individuals they see (age, race, and so on) and to use those descriptions to reach conclusions about the subjects' education, economic status, and so forth. Additionally, direct them to the positioning of the man and woman and point out that they are angled away from each other (not quite back-to-back). Ask students to identify what the subjects of the photo are doing. The cell phone in the woman's hand is quite apparent, and students will probably assume that the man is holding one as well. Students can speculate about whether they are talking to each other or to other people. Once students have explored the foreground, ask them to discuss the significance of the background. What is significant about the fact that the man and woman are outside instead of inside? As a class, students can contribute their ideas about the essential message conveyed in this photo. If you have Internet access in class, you might get the discussion going by entering the terms "cell phones" and "social interaction" into a search engine like <http://google.com> or <http://yahoo.com>.

Based on class discussion and students' interpretations, direct them to create captions, which will be a sort of thesis. Students may have had some experience writing a thesis but may be unsure of how to write a caption. Information about writing a caption can be found at various sites. Bill Walsh, a copyeditor at the *Washington Post*, has posted "The Nine Commandments of Caption Writing" to his blog, The Slot (<http://theslot.com/captions.html>). Students can also visit "What Makes a Good Caption" (<http://notrain-nogain.org/Train/Res/Write/caps.asp>). Lorie Oglesbee's "Writing Captions," found in *Journalism Education Today*, volume 32, number 2, pages 2–6 (Winter 1998), discusses the four parts of a good caption and provides sample captions and an assignment. Students can also scan their textbooks to study the various photo captions.

Web Search (p. 530)

Have students brainstorm their personal interests, perhaps using the mapping technique described on p. 301 of the text. Some topics are bound to yield overwhelming results. For example, entering the search term "scrapbooking" into <http://google.com> produces millions of hits, certainly too many to wade through in a timely manner. Suggest that students use additional terms, like "scrapbooking" plus "family photos," to narrow the results. Within Google, students can also search for blogs on a given topic by clicking on the "more" menu under "Web." Remind students to record the data necessary for them to fulfill this writing assignment. They should keep track of the sites they have visited, the types of activities they engaged in at those sites, the people — if any — with whom they have come into contact. Were students observers, or did they participate in online interaction in some way? They can also note if communication was static or dynamic. Students might also comment on their comfort level in each area — for example, in blogs versus discussion boards versus chat rooms. Guide students in forming a thesis that states their general impression of online communication. For more about using this activity, see page 244 of this manual.

HARVARD MAGAZINE *Creating Community, Online and Off* (p. 530)

This essay, originally published in *Harvard Magazine*, presents the rationale for Harvard Law School's use of blogs on campus. The original intent was to "build bridges" between departments. Originators haven't yet been able to determine whether they have achieved that purpose, but they are certain that blogging builds communities.

To prepare for discussion of this essay, you might want to read Carie Windham's "Reflecting, Writing, and Responding: Reasons Students Blog," published by Educause in May 2007 and available at <http://educause.edu/ir/library/pdf/ELI3010.pdf>. This article examines both student and faculty blogging.

As You Read (p. 530)

To analyze similarities and differences, students will first need to locate various quotations, so have them scan the essay in its entirety, or a few pages of it. Students should consider not only the source of the quotations but also their content or message. Based on their findings, students might concur with the first sentence of paragraph 23: "Despite the growing pains, most bloggers remain true believers in their medium's value and promise."

Pop Quiz

1. What, exactly, is a blog?

2. How do educators use blogs?

Questions to Start You Thinking (p. 535)

1. *Considering Meaning.* Ensure that students understand what blogs are and how they may be different from a discussion board, chat room, and so forth. Students can brainstorm their ideas about blogging's popularity and pitfalls, or they can refer to the essay. Paragraphs 9–16 include reasons for its popularity (it is simple, cheap, inclusive, and so on). Drawbacks to the medium are directly stated in paragraphs 20–22 (blogs can be boring, they are frequently abandoned, and bloggers can attract unwanted attention), and a related problem (censorship) is mentioned in paragraphs 17–19.

2. *Identifying Writing Strategies.* The essay begins with an example and then introduces the blog project (paragraphs 4–6), defines blogging (7–8), and then moves to discussing its popularity and drawbacks, as noted in the previous response to "Considering Meaning." In paragraphs 9–16, have students list the transitional expressions used to introduce each reason for the popularity of blogging. They should list words such as *first, in addition, also.* Ask students if further transitions are needed within that section to allow readers to follow the essay's organizational pattern. In paragraphs 20–22, transitions are included to introduce each drawback as well as to emphasize the extent of the drawback, such as "the biggest problem" (paragraph 20).

3. *Reading Critically.* Because the essay was published in the *Harvard Magazine*, the essay is directed to current students and graduates of Harvard University. Because of the scope of the essay, students might theorize that the essay's purpose is primarily to inform. However, given the thrust of the positives (data and quotes), some students might argue that it has a persuasive purpose. Ask students to defend their choices.

4. *Expanding Vocabulary.* The *Encarta* dictionary defines *grassroots* as "the ordinary people in the community." In what ways, then, do blogs appeal to ordinary people, if that is the definition upon which students agree? Students might also do a Google search to find other instances of "grassroots" to see if their definition of grassroots should be expanded or refined. The grassroots notion ties into the essay's point that blogging can build communities among regular folk.

5. *Making Connections.* Refer students to paragraphs 19 and 22 to discuss privacy issues related to blogging. Are these issues exclusive to blogging or are they general online issues? How might they be resolved?

Journal Prompts (p. 535)

1. Students' views about the positive and negative aspects of electronic communication will be related to the type and degree of their online communication. Have

students list the different types of online communication in which they engage and then state the benefits and pitfalls of each type. How might the pitfalls be prevented?

2. To get started, students can look at the various blogs in this essay. They can then think about their own interests to determine the type of blog they might create. Suggest that they name their blog and write the first entry about why they have created the blog. If students already have a blog, have them write a quick review of their blog, explaining what it is about, its strengths and weaknesses, and any problems they have encountered. If students don't understand what a blog is or how it works, they can search <http://google.com> with the word "blog," and then they can search within blogs for a particular topic.

Suggestions for Writing (p. 535)

1. Before students write, have them explore what it means to be part of a community. Suggest that they consider the various communities to which they belong and the characteristics of those communities. Students should then select one as the basis of this essay and discuss how the Internet in general and blogging specifically can build community.

2. Introduce this assignment to the class by giving examples of various blogs, showing some in class if your technology resources permit. (If students are unfamiliar with blogs, you may need to introduce some examples earlier.) Before showing any blogs in class, check first for appropriateness, ease of use, and so on. Because students will be writing a classification essay, remind them to identify the basis of their classification and to discuss the same principles (features) within each category.

DAVID GELERNTER *Computers Cannot Teach Children Basic Skills* (p. 536)

At a time when computers are considered an answer to the problems facing education, Gelernter offers a different perspective. In this 1994 essay from the *New Republic,* he contends that rather than improving children's academic skills, computers actually weaken their skills, specifically their reading skills. He doesn't totally discount the benefits of computers but suggests that certain conditions must be met first. His bottom line, however, is that "you cannot teach a child anything unless you look him in the face."

As You Read (p. 536)

Students, no doubt, have had some exposure to computers in the classroom. Ask them to share some of their experiences. Once they have read the essay, review the conditions for effective computer use that are mentioned in paragraphs 11–13. Given these conditions, would Gelernter have considered students' computer experiences academically sound?

Pop Quiz

1. What is hypermedia?

2. What one condition is necessary to counter computers' shortcomings?

Questions to Start You Thinking (p. 539)

1. *Considering Meaning.* Gelernter's use of headings, logical paragraphing with clear topic sentences, and fitting transitions allows students to identify the problems that computers can create: low reading scores and "allow me" programs that don't promote basic skills.

2. *Identifying Writing Strategies.* Again, the headings are the first clue that Gelernter is employing a problem-and-solution format. "Conditions on the Use of Computers" is the section where he discusses how computers should be used. Note that he begins this section by acknowledging computers' potential.

3. *Reading Critically.* Have students find these passages in the essay. If they have difficulty, direct them to paragraphs 4–7 and 13. Students can comment on Gelernter's comparison and try to predict what he might say about e-books and audio books.

4. *Expanding Vocabulary.* It is important that students understand the vocabulary used in the essay before they summarize. Have students identify the original source of publication (*New Republic*) and hypothesize about the readers' educational level. They might adapt their summary to readers of a more general publication.

5. *Making Connections.* From reading Dillard, students should recognize that she has solid reading and critical thinking skills — proficiencies that Gelernter thinks computers cannot promote. Students will likely conclude that she could not have learned the same thing by simply using a computer. However, if challenging and effectual science software programs were available to her, she might have developed her science skills even further.

Journal Prompts (p. 539)

1. As students explore the type of learning they have done on computers, mention that they are not limited to an academic setting. Is it possible to learn from playing computer games? If so, what, specifically, can be learned?

2. Gelernter is contending that people — teachers — are what make education possible. The simple act of a teacher talking to a student is more effective than any computer, he asserts. Point out that $2 billion have been invested in computers for the classroom. Would that money have been better spent on hiring teachers? Students can respond to this prompt based on their own learning experiences with both teachers and computers. Older students may not have had computers in the classroom during their elementary and secondary school years, but their children may have.

Suggestions for Writing (p. 539)

1. As a class, discuss the vast and varied use of computers in the classroom. Students can contribute to the discussion by providing examples based on their experiences (perhaps even related to their own major): writing and editing, math review, anatomy visualizations, music appreciation, graphic design, and so on. Since the writing prompt asks to what extent students agree or disagree with Gelernter's position, they can decide which of his points, either the problems or the conditions, they support and which they don't.

2. Because of the bulk of information available, you might have students narrow their topic to a particular discipline, such as language arts or science. (Students may find it interesting that the computer as a search tool — even in a search for a book — has been at least one advancement since 1994.) As students conduct their research, guide them to reputable sources. Urge them to seek the opinions of teachers, perhaps through interviews, since instructors will have the most insight into

whether and how computers have affected their students' learning. Because students have been asked to comment on how Gelernter would feel about computers today, remind them of the conditions he presents in his essay. Are they still necessary, or have those conditions been met already?

STEVEN LEVY   **From** *The Perfect Thing* (p. 540)

In this excerpt from a larger work, Levy recognizes that iPods have infiltrated our society and explores the implications. His contrast of life before and after iPods and his descriptions, quotations, and examples add to the essay's appeal.

As You Read (p. 540)

Refer students to the first and second paragraphs, where Levy describes what iPod users might look like to an observer. Is the description exaggerated to make a point, or is that how iPod enthusiasts look and act? Are students insulted or amused by the description?

Pop Quiz

1. How do many non-iPod users feel about iPods in their environment?

2. What does Levy think of Wayne Coyne's criticism?

Questions to Start You Thinking (p. 541)

1. *Considering Meaning.* Have students find places in the essay where iPods are criticized. What is the criticism and who are the critics? Do the iPod users in class find the criticisms valid? Do iPods exclude and isolate? How do students discount such criticism? Do students who do not use iPods have a different perspective to share?

2. *Identifying Writing Strategies.* Sullivan, whom Levy quotes here, presents a slightly humorous but negative portrayal of iPod users. Students might recognize the description as something that might come out of a horror movie like *Dawn of the Dead*. Placing these quotations at the beginning of the essay makes for a good segue into the key questions Levy asks in paragraph 3.

3. *Reading Critically.* Students can point to paragraph 6 as the place where Levy begins to counter the criticisms. He compares and contrasts life before and after iPods to make his point that the criticisms are not valid. Facilitate a class discussion about whether Levy's criticism is sufficient. Would a particular type of evidence help him make his point more effectively?

4. *Expanding Vocabulary.* Have students reread the paragraphs where the words appear. Would simple synonyms have matched the tone and purpose of the paragraph? Keeping with the science fiction flavor of the first few paragraphs, "discombobulated" and "transmogrified" seem fitting.

5. *Making Connections.* Students' responses will vary based on a number of factors: their age, their familiarity with technology, and the amount of confidence they have using such technology. Some may find that cell phones isolate, yet others could argue that they connect us. While iPods may seem to isolate people, they can allow people to share music with other. Have the class list each technology and then identify its ability to isolate or to create communities.

Journal Prompts (p. 542)

1. Students who own iPods will likely favor them, but they may find some of the criticisms valid. Have them imagine that they are writing an ad geared to those who are against iPods. What would they say in their ad to make the product appealing?

2. This is a fun question that should get students thinking about their life and what music best reflects it. While students can write their response as a journal entry, another option is for them to play selections from their chosen songs and to discuss their reasons for including them.

Suggestions for Writing (p. 542)

1. This assignment lends itself well to group work. Have each group pick an electronic device and discuss its pros and cons, providing as many examples as possible. Each group can then share its findings with the class. Allow students to select any of the discussed electronic devices as the basis of their essay.

2. Downloading music without permission or payment is against the law. Many students are unaware of this law or choose to ignore it. For this essay, students will need a general understanding of copyright laws related to music. Students can review a fact sheet concerning music piracy on the Web site of the Recording Industry Association of America (<http://www.riaa.com/faq.php>). One exceptional site is the Columbia Law Library Music Plagiarism Project (<http://ccnmtl .columbia.edu/projects/law/library/entrance.html>). It contains copyright infringement cases from 1845 to the present. If students click on the "Case List" tab, they can hear the music from copyright infringement cases and read the judge's verdict. Urge students to find additional sites and to share them with the class.

MERRILL MARKOE   *Who Am I?* (p. 542)

Markoe, a TV comedy writer and author, pokes fun at online and magazine quizzes designed to reveal people's personalities and aspirations. Using an extended personal example, she gives readers a humorous glimpse into her struggles to discover her true self via quizzes.

As You Read (p. 543)

Refer to the essay's title, which poses the question "Who am I?" Then have students summarize the various selves she discovers from various quizzes. Jump to the conclusion, where she summarizes her personality as one of contradictions ("extroverted" and "reserved").

Pop Quiz

1. What is the difference between Internet and *Cosmopolitan* quizzes?

2. What does it mean to have a Pitta constitution?

Questions to Start You Thinking (p. 545)

1. *Considering Meaning.* Do students recognize her last sentence, "All things considered, I have to say that it feels great to really get to know myself at last," as sarcastic, underscoring her point that no quiz can reveal her inner self?

2. *Identifying Writing Strategies.* In paragraph 4, Markoe describes the quiz as passing judgment, even sighing. In other words, she has given the quiz human characteristics, as if it were a good friend who might provide insightful advice. Ask students why Markoe may have used this technique. What is its intended effect?

3. *Reading Critically.* With appropriate humor, Markoe makes fun of the absurdity of such quizzes and, indirectly, of the people who take the results seriously. Students can speculate about how she wants her readers to respond. However, her use of humor, exaggeration, and examples that make fun of herself indicate that she would like readers to laugh along with her. Given her purpose, students might feel that the quizzes she quotes from are not real, but they should be able to defend their answers.

4. *Expanding Vocabulary.* Students will have little difficulty in recognizing that some adjectives contrast with others: extroverted/reserved, passive/active, risk-taking/afraid of change, calm/neurotic. The fact that the quizzes gave such polar results indicates that their results are not authentic measures of someone's personality, interests, goals, future, and so on. Is that the overall point that Markoe is presenting in this essay? Ask students to respond based on the reading and their interpretation of her writing purpose.

5. *Making Connections.* Challenge students to use Markoe's humorous tone as they write a response to Razdan. Considering what Markoe has revealed about online and magazine quizzes, would she endorse personality questionnaires as a way to romantically match people? In what ways are they similar to or different from the type of quizzes she writes about in this essay?

Journal Prompts (p. 545)

1. Students can select a quiz from a magazine that is of interest to them, or they can select one from a Web site, entering "personality quizzes" into a search engine like <http://google.com>. When they are finished, have them assess the results. Do they agree or disagree with the results or find them confusing? For a journal response, students can write a brief response to the quiz originator (or the magazine or Web site) about the validity of the results.

2. Ask students to consider how much time they spend online during a given day or period of time. What types of activities do they do, and for what purpose? For example, do they play games for fun, e-mail to stay connected to family and friends, search the Web for school assignments, or surf the Web for fun? Based on their purpose and length of time they spend online, they can determine whether being online is addictive to them. Have students share their responses with the class and discuss the addictive (or nonaddictive) nature of Internet surfing.

Suggestions for Writing (p. 545)

1. Suggest that students write for their college newspaper about their experience with online personality quizzes. If they are unsure where to find them, they can go to <http://google.com> and use "personality quizzes" for their search term. As students plan their essays, remind them to develop a thesis that gives their overall impression of the quizzes and to support the thesis with specific examples from the quiz title, questions, or results. If students would like to achieve a comic tone, they can reread Markoe's essay to see how her examples, vocabulary, and phrasing contribute to the humorous effect.

2. Students might readily note that quizzes and horoscopes appeal to people because they hope such instruments will provide them with some quick, inexpensive, and helpful insights about themselves, their personalities, their ideal mate,

and so on. Some people take the quizzes to amuse themselves, but some are more serious and take the results to heart. To develop their essay, students can use the information from varied sources: their own experiences, interviews with quiz takers, Web-related research, and data gathered from related class activities and discussions.

ALEX KOPPELMAN   *MySpace or Our Space?* (p. 546)

Students who use social-networking sites will be especially interested in this essay, which explores the privacy issues that stem from these sites. Using MySpace as his primary example, Koppelman cites various postings that have resulted in school disciplinary action and arrests. Drawing on students' reaction to what they consider a violation of their privacy rights and some legal interpretations of privacy, he provides insight into both sides of the debate over censorship and monitoring of social-networking sites.

As You Read (p. 546)

Koppelman's examples from MySpace highlight the privacy issue. Do students have the right to post what they want to these sites? Do authorities have the right to read them and to take action if they believe that a posting is defamatory or otherwise harmful? These are the key questions Koppelman poses. To foster a class discussion and to identify the primary concerns of each side, select a particular case from the essay and ask students to debate the issue. Have students defend their answers by referring to specifics within the essay or even to the Constitution or the Bill of Rights. These documents are available on the Library of Congress Web site at <http://memory.loc.gov/ammem/help/constRedir.html>.

Pop Quiz

1. What action is Illinois's Community High School District 128 taking?

2. According to the essay, do police have the right to patrol MySpace?

Questions to Start You Thinking (p. 551)

1. *Considering Meaning.* Ask students to refer to the essay to identify the people who are concerned about the authorities' visit to MySpace pages. What are their affiliations: school, police, government, an agency? Exactly what are their concerns? Do students think their concerns are justified? Have students state their own concerns based on their experiences with MySpace or Facebook.

2. *Identifying Writing Strategies.* The privacy issue is complex, so students may realize the value of interviewing various sources to get a full picture of the concerns. Ask students if the quotations help them to understand Koppelman's point. Why, or why not? Are there other types of people (parents or teachers) Koppelman should have interviewed? How might these other possible interview subjects have contributed to a fuller understanding of the issue?

3. *Reading Critically.* If students have responded to "Identifying Writing Strategies," they have probably scanned the essay for quotations. To determine whether Koppelman promotes one side over the other, suggest that students review the quotations, noticing what position each seems to be advocating. Does Koppelman offer balanced quotations — that is, an equal number for each side? Students' answer to

this question will be directly connected to what they consider his purpose to be: informative or persuasive.

4. *Expanding Vocabulary.* Ask students if they can define the words in context. Given that paragraph 15 raises the legal issue that Koppelman develops in paragraphs 16–24, students may find that using legal jargon seems fitting.

5. *Making Connections.* Ask students to defend their position about blogs and censorship. They can review various positions stated in Koppelman's essay to help defend their position. You might share a blog (or printouts from one) in class and ask students whether any postings should have been censored and why or why not. If students believe that censorship is sometimes necessary, ask them in what instances it should be used.

Link to the Paired Essay (p. 551)

Before students respond to these questions, be sure that they understand the difference between *privacy* and *privilege.* Can they give examples of each? Link this discussion to students' responses to "Considering Meaning" and "Writing Strategies." Next, to approach these questions in an organized manner, create three columns on the board, representing three people quoted in Koppelman's essay. The columns should be for each person's name, position on the issue, and extent of likely agreement with Turkle's quote. Additionally, ask students to volunteer their names, positions, and stances.

Journal Prompts (p. 551)

1. Ask students to brainstorm in their journals about the type of online communication they are involved in and to list of the type of information they share about themselves. Students can refer to their list as they reflect upon how safe they feel disclosing information about themselves in each particular online environment. Have they ever felt uncomfortable because of undesired feedback? Did they take any actions to prevent such feedback? Have students share some of their reactions and discuss whether or not Koppelman's essay has changed their opinion. Will it likely change their online behavior? If so, in what ways?

2. For this journal prompt, have students direct their response to a member of the school board that endorsed Arethas's suspension. In their response, remind students to explain why his suspension was fair or unfair. Students can refer to the essay itself to gather support for their position.

Suggestions for Writing (p. 552)

1. Students will have their own reasons for posting to MySpace and similar sites, if they post at all. To establish reasons for the popularity of MySpace, students could develop an anonymous in-class survey. They might also look to *A Nation of Idol-Worshippers* (p. 525) to determine whether there is a relationship between the popularity of social-networking sites and what Golway describes as a growth of narcissism in America. Decide whether students should write to a particular or general audience. Once students have their reasons, have them decide on a workable pattern of organization. Is one reason more important than another? If so, where should it be placed?

2. The courts have long grappled with free speech issues, so this writing prompt is meant to challenge students as they write about this topic, focusing on the school environment. Koppelman points out in paragraph 15 that "The question of what public-school students have the right to say, and where they have the right to say it, remains murky." To write clearly on this topic, students must consider whether free speech extends to all situations or to just some. If they select "some," they will

need to state the situations that are exempt from the free speech right. Therefore, suggest that students brainstorm various school-related free-speech issues, from newspapers to speeches, to clothing, to online communication. Students can conduct a basic search using "students' rights to free speech" to find cases and sites that explore the debate. However, they might want to begin their search at the American Civil Liberties Union Web site, <http://aclu.org/freespeech/index.html>.

SHERRY TURKLE   *How Computers Change the Way We Think* (p. 552)

In this thought-provoking essay from the *Chronicle of Higher Education,* psychologist and sociologist Sherry Turkle focuses on the computer's influence on our thought process. She incorporates examples from her own experiences, readings, surveys, and observations to reveal the psychological effects of computer technology, ranging from chat rooms to word processing. This essay underscores how "[i]nformation technology is identity technology" and consequently has profound repercussions for us and our culture.

As You Read (p. 552)

Students are bound to be intrigued and perhaps surprised by Turkle's conclusions, based on her extensive research. Her ideas are complex but not confusing because of her clear method of organization. The headings should make it easy for students to identify the six areas where she sees technology promoting changes in thinking. In paragraph 9, Turkle notes "There can be no simple way of cataloging whether any particular change is good or bad." Have students reread the changes that technology is promoting, according to Turkle, and determine whether she implies or states that each is good or bad. Students can then present their own opinions and back them up with their reasons. This activity also lends itself well to group work; divide the class into six groups and give each one a different change to explore.

Pop Quiz

1. Why are online worlds valuable, according to the essay?

2. According to Edward R. Tufte, what is wrong with PowerPoint?

Questions to Start You Thinking (p. 558)

1. *Considering Meaning.* If your students worked with the "As You Read" prompt (p. 552), have them return to their responses to identify the six areas. Ask them to write a quick summary geared to general readers. Direct students to paragraphs 31–33 in order to respond to the question of why Turkle thinks paying attention to these changes is important. What significance do these shifts have for us as individuals and for society?

2. *Identifying Writing Strategies.* These questions are challenging because students must first be able to understand what they have read and reach some conclusions about Turkle's purpose. Write the six areas of change on the board and have a student briefly summarize each. Lead a class discussion on the logic behind the arrangement of these ideas. Is it random? General to specific? Most important to least important? Most complex to least complex? Be sure that students provide a rationale for their response.

3. *Reading Critically.* Before students assess clarity, they need to determine the specific causes and effects. They will likely note that computers are the general cause, but each specific change has its own effects. Students can refer to the "As You Read" activity as a basis for considering whether they find her arguments effective. If you divided the class into groups for the "As You Read" activity, have students in those groups assess the extent to which Turkle's arguments are or are not convincing. For example, given the topic of word processing (paragraphs 20–22), what type of evidence does Turkle present? What is the purpose of opening with the Vermont Country Store example and ending with the example from the seventh grader? Are these examples compelling, illustrative, sufficient, and ultimately convincing? If not, what other type of evidence might be convincing? Does Turkle's own expertise lend her argument sufficient credibility, aside from other evidence she cites?

4. *Expanding Vocabulary.* Turkle makes the point that "we don't have to know how a computer works." Ask students if they agree with her statement. Do students with expertise in computers have a different opinion from those who are more casual users? Students will most likely be able to define transparency and opacity based on these words' context. Epistemic (involving or relating to knowledge) might be more difficult to define without using a dictionary. Once students understand the words, have them discuss how "transparency means epistemic opacity" relays Turkle's point about "taking things at face value."

5. *Making Connections.* A Venn diagram might be a helpful way to begin thinking about the connection between the two essays. Have students revisit Gelernter's piece to list the problems he finds with computers and then compare them to the problems Turkle presents. Students will then be able to see similarities and differences, both specific and general, between the authors' points. Additionally, you might ask students to act as one author writing a response to the other.

Link to the Paired Essay

This activity ties in well with discussions of organizing a comparison-and-contrast essay. (See Chapter 7 of the text.) Brainstorm points of comparison-and-contrast on the board. Begin with the ones listed here, but have students generate more. They might also consider the authors' credentials, types of evidence used, focus, and whatever else students might contribute. Discuss with them what type of comparison-and-contrast format would work best. As students write their drafts, remind them to include specific examples from the essays themselves (or from the introduction to the essay) to make their point.

Journal Prompts (p. 558)

1. Have students freewrite about their general reaction to Turkle's point that computers change the way we think. Then ask students to explore, individually, their reactions to one technology change that she mentions, selecting a technology with which they have some experience. Finally, have students share their reactions.

2. Suggest that students list their computer use in chronological order, from the beginning to the end of a typical school day. Students can then compare their lists to determine the extent and variety of use. Ask them what implications computer use might have on their lives. What might Turkle say in response?

Suggestions for Writing (p. 559)

1. Computer enthusiasts may not recognize or agree that there are negative effects of computer use. Have those students especially review the essays in this chapter to gather possible negative effects of computer technology. Encourage students to

consider their own lives as well. Do they use computers or cell phones as their main form of social interaction and spend less time going out with friends as a result? If students are unable to list negative effects, suggest that they conduct some online research at reputable sites. They might also read other articles or books by the authors in this section, such as Turkle's *Life on the Screen: Identity in the Age of the Internet.*

2. It might be best to approach this assignment after students have discussed some challenges (ecological, political, social, academic, and so forth) that the world faces. Given the complexity of some of the challenges, students might need to select just one. For example, rather than consider several ecological changes, students might focus on global warming. Regardless of what challenge or challenges students select, their research should be sound and appropriately documented. Peer editing will help students ensure that their topic is focused, developed, and organized.

CHAPTER 27: EDUCATION (p. 560)

The essays in this chapter represent a variety of viewpoints on the role of education in our lives. Tamara Draut figures the real cost of a college degree, and Susan Brady Konig wryly suggests that multicultural education is wasted on three-year-olds. William Zinsser makes a case for rethinking our perception of the dropout, and Richard Rodriguez presents a poignant case against bilingual education. In the paired essays, Annie Dillard recalls the excitement of discovering nature on her own, while Carl T. Rowan remembers a courageous and beloved teacher who made his education possible.

Responding to an Image (p. 560)

Allow your students to use their imagination while examining these visual activity prompts. If necessary, have students free-associate responses to elements of each image. If they are given free rein for their own interpretation, they will most likely view analyzing these images as a rewarding way to begin thinking about writing in these modes.

Have students think about their high school or college athletic experiences, either as participants or observers. Ask them if this cartoon brings to mind experiences from their own lives that highlight the tension between academics and sports. Do these experiences influence their interpretation of the image, or is their interpretation based solely on elements in the visual? Have students consider whether the image includes a prominent focal point. Are their eyes attracted to one side of the court more than the other? Discuss whether the focal point is related to the message behind the cartoon.

Web Search (p. 561)

Because students are bound to find an overwhelming number of topics for this exercise, ask them to focus on just one or two issues that affect their lives in some way, such as financial aid or exit exams. To help them find credible sources, refer them to the Evaluation Checklist in the Quick Research Guide. You might have students write a summary of what they learned about their topics, and then hold a class discussion about the types of information (statistics, testimony, links, and so on) they found at each Web site. For more about using this activity, see page 244 of this manual.

TAMARA DRAUT   *What's A Diploma Worth Anyway?* (p. 561)

Draut's economic background enables her to explain the bleak outlook for today's college graduates. She contends that a college education, hard work, and a bank account do not guarantee graduates a secure financial future. In fact, she points out that they are likely to have a lower standard of living than their parents' generation.

As You Read (p. 561)

Students will likely recognize the philosophy expressed in Draut's first three sentences as words echoed by their own parents. Unfortunately, as Draut effectively points out, the "tried-and-true recipe" for success no longer holds true in today's economy. Specifically, her concerns are that college graduates often have serious debt loads, face a labor market with stagnating wages (despite increased productivity), and generally do not have the savings needed for financial security. Have students comment on the dismal picture that Draut presents. Do they accept it, challenge it, or feel a sense of resignation?

Pop Quiz

1. Why are so many middle-class college graduates in debt?

2. How does Draut define "Generation X"?

Questions to Start You Thinking (p. 563)

1. *Considering Meaning.* Have students scour the essay to identify reasons college graduates are not as financially stable at their parents are. (If students responded to the "As You Read" prompt on p. 561, they might want to return to their answers for that.) Is such a bleak picture inevitable? Are all of these causes beyond students' control, or can they make changes in their lives to alter Draut's forecast? For example, what might they do about their savings?

2. *Identifying Writing Strategies.* The complexity of the issue Draut takes on is in direct contrast to the simplicity of her essay's three-part structure. Have students scan the essay to mark each section before discussing the pattern Draut employs. Each of Draut's first three sentences (the "rules" of success) previews her three main points and the order in which she will develop them. In the essay itself, she dissects each rule to show why it no longer applies to today's college graduates: "go to college" (paragraphs 4–5), "work hard" (paragraphs 6–8), and "save money"(paragraph 9). Urge students to comment on the effectiveness of her approach.

3. *Reading Critically.* Students may be surprised to read Draut's comment, in paragraph 10, that "in all likelihood, this will be the first generation to not surpass their parents' standard of living." This prediction will be difficult for many students to accept given their own standards and the high cost of their college education — an education they were assured would bring them up to and beyond their parents' financial status. Question students about Draut's evidence for her assertion and her interpretation of that evidence. Is it sufficient? Why does Draut use the phrase "in all likelihood"? Does that phrase give students some hope?

4. *Expanding Vocabulary.* The term "baby-boom generation" refers to people born between the end of World War II and 1964. Call for volunteers to provide a defini-

tion for the class. A visit to Wikipedia <http://en.wikipedia.org/wiki/Baby_boomers> could add to the discussion.

5. *Making Connections.* Just by glancing at the numbers in this essay, students will conclude that Draut is approaching this topic from an economic perspective, which is directly connected to her background. She has an MPA (master's in public administration) and a BSJ (bachelor's of science in journalism) and writes frequently on economic issues (refer to her biography on p. 561). On the other hand, Zinsser, as his brief biography points out, is a writer and teacher. This question gets to the essence of the purpose of a college education. While an education is often sold to students as "the required ticket for entry into the middle class" (paragraph 4), is it really more than that? Students might comment that to Zinsser an education is more than a means to an economic end. If Draut measures success in terms of dollar amounts, how does Zinsser measure success? Challenge students to provide a definition of "success" from each writer's perspective.

Journal Prompts (p. 563)

1. Draut's point about the lack of economic benefits associated with a degree might alarm some students. Have students reflect on their own college application letters. What did they include as their reasons for wanting to attend college or to pursue a particular degree? If they had known Draut's points then, might they have made a different choice?

2. You might ask students to imagine that they are attending their high school's fifth-year class reunion and need to write a brief story of their lives after high school. Remind them to use past tense appropriately and consistently. Students can share their biographies in small groups or with the entire class.

Suggestions for Writing (p. 564)

1. If students completed the first journal prompt, they can reflect on that as they begin responding to this essay assignment. As students generate ideas for this essay, remind them to consider the general purpose of a college degree as well as their own specific major and/or minor. Have them explore their immediate short- and long-term goals and how a diploma will help them to achieve these goals.

2. As with all comparison-and-contrast essays, students will need to determine the basic points of comparison or contrast: age, values, goals, interests, influences, educational level, employment, average salary, and so on. Suggest that students do a general search on the Web and then narrow their topics. (They should include the terms "baby-boom generation" and "Generation X" in their searches.) Once they have specific characteristics to explore, they can develop them through interviews, additional Web searches, and other strategies. Two blogs might facilitate their research: <http://aginghipsters.com/blog/archives/000018.php> and <http://gen-y.org/blog2/category/gen-y-characteristics/>.

SUSAN BRADY KONIG *They've Got to Be Carefully Taught* (p. 564)

In an essay bound to elicit some chuckles, writer and editor Konig pokes fun at a cultural diversity event at her daughter's preschool. She indirectly ponders the value of such activities, questioning whether they divide rather than unify.

As You Read (p. 564)

In this extended example, Konig presents a humorous glimpse into Cultural Diversity Month at her daughter's preschool. Once students have identified the various activities designed to make students culturally aware, ask them to reflect on their appropriateness, effectiveness, and necessity. (They might refer to examples of the preschoolers' reactions in paragraphs 20 and 24.) Ask students to recall special occasions (such as Christmas and Hanukkah) where their own schools might have introduced cultural diversity. Did such activities increase the students' awareness of different cultures or affect them in any other way?

Pop Quiz

1. How does Konig respond to the letter requesting that she provide information about her family background?

2. What is significant about Konig's use of the word *interrogation*?

Questions to Start You Thinking (p. 566)

1. *Considering Meaning.* Based on their reading and the specific example it relays, ask students to reflect on Konig's position. Certainly, she uses humor to make her point, but exactly what is her point about teaching cultural diversity in the classroom? Consider singling out the title of this essay "They've Got to Be Carefully Taught" and introducing the lyrics (<http://stlyrics.com/lyrics/southpacific/youvegottobecarefullytaught.htm>) from "You've Got to Be Carefully Taught" from the musical *South Pacific.* Ask students in what way, if any, Konig's title/essay relates to the song's title/lyrics.

2. *Identifying Writing Strategies.* Draw students' attention to paragraphs 4–19, noting Konig's incorporation of dialogue and how it contributes to the impression of a person. What does this exchange reveal about Miss Laura? How else do we learn about her? If students could pick one adjective to describe her, what would it be? Have them defend their choice.

3. *Reading Critically.* Ask students if they would label Konig's view "conservative." What clues or statements in the essay have influenced their opinion? A related activity is to have students imagine that they have just read Konig's essay in the *National Review* and are writing a letter to the editor. What would they say? Suggest that they share their letters with the class.

4. *Expanding Vocabulary.* Provide students with a definition of the word *indigenous* (perhaps "originating from a particular country or other location") and have them give examples of indigenous items from different cultures. Can they also include indigenous songs? Do students see the irony in the description of "Take Me Out to the Ballgame" as indigenous? If not, ask them whether indigenous is ever used (outside of Konig's essay) to describe cultural artifacts that are perceived as quintessentially American.

5. *Making Connections.* Both Tan and Rodriguez write about ethnicity and adapting to American culture. Would students in Tan's and Rodriguez's elementary classrooms have benefited from a Cultural Diversity Month? Would it have changed the way Tan and Rodriguez assimilated American culture and language? Have students respond to these questions as if they were Konig. Ask students, based on these readings and their own experiences, whether students benefit by learning about different cultures. If so, how should such learning occur — in the manner it does in Miss Laura's class or in some other way?

Journal Prompts (p. 567)

1. The topic of cultural diversity may or may not have been addressed in students' elementary or secondary schools, depending on their age and where they went to school. If it was, have them discuss whether their introduction to cultural diversity was successful, a turnoff, a waste of time, or something else.

2. As students prepare to respond to this journal prompt, encourage them to consider that moment when they recognized a racial or ethnic difference between them and someone else — for example, when they realized that a friend celebrated a holiday differently from the way they did. Suggest that students go beyond identifying the moment of recognition to include the effects.

Suggestions for Writing (p. 567)

1. This topic is a broad one because it could relate to any year in school and any subject. Urge students to narrow their topic so that they focus on one particular event. Suggest that they reread Konig's essay, paying particular attention to her use of details and dialogue — both of which make her essay come to life as she shares her experiences with readers.

2. Before students voice their opinions, survey the readings in the text thus far. Have students consider the points made by Tan, Senna, Staples, and La Ferla and imagine how these authors would respond to these questions. Would they eschew or embrace a specific adjective, such as *Asian, African,* or *Hispanic* in favor of the general *American*? What would be their rationale? Why are people asked to check off their ethnicity or race on forms, such as college applications? Once students have considered both the positive and negative consequences of specifying ethnic or cultural backgrounds, have them draft their essay. For support, suggest that they incorporate information from their readings and their own experiences.

WILLIAM ZINSSER *The Right to Fail* (p. 567)

While many people consider failure to be the antithesis of the American dream, Zinsser holds that failure can sometimes be the path to success. He draws on examples from literature, media, and politics to clarify his position.

As You Read (p. 567)

Students may have difficulty imagining how they might benefit from flunking a test, failing a class, or dropping out of school. Zinsser offers numerous examples to support his position that people should create their own definition of success rather than abide by society's definition. Discuss whether students accept or at least understand Zinsser's point that failure can open up new doors by reducing stress, encouraging exploration, and creating new standards for success.

Pop Quiz

1. What example from literature does Zinsser use to support his position?

2. Name two benefits of failure that Zinsser points out.

Questions to Start You Thinking (p. 570)

1. *Considering Meaning.* Ask students to define the term *drop out* and to look up some synonyms in a thesaurus. How would Zinsser react to such derogatory adjectives, given the positive effects that he says can result from dropping out?

2. *Identifying Writing Strategies.* Students should have little difficulty identifying the examples because they appear in almost every paragraph. To evaluate how varied they are, ask students to label each type of example. In paragraph 4, for instance, Zinsser mentions figures from American history, and in paragraph 8 he discusses an example from literature. In paragraphs 2 and 13, he cites a general example — students who volunteer for VISTA. When students finish categorizing and labeling the examples, ask them to comment on their overall effect. Do they help Zinsser make his case? Which ones were particularly strong or weak, and why?

3. *Reading Critically.* Zinsser acknowledges his opposition up front (para. 3), then later directly addresses parents who instill in their children a fear of failure (paras. 5–6). In paragraph 9, he softens the tone of his argument, assuring the opposition that he is not "urging everyone to go out and fail just for the sheer therapy of it." Anticipating the older generation's viewpoint that dropouts are "just plumb lazy," he counters that response with his alternative take (para. 12).

4. *Expanding Vocabulary.* Students will easily recognize Zinsser's implication that Americans worship material success, a goal that is created and reinforced by advertising. Ask students to discuss specific print ads, commercials, or televisions shows that can be viewed as "hymns" to a product, brand, or value. What are their "lyrics" (literal or metaphorical)?

5. *Making Connections.* You might have students actually write a letter from Carl T. Rowan to Zinsser. Rowan was at risk of failing before the intervention of a tough but caring teacher, Miss Bessie. He seems to have viewed his rescue from potential failure as a lesson, but what other views are possible? Ask students whether groups like African Americans, who have faced discrimination or other barriers to advancement, have as much luxury to fail. For such groups, academic success may be seen as a societal "stamp of approval" needed for economic and social advancement.

Journal Prompts (p. 571)

1. For this assignment, refer students to the discussion of defining a term in Chapter 19, "Strategies for Developing." Remind them that they can form their definition by negation — stating what the term is not — as in "The American dream is not about money."

2. Before students begin this journal response, have them paraphrase Zinsser's thesis. With the thesis in mind, they should identify someone who might benefit from the essay's main idea. Suggest that students end their response with a relevant quotation from the essay and be prepared to explain their choice of quotation.

Suggestions for Writing (p. 571)

1. Students have probably experienced failure at some point in their lives — in school, sports, a relationship, and so on. Suggest that they use the reporter's questions (p. 303) to generate ideas and to use description and/or dialogue to detail their experience. Remind students that their essay must go beyond a mere recounting of the experience to show what they learned from it.

2. Introduce this assignment by asking students which of Zinsser's examples are unfamiliar to them, and then brainstorm some individuals whose "failure" ulti-

mately led to their success. Research via the Internet will help students identify additional examples and will provide essential facts about the people they select to write about. You might ask students to identify their specific audience in a note to you that accompanies their essay. Remind students to keep in mind their audience's knowledge and attitude about the subject throughout the essay.

RICHARD RODRIGUEZ   *Public and Private Language* (p. 571)

In this eloquent reflection on his childhood experiences with language, Rodriguez shows the benefits of his English-only schooling. At the same time, however, learning English — his "public" language — diminished the need for his "private" home language, changing his relationships with family members. Rodriguez calls on his personal experience to challenge the benefits of bilingual education.

As You Read (p. 571)

In the beginning of the essay, Rodriguez's reluctance to speak English makes him "diffident and afraid" (para. 3). As he realizes that others can understand his English, however, his confidence in his ability to learn the language quickly increases (para. 10). In turn, this confidence boosts Rodriguez's esteem in his "public identity" (para. 13). Have students refer to those passages and note what is happening in his home life during these periods. Do events in Rodriguez's family life correspond to his accomplishments in learning English?

Pop Quiz

1. Why did the nuns visit the Rodriguez family's home?

2. What is Rodriguez's "public" language?

Questions to Start You Thinking (p. 576)

1. *Considering Meaning.* Encourage students to discuss whether Rodriguez uses the term *silence* literally, figuratively, or both. Ask them to point out references to auditory senses, such as "hear," "loud," "silence," and "quiet," and have them speculate as to why Rodriguez included them so frequently.

2. *Identifying Writing Strategies.* List on the board all the comparisons and contrasts that students find in the essay, discussing what each reveals. If students need hints to get started, you might note that the title of the essay reveals the contrast at the essay's center. Rodriguez also contrasts his public identity before and after learning English, his family relationships before and after the Rodriguezes started speaking English in their home, and his parents' different reactions to the "Americanization" of their children.

3. *Reading Critically.* Dialogue allows readers to hear the contrast between Rodriguez's public and private languages. For example, the nuns' pronunciation of Rodriguez's name — "Rich-heard" (para. 8) — illustrates how foreign and impersonal English sounded before he became fluent in it. Rodriguez also uses dialogue to illustrate his teachers' and parents' commands, reinforcing the point that English was the language that shaped his public identity: "Richard, stand up. Don't look at the floor. Speak up" (para. 3). And the combination of English and Spanish in his

parents' repeated command to "Speak to us *en ingles*" (paras. 7, 9) conveys the confusion Rodriguez felt as a child divided between two languages.

4. *Expanding Vocabulary.* Students may have an easier time applying these terms to others than to themselves. You might begin by asking students whether a media personality has a public and a private self or if they have ever noticed that a certain group of people has a private language. Ask students whether they use language differently in different environments: at home and at work, for example. Does their behavior in these environments differ in other ways? Use this discussion to help students understand the polarity that bilingualism created for Rodriguez.

5. *Making Connections.* To connect the issues presented in these two readings, ask students to create a two-column chart, devoting one column to each author. Have students list instances where the authors reveal the effects of their language acquisition on their mothers. When students have finished, ask them to report and analyze their findings. Were the effects on Rodriguez's and Tan's mothers largely positive, negative, or a combination of both? How do students account for the differences or similarities in the mothers' reactions?

Journal Prompts (p. 576)

1. Ask students to go beyond narrating for this assignment and evaluate whether the division between a public and a private self has negative or positive effects.

2. This assignment will help students empathize with Rodriguez, showing them how a positive accomplishment can often elicit mixed feelings. When students have finished their entries, ask them to volunteer their responses.

Suggestions for Writing (p. 576)

1. Tell students that they can modify this topic on the basis of their own experience (or lack of experience) with other languages. Students from a bilingual home might relay experiences quite different from those of classmates who learned a second language in an educational environment. Those who are monolingual may approach the topic from another perspective: Do they feel that it is important to learn another language? Why, or why not?

2. Students' arguments will be stronger if they do some research to expand their understanding of this topic. In fact, without researching bilingual education, some students may have only a faint idea of what the term means. Guide students to credible Web sites on the topic, such as Education Week on the Web at <http://edweek.org/context/topics/issuespage.cfm?id=8>, the National Association for Bilingual Education at <http://www.nabe.org/>, Bilingual Education Resources at <http://www.ecsu.ctstateu.edu/depts/edu/textbooks/bilingual.html>, and Issues in U.S. Language Policies — Bilingual Education at <http://ourworld.compuserve.com/homepages/JWCRAWFORD/biling.htm>.

ANNIE DILLARD *From An American Childhood* (p. 577)

In this excerpt from her memoir *An American Childhood,* Dillard writes of receiving her first microscope and the scientific adventures that followed. She gives explicit details about how the microscope ignited her passion for learning, which was given room to grow as a result of her parents' hands-off philosophy. With the freedom granted by her parents, Dillard was able to set her own goals and, as she implies, reach for the stars.

As You Read (p. 577)

Dillard's ability to recall specifics is impressive. Because of her plentiful and robust details, readers can picture an inquisitive child whose desire to learn is bolstered by each new discovery, whether it was an amoeba, diatom, or the common worm. Have students share their adjectives to describe Dillard: precocious, nerd, curious, determined, and so on. Then ask students what adjectives Dillard might select from the list to describe herself.

Pop Quiz

1. Why did Dillard want a microscope?

2. What does it mean to "hit pay dirt" (paragraph 14)?

Questions to Start You Thinking (p. 579)

1. *Considering Meaning.* In paragraph 3, Dillard explains how she begins her search for a one-celled animal and then later, in paragraph 7, her joy at finding one, the amoeba. Ask students to state the short- and long-term effects of this discovery on Dillard. What role did her parents play?

2. *Identifying Writing Strategies.* From the simplicity of "a white enamel table" (paragraph 2) to the complexity of her description of the amoeba "rolling his grains . . . extending an arc of his edge for a foot and drawing himself along by that foot" (paragraph 13), Dillard's essay is full of vivid descriptions that are especially helpful for those readers who have little scientific background. Are students impressed or overwhelmed by the details?

3. *Reading Critically.* In paragraph 8, Dillard reveals the scene following her discovery. Students will note that she "ran" upstairs. She was so excited that she was "bursting" with the news of her discovery. Her use of language makes it seem as if she is a barker at a carnival, trying to attract people to the tent to see a thing of wonder. See if students can identify how the phrases "see the famous amoeba," "hurry before his water dried," and "It was the chance of a lifetime" contribute to this effect. Encourage a student to read the paragraph aloud to hear the excitement in Dillard's words.

4. *Expanding Vocabulary.* Most likely students will need a dictionary to define these words as well as other scientific terms used in this essay. In terms of Dillard's scientific vocabulary, ask students if it is important to her point that readers are familiar with these words, or do they just need to recognize them as part of the vernacular of a scientist? At a young age, Dillard is speaking as a scientist, as she has immersed herself in the world of science. She has picked up the language found in *The Field Book of Ponds and Streams,* her various collected books, and her microscope booklet. Reinforce the point that when writing in a scientific field, it is difficult to *not* use scientific terms. For example, right-clicking on the word *siliceous* will not produce a synonym that will make this word's meaning understandable to most readers, so Dillard is forced to use the appropriate scientific label. In addition to using scientific vocabulary, she also uses sophisticated language. For example, she could have substituted *crumbly* for *friable.* Ask students if they are frustrated, amused, or educated by her language. Would this essay have a different effect if she used more common terms when possible?

5. *Making Connections.* While it is true that both Dillard and Rodriquez live a life independent from their parents, they came about their independence differently. Ask students to determine how Dillard and Rodriquez arrived at their independence. They might point out that Dillard's parents gave her independence while Rodriquez sought his.

Link to the Paired Essay (p. 579)

Students might note that both Rowan and Dillard, despite their social, economic, and educational backgrounds, showed perseverance, self-direction, and a passion for learning. One difference, however, is that Dillard developed these attributes largely on her own (through her parents' lack of involvement), while Rowan had an outside influence, Miss Bessie, who helped him to foster these attributes. Ask students if he would have been able to achieve his educational goals if Miss Bessie embraced a hands-off philosophy.

Journal Prompts (p. 579)

1. For this journal entry, have students list their activities and then freewrite about the one they found the most riveting or enjoyable.

2. To introduce this journal entry, consider sharing an excerpt from the 1983 movie *A Christmas Story,* based on Jean Shepherd's book *In God We Trust: All Others Pay Cash,* where young Ralphie yearns for a Red Ryder BB gun. What similarity do they see between his reaction when he finally gets the gun and Dillard's when she receives the coveted microscope?

Suggestions for Writing (p. 580)

1. Ask students if they can identify with Dillard's pride in her accomplishment and if they have ever felt a similar way about something that they achieved. The key phrase in this assignment is "important to you." Be sure that after students brainstorm topics, they choose one of personal significance. Also, remind them to use specific details and examples to relay their struggles so readers can identify with both their motivations and the situation. As they write, suggest that students consider the following questions and incorporate relevant responses: Did they accomplish what they set out to achieve? What was the outcome? How did they feel about it at that moment? How do they feel about it now? Were there any lasting effects?

2. Suggest that students reflect on some of the other readings in the text. What other authors echo Dillard's point about the connection between freedom and learning? Also, have students explain the phrase "without their parents watching over their every move." What do students think about Dillard's parents' hands-off philosophy? In paragraph 12, Dillard states that they did not "inquire about my homework or term papers or exams . . . nor attend my field hockey games." Is this parenting approach desirable? Does it always have the same effect? Students should feel free to disagree with Dillard's position or to reach some type of compromise.

CARL T. ROWAN   *Unforgettable Miss Bessie* (p. 580)

Rowan's essay captures the spunk and spirit of a quintessential teacher, one who taught him "more than [he] realized." His vivid portrayal is sure to impress students, and it may make them think of teachers who made a difference in their lives.

As You Read (p. 580)

This essay is fundamentally Rowan's tribute to a memorable teacher, Miss Bessie. His well-chosen examples, dialogue, quotations, and description bring her to life. The combination helps students understand her character, which is essential to their understanding her influence. Students can skim the essay and find numerous examples of her influence — from Rowan's grammar aptitude, his love of literature, his ability to read and write, as well as his lifelong love of learning.

Pop Quiz

1. According to Miss Bessie, what takes guts?

2. What is the "measure of a great teacher"?

Questions to Start You Thinking (p. 584)

1. *Considering Meaning.* Rowan paints a vivid picture of Miss Bessie. Have students identify descriptive passages that suggest her influence. Then have them find directly stated reasons for her importance in Rowan's life. Her influence seems almost immeasurable, but students can select certain sentences or sections that capture part of it (such as paragraphs 10, 14, and 16). Another option is to have students write to Miss Bessie as Rowan might have after receiving her note (paragraph 20) to explain how she influenced him.

2. *Identifying Writing Strategies.* Frequently, Rowan uses both recall and dialogue to make points about Miss Bessie and her influence on him. For instance, he follows his second paragraph ("I shall never forget the day she scolded me into reading Beowulf") with dialogue between the two of them, explaining what happened that day. Ask students to select what they consider to be especially powerful, moving, or amusing dialogue. Also, ask students to point to causes and effects that Rowan portrays. Specifically, what were some causes of Rowan's potential academic failure? What effects did Miss Bessie's words and actions have on him? Additionally, encourage students to note the organizational structure of the essay. They might readily recognize Rowan's introduction, where he gives background on Miss Bessie. He then gives specific examples of her behavior and influence on him, discusses "things [he] did not have" (paragraphs 15–18), and then fast-forwards to the future.

3. *Reading Critically.* Rowan's portrayal of Miss Bessie is powerful because of his use of specifics (details, dialogue, situations). Readers can imagine her commanding presence in the classroom and in his life. In terms of why Rowan has written this essay, ask students to find hints within the essay itself, especially paragraphs 25–28. Is he merely providing a commentary about her or does he have a larger purpose?

4. *Expanding Vocabulary.* The word *dignity* can easily be defined by looking it up in the dictionary, but a one-word definition cannot capture the essence of dignity. Refer students to Rowan's use of the word in paragraph 11. Using Miss Bessie and Rowan as examples, have students expand on the simple definition of *dignity* so that it applies to both of them. Students may have an easy time explaining how and why dignity is used to define Miss Bessie. However, they may need some prodding to understand how it applies to Rowan. Remind them that his essay focuses on her influence on him so they can understand how dignity has been transferred from her to him.

5. *Making Connections.* In paragraph 3, Rowan uses the phrase "I ain't," which Miss Bessie considers to be substandard English that has no place in education or the workforce. In fact, her statement "you've got to live and be somebody" (para. 6) suggests that such words have no place anywhere. Ask students to discuss if she would consider such phrases "private" or never acceptable. In terms of how Rodriguez might respond to Miss Bessie, ask students to determine whether the situations are the same and whether language needs to be adapted for a "public self."

Link to the Paired Essay (p. 584)

Students may note that both Rowan and Dillard likely had strong internal motivations to succeed; however, Rowan (at least in this essay) focuses on an important external motivator, Miss Bessie, while Dillard describes internal motivation primarily. Dillard notes how the hands-off attitude of her parents helped to foster her independence. As an extension of this assignment, you might ask students whether they would describe themselves as either internally or externally motivated learners (or some combination). They should give specific examples to support their conclusions.

Journal Prompts (p. 584)

1. For this journal entry, point out that an accomplishment doesn't have to be something major. It can be winning an award or something as simple as getting a passing grade on a math test.

2. Rowan provides a dramatic example of learning to read and write. Students' examples of a special effort may not be as remarkable. Have them brainstorm to discover times when they applied more than the usual effort in order to reach a personal goal. Topics could range from losing weight to achieving some type of academic success.

Suggestions for Writing (p. 584)

1. Rowan was lucky that he had someone like Miss Bessie in his life, someone who guided and influenced him. In this essay, students are asked to write about a "Miss Bessie," a person who — for whatever reason and in whatever way, knowingly or unknowingly — gave them what they needed to succeed. This person could be a family member, a coach, a teacher, a boss or coworker, or even a friend. Underscore the importance of using vivid details to bring the person to life and to show the effects that he or she had on the student.

2. Before writing, have students review some of the essays in this section to assess what they say about education and success. Which authors would assert that education is the key to success? Which ones might not? Students should have a clear definition of "success" and be sure that they relay this definition to their readers. To argue their point effectively, students will need to use logical, ethical, and emotional appeals — all of which are used effectively in various essays within this chapter. If desired, have students target their writing toward a particular publication, such as *Reader's Digest,* the *National Review,* or *TomPaine.com.* Or students might also select a school, community, or city newspaper. With particular readers in mind, students can select suitable support, persuasive appeals, and organizational strategies.

CHAPTER 9

Teaching *A Writer's Research Manual*

We encourage you to incorporate some writing from investigation into your course, even if students will be focusing on the research process in a later course. How college instructors use and require research writing varies widely from campus to campus and from discipline to discipline within an institution. Different instructors' different requirements might intimidate students — many in fact might be terrified of doing research. You can help them to overcome their anxiety by introducing them to a successful system for academic inquiry based on the writing process they have been practicing in your course.

Emphasize that research is more than collecting a bunch of notes from several books and articles; it is an active process of investigating to learn. Remind students that the recursive nature of the writing process applies to the research process as well; they should allow themselves time and space for necessary backtracking and leaping forward in their investigations. Focusing on the sequence of steps laid out in *A Writer's Research Manual* will help them to develop an organized and sequential system to effectively search for information. In this section of *Practical Suggestions,* you will find descriptions of the resources available for students in *The Bedford Guide* as well as ways for you to introduce and reinforce the research process in your course.

Whether or not your version of the text includes *A Writer's Research Manual,* your students will find the Quick Research Guide to be a convenient minireference to the key steps of the research process. The appendix offers clear advice, checklists, and charts that will help them define their research goals, search for and evaluate sources, incorporate source material effectively, and document sources according to MLA or APA style. Students can use this reference when writing any kind of research paper, but they may find it especially useful for assignments drawing on just a few sources. For short position papers drawing on a few sources, refer students to Chapter 12.

IMPORTANT FEATURES OF *A WRITER'S RESEARCH MANUAL*

The seven chapters of the research manual guide students through the process of generating a fully documented research paper. Building on the skills students have learned in previous writing assignments, the authors explain how to choose a research topic and explore a variety of sources to compile information about it, how to shape their material into a thesis statement and draft, how to use and document their evidence, and how to revise and edit a final draft in correct manuscript form. You will find the same helpful resources in these chapters that you have relied on throughout the textbook: checklists focused on each part of the research process, from generating a topic to revising and editing; tips for using the computer to expedite research, drafting, and documentation tasks; and a student paper as a model. The student MLA research paper by Maegan Kinkelaar relies on library and Internet sources. Also, new to the book are extracts from a paper modeling APA style.

Chapter 28, "Planning and Managing Your Research Project," introduces students to the first step in the process: generating a question and locating and managing information. Chapter 29, "Working with Sources," guides students as they begin a working bibliography and recording information from their sources by quoting, paraphrasing, and summarizing. It also includes Source Navigators to help students find the information that they need to document their sources fully and correctly. In Chapter 30, "Finding Sources in the Library, on the Internet, and in the Field," a variety of sources are covered, including library and field sources, as well as information on searching the Internet. Chapter 31, "Evaluating Sources," provides clear criteria for critically questioning the reliability of each type of source, and in Chapter 32, "Integrating Sources," students will find advice on ethically incorporating source material into their drafts. Chapter 33, "Writing Your Research Paper," guides students through the process of shaping the mass of information they have collected and acknowledging source material in their drafts. Chapter 34, "Documenting Sources," a complete documentation stylebook, contains information about how to cite sources using either MLA or APA style. It also includes an MLA paper and extracts of an APA paper.

The research skills these chapters teach will serve students well not only in the academic community but in their work communities as well. Good research skills and critical thinking are of a piece, and both are crucial for an educated person. In all of your conversations about research and writing, continue to emphasize the role of the intellectually curious writer.

INTRODUCING STUDENTS TO THE RESEARCHING AND WRITING PROCESS

Even if you have not normally been holding conferences with your students, it is essential that you plan at least three conferences with writers working on research papers. Whether you hold these conferences during class or in your office, the high-caliber papers that result will certainly be worth the extra time you spend.

The first conference should be short and scheduled early on to discuss possible research topics and to help students hone their research questions. Many students have trouble narrowing and specifying a topic for research. Ask them to do an overview of two topics and to phrase each topic as a research question. Have them make a preliminary search of the two topics to discover the following:

- Are materials accessible and available in the time given?
- Has the topic been underresearched or overreported?
- Can the writer generate a fresh view on the topic and convince a reader of its validity?

In the conference, ask each student what he or she has discovered so far. React honestly to the topic. Let the writer know whether the topic is an appropriate response to the assignment and whether it would allow him or her to flex some cognitive muscles.

The second conference should be held after students have gathered all (or at least most) of their material and have handed in a working outline for the essay and a list of works cited (students should be simultaneously drafting their essays). Often the working outline can alert you and the writer to potential problems. The outline might show an imbalance of discussion, an insufficiency of evidence, a direction the paper might go that's not predicted by the thesis, a breakdown of classifications, and so on. Obviously, you will want to discuss with writers the direction in which they see their essay moving and any additional questions that might be developing as they work with the research. Often in this conference you can provide specific advice about additional resources, ask questions that might help writers clarify their thesis or pattern of organization, and comment on the manner in which sources are quoted or paraphrased, perhaps suggesting smoother introductions.

If any writer's topic includes an interview, survey, or questionnaire, plan to hold an additional conference after he or she has drafted the interview questions or the survey to have the writer explain what information he or she wants to gather and determine whether the questions will elicit that information. Talk with writers about what background information they might need about respondents. If some writers have conducted interviews, talk with them about selecting materials from the interviews. Most important, conduct your discussions so that students discover more about their research purposes and methods as well as the significance of their research. Direct students to Chapter 6, "Interviewing a Subject," for tips on interviewing. Part II, Chapter 7 of this manual contains activities to help students with interviewing techniques.

Hold the third conference after students have completed a final draft and before the final paper is due. Use this conference to focus writers on the revision process. Before the conference, read and evaluate the drafts. Then discuss with each student your evaluation and make specific suggestions before he or she turns in the final paper.

Most of our students use conference advice and written comments to revise their essays. Some college instructors who require research papers call for them in the last week of classes and return them graded — and perhaps with evaluative comments — only at the end of the finals period. We strongly discourage this procedure because it does not give students a chance to talk with the instructor and to think further about how to improve their papers. They are not, therefore, encouraged to make revision a part of their process of writing from research. A conference about the submitted essay with an option or requirement for revision helps student writers learn how important the rewriting stage is.

In a portfolio class, writers must decide — with the advice of peer respondents and under your guidance — how to revise the draft before putting it into the portfolio for evaluation. Students should not be left to flounder at this point but should be given specific guidance, both orally and in writing (so they can refer to it when they are actually revising). If you use portfolios, consider assigning the research paper during the first half of the course to give students ample time to revise as their writing skills improve.

Instructors who use portfolios often require that the finished research paper be turned in with the other writings in the portfolio. Generally, student portfolios are due one or two weeks before the end of the semester, so if you choose this method, be sure to create time in the schedule to allow for your students' research papers. Other colleagues set the deadline for the finished research project one or two weeks before the final portfolio is due. By collecting the research papers earlier, they can complete this part of the grading while the students revise their final portfolios. The instructors then average the grade for the research paper into the portfolio grade.

You will need to provide students with clear criteria for evaluating each step of the process. Some instructors prefer to grade by letter or percentage; others prefer a simple satisfactory/unsatisfactory system of assessment, or one with a third category of "needs improvement." Use an evaluation system that both you and your students are comfortable with, and be sure to make your system clear to them. (See Chapter 6 of this manual for more about evaluating student writing.) If you decide to assign letter grades, remind students that just because they receive all A's on the preliminary steps doesn't automatically mean they will receive the same overall grade for the course. The grade from the final revision becomes the grade of the essay.

Planning and Managing Your Research Project (Ch. 28, p. 589)

When a researcher plans a research project, she or he must be willing to live with it. Chapter 28 will encourage students to discover suitable research questions, to record and organize information from sources, and to schedule their tasks so that they complete their project on time. You might also want to refer students to information in Chapter 28 as they generate ideas for the assignment in Chapter 9, "Taking a Stand," or Chapter 12, "Supporting a Position with Sources."

Chapter 28, "Planning and Managing Your Research Project," contains these activities:

- For Group Learning (p. 599). See page 39 of this manual for advice about how to use this feature.

BEGINNING YOUR INQUIRY (p. 590)

The Assignment: Writing from Sources (p. 590)

Notice that the authors assign a researched writing based on critical thinking. College-level writers shouldn't be wasting their time with researching only to report and summarize. Some college instructors do ask for summary research papers as a way of gauging students' reading and basic comprehension of characteristic field research. More and more instructors are, however, encouraging critical thinking through research and writing. Particularly on campuses with writing-across-the-curriculum programs, college faculty are thinking more carefully about how to use research assignments to elicit higher-order thinking. The research paper assignment that mandates critical thinking forces students to take control of their learning. They can write a summary paper without having to alter any of their initial opinions; for an investigative research paper, they must evaluate and perhaps reassess their opinions and locate and read up on the opinions of others — opinions they might not have encountered before.

Here's an Idea . . .

To demystify the research paper and to promote more enthusiasm for conducting research, ask students early in the semester to write you a letter or a reflection describing any research projects — individual or collective —that they've participated in. Ask them to describe in particular any experience in which they have discovered more than they expected to find when they began — whether it was more about the library, about field research, about planning or drafting, about the conventions of the research paper, or about the joy of researching their topic. Make use of these anecdotes and descriptions whenever you work on research activities.

Consider surveying colleagues in several disciplines for examples of research assignments and of typical student responses to share with your students. Refer frequently to your own research for classes you might now be taking, the thesis or dissertation you wrote, the proposal you drafted for curricular improvement or some civic reform, and so on. Let your students see that the research process is a practical and useful skill that you enjoy and use in your life.

GENERATING IDEAS AND ASKING A RESEARCH QUESTION (p. 590)

Encourage students to generate topics by scanning their fields of expertise or interest. You might even urge those who have been given a research assignment for another course to use the same topic in both courses and thus work intensively on developing and reimagining the topic for at least two audiences. Suggest that writers who want to rethink a question they attempted in high school should investigate new research and develop new insights.

Consider beginning the research assignment by writing a list of "forbidden topics" on the board. Compiling this list with students often cures them of the temptation to play it safe or simply to recycle an old paper. Include topics that might be difficult for you to read and respond to objectively as an adviser and editor and topics that are so worn out you could write the introduction in your sleep. Challenge students to find some way of addressing a topic that will make their research and their writing unique. Remind them to make you want to read the paper, not just be obligated to do so.

It's important for students to begin with two topics; although a preliminary search might suggest that they will have no difficulty researching and writing about one topic, something can always go wrong. Having a backup topic approved in advance can save a student from getting into time trouble later on. Help each writer think about his or her research questions. If a question is stated in such a way that it would lead only to a report, help the writer revise the question until the research and writing task includes more critical thinking. If the question has been asked too often, help the writer find a way to ask an allied but original question.

Choosing Your Territory (p. 592)

Students often flounder at this stage of a writing project, and some instructors, not realizing that many students do not know how to choose a suitable topic and to generate ideas for it, do not provide sufficient guidance to help students at this critical juncture. Start by brainstorming together.

Have students spend fifteen minutes in class or outside listing the themes that organize their classes. Ask them to list any idea that was new to them at the beginning of the semester but that they keep running into. For a second and third session of listing, ask them to choose one of the topics suggested by the Discovery Checklist on "Choosing Your Territory" (p. 592). Then ask students to choose two topics from their lists and write seven questions for each using reporter's questions. This practice might or might not lead students directly to research questions, but it shows them how to narrow the territory. Check each student's topic to see that he or she is on the right track. You might need to work with some students individually to discover a suitable topic.

Here's an Idea . . .

After discussing the importance and excitement of research, ask students to write their name and two research questions on an index card. Students assume that you will compile a list of the selected research topics for the class, and they are correct, in a way. Collect the cards, shuffle them, and then ask each student to select a card from the deck. They should not look at the card while choosing, and if they select their own card, they must return it to the deck. Inform students that they have just selected the topics for their research assignment. After the moaning and groaning subside, suggest to them that they might trade cards but that they must not trade for their own topics. If they are confused about a research question, then they must talk with the writer of the question and ask about the question and the focus of the research.

This process moves students into a dialogue with one another. Writers are encouraged to narrow their topics when they have to explain what they wanted to investigate. Once this procedure is finished, record the topics and the name of the person who suggested it. Tell students that their finished paper will also be read by the student who created the initial question. This expands the audience for the research and allows students to work as a community of researchers. If you find this card-shuffling procedure too harsh, allow students to return to their original topics after they have clarified them for their classmates. This topic will not necessarily be the one that the student will investigate, but the discussion and thinking engendered can be valuable in refining students' thinking.

Taking an Overview (p. 592)

Indicate to your students how important the early overview is by starting each day's discussion of research with a report of each writer's progress. Ask each student simply to tell what he or she has learned so far about what the library can reveal about his or her topic. Often students will notice materials for others in the class while they work on their own topic, and a sharing community emerges.

It is important to get students into the habit of what the authors call "reconnaissance" as early as possible. Many instructors structure this experience with a scavenger-hunt assignment. The three following scavenger hunts will introduce students to a variety of resources available at their college library.

Hunt No. 1   You want to learn three things about your students from this assignment: (1) how confidently and successfully they can research materials in the library; (2) how well they can abstract ideas, restate research, and document sources; and (3) how well they collaborate on a research assignment.

Have groups of students choose five of the topics listed here and search the library and any other resources they know to discover the topic's significance. Tell them to use whatever library resources might help give them a full picture, such as the library catalog, periodical indexes, dictionaries, videotapes, databases, and so on.

Then have them use a word-processing program to write two or three paragraphs explaining the significance of the topic and to append a carefully detailed list of sources used for each identification and evaluation. Each group should work together to hand in one set of materials, carefully written and edited, as each member of the group shares the grade earned by the group.

Research Topics

Wounded Knee	neoteny	Frederik Pohl
Margaret Sanger	Gabriel García Márquez	Molly Bloom
Teilhard de Chardin	Itzhak Perlman	quarks
Khmer Rouge	Wilma Mankiller	Rita Dove
Henry Moore	Sojourner Truth	Barry Commoner
Ntozake Shange	David Levine	Hannah Gray
Lewis Thomas	Grace Paley	August Wilson
blogosphere	serotonin	Nelson Mandela
Rosalind Franklin	Raymond Loewy	Saul Steinberg
Daniel Boorstin	Thurgood Marshall	Amnesty International
antioxidant	Chinua Achebe	Cubism

Hunt No. 2   This is a more sequential scavenger hunt designed to familiarize students with a wide variety of basic sources common to most libraries. Generate a list of questions and answers for each resource that you want students to use. At Dodge City Community College, instructors use the *Oxford English Dictionary*, Shakespeare plays, and *Bartlett's Familiar Quotations*; electronic indexes such as *InfoTrac*, *FirstSearch*, and *NewsBank*; print indexes such as the *New York Times Index*, *Education Index*, and *Humanities Index*; specialized dictionaries and encyclopedias; statistical and biographical sources such as *Kansas Legislative Handbook* and *Current Biography*; SIRS; and the Web catalog. They generate a bank of twelve or fifteen questions from each of thirty sources. (Colleagues who use the hunt help update the bank each year.) From the bank, they create a set of thirty questions, using one question from each source.

Each pair of students in the class is given a different set of questions. They must record the answer, the source in which they found it, and the page and volume number if there is one. Sometimes a student will find an answer in an unanticipated source, and statistics can vary slightly from source to source. Students aren't allowed to use the Internet, as the objective is to acquaint them with a variety of sources. The classes have two weeks to complete the hunt. The hunt is hard, so it is worth plenty of points. Each student's hunt is graded separately, and all are told that they are under no obligation to share answers with their partner if that person is not doing his or her share.

If you assign this project, be sure to warn the librarians; give them a copy of the scavenger hunt with answers and ask them to help students on an emergency basis only. Although classes are instructed in library tours or lectures, a hands-on activity with the support and safety of a partner prepares students to start the research project with less anxiety and a working knowledge of library sources.

Hunt No. 3   Explain to students that they will work in pairs to learn more about their library. Remind them that the library is a network; in fact, it is a collection of networks within networks. Each pair will move through the library together and discover the answers to the questions that follow. Only as a last resort should students approach the librarian. Remind students to remain quiet as they search. Have each pair return the paper to you before class is over. If they have not finished, have them work on this assignment again during your next class meeting.

1. Where is the unabridged *Webster's Third International Dictionary* located? What is the copyright date?

2. What information can you obtain from the ERIC database? Write down one of the entries from the index to this resource.

3. What information does the periodical guide scanning index contain? How many years' worth of articles are indexed? How are they arranged?

4. Look up the subject "Dog Psychology" in the *NewsBank* index. Print out the sources given for this subject.

5. How are the current magazines arranged on the shelves?

6. Who is on the cover of the most recent issues of *Rolling Stone* and *Newsweek?*

7. Choose the print or online *Readers' Guide to Periodical Literature* and write down the title and author of a magazine article listed under "Education." Do not forget the date of publication.

8. Locate the shelves with bound periodicals. Find the shelf that has copies of *Parents* magazine. Look at the cover of the May 2007 issue and write down the title of at least one article listed on the cover. If your library does not have bound copies, use microfiche or see if *Parents* is available through a database.

9. Move into the bookshelves and locate these two books:
RC 552.567 M37 1988
RC 565.F563 1988
Write down the titles, authors, and places of publication.

10. What are the dates of the *New York Times* that are kept in the library, in print and/or electronic form? List only the earliest date and the most recent date.

Note: To avoid a stampede at one location, vary the sequence of questions. The librarians also appreciate this avoidance of large research mobs.

Turning a Topic into a Question (p. 593)

Using one of the topics generated from brainstorming (see "Choosing Your Territory," p. 592) or one of the topics from the students' scavenger hunt in the library (see p. 313 of this manual), conduct a systematic discussion of that research topic to model questions that students might use for research. For example, a class might ask questions about a broad topic like global warming: "What are the least dire predictions about global warming?" "What are the most dire predictions?" "Which people or groups downplay the threat?" "Which people or groups take the threat seriously?" "What are the purported causes of global warming?" "What processes are involved in the phenomenon?" "What are the effects of global warming?" "What, if anything, can be done to reduce the threat?" Any one of these questions might inform research. Students could generate additional questions from those materials. Spend enough class time on stating the question so that writers can see that by revising or shifting directions of the research questions, they might come to discover a strong writing purpose.

Some of the questions from the Research Checklist on "Questioning Your Question" (p. 595) could be used for collaborative workshops. Have students talk in groups about what they have written as their research questions. Often group members will be able to ask the crucial question that will help the writer clarify his or her purpose. Of course, you should return the students' statements of their research questions during the next class period with your response and your questions about them.

Surveying Your Resources (p. 596)

We advise you to monitor this search — for example, through a preliminary bibliography or conferences. Many students will not have had experience selecting materials. Such students might arbitrarily pull books off the shelves and articles from a periodical database. You want them to show that they are uncovering a range of materials and that they are evaluating these materials.

Some students will badger you with the question "How many sources will I need?" They will grimace when you tell them that they need as many sources as the research question demands. That behavior probably means they lack confidence in their research skills and critical thinking. To provide them with the structure they might need to get back to work, set a minimum number of entries for a preliminary bibliography and tell them that by meeting this standard they will show that they're finding their way around the library. Tell them that the list of, say, twenty sources must include books and magazine or journal articles; tell them that at least one-third of the sources must be from the past two years. Then look over the bibliographies to see whether the students seem to be selecting materials carefully. When the list stops at the letter F for the author, you might wonder if the student has just copied the first two dozen titles from the library catalog.

Avoid, however, setting up arbitrary numbers and kinds of sources that might not be appropriate for some research topics. For example, a student who is researching AIDS treatment will not benefit from having to cite one book, one encyclopedia article, one chapter from a book, one newspaper article, one magazine article, and one interview. He or she might find the most valuable information only in current periodicals. Arbitrary and unrealistic requirements such as this will make students spend more time searching for types of information than evaluating and comprehending available sources that are relevant to their objective. It will ultimately cause them to waste valuable time.

Using Keywords and Links (p. 597)

A hands-on experience is essential to show students how to use keywords and links. Arrange for your librarians or writing center director to demonstrate for students these techniques in one of the computer labs on campus. Students should come to the lab armed with their research questions and a list of keywords. Direct them to bring their research journals so that they can record which keywords and search engines produce the most useful results.

Students will need some hands-on time to experiment after the demonstration. Move among them to provide direction and answer questions.

Your librarian will be able to advise your students on reliable databases. Caution students to ascertain the reliability of each source. For more on evaluating sources, refer them to "Evaluating Sources" in Chapter 31 (p. 650).

MANAGING YOUR PROJECT (p. 598)

Even for students who have learned time-management skills, a research paper is a big project. Spending some class time to discuss project management up front will save time in the end.

Creating a Schedule (p. 599)

Students need some direction. Develop a schedule for them to follow. Although many students might vaguely know what to do, they need deadlines to keep their focus on the large task. Setting a series of deadlines forces even the most procrastinating students to structure their time so that something besides panic and lack of confidence results from the research assignment. In particular, students need to commit early to a research question so that they have enough time for the research and for shifting their topic, direction, or perspective if the first question doesn't work out.

We strongly recommend that you use a schedule similar to the one on page 318, which requires an early statement about the subject and an early formal statement of tentative thesis. You might also want to require early demonstrations of research and note taking and talk with writers about their working outlines and the possible shape of their essays.

After the research questions have been selected, give students a research checklist on which they can write in the dates and quantity requirements for each step of the process. This checklist should be turned in with the rough draft as a record of the students' progress and will remind you of the areas of the students' writing that you should double-check. Tell students that they must complete the stages sequentially and that you will initial each deadline when the work for that date is submitted. Do not collect the materials and take them home; use the class time to check their deadlines and the format. Also establish the minimum number of sources to be used to ensure that you are providing students with a broad base of research experience. Schedule each major deadline on a Monday, giving students the weekend to complete the assignment. If students need an extension, you can give them a later deadline and write it on the checklist. This method will show students that they are investigating with an organized system.

Plan on responding to at least one draft, in addition to the completed paper, and set your deadline according to how "rough" a draft you are willing to read. Ask that each draft be typed and completed by the established deadline. And ask for at least a "finished" draft — the result of shaping and multiple drafting. Although 97 percent of the time this draft will not be finished, your job as instructor, editor, and coach is to show writers how to improve what is basically a competent paper until it is the best paper they can produce. By organizing a schedule that gives you time to look at a rough draft, you encourage students to draft and redraft.

Of course, you can always choose to be flexible with a schedule. Plan for the unexpected to push the deadlines further into the semester. Stagger the deadlines if you are teaching more than one course with a research assignment. If you learn through conferences with students that a logjam in the interlibrary loan department has slowed down research, extend the deadline for the preliminary outline and bibliography. If you discover via an impromptu chat with a student that he or she has hit upon a better proposal and is sensibly dumping two-thirds of the essay, make an individual arrangement. Because you have been monitoring the research and the writing, you'll know which students are having bona fide problems related to the research process and which have not yet begun to work. Still, don't be surprised if, even after clear messages about keeping a schedule and pacing the work, a distraught and perhaps angry student shows up two days before the deadline to rant at you for expecting too much and forgetting that "I'm taking other classes, too." Research projects call for very responsible behavior, and it often falls to writing instructors to remind students that they must practice that behavior if it's to become habitual.

RESEARCH SCHEDULE AND CHECKLIST

Date Due   *Stage of Process*   *Instructor's*
                                                                               Initials

_____   Topic stated as a research question: _____   _____

             _____

_____   Thesis statement: _____   _____

             _____

_____   Source or bibliography cards (#   )   _____

             Periodicals: # _____   Books: # _____

             Interviews: # _____   Internet: # _____

             Other: # _____

_____   Notes (#   )   _____

             Paraphrase: # _____   Summary: # _____

             Direct Quote: # _____

_____   Preliminary outline   _____

_____   Formal three-level sentence outline and introductory   _____

             paragraph

_____   First completed draft with works cited   _____

_____   Revised finished paper, prewriting materials, and   _____

             peer reviews

Here's an Idea . . .

The following are suggestions for managing team research projects.

- Decide whether teams will be self-selected or arranged by you. (You might want to ask colleagues about their experiences: Which did they choose, and why?) Let students know the purpose behind your choice.
- Explain your expectations and grading policy at the beginning.
- Allow at least eight weeks for the project. Ironically, a team effort often requires more time than an individual effort. In addition to the planning, information-gathering, and writing stages, you will also need to build in time for project coordination, role assignments, and peer review.
- Assign team-building activities in the beginning weeks.
- Meet briefly with teams on a regular basis to check progress.
- Today's students have busy lives. In addition to attending school, many of them work and have families to care for. Consider building team time into an occasional class.
- Remind yourself and your students that research in a professional setting is often a collaborative effort.

Setting up a schedule and monitoring the steps in the process also seriously reduce the chances that students will submit plagiarized materials. The schedule that includes several reports on work-in-process and several deadlines for reporting part of the research might catch that rare student who plans to buy a research paper from one of the companies that advertise on every free inch of bulletin board. Such a student would have to break apart the paper, at least rearrange parts, at most "fake" earlier drafts, and certainly get involved with the paper if he or she were to try to complete your assignments. Most students will conclude that it is just as easy to go with the program. More frequent are the students who are having legitimate problems assimilating and restating the materials they've researched. Those students and you have more opportunity to identify their problems and correct them when they must meet several deadlines.

Recording Information (p. 600)

Should you look at students' research notes early in the process? That question always seems to get a split vote. Instructors who say yes point out that by checking notes they can monitor not only the search but also the early use of materials and help

Here's an Idea . . .

Have your students write their research question or preliminary thesis on a note card and place it in front of them as they take notes. As they research, they can refer to the card to be sure their note taking is focused and includes only evidence relevant to their thesis. You might want to have them generate a brief list of subtopics and add it to the card. These can serve as subject headings in the upper left corner of their note cards.

Here's an Idea . . .

Help students develop their critical thinking skills by having them watch an informative television program, summarize its contents, and evaluate its credibility. They will enjoy sharing what they have learned with their classmates. A caveat: Some students will not have time to watch television because of work, family, and school pressures, so be sure to provide an alternative assignment for these students and don't penalize them if they can't do a television-based assignment. One alternative might be for them to do the assignment by listening to a talk-radio program, possibly as they are driving to work or taking care of children.

---

to guide students toward a satisfactory paper. At this point, they can also give much-needed help to students who are not reading critically enough. Instructors who say no argue that asking students to hand in their notes is perceived by students as another hurdle rather than a necessary part of the process. If you choose not to check all notes, ask students to show you the first half of their notes and insist that they include each type of note taking in this first group. If you do look at the early notes, you can alert students to any dangers and also comment on their form and content.

Checking notes is a time-consuming task for you, but we think it pays off for both students and instructors. Check the notes for scope, content, and format. Remind students of the danger of taking three-fourths of their notes from a single source. The challenge of a research paper is to skillfully weave a variety of sources into a smooth, coherent paper that supports and answers a research question.

Indicate to students that you will expect them to turn in all of their notes and other prewriting materials when they hand in the finished paper. Suggest that they put their notes on a CD if they have access to a computer.

Many students use personal computers and laptops in their research assignments to streamline certain steps of the process. Students who have access to a computer often find themselves ahead of most deadlines. Evaluating notes and subsequent material can take half as long when students work with a computer file. Consider allowing students to compile their notes on a computer and print them out to hand in instead of copying them to cards. Some students are more comfortable with note cards they can shuffle into various orders. Because most printers can be set to print envelopes or note cards, suggest that these students adjust the margins of their files to fit their note cards and print their notes. If they cannot print note cards, suggest that they cut their printed notes apart so that they can shuffle them.

Starting a Research Archive (p. 601)

If your students have chosen a research question from their major field of study, point out that their archive will be a welcome resource for future investigative assignments in their classes. They can continue to build it as they progress through their coursework.

Emphasize the importance of making marginal notes and highlighting archive material. If students have a preliminary outline or list of subtopics, have them highlight each one with a different color marker. Then they can key information in their archival papers with corresponding colors on the edge of papers or on paragraphs or subhead-

---

Here's an Idea...

To manage material in their research archives, students might label a file folder for each subtopic in their preliminary outline. They can place copies of articles, notes, and other evidence they will use to support that subtopic in the folder. They should stack the folders in the order in which they will address each subtopic in their paper. When they draft, they can draw on relevant evidence from each folder as they move from subtopic to subtopic.

---

ings in the text of copies. These colors can also cue file folder tabs, bibliography cards, and annotations.

Remind students that they can e-mail Web addresses and material from databases to their own e-mail boxes for future access. For more information on using the Internet, see Chapter 5 of this manual.

Working with Sources (Ch. 29, p. 603)

Chapter 29 lays the groundwork for gathering and incorporating sources of information. When students create a working bibliography, they record the location of source information in a format recognized and expected by research communities. Armed with this skill, they can move to other documentation styles with minor adjustments. Students must also record information from their sources to support their claims. The authors lead students through this process, suggesting a variety of ways they can record their notes and emphasizing the skills of judiciously quoting, paraphrasing, and summarizing. If you assigned Chapter 12, "Supporting a Position with Sources," your students may have already practiced some of these skills and will now be able to refine them further. Chapter 29 also gives students advice on how to create an annotated bibliography, a skill they will use repeatedly throughout their college coursework.

Starting a Working Bibliography (p. 603)

Organize students into groups of three or four and ask them to take a topic of their choice and generate a five- or seven-item annotated bibliography (one item for each group member). This assignment has three objectives that each group must meet:

1. to critically evaluate a research source
2. to briefly but significantly describe the work
3. to use the conventions of bibliographical citation

Ask the groups to select a range of books and articles that would be essential reading for any student who decided to research that topic for a class assignment. Give the groups three days to work and time at the end of each class period to confer and plan. Have each group hand in one typed bibliography. Each entry should document the source following the conventions for citing works and be followed by a one- or two-paragraph abstract explaining what makes the material useful for research. The annotation should include an evaluation of the material, specify the audience for the writing, and gauge the readability of the source. Read your class the following two annotations for the topic "Sexism in the English Language" as examples:

Farb, Peter. *Word Play: What Happens When People Talk.* **New York: Knopf, 1977.**

Written in a humorous and lively style for a large and general audience, this book includes several discussions of sex differences in language. Farb writes about "the unequal treatment [that] many languages give to the two sexes." For evidence, he cites the use of male generic words, the assumption that the average person is always masculine (like "man on the street" and the hypothetical man in the riddle about a woman surgeon), and the connotations of words (males roar, bellow, and growl, whereas females squeal, shriek, and purr). He discusses etymology that fossilizes sexist assumptions. The book covers a wide range of topics and includes many interesting examples for each major idea. It would be a good introduction to the topic of sexist language because the writer shows how sexism is one feature of the language. Chapters 3 and 4 are particularly helpful.

Lawrence, Barbara. "Dirty Words Can Harm You." *Redbook* **May 1974: 33.**

This essay was originally written as an editorial for the *New York Times* and then revised for readers of *Redbook* magazine. It is easy to read but full of weighty issues. The essay gives a good example of how to start researching and questioning "sexist language." Lawrence points out the systematic denigration of women through the use of many obscenities. Various tabooed sexual verbs (which she carefully does not say but which carefully suggest meaning) involve origins and imagery with what she labels "undeniably painful, if not sadistic, implications, the object of which is almost always female." She points out that when they don't directly denigrate women, tabooed male descriptions might serve to "divorce a male organ or function from any significant interaction with the female" (for example, testes suggesting "witnesses to the sexual and procreative strengths of the male organ"). Parallel female descriptive terms are usually contemptuous of women (for instance, "piece"). Lawrence points out that many people who are shocked at racial or ethnic obscenities do not question obscenities that denigrate women. She questions them.

Ask students to print out multiple copies of the bibliographies. Review them in class for specificity of annotation, clarity of the evaluation, and correct usage of the conventions of documentation. Grade each bibliography as a class, using those criteria. Each group member shares the group's grade.

Because the activity is shared by class members, it's more easily completed and it's perceived as less drudgery than if each student had to develop his or her own bibliography. No student feels that a judgment is being made on his or her ability to research and to read, but each student is able to see competent, more than competent, and less than competent responses to the assignment. The discussion of note taking is grounded in a real activity, and students should be able to use the skills they practiced in their individual projects. The side effects of the assignment — students talking with one another about how to use the library, sharing information discovered serendipitously, talking about their own research projects, negotiating to share the research, writing, and editing tasks — cannot be underestimated for their influence on student learning.

Drawing the Details from Your Sources (p. 604)

The Source Navigators in this section will provide your students with a clear, easily accessible method of extracting the necessary information from a variety of sources to write their bibliography entries. Take class time to show them this resource and have them practice with the sources they have located. Move among your students as they work, helping them find the Navigator that matches their source and checking that they record all the information accurately. You may have to guide them to Chapter 34, "Documenting Sources," to help them find a source not covered by the Navigators. Advise your students to follow the examples by including a note at the bottom of the entry to remind them of the contents. The extra care that students take as they extract and record the details described in the Navigators will pay off later. An accurate bibliography entry will make it possible for them to locate the source again, and in addition, it can be cut and pasted into their Works Cited list when they complete their draft.

Capturing Information by Quoting, Paraphrasing, and Summarizing in Your Notes (p. 615)

Whether or not you decide to ask for students' notes, be sure to design a class exercise for note taking. Have students practice these skills using the activity on page 620. Time spent on this will pay off later both for your students and for you.

Developing an Annotated Bibliography (p. 621)

Have students practice annotations by first summarizing, then summarizing with evaluation, and finally summarizing with interpretation. Before they summarize with evaluation, have them review the criteria for evidence found in Chapter 3, "Critical Thinking Processes" (p. 39).

Finding Sources in the Library, on the Internet, and in the Field (Ch. 30, p. 624)

Knowing where to find information may be the most important skill we can teach our students. In Chapter 30, the authors guide students in finding information in the library, on the Internet, and in the field. Encourage your students to become seekers. Let them know that the skills they learn here will serve them well beyond this research project, and even beyond their college careers. If they know how to access information, they will be more likely to become lifelong learners.

Chapter 30, "Finding Sources in the Library, on the Internet, and in the Field," contains this activity:

- For E-Writers (p. 642). See page 73 of this manual for advice about how to use this feature.

In addition to Chapter 30, the Quick Research Guide provides easily accessible information on finding sources. Refer students to the charts "Understanding Print Sources and Their Applications" (p. A-10) and "Understanding Electronic Sources and Their Applications" (p. A-11).

SEARCHING THE ONLINE LIBRARY CATALOG (p. 624)

Your students, guided by this section, will navigate the library easily. As an instructor, you simply need to encourage students who have not yet found their way to the library to go there and discover it. To do so, you might arrange a field trip with the reference staff. Most reference librarians will bend over backward to help students learn to use the library for research. Send over a possible topic for research that you have culled from class discussion and ask the reference librarian to individualize the tour to show how students might research that topic.

While much of their research will be conducted using the library catalog, students should not rely on it exclusively. Encourage them to use the other library resources, such as periodical indexes and databases. Too many students become frustrated when they can't find books on the topic they have chosen; they need to understand that books are only one source.

Encourage students to locate the books they have identified in the stacks and simply browse the shelves nearby. They will invariably discover other promising resources there that their catalog search has not uncovered.

Here's an Idea . . .

Ask each student to make a copy of one entry from the library catalog for a book on his or her research topic. Then have him or her explain in a paragraph each item in the entry. Students' explanations should include each of the following: call number, author, title, publication information, number of pages, illustrations, size of book, the International Standard Book Number, special features, subject headings, Library of Congress number, Library of Congress catalog number, and Dewey Decimal System number.

Here's Another Idea . . .

To provide practice in exploring periodical indexes and databases, ask each student to see how many relevant references he or she can find on one of the following topics:

- teaching techniques for adult education
- recent treatment of Alzheimer's disease
- fourteenth-century misunderstandings of the Black Death
- educational requirements for becoming an FBI agent
- recent Supreme Court rulings on the First Amendment
- global weather changes over the past decade
- the winner of the 2006 Nobel Prize for Literature
- how to find an agent for publishing music
- theories of the John F. Kennedy assassination
- the debate over the effect of violent lyrics in rap music

Ask students to keep a record of each combination of descriptors they try in the search and to note which one provided the most useful information.

Searching Databases: Periodical Indexes and Bibliographies (p. 631)

The second most used tools for locating information in the library are periodical indexes and databases. One of the main search techniques students need to learn for efficient use of these tools is finding useful descriptors or keywords — the word or words that will identify and limit the sources for their investigation. Explain to them that they might need to try different combinations of their keywords to find information on specific topics. Direct their attention to "Conducting Advanced Electronic Searches" (p. 639) for information on using keywords.

Another assignment that familiarizes students with database research is to send teams of students (two or three per team because of elbow room at terminals) to search assigned topics in computer databases. In a research writing journal, assign entries in which the writers describe the process used to access a database, receive hard copy, and use the information to obtain useful materials.

USING OTHER LIBRARY RESOURCES (p. 634)

You might need to nudge students to use the resources listed here, but once they discover the wealth of information these sources can provide, they will be glad they explored them.

Consulting Reference Materials (p. 634)

Most students are familiar with general encyclopedias from high school, but few are aware of the breadth of material available in the college library reference section. Make sure that students understand that general encyclopedias are useful as an early introductory source to provide an overview of a topic but that they are probably too general to be cited in their final paper. Stress instead the more in-depth specialized sources on which they should concentrate their research energies.

Provide a quick introduction to the reference section that will help students to begin to understand what is available and how to use it wisely. Assign groups of two or three students to look up the same topic in a generalized encyclopedia (such as *Encyclopedia Americana* or *Compton's*) and in a specialized encyclopedia (such as *The New Grove Dictionary of Music and Musicians* for Brahms or baroque music or *Encyclopedia of the American Constitution* for the Bill of Rights) and to compare and contrast the entries in the two sources. Then have them look up the same topic or a related topic in a specialized handbook, in a statistical source, an atlas, and a biographical source to discover other information that is available about this topic. For example, they might look up Thomas Jefferson in *Encyclopedia Americana, The Dictionary of American History, Encyclopedia of the American Constitution, Biography Index*, and a handbook of American architecture; then they could look up the population of Virginia in the seventeenth century in *Statistical Abstract of the United States*, the University of Virginia in a sourcebook on American colleges and universities, and Charlottesville in an atlas of the United States. Have them report to the class or write a brief collaborative report on their findings.

You can also organize a research assignment that will take students into the dictionary section of the reference room. Assign each student a word that can be researched in the *Oxford English Dictionary*. The students will, of course, find more data than they want. Their task is to select the most important data: the record of important changes in the word's shape and meaning. Tell the writers to be specific in citing the history of the word and to conclude the report with some speculation about why the word changed and what it might tell us about the people who changed its meaning. When students discover, for example, that the early English word *bonefire* referred to the fire on which invaders threw their vanquished foes, and that its meaning has shifted to apply to the punishment for witches and heretics and then to throwing a leaf-stuffed effigy of the opponent's coach into the football homecoming bonfire, they might be surprised at the generalizations they make about "civilization."

Be sure to request a photocopy of the entry to accompany the short essay, and advise any student whose analysis is too detail-laden, misguided, or general. Here are some suggestions for words to assign: *moral, virtue, diaper, boycott, cardigan, henchman, coroner, silly, foolish, nice, mistress, pollution, buxom, churl, doom, humor, disparage, shimmy, zealot, genteel, magazine, fret, frank, siege, guy, talent, strange, cunning, harlot, varlet, wife, family, enthusiasm, phony, lynch.*

Locating Special Materials (p. 636)

To familiarize students with microform resources, Charles Bazerman in *The Informed Writer*, 5th ed. (Boston: Houghton, 1994), sets up a project in which students research the week of their birth. Such a project takes writers to the microfilm and microfiche collections of national and local newspapers.

Hands-on inquiry with government documents might not only generate pertinent materials for analysis but also train citizens to evaluate government process and policy. Many libraries have joined the computer-based information network called American Memory. Some students enjoy using this tool as part of political science classes, and many have used it successfully in American literature classes.

Students who need to use pamphlets and annual reports should consider e-mailing or faxing their request. With an e-mail or a fax, requests for brochures, handouts, and annual reports can reach the appropriate offices in time for receipt of materials. We've had conscientious students discover a need for certain material during their drafting, send off a request for such material, and then not receive it until long after the final draft had been evaluated. E-mail and fax machines speed up communication in both ways. Increasingly, many organizations are making full texts of reports and other publications available on their Web sites.

Consider having students fill out a mock interlibrary loan form in one of the library orientation or hunt activities (pp. 313–15 of this manual). If they are familiar with the form, students will be more likely to use this resource.

USING THE INTERNET FOR RESEARCH (p. 637)

Your students will face two challenges when searching Internet sources: limiting the information to a manageable amount and discerning credible sources. To help students learn these skills, the authors provide in this chapter a range of strategies for managing a search, while in Chapter 31, "Evaluating Sources," they give specific guidelines for determining the credibility of those sources.

To give students more practice with directed searches on the Web, consider assigning a Web Search activity from A Writer's Reader (pp. 441, 475, 502, 530, and 561). These assignments ask students to locate specific sources on the Web and then to evaluate those sources using a series of questions designed to prompt critical thinking. For more about how to use these activities, see page 244 of this manual.

For more about using technology in your classroom, see Chapter 5 of this manual.

Finding Recommended Internet Resources (p. 638)

Many students will be tempted to begin every Web search by Googling their research topic. Stress to them how much time they can save by beginning their search by using recommended Internet resources. If you teach in a computer-equipped classroom, spend a few minutes of one class showing students your library's online research guides and some sites mentioned in this section and listed in the Quick Research Guide. Using a sample research topic, demonstrate the process of beginning a search at some of these recommended Internet resources.

Selecting Search Engines (p. 639)

Have students work in groups to compare and contrast three or four search engines. (See the "For E-Writers" box on page 642 for a list of search engines.) Have them read the "About" or "Search Tips" page for each search engine, comparing and contrasting the ways terms are entered, the order in which search results are presented, and the kinds and amounts of information yielded.

Conducting Advanced Electronic Searches (p. 639)

Have students write their research question at the top of a piece of paper and use it to brainstorm keywords. They can then use their lists to refine their question or thesis and search with various words and combinations in both electronic and print indexes, databases, and Web sites.

Your librarians can help you and your students with electronic searches. They can tell you which wildcard symbols or Boolean search defaults are used by the databases, search sites, and catalogs in your library. As the authors explain in the text, the results of your search can vary, depending on the Boolean term used. Library catalogs typically use *and* as a default, while most Web search sites use *or*, first showing results that contain all terms and then those that contain some of the terms. If a librarian is unavailable, consult online help to discover how the default is set on the database, search site, or catalog you are using. On most Web sites, you can read online help or access advanced searches by clicking on a button or label located near the search form.

Finding Specialized Online Materials (p. 643)

Encourage your students to visit some of the sites the authors list. Students who are having difficulty finding sources on a current issue may find expert opinion in blogs, newsgroups, or chat rooms before it is published in print format. Caution them to evaluate the sources critically, using the research checklist for evaluating sources in Chapter 31 (p. 651) and in the Quick Research Guide.

FINDING SOURCES IN THE FIELD (p. 644)

Field resources are often overlooked by both students and instructors as valid sources of information. Students in composition courses will benefit from becoming familiar with the techniques of field research for use in other courses and on the job, as well as to supplement and enhance library research investigations. Through observation, interviews, surveys, correspondence, and attending lectures, writers uncover information that deepens their knowledge and enhances their research writing. For example, a student who was researching the impact of pollution on the Gulf of Mexico recorded the trash he observed while out fishing, conducted an in-depth interview with a man who had been a commercial fisherman for thirty years, and surveyed ten other fishermen on pollution they had observed in the Gulf of Mexico. He then imagined what the gulf would be like if water pollution continues to increase and used an imagined futuristic scenario as the introduction to his research paper. Encourage your students to use field research sources to fill in gaps, to strengthen their papers, and give them life.

Field research demands a great deal more than library research, both from your students and from you as their guide. The authors define this type of research as "the sensitive, intelligent, and critical selection of meaningful ideas and information." Often this means that, even though your writers might have an "almost vast" idea, they need your help in talking through methods of clarifying the idea, of generating research data to explore the idea, of interpreting the data, and of organizing the material into an incisive essay. So if you plan to incorporate field research, plan to spend additional time working with students.

Interviewing (p. 644)

One complication of field research is that students will be taking notes from oral language rather than from written language, so remind them that they must learn to listen very carefully so that they do not misconstrue what they hear. Direct them to Chapter 6, "Interviewing a Subject," for tips on generating questions and interviewing. Chapter 7 of this manual suggests activities to hone students' interviewing skills.

Observing (p. 645)

A field trip in which the researcher can combine observation and conversation may provide invaluable, up-to-date information. Encourage students to use this field-research tool, but remind them to prepare themselves carefully beforehand so that the trip will be purposeful and they will come away with the information they are seeking. Also remind them that they must, out of courtesy and respect, plan the field trip at a time that is convenient for the group and its leaders or supervisors. They should also ask permission to photograph in some environments — museums, for example, and sensitive environments such as a safehouse. A few excursions that might provide valuable information are those to an elementary classroom for information on the impact of school on children, a rock concert for information on the behavior of fans, a high school prom, the county jail, a homeless shelter, an abuse safehouse, or a museum.

Direct your students' attention to Chapter 5, "Observing a Scene," for tips on observing and recording data. Chapter 7 of this manual suggests activities for sharpening observation skills.

Using Questionnaires (p. 646)

The authors provide very specific and helpful advice about shaping a questionnaire. Ask students to double-check their questionnaires against that advice. Talk with students about any questionnaires or surveys they write in a conference. Ask them what they are trying to discover and focus on how the questions are asked:

- Will they elicit the information the students need or desire?
- Should they be revised in any way?
- What background questions might provide classifications that will illuminate the data or that might suggest a new research direction?

You might also have students discuss these questions with their collaborative group.

Remind students to consider their chosen method of interviewing as they format the questionnaires. Will they be conducting their interviews by telephone, in person, or by e-mail? These choices should affect the design and content of their questions.

Corresponding (p. 648)

Many students neglect this source of research when, in fact, it often produces valuable brochures, pamphlets, and press releases. Word processing makes a mass mailing fairly easy. Encourage students who will be writing letters or sending out questionnaires to begin early. Offer to read drafts of letters and to evaluate them as you would questionnaires or surveys. Unfortunately, many students are not practiced letter writers and need to learn some basic skills. Refer them to Chapter 14, "Writing in the Workplace," for advice from the authors about letter writing.

Attending Public and Online Events (p. 649)

On the classroom bulletin board, post college and community lecture series, conferences, and meetings so that students will be aware of the variety of topics covered in such forums. Check campus and local newspapers weekly to update this list. Ask students to bring in other announcements from their workplaces, religious and civic organizations, political parties, and recreational groups. A student might be able to share a valuable source with a classmate, contributing to the atmosphere of a community of writers.

Television and radio programs, films, and recordings provide a wealth of information, not just entertainment. Some television channels, such as CNN, CNBC, and the Discovery Channel, are devoted completely to in-depth news, including business, cultural, and environmental and scientific coverage, and C-Span provides invaluable coverage of government and public figures. A student can even write or fax a request to the network or to an address given at the end of the program and receive a transcript or a videotape of a relevant program — for a small fee, of course. Some media outlets make transcripts available through their Web sites.

Encourage students not to overlook these sources, but warn them to evaluate and select the information from these sources critically — as they do in all research investigations. For example, comments from biologist E. O. Wilson on environmental issues would have more credibility than those from actor Martin Sheen. Warn students specifically about television and radio talk shows: The guests and callers are seldom credentialed experts in the field in which they are commenting.

Don't overlook the holdings of your own school. Most college libraries maintain an excellent stock of commercial and academic films, videos, and recordings. Encourage students to check the catalog for possible sources in the media library.

Evaluating Sources (Ch. 31, p. 650)

While the criteria that the authors lay out for evaluating sources apply equally to library, field, and Internet sources, the increasing popularity of the Web has created a sense of urgency about these skills: Now more than ever, students need to learn basic strategies for critical evaluation. Even if you do not assign a research paper in your course, refer students to Chapter 31 and the Quick Research Guide whenever their course work requires them to read and respond critically to new material.

EVALUATING LIBRARY AND INTERNET SOURCES (p. 650)

Students tend to accept whatever they see in print or on the Internet as authoritative, and they will need your guidance to begin to think critically about these sources. Ask them to review the criteria for selecting and evaluating evidence provided in Chapter 3, "Critical Thinking Processes" (pp. 39–40), as well as the Research Checklist "Evaluating Sources" (p. 651) in this chapter. Also refer them to the Quick Research Guide. Work with students on applying these questions to the sources in their bibliography. Ask them to give you one note card on which they have analyzed the magazine or journal in which they found a source. Some first-year writers might believe that *Reader's Digest* is a good source for condensed materials, but a simple analysis of the magazine might dispel that idea.

Warn students to evaluate carefully all of the information they use in their papers, but especially what they find on the Web. The Web offers exciting possibilities for access to previously unavailable material, such as document archives and conversations among communities of specialists, but the ephemeral nature of the Web can pose problems for serious researchers. Students might find that not only is checking the credibility of evidence or the credentials of an author difficult on the Web, but re-creating a particular Web search and locating other researchers' Web sources are difficult as well. Encourage students to use sources other than the Internet to check the information they obtain from it. If students can't track down any reliable background information about the source, they probably shouldn't use the evidence. Carol Luers Eyman uses these tips to help her students evaluate Web sites:

- Look at URL endings. Knowing that <.gov> indicates a government site, <.edu> an education site, <.org> an organization site, and <.com> a commercial or business site can alert you to possible purposes of the site.

- Look for URLs that contain tildes (~). They may be student Web sites operating off a university's server.

- Look at domain names. Sites with their own names (for example, <http://fsmith.com>) sometimes may be more credible than sites that are an extension of the ISP's domain name (for example, <http://aolk.com/users/fsmith>).

For practice evaluating Web sources in particular, assign students a Web Search activity from *A Writer's Reader* (pp. 441, 475, 502, 530, and 561).

To help students practice critically evaluating sources, copy a few paragraphs from a book, a journal article, an article found on the Web, and sections from two or three periodicals on the same topic. Include one or two from popular magazines designed to entertain and one from a questionable Web source. Have students work in groups to evaluate the sources, using the checklist "Evaluating Sources" (p. 652). Keep the periodicals on hand so that students can examine them to get an idea of their purpose and intended audience. Remind students that Chapter 20, "Strategies for Revising and Editing," contains more information about purpose and audience. Have students present their findings to the class and discuss the criteria they used for their decision.

EVALUATING FIELD SOURCES (p. 657)

Field sources can add the appeal of a human voice to your students' papers, but they must evaluate them carefully. Students inexperienced in thinking critically sometimes want to quote a favorite teacher or someone they admire and find it difficult to step back and consider the source objectively. Emphasize that they must consider all factors that may affect credibility; they are ethically bound to present only evidence they have evaluated carefully. Have students use the checklist on page 651 to determine the reliability of each source they use.

RECONSIDERING YOUR PURPOSE AND YOUR THESIS (p. 662)

The Quick Research Guide provides easily accessible help to reinforce students' efforts during each step of their research project. Have them use the purpose checklist on page 662 as they reconsider their purpose.

Integrating Sources (Ch. 32, p. 663)

This chapter speaks to one of the most difficult parts of the research process for student writers: synthesizing their own ideas with the ideas of others. Wading into the pool of information they have collected and evaluated, they may flounder as they try to determine which ideas are their own and which they have absorbed from their research. It is no easy task for students to sort through all that information and find their own path, and they will need your help in thinking through the process. In conferences, ask them to articulate their confusion. Encourage them to be specific as they identify problems they anticipate. While you listen, have them retrace their thinking as they researched. Thinking out loud will often help students clear away some of the confusion and give them the confidence they need to advance.

USING SOURCES ETHICALLY (p. 663)

Most plagiarism results from students not having a clear enough understanding of how to restate through summarizing or paraphrasing. Some students have trouble distinguishing the ideas they encounter in authoritative writing from their own ideas: that is, once they understand an author's ideas, they no longer see the difference between their new understanding and the original author's idea. When they lift whole chunks of text from the original source, they simply do not see where their source's ideas end and their own ideas begin. Often these students' egocentric thinking is interfering with their critical perceptions. They are not consciously plagiarizing with ill intentions. Students' essays will be less likely to have large chunks of unassimilated, and undocumented,

Here's an Idea . . .

Organize the class into small groups and ask them to choose one of the following essays in the textbook: "Last Rites for Indian Dead" by Suzan Shown Harjo (p. 140), "Kids in the Mall: Growing Up Controlled" by William Severini Kowinski (p. 122), "Why Prisons Don't Work" by Wilbert Rideau (p. 168), or "How Computers Change the Way We Think" by Sherry Turkle (p. 552). Although students might have read the essay before, ask them now to approach it as a potential source for a research paper. Have each group prepare collaboratively three note cards: one with a quotation, one with summary, and one with a paraphrase. The groups should decide not only how to take the notes but also why the different types of notes are needed, just as researchers must determine which information is too powerful to be paraphrased or summarized and which examples of technical language might need paraphrasing.

After groups have finished their notes, show students on the board or overhead projector samples of the documentation style required for their papers. Then have them use that style to document the source of their different notes. This final step will remind students that documentation is necessary for paraphrasing and summarizing as well as for direct quotes.

Here's an Idea . . .

Ask students to memorize these Rules for Preventing Plagiarism:

1. I cannot *copy* material from any source unless:
   a. I cite the source in the body of my paper AND
   b. I list the source on my reference list AND
   c. I enclose the copied material in quotation marks or indent the entire quotation.
2. I cannot *paraphrase* material except common knowledge from any source unless:
   a. I cite the source in the body of my paper AND
   b. I list the source on my reference list.

materials if you give them adequate help during the note-taking stage. Emphasize how important it is for students to keep records for themselves (on note cards, on a CD, in the margins) of when they're borrowing, how much they're borrowing, and from whom they're borrowing.

CAPTURING, LAUNCHING, AND CITING EVIDENCE FROM SOURCES (p. 666)

First-year writers often rely too heavily on their sources. They are awed by the authority of their evidence and lack the confidence to advance their own ideas. You can help students integrate their sources by having them first shape a draft of their own ideas, then consider how the evidence they find will support or reshape their thinking. Committing their ideas to paper will help them clarify their own opinions and gain the confidence to state their own ideas and use source information as support.

Many students believe that they must fill their essay with quotations and paraphrases to prove they have researched the topic. It is often difficult for them to determine when and why to quote. Help students determine the general knowledge in a field that was new to them when they began their research. Remind them that, to be safe, they should document every idea or fact — whether quoted, paraphrased, or summarized — that they state in the paper but were unaware of when they started the research.

Here's an Idea . . .

Have students analyze the quotations and paraphrases used and acknowledged in either the research paper included in Chapter 34 or several essays in *A Writer's Reader*, such as Evelyn F. Murphy's "Why Not a Dollar?" (p. 488), Anjula Razdan's "What's Love got to Do with It?" (p. 453) or Alex Koppelman's "MySpace or OurSpace?" (p. 546). For each quotation, have students discuss why the writer thought it helpful to bring in the voice he or she chose. For each paraphrase, ask what in the paraphrase demonstrates clearly that the ideas are borrowed.

As students try to integrate their source material with their own words and ideas, it can become difficult for readers to distinguish whose words they are reading — the student's or the source's. Emphasize that students must launch their sources to clearly distinguish for the reader where the student's own voice leaves off and the source material begins. They may also need to cue the reader when they begin developing their own ideas again after presenting source material. Have them ask peer readers to watch for places where the voice is unclear and alert them.

Students will find more advice on incorporating source material in the Quick Research Guide. Encourage them to consult the checklists on pages A-16–A-17 and "Accepted Methods of Adding and Crediting Source Material" on page 4–14.

In addition, the Draft Doctor on page 674 will help your students recognize, diagnose, and remedy problems with integrating and synthesizing sources in their papers. The authors identify a variety of common problems when students deal with sources and suggest strategies for remedying them. Show this tool to your students and encourage them to use it.

Writing Your Research Paper (Ch. 33, p. 677)

With your guidance and the collaboration of classmates, most students feel prepared to begin writing their research paper at this point. They have conquered their terror of academic research, have lessened their anxiety over such a lengthy project, and have implemented a successful search for information using library, field, and Internet sources. They are experiencing the excitement of actively investigating and discovering new types of sources for information. Now they must interpret, evaluate, select, synthesize, and integrate the materials they have gathered. This is the point at which they, in the words of Richard W. Paul, exercise both their creativity and their criticality. Now more than ever they will need your guidance through conferences and specific comments on their drafts.

In all your discussions and conversations about research and writing, continue to emphasize the role of the intellectually curious writer. Stress the importance of students' sticking to a schedule (with reasonable flexibility for the unexpected problem or insight that might require more time to investigate but will result in a better paper) and of giving themselves time and space for necessary backtracking and leaping forward. Remind them, too, that they might have to return to the library or follow up on a field-research interview to fill in information necessary for a coherent and persuasive paper.

Chapter 33 focuses students' attention on the process of drafting and revising their papers. A review of Chapter 3, "Critical Thinking Processes," will also be helpful now to encourage students to use both their creative and critical skills. To foster your students' critical thinking skills and help them to move beyond the recall and comprehension levels of Benjamin S. Bloom's taxonomy to application, analysis, synthesis, and evaluation, see Chapter 3 of this manual.

Chapter 33, "Writing Your Research Paper," contains these activities:

- For E-Writers (pp. 679, 683, and 684). See page 73 of this manual for advice about how to use this feature.
- For Peer Response (p. 682). See page 39 of this manual for advice about how to use this feature.

PLANNING AND DRAFTING (p. 677)

The authors discuss writing the research paper in the same way that they discuss writing any paper, focusing on a flexible, recursive process for writing. Only the discussion of generating ideas looks different because of the different types of sources of information used in research papers.

For research writing, it is particularly helpful for students to think about and state a thesis as a point of focus and a guide. (For more about theses, refer students to Chapter 17, "Strategies for Stating a Thesis and Planning.") Emphasize that a thesis for research grows out of the gathered information; warn them against choosing information from their notes to fit a preconceived thesis. Recommend that they start writing by trying to state a one-sentence answer to the question they used to guide their reading and note taking. Alert students to the tendency of some writers to stick with their original thesis no matter what. Encourage them to view their theses as open to revision if they discover additional supports or qualifications while they're examining their research data and shaping their drafts. Revision is crucial for writers who use the thesis method. Often writers will see that in writing their papers they have in fact developed a different thesis from the one they stated in the introduction. They then must decide whether to change the paper to support the new thesis or to rethink the development of ideas to support the original thesis.

Some writers prefer to use the question-and-answer method for shaping a draft. Then when they reread the essay they aren't surprised by any discrepancy of thesis and proof. Because they haven't set a specific course in the introduction, they don't regard themselves as lost. They simply introduce the reader to the essay they wrote and then conclude it. Writers who use this method must be sure that, once the draft is completed and revised, there is a main point, focus, and unity.

Each writer must decide which method to follow. You can help students monitor the shaping of their drafts by asking "What's happening with your essay now?" each time the class meets. Let writers know that they have not committed themselves to an absolute thesis or an absolute way of developing the thesis. Of course, they must remain committed to an area for research questioning; otherwise, they might vacillate between topics long past the time when it becomes impossible to change topics. While it is important to be flexible about topics, be sure to indicate to students that they need to confer with you before they do anything as drastic as changing their topic two weeks into the assignment.

Here's an Idea . . .

To help students apply critical thinking skills to research writing and to give them a start on drafting, ask each student to pull three note cards on the same subtopic or subject heading, each from a different source, and write a paragraph in which he or she synthesizes the information. Then, working in groups of three or four, have students review one another's attempts at synthesizing by answering the following questions:

1. Does the paragraph have a topic sentence that makes a generalization about the material and unifies the detailed information on the note cards?
2. Is the information organized in a logical, easy-to-follow order?
3. Is the information expressed clearly for someone who is not familiar with the subject?
4. Is the information integrated with transitions and other devices for coherence? (That is, has the writer done more than merely string together the three bits of information?)
5. Has the writer made the passage his or her own by including some personal ideas, observations, or conclusions in addition to the ideas from the research sources?
6. Are the sources for the ideas cited within the paragraph — either in the text or in parenthetical references?

Remind students to ask themselves these questions as they draft the various sections of their research papers.

A second conference is crucial at this stage of the process. Students are looking at research material and deciding not only if there's enough but also how to use it, organize it, and combine it. Direct students to come to this conference ready to report on how they are working with their research material. You can often save them anguish at this point by letting them know if they are needlessly panicked or if they are not concerned enough about the amount of material generated or about their sorting of it into meaningful classifications and relationships. If students discover that they need more material, this discovery will be much less painful now than being told later with a graded response that their research is scanty. Remind them that their schedules need to include time for spontaneous research trips while they are drafting their papers.

Using Your Sources to Support Your Ideas (p. 678)

The authors show outlining as a natural process. Arranging and rearranging notes into some order helps writers see gaps in their research or their evaluation of readings. This process also provides a scaffolding for the unconfident writers who are intimidated by shaping a large amount of material into an essay. Even if you require outlining nowhere else in the course, have students use outlines while organizing drafts of research papers; otherwise, the amount of information and the multiple sources students must manage will become overwhelming. (For more about outlining, refer students to Chapter 17, "Strategies for Stating a Thesis and Planning.")

One problem with outlines is that many were taught outlining outside the context of shaping a draft. Some consider outlining a hurdle instead of the useful tool it can be for planning, drafting, and revising. Particularly because of the complexity of the research assignment and the large body of information and insights that students are juggling, research writers need some sketch to tell them or remind them where they think they will go in the essay.

Some instructors require a formal sentence outline before students begin to draft. Each sentence in the outline then becomes the topic sentence of a paragraph. If you do this, remind students not to adhere slavishly to their outlines. At this point the outline should serve as a guide; students might make significant changes as they shape their material and draft.

Ask students to compile and hand in outlines. Discuss these preliminary plans with students in conference. Notice possible problems with research or with evaluations of

---

Here's an Idea . . .

Help students practice arranging materials for drafts by asking them to edit some formal outlines that have been previously submitted to you with finished essays. When students attempt to complete and then to revise and edit the outlines, they can see any major problems with organization or logic. In class discussion, our students usually talk about the illogic they see in the outlines and how they would revise parts of the outlines to present a logically articulated view. What they are doing, of course, is thinking about thinking. They carry back to their own drafts what they have observed about the need to present materials in some necessary and definable sequence.

the research, problems with lack of unity (that is, units of development not related to the main idea, such as irrelevant historical background), any large problems of organization, possible problems of transition, and certainly problems of development of the research thesis or question.

Ask students to read over their drafts-in-progress in class and to make a short outline of the parts and the major topics of each part. Ask them to compare these outlines with their working outlines and to think about rearranging notes or chunks of writing. While many writers don't want to revise until they finish, most writers profit from breaking longer writing into parts and revising as they continue to draft. Encourage students to try various writing strategies in order to discover a process suited to their way of thinking and for formulating ideas.

The following pages contain a handout with exercises that you can adapt for your students. Have them work in small groups to complete these incomplete outlines. Students will have to wrestle with these ideas to get them into some clear and logical sequence. Encourage them to add or revise as necessary. Explain the logic behind the formal conventions: for example, no "A" without "B," because the letters signal an analysis into parts. Expect students to see the serious problems of logic in the first outline, section IV; have them recommend several revisions.

Launching and Citing Your Sources As You Draft (p. 680)

Often first-year writers have a tendency merely to string together their notes —paraphrase, quotation, and summary — with transitions, rather than developing the paper with their own thoughts and ideas and incorporating their evidence as support. Try asking them to write their first draft without any of their source notes. They should use only their own words. Then have them revise by inserting and documenting evidence from notes to support each point they have made.

When they add source material, emphasize to students the importance of launching the material. Tell them that doing so not only establishes the reliability of the evidence by giving the credentials of the source, but it also shows the reader where the student's ideas end and the source's ideas begin. This clear distinction is especially necessary when students use paraphrase or summary, and when they use Internet evidence with no page numbers cited parenthetically at the end of the captured material. In those cases, caution them to make clear where the source material ends and their words begin as well.

Beginning and Ending (p. 680)

Even students who wrote introductions and conclusions after drafting their essays need to look a second time at introductions and conclusions. Notice that in this discussion of drafting the authors talk about redrafting, demonstrating again that the writing process is recursive. Consider asking students to write alternative introductions and conclusions to their own essays, using one of the different methods for introductions or conclusions discussed in Chapter 18, "Strategies for Drafting."

Often the revised versions tighten sentence structure, make more precise statements, and suggest some way to keep the reader interested. Sometimes the revised versions suggest ways of highlighting the research question or of broadening or narrowing it, and thus can lead the writer to revise even further.

1. Complete the following outline by inventing ideas that would be of parallel significance or logic to those listed. Look carefully at the sentences and topics used to show relationships of parts. Revise where needed.

Thesis: Nuclear energy today can be considered an ecologically sound source of energy.

Introduction

I. The energy crunch continues to be a serious problem.

  A.

  B.

  C.

II. Nuclear energy is a solution.

  A.

  B.

  C.

III. Nuclear energy is already working in the United States.

  A. 1980s nuclear power plants

  B. 1990s nuclear power plants

  C. Plans for future plants

IV. Poor alternatives

  A. Solar energy

  B. Fossil fuels

  C. Wind energy

Conclusion

2. State the thesis and correct any parts of the following outline that might indicate problems in logic or organization in the essay.

Thesis:

  I. What is natural childbirth?

     A. What natural childbirth does

  II. Natural childbirth differs from traditional childbirth.

     A. Differences before

     B. Differences in mind

  III. Why is natural childbirth considered healthier?

     A. For the mother

     B. Medications

  IV. What are some reasons for the recent trend toward natural childbirth?

REVISING AND EDITING (p. 681)

As you are aware, many writers — especially inexperienced ones — limit the rewriting process. Sometimes this results from their not understanding the necessity of revising, sometimes from their unsuccessful time management, and sometimes from their being overwhelmed by the length of what they have written. Unfortunately, some students will have had no previous experience writing anything longer than five or six hundred words, and now they might be worn out and even a little bored with this new experience. Revision might seem a large task for them.

To emphasize the revision process, hold a third conference with each student after a draft is complete. Show the student how well the draft at this point fulfills the criteria of a successful research project. Talk about what in the paper needs improvement. Look for and address the following:

- problems with paraphrase or unintentional plagiarism
- problems with introducing and interpreting quoted or paraphrased materials
- problems with scanty development of thesis or of major ideas
- problems with the conventions of documentation

Don't underestimate the practicality of having students outline their drafts as a revision tool. It is easier to work with ideas in outline form and to work them into a sensible order in skeletal form than in paragraphs. We have seen many students identify problems with organization and development of ideas when they have outlined. We've even seen them whoop with surprise when they realized they had overlooked a large chunk of their evidence in drafting the essay. With the aid of the outline, writers can move paragraphs around — with scissors and tape or with computer commands — until their paper coheres.

As with other types of writing, you should devote at least one class period to students reading one another's drafts. Ask them to use both the For Peer Response activ-

---

Here's an Idea . . .

Research paper conclusions in particular profit from peer revisions. Probably 90 percent of the conclusions we read say, "I told you I would do this. See point A. See point B. See point C. See? I did it." Encourage writers to be a bit more original. Ask them to trade the conclusions for their essays. Tell them no one can write a conclusion that only restates and summarizes. Challenge them to rewrite the conclusion to do the following:

- place the research question and answer in a larger context
- extrapolate imaginative consequences from what has been stated
- introduce the critical inquiry that should follow
- discuss the effects of the insights proffered in the essay
- generate some imaginative and satisfying way of easing the reader out of the paper

ity (p. 682) and the Revision Checklist (pp. 681–82). Encourage writers also to have readers outside class look at their essays.

Remind students that proofreading a paper is a crucial step in the process —and that it takes time. We've often encouraged students to proofread by reading lines backward, because this technique works. For more proofreading and manuscript guidelines, refer students to Chapter 20, "Strategies for Revising and Editing," and the Quick Editing Guide at the end of their textbook. In addition, the Quick Research Guide provides checklists for editing in-text citations and Works Cited entries.

Finally, advise writers to read their essays cold and aloud, or better yet, to have someone read the text to them. Tell them to pay particular attention to transitions between parts and to the tone they've established. Caution them against using a rigidly formal and impersonal tone. They're likely to have gotten the mistaken notion somewhere that research papers must be "stuffy."

DOCUMENTING SOURCES (p. 683)

Don't be surprised if students ask you more questions about documentation form and manuscript preparation than they have about interpreting materials or shaping a draft. This concern about how a manuscript looks is part of the "writing-as-product" legacy and also part of the students' need to hang onto some solid structures during what may seem to be an open-ended and unpredictable investigating process.

Students will be particularly worried about when, why, and how to document sources. Notice the authors' advice that students need to be aware of the several styles available and to learn which of those styles the instructor expects or the discipline requires. Emphasize that students must be consistent in their documentation and flexible about shifting styles according to writing purpose and audience. Many students will want to commit documentation "rules" to memory; some will have instructors who expect those rules to be part of a student's mental baggage. Remind students that *The Bedford Guide* offers most of the models they'll need and that up-to-date manuals are always available if they aren't certain how to proceed. Many software programs also offer documentation-style functions. Explain to students that it's most important to understand the ethics and logic of documentation, to consistently follow whatever style is chosen, and to be ready to consult style sheets for particularly vexing situations.

Other Assignments (p. 683)

These alternative assignments encourage library, field, and Internet research, but many could be managed in an essay shorter than the typical research paper. Some students will be turned on by some of these personal or career-related topics and by some of the unusual resources (such as interviews or television or videos). These assignments could be just the thing to get your recalcitrant students excited and involved in active research. Be aware that some of the assignments will lead to research reports of information (perhaps similar to technical reports) instead of researched thesis essays. If you prefer your students to write thesis-based essays, limit their choices.

APPLYING WHAT YOU LEARN: SOME USES OF RESEARCH (p. 684)

Spend some time going over these applications with your students to show them some of the realistic and valuable uses of research in various fields, not just in English composition or other college courses.

Here's an Idea . . .

Have each writer append a letter of self-evaluation or a reflective essay to the submitted manuscript, basing the letter on the research checklists throughout this chapter. Ask them to work with Tori Haring Smith's prompt, "If I had twenty-four hours to work more with this paper, here's what I'd do."

Reinforce the message that research is an enlivening and necessary activity by asking students to interview their adviser or a favorite instructor about how he or she uses research on the job and what research project he or she cares most about and to report back to the class. Print out a list of the research projects reported, add others you are involved in or know students or colleagues to be involved in, and give the list to your students. Then have them survey that list and make some generalizations about the state of research at your college. Several things will happen as a result: Students learn implicitly that research is integral to "higher learning," they connect with faculty in an informal learning situation, and they see that a community of researching writers is there as a resource to them in their careers. If students have interviewed faculty in the discipline they plan to follow, they also see models of professional scholarship even before they are completely immersed in their major.

Alternatively, survey students about the field research they find reported in their textbooks, and then ask them to interview their other instructors about the kinds of field research they or their students conduct. Some of your students who perceive research and research writing as boring and static might come to see it as an important way of imagining new ideas and of practicing the skills of the professions that they admire and hope to emulate. The next time they are required to write a research paper for a course, they should feel empowered to do so.

Documenting Sources (Ch. 34, p. 686)

Students persist in thinking of documentation as an enigma. Remind them that it is an intrinsic part of the research process. Students must learn the conventions of the language they use to convey their ideas. To help them understand different documentation styles, ask them to compare their experiences as employees, tourists in another country, or first-time users of some machine or equipment, especially the languages used in the various contexts.

In the authors' discussion of stylebooks, the implication is clear: Writers always need to adapt their styles to fit the publication or their audience. Style for a political science paper differs from that for a philosophy paper and from that for a paper on Shakespeare. Documentation styles can be described in ways that look like rules, which actually makes them more accessible than the "secrets" of how a political scientist thinks, organizes that thinking on paper, and revises it to meet the needs of other professionals. Use the fact that different documentation styles exist as a way to introduce students to the idea that various disciplines require different writing styles.

Student writers panic thinking that they must memorize correct documentation for each source in their bibliographies. Explain to them that few writers know how to document all of their sources without referring to a style manual — and that Chapter 34 of *A Writer's Research Manual* is in effect such a manual, containing the most frequently needed examples of documentation. Show students the MLA and APA directories in Chapter 34 and at the back of their textbook, and explain how to find the examples they need. The directories in Chapter 34 are organized by questions students might ask about a source, such as "Who Wrote It?" and "What Type of Source Is It?" The directories at the end of the book are organized by source type. Encourage them to use sections E1 and E2 of the Quick Research Guide as a convenient way to double check their documentation. The Draft Doctor on page 690 will help relieve your students' anxiety by answering questions about their documentation and providing advice for locating and fixing errors. Point out the Draft Doctor and show students how to use it. During the revision process, set aside a class period for students to use the Draft Doctor with their drafts as you move through the room answering their questions. Keep your sense of humor and help students develop a logical pattern of documentation. The authors provide a wide range of models in this chapter. Your students can find additional examples at *Research and Documentation Online* at <http://dianahacker.com/resdoc>.

Working with student writers on documentation might be the closest thing to drill and practice of any of our teaching activities. Even if you introduce the styles by focusing on them as initiation into a discourse community, writers still have to learn the conventions and how to apply them — and how to follow them precisely. When you are ready to turn your eye away from the whole essay and the quality of thought and expression, take a break before you look closely at how students documented their work. Reconsider before you decide to penalize students for problems with documentation. You want students to learn to take the time in revising their papers to edit and to proofread for consistency, and this includes documentation forms. Allow students to practice these editing skills before you judge the research essay completed and ready to be graded. Treat documentation as a competency check.

When students hand in their final papers, read them only for documentation, observing where and how students have introduced quotation, fact, statistics, and paraphrase. Use a highlighter to indicate problems they created or failed to correct, but don't correct the problems. Tell writers to correct the problems and return the essays to you for the final grade.

To help students with spotting and correcting documentation problems, assign the exercise on the following handout to groups during a class period. The sample research essay contains errors that often appear in student papers. By working together in groups, students begin to talk about research as scholars and editors.

A SAMPLE RESEARCH PAPER

MAEGAN KINKELAAR *Higher Education: Pricey or Priceless?* (p. 708)

The authors have included a completed research paper by a student, Maegan Kinkelaar. "Higher Education: Pricey or Priceless?" shows students a possible format for their paper, ways of incorporating a variety of evidence, methods of in-text documentation, as well as a Works Cited page and an outline. Refer to this paper to answer students' specific questions. Having this example at their fingertips will relieve more of their anxiety. (If you teach APA style, you might show style and formatting features of the APA sample on p. 733.)

Make transparencies of Kinkelaar's paper for overhead projection and take some time to go through it with your students. Ask them to answer the following questions:

- Find Kinkelaar's thesis. Where does she place it in the text?

- Find a place in which Kinkelaar uses paraphrase. Does she make it clear that the thoughts are a source's rather than her own? How does she do so?

- Find a place in which Kinkelaar uses direct quotation. Does she incorporate it smoothly into her text? How?

- How does Kinkelaar identify the credentials of the experts she uses? Is this effective?

- How does Kinkelaar identify figures? What kind of in-text citation does she use?

- Pick one of Kinkelaar's in-text citations and find the source in her Works Cited list.

- How are Kinkelaar's pages numbered? Look at the outline and Works Cited pages.

- Find a quotation that is indented block style. How long is the quotation? Does Kinkelaar use quotation marks? How does she handle the citation? How does she introduce the quotation?

- Where does Kinkelaar use page numbers in her citations? Where does she omit them? Why?

- Find a place in which Kinkelaar uses a page number without a name in her citation. Find this source on her Works Cited page.

- Compare and contrast entries on Kinkelaar's Works Cited page. Account for the differences by identifying each type of source.

Find the errors in the following MLA research essay and correct them as in the example in the first paragraph. Expect to find mistakes not only in parenthetical references and in the bibliography but also in the paper itself: incorrect quoting, misuse of parentheses, and so on. You might have to refer back and forth between the bibliography and the parenthetical references.

Portrait of the Past

(Courtesy of Julie Nieves, St. Petersburg Junior College)

Scholars have long realized that the literature produced during a given era can be a valuable resource in recreating that time period. Skillful authors can "mirror their world with the accuracy of the historian together with the sensitivity of the artist" (42 Westcott). No one serves as a better example of this combination than British author Oliver Jordan. From his first story, "Pilgrim's Passion," to his last novel, The Tears of London, Jordan created a strikingly faithful picture of turn-of-the-century England.

Throughout this Victorian's work, he took care to depict with awesome detail the values of the time. Among these is the surface respectability worshiped by the middle classes (Armitage, 642). Character after character plays the hypocrite to ensure that his reputation is maintained among his peers, for "to this class caught between the paupers and the aristocrats, respectability (not God) has become the shaper of their destinies" (87). In *Earthly Endeavours*, Julian Frank shivers at the idea that his secret affair will be discovered; when he is nominated for membership in the exclusive Hercules Club, he feels no compunction at dismissing his mistress of fifteen years.

> You know, Adele, that I cannot let our relationship blacken my family name. Sooner or later, the gossip will build to a crescendo. Of course I care for you, am grateful for your kindness, but the Franks' reputation, my dear, is worth so much more than our little emotional flurries (*Earthly* 42).

Similarly, another Victorian mania revealed by Jordan is the worship of status. Especially in the works written after 1890, he describes with charming precision the obsession with titles. "'Jordan's characters lie, cheat, and steal to win an earldom. To become a duke, they would probably murder any number of white-haired mothers'" ("The Literary Reputation of Oliver Jordan" 19). In his story *Lulu's Luck*, the ambitious Lulu tells the Prime Minister, "Put my husband on this year's honors list, and all I have is yours" (*Collected* 348).

A further evocation of his time is his continuing reference to contemporary history. The 1887 play "Dream and Dream Again," demonstrates the average Briton's dissatisfaction with the monarchy.

"The Queen? Haven't seen her in ten years. Not since her husband died. We pay for her jewels, her palaces, and her servants, but do we get so much as a glimpse of her? And her son's even worse! The Prince is a womanizing wastrel who's only fit for swilling whiskey and flirting with his friends' wives." (London, 1887, 48) No more telling criticism of the dynasty appears in the nineteenth-century literature (Varner, Crane, Haskill, Byrne 271). Yet another reference to real situations concerns the emergence of England as the world's greatest colonial empire. "Jordan's young male characters believe that Englishmen were sent by God to civilize the planet. They rush to the far ends of the earth to teach black and brown men to play cricket while ignoring the beauty of cultures far older and far more graceful than their own" (Varner, Crane, Haskill, Byrne 271). . . .

Works Cited

Armitage, Bradley. *Victorian Gentlemen.* Los Angeles, CA: Mills, 1980.

Brent, Carole. *Radicals and Writers.* Toronto: Jessup, 1988.

Brent, Carole. *Jordan and His Age.* Bantam, 1987. *Critical Essays.* Ed.

Critical Essays. Ed. Raymond Forbes. Random: New York, 1958.

Westcott, Adam. *The Life of Oliver Jordan.* Phildelphia: Kramer 1980.

Jordan, Oliver. *Collected Stories,* ed. James Harris. London: Pratt, 1898.

———. *Dream and Dream Again.* London: Worthington, 1887

———. *Earthly Endeavours.* London: Pratt, 1873.

———. *The Tears of London.* London: Worthington, 1900.

Lowell, Patrick, trans. *Politics in the Jordan Novels* by Jean Renaud. New York: Caldwell Publishers International, Inc. 1980.

Morgan, Dell. *The Great Victorians.* 2 vols. Reading: Franklin, 1945.

Peters, Pauline. "Characterization in *Class Crimes.*" *Atlantic* June, 1988: 37–39.

"The Literary Reputation of Oliver Jordan" *Saturday Review* February, 1985:19–26.

Varner, Philip et al. *Victorian Literature.* Rye, NY: Poole, 1978.

Wharton, James. *A Study of Dream and Dream Again and Its Influence on British Writers.* Bentley: Chicago, 1990.

CHAPTER 10

Teaching with *A Writer's Handbook* and the Appendices

In teaching writing as a process, we ask our students to focus on a hierarchy of concerns: (1) content and meaning, (2) structure, (3) stylistic issues such as sentence fluency and word choice, and (4) the conventions of grammar, punctuation, and spelling. In the shift away from Miss Grundy–style teaching, which focuses only on "correctness," some would argue that students have not been held accountable for this final part of the writing process. Many students enter our classrooms without a sound knowledge of grammar, and a few have the notion that grammar is somehow superficial. When we ask students to write about themselves as writers on the first day of class, however, most of them express the fear that their command of grammar, punctuation, and spelling is inadequate.

While it is true that research has shown little connection between learning grammatical rules and writing well, at some point students must acquire the skills that will allow them to polish their writing. Using correct grammar and punctuation is not simply a courtesy to the reader; grammatical and mechanical mistakes impede the paper's ability to convey meaning. Good writing requires clarity, grace, and style — all of which are difficult without a basic understanding of grammar and punctuation. This section of *Practical Suggestions* describes features in the textbook that give students practice with basic grammar and punctuation skills and provides you with advice about how to use *A Writer's Handbook* to teach grammar, in addition to the answers to the exercises in the handbook.

IMPORTANT FEATURES OF *A WRITER'S HANDBOOK*

The strength of *A Writer's Handbook* is that it is designed for students to use on their own. The table of contents at the beginning of the handbook makes it easy for them to find the advice they need, and the tabs at the top of the pages provide a quick guide for finding specific information. The connected discourse of the exercises also helps students to see how grammar and punctuation work in context to convey meaning.

Encourage students to use the handbook to become more autonomous — and more articulate — writers. Don't be surprised if some students recognize an editing problem but don't have the vocabulary to find the solution in the handbook. Make a habit of using the same grammatical terms as those used by the authors so that your students will learn to recognize them. When you introduce a term, explain what it means and use it whenever possible to describe your students' errors. Point out the term definitions annotated in the margins for students to use on their own.

The following features of the handbook will help students build their skills.

ESL Guidelines

These boxes in *A Writer's Handbook* contain information specifically for ESL students, who often have difficulty with particular aspects of English grammar. See the Index to ESL Guidelines at the back of the textbook. In addition, Exercise Central at the *Bedford Guide* Web site, <http://bedfordstmartins.com/bedguide>, contains ESL exercises that correspond to the ESL Guidelines in the handbook. To help you identify your

---

Here's an Idea . . .

If most of your class makes the same kind of error, take a class period and work on correcting it with the entire class. For example, if students have difficulty with unclear pronoun reference, copy some of their incorrect sentences on an overhead transparency, without names, to use as examples. Direct students to the sections in the Quick Editing Guide and in *A Writer's Handbook* that contain information on pronoun reference. (If you have not already shown them how to use the page tabs and table of contents to find specific information in *A Writer's Handbook* for themselves, you should do so now.) Go through the explanations with them, and then ask the class to identify the problem in the sentences on the overhead transparency and to suggest corrections.

Next, ask students to find an example of the error in their own drafts and to correct that error. Move around the room and make yourself available to students who need more help or tutoring. When the class has finished, have each student read the corrected version of his or her sentence. If a student is having trouble correcting a sentence, ask the class to suggest several ways to restructure it. (Later, check with the writer to make sure he or she understands the error.) Finally, direct your students to find the other pronoun reference mistakes in their drafts while you move through the classroom helping those who are still having trouble. Ask those students who do not have problems with pronoun reference to use the Quick Editing Guide to identify their own most common error.

You might also want to use the PowerPoints on the instructor side of the book's Web site (<bedfordstmartins.com/bedguide>). These include class practices on common grammar errors.

ESL students' patterns of error and determine which exercises you should assign to them, read the information on error analysis on page 60 of this manual.

For more on providing support for ESL students, see Chapter 4 of this manual.

Web Site Key Words

In the margins of *A Writer's Handbook*, students will find Key Words marked with a magnifying glass icon that link them to the text's companion Web site for additional help with certain grammar and punctuation problems. The keywords in these references allow students to quickly access the specific advice and practice they need.

USING *A WRITER'S HANDBOOK* TO TEACH GRAMMAR

How much grammar should you teach? This will be determined by the skill levels in each class and the constraints on your time. Building time into your syllabus for grammar lessons might be difficult. You cannot make up in one semester what a student has failed to learn in ten years of English classes. Take heart in the fact that grammar must be taught in conjunction with writing. Without a context, students do not retain rules. Grammar instruction is useless unless students can transfer what you are teaching to their own writing. Always have students work on grammatical and mechanical issues by focusing on either their own drafts or those of their peers.

The best way to teach grammar is through individualized instruction: Determine your students' particular weaknesses and ask them to practice correcting these faults. First-year writers often have difficulty with verb tense, pronoun reference and agreement, subject/verb agreement, sentence fragments, comma splices, and punctuation. As you read students' drafts, try to evaluate any patterns of mistakes. For a detailed discussion of error analysis, see page 60 of this manual.

If a student consistently makes the same kind of error, arrange to meet with him or her in an individual conference or with a group of students who make the same error. Show them one instance of the common error in their draft and explain the error. Also point out where in the textbook they can find information about that kind of error. Then ask students working in groups or on their own to locate other places in their drafts where the same error occurs, to correct the errors, and to resubmit their drafts. Focus on only one editing problem at a time. After the groups have corrected the errors in their drafts, have them exchange papers with their peers for another round of editing. Caution students to explain — not just to fix — mistakes for the writer they work with.

If, after focused instruction and extra practice, students are still having difficulty with particular errors, you will need to work with them further or make arrangements for tutoring. Talk with them to discover what they find difficult about the choices they are making, and explain the correct choice to them again. If a student has a problem with sentence fragments, show him or her how to locate in the table of contents, the end sheets, and the Quick Editing Guide the sections on sentence fragments. Have the student read through the explanation and examples in the handbook and work through the lettered exercises, checking his or her work against the answers in the back of the textbook. Then ask him or her to do the numbered exercises and submit them to you.

USING THE APPENDICES TO TEACH GRAMMAR AND RESEARCH

Quick Editing Guide

The Quick Editing Guide is contained in a separate dark-blue-edged section at the end of the book and provides students with more information about their most common grammatical errors: incorrect verb tense, lack of pronoun and subject/verb agreement, unclear pronoun reference, sentence fragments or comma splices, and misused punctuation. A checklist in the front of the guide helps students to identify specific problems and directs them to the subsection of the guide with the editing advice they need. Each subsection also contains an Editing Checklist to focus the writer on his or her particular problem.

Insist that students use the Quick Editing Guide. Tell them that no piece of writing is finished until they have completed the checklist on page A-26. Give them a paper clip, courtesy of Miss Grundy, to attach to this page so that they can find it quickly and easily.

In the Quick Editing Guide, students will also find detailed information on using word-processing software to edit their papers. While these E-writer boxes suggest ways to make the editing task easier, the authors are also careful to warn students about the unreliable aspects of using grammar and spell checkers. You might want to refer them to these warnings if you assign specific word-processing activities.

New to this edition, the Draft Doctors on pages A-38 and A-42 provide a tool for students to find and remedy common grammar and sentence errors. These charts ask questions to help students search for a problem, offer strategies to determine whether

> *Here's an Idea...*
>
> Require students to read and write a one-page summary of an essay from *A Writer's Reader* each week. Collect the summaries and go through them quickly, marking a check in the margin of each line with a grammar error. Students must find and correct each error in the returned draft, noting the number and letter of the handbook rule in the margin, and then return the draft to you. This exercise requires students to focus on errors in their writing and apply grammar rules to their own drafts; it also gives students practice in reading for main ideas and summarizing them.

the sentence contains the problem, and provide suggestions for fixing it. The Draft Doctors are designed to enable students to independently correct their own writing.

Quick Research Guide

The Quick Research Guide is a concise, easily accessible resource that students will find handy whether they are producing a short research paper, navigating a more lengthy research project, or merely adding a few supporting sources to bolster the effectiveness of an essay. The Quick Research Guide is contained in a separate dark-red-edged appendix at the end of the text and includes checklists, charts, and advice to help inexperienced researchers define a research task, find and evaluate sources, use evidence to support writing, and handle the technicalities of citing sources and compiling an MLA-style Works Cited list or APA-style Reference list.

Show your students the Quick Research Guide and briefly touch on each of its features. Point out the charts explaining types of evidence (pp. A-2–A-3), the statement-support pattern (p. A-5), print and electronic sources and their applications (p. A-10 and p. A-11), and methods of adding source material (pp. A-13–A-18). Your students will find these resources invaluable as they tackle writing assignments for your class and throughout their academic career.

USING ANCILLARIES TO *THE BEDFORD GUIDE* TO TEACH GRAMMAR

In addition to the features in the textbook, several ancillaries also provide ways to help students improve their grammar. Written to correspond with *A Writer's Handbook*, the grammar exercises in Exercise Central at <bedfordstmartins.com/bedguide> are an invaluable resource. Comment for *The Bedford Guide* lets you (as well as peer reviewers) link to specific parts of *A Writer's Handbook* in your responses to students' papers. *Testing Tool Kit: A Writing and Grammar Test Bank* provides even more grammar support, allowing you to create secure, customized tests and quizzes from a CD-ROM. A chart at the end of this manual correlates topics in *Testing Took Kit* with chapters and sections of *The Bedford Guide*. For more on these and other resources, see pages 74–76 of this manual. To help students get the most out of these ancillaries, spend part of a class period early in the semester orienting students to them.

Grammar instruction will be meaningful only if students recognize that using proper grammar is an essential skill. Always stress that you are finding time to help students acquire grammar skills because you have discovered that students will need these skills in their college work and careers.

Answers for Lettered Exercises

Exercise 1–1 *Eliminating Fragments* (p. H-9)

Suggested revisions:

a. Michael had a beautiful Southern accent, having lived many years in Georgia.
b. Pat and Chris are determined to marry each other, even if their families do not approve.
c. Jack seemed well qualified for a career in the Air Force, except for his tendency to get airsick.
d. Lisa advocated sleeping no more than four hours a night until she started nodding through her classes.
e. Complete Sentences

Exercise 2–1 *Revising Comma Splices and Fused Sentences* (p. H-13)

Suggested revisions:

a. We followed the scientist down a flight of wet stone steps. At last he stopped before a huge oak door.
   We followed the scientist down a flight of wet stone steps, until at last he stopped before a huge oak door.
b. Dr. Frankenstein selected a heavy key; he twisted it in the lock.
   Dr. Frankenstein selected a heavy key, which he twisted in the lock.
c. The huge door gave a groan; it swung open on a dimly lighted laboratory.
   The huge door gave a groan and swung open on a dimly lighted laboratory.
d. Before us on a dissecting table lay a form with closed eyes. To behold it sent a quick chill down my spine.
   Before us on a dissecting table lay a form with closed eyes; beholding it sent a quick chill down my spine.
e. The scientist strode to the table and lifted a white-gloved hand.
   The scientist strode to the table; he lifted a white-gloved hand.

Exercise 3–1 *Using Irregular Verb Forms* (p. H-18)

a. In those days, Benjamin wrote all the music, and his sister *sang* all the songs.
b. Correct
c. When the bell rang, darkness had already *fallen*.
d. Voters have *chosen* some new senators, who won't take office until January.
e. Carol threw the ball into the water, and the dog *swam* after it.

Exercise 3–2 *Identifying Verb Tenses* (p. H-26)

a. has been living: present perfect progressive; hacked: simple past; change: simple present
b. have never appeared: present perfect; never will appear: simple future; gets: simple present
c. had been: past perfect; pitched: simple past d. will have been studying: future perfect progressive; will be taking: future progressive e. was running: past progressive; strolled: simple past

Exercise 3–4 *Using the Correct Mood of Verbs* (p. H-31)

a. Dr. Belanger recommended that Juan *floss* his teeth every day. (Incorrect *flosses*, indicative; correct *floss*, subjunctive)
b. If I *were* you, I would have done the same thing. (Incorrect *was*, indicative; correct *were*, subjunctive)
c. Tradition demands that Daegun *show* respect for his elders. (Incorrect *shows*, indicative; correct *show*, subjunctive)
d. Please *attend* the training lesson if you plan to skydive later today. (Incorrect *attends*, indicative; correct *attend*, imperative)

Exercise 4–1 *Making Subjects and Verbs Agree* (p. H-36)

a. For many college graduates, the process of looking for jobs *is* often long and stressful.

b. Not too long ago, searching the classifieds and inquiring in person *were* the primary methods of job hunting.

c. Today, however, everyone also *seems* to use the Internet to search for openings or to e-mail his or her résumés.

d. My classmates and my cousin *send* most résumés over the Internet because it costs less than mailing them.

e. All of the résumés *arrive* quickly when they are sent electronically.

Exercise 5–1 *Using Pronouns Correctly* (p. H-39)

a. I didn't appreciate *your* laughing at her and *me*. (*Your* modifies the gerund *laughing; me* is an object of the preposition *at*.)

b. Lee and *I* would be delighted to serenade *whoever* will listen. (*I* is a subject of the verb phrase *would be delighted; whoever* is the subject of the clause *whoever will listen*.)

c. The managers and *we* servers are highly trustworthy. (*We* is a subject complement.)

d. The neighbors were driven berserk by *his* singing. (The gerund *singing* is the object of the verb *driven;* the possessive pronoun *his* modifies singing.) *Or* Correct as is. (*Him* is the object of the verb *driven; singing* is a participle modifying *him*.)

e. Jerry and *I* regard you and *her* as the very people *whom* we wish to meet. (*I* is a subject of the verb *regard; her* is a direct object of the verb *regard; whom* is the object of the infinitive *to meet*.)

Exercise 6–1 *Making Pronoun Reference Clear* (p. H-43)

Suggested revisions:

a. As the moon began to rise, I could see the faint shadow of the tree.

b. While she spent the summer in Paris, Katrina broadened her awareness of cultural differences by traveling throughout Europe.

c. Most managers want employees to work as many hours as possible. They never consider the work their employees need to do at home.

d. Working twelve hours a day and never getting enough sleep was worth it.

e. Kevin asked Mike to meet him for lunch but forgot that Mike had class at that time. *Or* Kevin forgot that he had class at the time he asked Mike to meet him for lunch.

Exercise 7–1 *Making Pronouns and Antecedents Agree* (p. H-46)

Suggested revisions:

a. Correct

b. Neither Melissa nor James has received an application form yet. *Or* Melissa and James have not received their application forms yet.

c. He is the kind of man who gets his fun out of just sipping his beer and watching his Saturday games on TV.

d. Many a mother has mourned the loss of her child. *Or* Many mothers have mourned the loss of their children.

e. When you enjoy your work, it's easy to spend all your spare time thinking about it. *Or* When one enjoys one's work, it's easy to spend all one's spare time thinking about it.

Exercise 8–1 *Using Adjectives and Adverbs Correctly* (p. H-50)

a. Change *increasing* to *increasingly*. **b.** Correct **c.** Change *lower* to *lowest*. **d.** Change *rapid* to *rapidly*. **e.** Change *well* to *good*.

Exercise 9–1 *Maintaining Grammatical Consistency* (p. H-56)

Suggested revisions:

a. Dr. Jamison is an erudite professor who tells amusing anecdotes in class. (Formal) *Or* Dr. Jamison is a funny teacher who cracks jokes in class. (Informal)
b. The audience listened intently to the lecture but did not understand the message.
c. Scientists can no longer evade the social, political, and ethical consequences of what they do in the laboratory.
d. To have good government, citizens must become informed on the issues. Also, they must vote.
e. Good writing is essential to success in many professions, especially in business, where ideas must be communicated clearly.

Exercise 10–1 *Placing Modifiers* (p. H-59)

Suggested revisions:

a. The bus full of passengers got stuck in a ditch.
b. In the middle of a staff meeting, he was daydreaming about fishing for trout.
c. With a smirk, the boy threw the paper airplane through an open window.
d. When the glare appeared, I reached for my sunglasses from the glove compartment.
e. Sally and Glen watched the kites high above them drift back and forth.

Exercise 10–2 *Revising Dangling Modifiers* (p. H-60)

Suggested revisions:

a. As I was unpacking the suitcase, a horrible idea occurred to me.
b. After preparing breakfast that morning, I might have left the oven on at home.
c. Although I tried to reach my neighbor, her telephone was busy.
d. Desperate to get information, I asked my mother to drive over to check the oven.
e. I felt enormous relief when my mother's call confirmed that everything was fine.

Exercise 11–1 *Completing Comparisons* (p. H-62)

Suggested revisions:

a. The movie version of *The Brady Bunch* was much more ironic *than the television show*.
b. Taking care of a dog is often more demanding than *taking care of* a cat.
c. I received more free calendars in the mail for the year 2008 than *I have for* any other year.
d. The crime rate in the United States is higher than *it is in* Canada.
e. Liver contains more iron than any *other* meat.

Exercise 11–2 *Completing Sentences* (p. H-64)

Suggested revisions:

a. Eighteenth-century China was as civilized *as* and in many respects more sophisticated than the Western world.
b. Pembroke was never contacted *by*, much less involved with, the election committee.
c. I haven't yet *finished* but soon will finish my research paper.
d. Ron likes his popcorn with butter; Linda *likes hers* with parmesan cheese.
e. Correct

Exercise 12–1 *Correcting Mixed Constructions and Faulty Predication* (p. H-68)

Suggested revisions:

a. Health insurance protects people from big medical bills.
b. His determination to prevail helped him finish the race.
c. AIDS destroys the body's immune system.
d. The temperatures are too low for the orange trees.
e. In a recession, economic growth is small or nonexistent, and unemployment increases.

Exercise 13–1 *Making Sentences Parallel* (p. H-71)

Suggested revisions:

a. The border separating Texas and Mexico marks not only the political boundary of two countries but also the last frontier for some endangered wildlife.
b. In the Rio Grande Valley, both local residents and tourists enjoy visiting the national wildlife refuges.
c. The tall grasses in this valley are the home of many insects, birds, and small mammals.
d. Two endangered wildcats, the ocelot and the jaguarundi, also make the Rio Grande Valley their home.
e. Many people from Central America are desperate to immigrate to the United States by either legal or illegal means.

Exercise 14–1 *Using Coordination* (p. H-75)

Suggested revisions:

a. Professional poker players try to win money and prizes in high-stakes tournaments; however, they may lose thousands of dollars.
b. Poker is not an easy way to make a living, and playing professional poker is not a good way to relax.
c. A good "poker face" reveals no emotions, for communicating too much information puts a player at a disadvantage.
d. Hidden feelings may come out in unconscious movements, so an expert poker player watches other players carefully.
e. Poker is different from most other casino gambling games, for it requires skill and it forces players to compete against each other. Other casino gambling pits players against the house, so they may win out of sheer luck, but skill has little to do with winning those games.

Exercise 14–2 *Using Subordination* (p. H-77)

Suggested revisions:

a. Cape Cod is a peninsula in Massachusetts that juts into the Atlantic Ocean south of Boston, marking the northern turning point of the Gulf Stream.
b. Although the developer had hoped the condominiums would sell quickly, sales were sluggish.
c. Tourists love Italy because it has a wonderful climate, beautiful towns and cities, and a rich history.
d. At the end of Verdi's opera *La Traviata*, Alfredo has to see his beloved Violetta again, even though he knows she is dying and all he can say is good-bye.
e. I usually have more fun at a concert with Rico than with Morey because Rico loves music while Morey merely tolerates it.

Exercise 16–2 *Avoiding Jargon* (p. H-84)

Suggested revisions:

a. Everyone at Boondoggle and Gall attends holiday gatherings in order to meet and socialize with potential business partners.
b. This year, more than fifty employees lost their jobs after Boondoggle and Gall's decision to reduce their number of employees by September 1.
c. The layoffs left Jensen in charge of all telephone calls in the customer service department.
d. Jensen was responsible for handling three times as many telephone calls after the layoffs, yet she did not receive any extra pay.
e. Jensen and her managers could not agree on a fair compensation, so she decided to quit her job at Boondoggle and Gall.

Exercise 16–3   *Avoiding Euphemisms and Slang* (p. H-85)

Suggested revisions:

a. Our security forces have arrested many political dissidents.
b. At three hundred dollars a month, the apartment is a bargain.
c. The soldiers were accidentally shot by members of their own troops while they were retreating.
d. Churchill was an excellent politician.
e. The president's tax plan was doomed; Congress would not approve it.

Exercise 18–1   *Avoiding Bias* (p. H-93)

Suggested revisions:

a. Our school's extensive athletic program will be of interest to *many* applicants.
b. The new physicians on our staff include Dr. Scalia, *Dr.* Baniski, and Dr. Throckmorton.
c. Joni believes in the healing properties of herbal remedies.
d. Philosophers have long pondered whether *humans are* innately evil or innately good.
e. *Diligent researchers* will always find the sources *they* seek.

Exercise 20–1   *Using End Punctuation* (p. H-98)

a. The question that still troubles the community after all these years is why federal agents did not act sooner. (Not a direct question)
b. Correct
c. I wonder what he was thinking at the time. (Not a direct question)
d. One man, who suffered a broken leg, was rescued when he was heard screaming, "Help me! Help me!" (Urgent directive)
e. Correct

Exercise 21–1   *Using Commas* (p. H-99)

a. Farmers around the world tend to rely on just a few breeds of livestock, so some breeds are disappearing.
b. Correct
c. For instance, modern breeds of cattle usually grow larger and produce more meat and milk than older breeds.
d. In both wild and domestic animals, genetic diversity can make the animals resistant to disease and parasites, so older breeds can give scientists important information.
e. Until recently, small organic farmers were often the only ones interested in raising old-fashioned breeds, but animal scientists now support this practice as well.

Exercise 21–2   *Using Commas* (p. H-101)

a. Mrs. Carver looks like a sweet little old lady, but she plays a wicked electric guitar.
b. Her bass player, her drummer, and her keyboard player all live in the same retirement community.
c. They practice individually in the afternoon, rehearse together at night, and play at the community's Saturday night dances.
d. The Rest Home Rebels have to rehearse quietly and cautiously to keep from disturbing the other residents.
e. Correct

Exercise 21–3   *Using Commas* (p. H-103)

Suggested revisions:

a. We are bringing a dish, vegetable lasagna, to the potluck supper.
b. I like to go to Central Bank on this side of town because this branch tends to have short lines.
c. The colony that the English established at Roanoke disappeared mysteriously.

d. If the base commanders had checked their gun room, where powder is stored, they would have found that several hundred pounds of gunpowder were missing.
e. Brazil's tropical rain forests, which help produce the air we breathe all over the world, are being cut down at an alarming rate.

Exercise 21–4   Using *Commas* (p. H-104)

a. The university insisted, however, that the students were not accepted merely because of their parents' generous contributions.
b. This dispute, in any case, is an old one.
c. It was the young man's striking good looks, not his acting ability, that first attracted the Hollywood agents.
d. Gretchen learned, moreover, not to always accept as true what she had read in celebrity magazines.
e. The hikers, most of them wearing ponchos or rain jackets, headed out into the steady drizzle.

Exercise 21–5   Using *Commas* (p. H-106)

a. César Chávez was born on March 31, 1927, on a farm in Yuma, Arizona.
b. Chávez, who spent years as a migrant farmworker, told other farm laborers, "If you're outraged at conditions, then you can't possibly be free or happy until you devote all your time to changing them."
c. Chávez founded the United Farm Workers union and did, indeed, devote all his time to changing conditions for farmworkers.
d. Robert F. Kennedy called Chávez "one of the heroic figures of our time."
e. Correct

Exercise 22–1   Using *Semicolons* (p. H-109)

a. By the beginning of 2006, Shirley was eager to retire; nevertheless, she agreed to stay on for two more years.
b. In 1968 Lyndon Johnson abandoned his hopes for reelection because of fierce opposition from within his own party.
c. The committee was asked to determine the extent of violent crime among teenagers, especially those between the ages of fourteen and sixteen; to act as a liaison between the city and schools and between churches and volunteer organizations; and to draw up a plan to reduce violence, both public and private, by the end of the century.
d. The leaves on the oak trees near the lake were tinged with red; swimmers no longer ventured into the water.
e. The football team has yet to win a game; however, the season is still young.

Exercise 23–1   Using *Colons* (p. H-112)

Suggested revisions:

a. The Continuing Education Program offers courses in building and construction management, engineering, and design.
b. The interview ended with a test of skills: taking messages, operating the computer, typing a sample letter, and proofreading documents.
c. The sample letter began, "Dear Mr. Rasheed: Please accept our apologies for the late shipment."
d. Correct
e. These are my dreams: to fly in a small plane, to gallop down a beach on horseback, and to cross the ocean in a sailboat.

Exercise 24–1   Using the *Apostrophe* (p. H-115)

a. Joe's and Chuck's fathers were both in the class of '73.
b. Correct
c. It was a strange coincidence that all three women's cars broke down after they had picked up their mothers-in-law.

d. Don't forget to dot your *i*'s and cross your *t*'s.
e. Mario and Shelley's son is marrying the editor in chief's daughter.

Exercise 25–1   *Using Quotation Marks* (p. H-120)

a. "What we still need to figure out," the police chief said, "is whether the victim was acquainted with his assailant."
b. A skillful orator, Patrick Henry is credited with the phrase "Give me liberty or give me death."
c. "I could hear the crowd chanting my name — 'Jones! Jones!' — and that spurred me on," said Bruce Jones, the winner of the 5,000-meter race.
d. The video for the rock group Guns and Roses' epic song "November Rain" is based on a short story by Del James.
e. In response to a possible asteroid strike on Earth, former astronaut Rusty Schweickart says, "Every country is at risk."

Exercise 26–1   *Using the Dash* (p. H-121)

Suggested revisions:

a. I enjoy going hiking with my friend John, whom I've known for fifteen years.
b. Pedro's new boat is spectacular — a regular seagoing Ferrari.
c. The Thompsons devote their weekends to their favorite pastime — eating bags of potato chips and cookies beside the warm glow of the television.

Exercise 27–1   *Using Parentheses* (p. H-123)

Suggested revisions:

a. Our cafeteria serves the four basic food groups: white (milk, bread, and mashed potatoes), brown (mystery meat and gravy), green (overcooked vegetables and underwashed lettuce), and orange (squash, carrots, and tomato sauce).
b. The hijackers will release the hostages only if the government (1) frees all political prisoners and (2) allows the hijackers to leave the country unharmed.
c. Correct

Exercise 28–1   *Using Abbreviations* (p. H-130)

a. At 7:50 p.m. [*or* 7:50 in the evening] on election day, the media first awarded Florida to Al Gore, only to reverse that statement and declare George W. Bush the president a few hours later.
b. Biology lectures are only ninety *minutes* long because lab sessions immediately follow them.
c. *Professor* James has office hours on *Monday* and *Tuesday*, beginning at 10:00 a.m.
d. Emotional issues, *for example*, abortion and capital punishment, cannot be settled easily by compromise.
e. The red peppers are selling for $3.25 a *pound*.

Exercise 29–1   *Using Capitalization* (p. H-133)

a. At our family reunion, I met my cousin Sam for the first time, as well as my father's brother George.
b. I already knew from Dad that his brother had moved to Australia years ago to explore the Great Barrier Reef.
c. I had heard that Uncle George was estranged from his mother, a Roman Catholic, after he married an atheist.
d. She told George that God created many religions so that people would not become atheists.
e. When my uncle announced that he was moving to a continent thousands of miles southwest of the United States, his mother gave him a Bible to take along.

Exercise 30–1   *Using Numbers* (p. H-135)

a. If the murder took place at approximately *6:20* p.m. and the suspect was *half* a mile away at the time, he could not possibly have committed the crime.

b. A program to help save the sea otter transferred more than eighty animals to a new colony over the course of *two* years; however, all but *thirty-four* otters swam back home again.

c. *Twelve percent* or so of the estimated *15* to *20* billion pounds of plastic discarded annually in the United States is recycled.

d. The Reedville Rockets beat the Botton Blasters 94–4 before a crowd of *550*.

e. In act II, scene ix, of Shakespeare's *The Merchant of Venice*, Portia's *second* suitor fails to guess which of *three* caskets contains her portrait.

Exercise 31–1   Using Italics (p. H-138)

a. Does *avocado* mean "lawyer" in Spanish?

b. During this year's First Night celebrations, we heard Verdi's *Requiem* and Monteverdi's *Orfeo*.

c. You can pick out some of the best basketball players in the NBA by the *33* on their jerseys.

d. It was fun watching the passengers on the *Europa* trying to dance to "Blue Moon" in the midst of a storm.

e. In one episode of the sitcom *Seinfeld*, Kramer gets a job as an underwear model.

Exercise 32–1   Using Hyphens (p. H-141)

a. The strong-smelling smoke alerted them to a potentially life-threatening danger.

b. Burt's wildly swinging opponent had tired himself out before the climactic third round.

c. Tony soaked his son's ketchup- and mustard-stained T-shirt in a pail of water mixed with chlorine bleach.

d. Correct

e. Tracy's brother-in-law lives with his family in a six-room apartment.

Answers for Numbered Exercises

Exercise 1–1   *Eliminating Fragments* (p. H-9)

Suggested revisions:

1. Being the first person in his family ever to attend college, Alex is determined to succeed.
2. Does our society rob children of their childhood by making them aware too soon of adult ills?
3. Richard III supposedly had the young princes murdered, though no one has ever found out what really happened to them.
4. For democracy to function, two elements are crucial: an educated populace and a collective belief in people's ability to chart their own course.
5. You must take his stories with a grain of salt, as others do.

Exercise 1–2   *Eliminating Fragments* (p. H-9)

Suggested revision:

Some people assume that only women are overly concerned with body image. However, men often share this concern. While women tend to exercise vigorously to stay slender, men usually lift weights to "bulk up" because of their desire to look masculine. Both are trying to achieve the "ideal" body form: the muscular male and the slim female. Sometimes working out begins to interfere with other aspects of life, such as sleeping, eating regularly, or going to school or work. These are warning signs about too much emphasis on physical appearance. Preoccupation with body image may turn a healthy lifestyle into an unhealthy obsession. Many people believe that looking attractive will bring them happiness. Unfortunately, when they become compulsive, they learn that beautiful people are not always happy.

Exercise 2–1   *Revising Comma Splices and Fused Sentences* (p. H-13)

Suggested revisions:

1. When Dr. Frankenstein flung a power switch, blue streamers of static electricity crackled about the table. The creature gave a grunt and opened smoldering eyes.
2. "I've won!" exclaimed the scientist. In triumph, he circled the room doing a demented Irish reel.
3. The creature's right hand strained. The heavy steel manacle imprisoning his wrist groaned in torment.
4. Correct
5. The creature sat upright and tugged at the shackles binding his ankles. Frankenstein uttered a piercing scream.

Exercise 2–2   *Revising Comma Splices and Fused Sentences* (p. H-13)

Suggested revision:

Have you ever wondered why you drive on parkways and park on driveways? That's about as logical as your nose running while your feet smell! When you stop to think about it, these phrases don't make sense, yet we tend to accept them without thinking about what they literally mean. We simply take their intended meanings for granted. Think, however, how confusing they are for a person who is just learning the language. If, for example, you have just learned the verb "park," you would logically assume that a parkway is where you should park your car. Of course, when most people see a parkway or a driveway, they realize that braking on a parkway would be hazardous, while speeding through a driveway will not take them very far. Our language is full of many idiomatic expressions that may be difficult for a person from another language background to understand. Fortunately, there are plenty of questions to keep us all confused, such as why Americans commonly refer to going to work as "punching the clock."

Exercise 3–1 Using Irregular Verb Forms (p. H-18)

1. Correct
2. By the time the sun set, the birds had all *gone* away.
3. Teachers had *spoken* to his parents long before he stole the bicycle.
4. While the cat *lay* on the bed, the mouse ran beneath the door.
5. For the past three days, the wind has *blown* hard from the south, but now the clouds have *begun* to drift in.

Exercise 3–2 Identifying Verb Tenses (p. H-26)

1. will have been going: future perfect progressive 2. will be working: future progressive; need: simple present 3. have been hoping: present perfect progressive; will come: simple future
4. know: simple present; will have returned: future perfect 5. had been expecting: past perfect progressive; heard: simple past; was waiting: past progressive

Exercise 3–3 Using Active and Passive Voice Verbs (p. H-29)

Suggested revision:

Many scientists *have studied* the unique creatures of the Galápagos Islands. Charles Darwin *explored* the islands in 1835. His observations led to the theory of evolution, which he explained in his book *On the Origin of Species.* Darwin *discovered* thirteen species of finches on the island, all descended from a common stock; even today visitors to the islands *can see* this great variety of species. Each island species has evolved by adapting to local conditions. The woodpecker finch *uses* a twig to probe trees for grubs. The marine iguana *feeds* on algae on the ocean floor. The Galápagos cormorant *can drink* salt water, thanks to a salt-extracting gland. Because of the tameness of these animals, visitors *can study* them at close range.

Exercise 3–4 Using the Correct Mood of Verbs (p. H-31)

1. If she *were* slightly older, she could stay home by herself. (Incorrect *was*, indicative; correct *were*, subjunctive)
2. If they *had* waited a little longer, they would have seen some amazing things. (Incorrect *have*, subjunctive; correct *had*, indicative)
3. Emilia's contract stipulates that she *work* on Saturdays. (Incorrect *works*, indicative; correct *work*, subjunctive)
4. If James *had invested* in the company ten years ago, he would have made a lot of money. (Incorrect *invested*, indicative; correct *had invested*, subjunctive)

Exercise 4–1 Making Subjects and Verbs Agree (p. H-36)

1. There are many people who *think* that interviewing is the most stressful part of the job search.
2. Sometimes only one person conducts an interview, while other times a whole committee *conducts* it.
3. Either the interviewer or the committee usually *begins* by asking simple questions about your background.
4. Making eye contact, dressing professionally, and appearing confident *are* some of the qualities an interviewer may consider important.
5. After an interview, most people *send* a thank-you letter to the person who conducted it.

Exercise 5–1 Using Pronouns Correctly (p. H-39)

1. Have you guessed the identity of the person of *whom* I am speaking? (*Whom* is the object of the preposition *of*.)
2. It was *his* asking about the clock that started *my* suspecting him. (*His* and *my* are possessive pronouns modifying the gerunds *asking* and *suspecting*, respectively.)
3. They — Jerry and *she* — are the troublemakers. (*She* is an appositive to the subject *They*.)

4. Mrs. Van Dumont awarded the prize to Mona and *me*. (*Me* is an object of the preposition *to*.)
5. The counterattack was launched by Dusty and *me*. (*Me* is an object of the preposition *by*.)

Exercise 6–1 *Making Pronoun Reference Clear* (p. H-43)

Suggested revisions:
1. Bill's prank frightened Josh and made Bill wonder why he had done it. *Or* Bill's prank frightened Josh and made Josh wonder why Bill had done it.
2. Korean students study up to twenty subjects a year, including algebra, calculus, and engineering. Because these subjects are required, students must study them year after year.
3. Pedro Martinez signed a baseball for Chad that Martinez had used in a game.
4. The bottle shattered when it hit the windshield.
5. My friends believe they are more mature than many of their peers because of the discipline enforced at my friends' school. However, the emphasis on discipline can also lead to problems.

Exercise 7–1 *Making Pronouns and Antecedents Agree* (p. H-46)

Suggested revisions:

1. All students are encouraged to complete *their* registration on time.
2. *Babies* who don't know *their* own mothers may have been born with some kind of vision deficiency.
3. Correct
4. If you don't like the songs the choir sings, don't join in.
5. Young people should know how to protect *themselves* against AIDS.

Exercise 8–1 *Using Adjectives and Adverbs Correctly* (p. H-50)

1. Change *secret* to *secretly*. 2. Change *increasingly* to *increased*. 3. Change *most* to *more*.
4. Change *more* to *most*. 5. Change *breathless* to *breathlessly*.

Exercise 9–1 *Maintaining Grammatical Consistency* (p. H-56)

Suggested revisions:

1. Our legal system *makes* it extremely difficult to prove a bribe. If *the prosecutor does not prove* the charges to the satisfaction of a jury or a judge, then we jump to the conclusion that the absence of a conviction demonstrates the innocence of the subject.
2. Before Morris K. Udall, Democrat from Arizona, *resigned* his seat in the U.S. House of Representatives, he helped preserve hundreds of acres of wilderness.
3. Anyone can learn another language if *he or she has* the time and the patience.
4. The immigration officer asked how long we planned to stay, so I *showed* him my letter of acceptance from Tulane.
5. Archaeologists spent many months studying the site of the African city of Zimbabwe and *uncovered* many artifacts.

Exercise 10–1 *Placing Modifiers* (p. H-59)

Suggested revisions:

1. She found a fly in her soup at one of the best French restaurants in town.
2. From the pages of an old book Andy learned how to build kites.
3. On the day he left the island, Alex vowed to return to it sometime soon.
4. The fish, wrapped in newspaper, was carried in a suitcase.
5. The reporters were informed by a press release of the crimes committed.

Exercise 10–2 *Revising Dangling Modifiers* (p. H-60)

Suggested revisions:
1. After they worked for six hours, the job was done. *Or* After working for six hours, they finished the job.

2. You can obtain further information by calling the specified number.
3. To compete in the Olympics, you need talent, training, and dedication.
4. Pressing hard on the brakes, he spun the car into a hedge.
5. Because the student showed a lack of design experience, the architect advised her to take her model back to the drawing board.

Exercise 11–1 Completing Comparisons (p. H-62)

Suggested revisions:

1. Driving a sports car means more to Jake than *it does* to his professors. *Or* Driving a sports car means more to Jake than his professors *do*.
2. People who go to college aren't necessarily smarter *than those who don't*, but they will always have an advantage at job interviews.
3. I don't have as much trouble getting along with Michelle as *I do with* Karen. *Or* I don't have as much trouble getting along with Michelle as Karen *does*.
4. Correct
5. Singing is closer to prayer than *it is to* a meal of Chicken McNuggets. Or Singing is closer to prayer than a meal of Chicken McNuggets *is*.

Exercise 11–2 Completing Sentences (p. H-64)

Suggested revisions:

1. You have traveled to exotic Tahiti; Maureen *has traveled to* Asbury Park, New Jersey.
2. The mayor refuses to negotiate *with* or even talk to the civic association.
3. Building a new sewage treatment plant would be no more costly *than* and just as effective as modifying the existing one.
4. You'll be able to tell Jon from the rest of the team — Jon wears white Reeboks; the others *wear* black high-tops.
5. Erosion has *reshaped* and always will reshape the shoreline.

Exercise 12–1 Correcting Mixed Constructions and Faulty Predication (p. H-68)

Suggested revisions:

1. The new shopping mall should draw out-of-town shoppers for years to come.
2. The referendum was defeated because voters are tired of paying so much in taxes.
3. The glacier's retreat created the valley.
4. Correct
5. The researcher's main interest is cancer.

Exercise 13–1 Making Sentences Parallel (p. H-71)

Suggested revisions:

1. Because the land along the Rio Grande has few human inhabitants and the river is often shallow, many illegal immigrants attempt to cross the border there.
2. To capture illegal immigrants more easily, the U.S. government has cut down tall grasses, put up fences, and increased the number of immigration patrols.
3. For illegal immigrants, crossing the border at night makes more sense than entering the United States in broad daylight, so the U.S. government has recently installed bright lights along the border.
4. The ocelot and the jaguarundi need darkness, hiding places, and solitude if they are to survive.
5. Neither immigration officials nor wildlife conservationists have been able to find a solution that will protect both the U.S. border and these endangered wildcats.

Exercise 14–1   *Using Coordination* (p. H-75)

Suggested revisions:

1. The rebels may take the capital in a week; however, they may not be able to hold it.
2. If you want to take Spanish this semester, you have only one choice: you must sign up for the 8 a.m. course.
3. Peterson's Market has raised its prices: last week tuna fish cost $1.29 a can, but now it's up to $1.59.
4. Joe starts the morning with a cup of coffee, which wakes him up. Then at lunch he eats a chocolate bar, so that the sugar and caffeine will bring up his energy level.
5. The *Hindenburg* drifted peacefully over New York City and exploded just before landing.

Exercise 14–2   *Using Subordination* (p. H-77)

Suggested revisions:

1. We occasionally hear horror stories about fruits and vegetables being unsafe to eat because they were sprayed with toxic chemicals or were grown in contaminated soil. The fact remains that, given their high nutritional value, these fresh foods are generally much better for us than processed foods.
2. English has become an international language, although its grammar is filled with exceptions to the rules.
3. Some television cartoon shows, such as *Rocky and Bullwinkle* and *Speed Racer*, have become cult classics years after they went off the air.
4. Although stock prices have gone up, investors have not fully regained confidence in the stock market.
5. After giving away her money and bidding adieu to her faithful servant, Violetta dies in her lover's arms.

Exercise 15–1   *Increasing Sentence Variety* (p. H-80)

Suggested revision:

How terrified we are of death! We do not think of it or speak of it: We do not mourn in public or know how to console a grieving friend. In fact, we have eliminated or suppressed all the traditional rituals surrounding death.

The Victorians coped with death differently. The elaborate Victorian funeral, with its yards of black crepe around the hearse, its hired professional mourners, and its solemn procession leading to an ornate tomb, is now only a distant memory. Victorians wore mourning jewelry and had complicated dress codes for the grieving process, which governed what mourners wore and how long they wore it. Many of these Victorian rituals may seem excessive or even morbid to us today, but they served a psychological purpose in helping the living deal with loss.

Exercise 16–1   *Choosing an Appropriate Tone and Level of Formality* (p. H-82)

Suggested revisions:

1. Dear Senator Crowley:
   I am writing to urge you to support the passage of the new environmental law. The damage we are inflicting on forests and wetlands may be permanent and irreversible. Let us act now for the sake of future generations.
   Sincerely,
   Glenn Turner
2. The United States Holocaust Memorial Museum in Washington, D.C., is a remarkable memorial to one of the greatest atrocities in human history. It is very difficult to remain unmoved by the exhibits or to forget what you have seen.

3. Dear Elaine,

   I am looking forward to going to the homecoming dance with you on Friday. I think we're going to have a great time. I hear that Electric Bunny will be playing there. Bring your earplugs! Give me a call before Friday and let me know what time I should pick you up.
   Take care,
   Bill

Exercise 16–2   Avoiding Jargon (p. H-84)

Suggested revisions:

1. The driver education course teaches the student how to drive.
2. We the State Department staff have investigated the riots in Lebanon, and all our data indicate that they are rapidly becoming worse.
3. I recommend multiple bypass heart surgery for Mr. Pitt.
4. Praying is the best way for a person to be close to God.
5. The hunters killed enough deer so that the remaining deer will neither starve nor destroy all the vegetation in the area.

Exercise 16–3   Avoiding Euphemisms and Slang (p. H-85)

Suggested revisions:

1. To prevent spending from exceeding income next year, the governor favors a tax increase.
2. The course was ridiculously easy; the professor passed everyone and didn't even grade the work we turned in.
3. Saturday's forecast calls for rain.
4. The caller to the talk-radio program sounded very disturbed.
5. We expect a recession.

Exercise 17–1   Selecting Words (p. H-90)

Suggested revision:

We spent the first day of our holiday in Mexico arguing about what we wanted to see on our second day. We finally agreed on a day trip out to some Mayan ruins. The next day we arrived at the ancient city of Uxmal. It is an impressive site, in the midst of a jungle, with many buildings still covered in vegetation and iguanas scuttling over the crumbling ruins. The view from the top of the Soothsayer's Temple was spectacular, although we noticed storm clouds gathering in the distance. The rain held off until we climbed down from the pyramid, but we drove back to the hotel in a torrential downpour. After a day of sightseeing, we were ravenously hungry, so we had a good meal before we turned in.

Exercise 18–1   Avoiding Bias (p. H-93)

Suggested revisions:

1. Simon drinks quite a bit.
2. The television crew interviewed a number of average passersby about the new tax proposal.
3. Whether the president of the United States is a Democrat or a Republican, he or she will always be a symbol of the nation.
4. Soon Li excels at music and mathematics.
5. Dick drives a Porsche because he likes the way it handles on the road. He gets pretty upset at the cautious drivers who slow down traffic.

Exercise 19–1   Eliminating Wordiness (p. H-95)

Suggested revision:

The media have recently become obsessed with the conflict on campuses across the nation between freedom of speech and the attempt to protect minorities from verbal abuse. Innocent or humorous remarks, sometimes taken out of context, have gotten many students into trouble for violating college speech codes. Many students have become vocal in attacking these "politically correct" speech codes and defending the right to free speech. But is the campaign against the politically correct really about freedom of speech, or is it itself a way to silence debate? Because the phrase "politically correct" has become associated with liberal social causes and sensitivity to minority feelings, it now carries an extraordinary stigma in the eyes of conservatives. It has become a condemnation against which no defense is possible. To accuse someone of being politically correct is to refute their ideas before hearing their argument. The attempt to silence the opposition is a dangerous sign of our times and suggests that we are indeed in the midst of a cultural war.

Exercise 20–1 Using End Punctuation (p. H-98)

1. What will Brad and Emilia do if they can't have their vacations at the same time? (Question)
2. When a tree falls in a forest, but no one hears it, does it make a sound? (Question)
3. If you have a chance to see the new Ang Lee film, you should do so. The acting is first-rate. (Exclamation point unnecessary)
4. Correct
5. On what day does the fall term begin? (Question)

Exercise 21–1 Using Commas (p. H-99)

1. During the summer of the great soybean failure, Larry took little interest in national affairs.
2. Unaware of the world, he slept and grew within his mother's womb.
3. While across the nation farmers were begging for mortgages, he swam without a care.
4. Neither the mounting agricultural crisis nor any other current events disturbed his tranquillity.
5. In fact, you might have called him irresponsible.

Exercise 21–2 Using Commas (p. H-101)

1. When she breaks a string, she doesn't want her elderly crew to have to grab the guitar, change the string, and hand it back to her before the song ends.
2. The Rest Home Rebels' favorite bands are U2, Arcade Fire, and Lester Lanin and his orchestra.
3. They watch a lot of MTV because it is fast-paced, colorful, exciting, and informative, and it has more variety than soap operas.
4. Just once, Mrs. Carver wants to play in a really huge, sold-out arena.
5. She hopes to borrow the community's big white van to take herself, her band, and their equipment to a major professional recording studio.

Exercise 21–3 Using Commas (p. H-103)

Suggested revisions:

1. The aye-aye, which is a member of the lemur family, is threatened with extinction.
2. The party, a dismal occasion, ended earlier than we had expected.
3. Secretary Stern warned that the concessions that the West was prepared to make would be withdrawn if not matched by the East.
4. Although both of Don's children are blond, his daughter, Sharon, has darker hair than his son, Jake.
5. Herbal tea, which has no caffeine, makes a better after-dinner drink than coffee.

Exercise 21–4 Using Commas (p. H-104)

1. The lawsuit demanded, furthermore, that construction already under way be halted immediately.
2. It is the Supreme Court, not Congress or the president, that ultimately determines the legality of a law.
3. Correct

4. The actor, kneeling, recited the lines with great emotion.
5. Both sides' patience running thin, workers and management carried the strike into its sixth week.

Exercise 21–5   Using Commas (p. H-106)

1. Yes, I was born on April 14, 1983, in Bombay, India.
2. Move downstage, Gary, for Pete's sake, or you'll run into Mrs. Clackett.
3. Vicki, my precious, when you say "great" or "terrific," look as though you mean it.
4. Perhaps you have forgotten, darling, that sometimes you make mistakes, too.
5. Well, Dotty, it only makes sense that when you say "Sardines!" you should go off to get the sardines.

Exercise 22–1   Using Semicolons (p. H-109)

1. Correct
2. When the harpist began to play, the bride and her father prepared to walk down the aisle.
3. The Mariners lost all three games to Milwaukee; worse yet, two star players were injured.
4. Correct
5. Chess is difficult to master, but even a child can learn the rules.

Exercise 23–1   Using Colons (p. H-112)

Suggested revisions:

1. In the case of *Bowers v. Hardwick,* the Supreme Court decided that citizens had no right to sexual privacy.
2. He ended his speech with a quotation from Homer's *Iliad:* "Whoever obeys the gods, to him they particularly listen."
3. Professor Bligh's book is called *Management: A Networking Approach.*
4. George handed Cynthia a note: "Meet me after class under the big clock on Main Street."
5. Rosa expected to arrive at 4:10, but she didn't get there until 4:20.

Exercise 24–1   Using Apostrophes (p. H-115)

1. The Hendersons never change: they're always whining about Mr. Scobee's farming land that's rightfully theirs.
2. It's hard to join a women's basketball team because so few of them exist.
3. I hadn't expected to hear Janice's voice again.
4. Don't give the Murphys' dog its biscuit until it's sitting up.
5. Isn't it a mother's and father's job to tell kids to mind their *p*'s and *q*'s?

Exercise 25–1   Using Quotation Marks (p. H-120)

1. That day at school, the kids were as high as kites.
2. "Notice," the professor told the class, "Cassius's choice of imagery when he asks, 'Upon what meat doth this our Caesar feed, / That he is grown so great?'"
3. "As I was rounding the bend," Peter explained, "I failed to see the sign that said 'Caution: Ice.'"
4. John Cheever's story "The Swimmer" begins with the line "It was one of those midsummer Sundays when everyone sits around saying, 'I drank too much last night.'"
5. Who coined the saying "Love is blind"?

Exercise 26–1   Using Dashes (p. H-121)

Suggested revisions:

1. The sport of fishing — or at least some people call it a sport — is boring, dirty, and tiring.
2. At that time, three states in the Sunbelt — Florida, California, and Arizona — were the fastest growing in the nation.
3. Lulu was ecstatic when she saw her grades — all A's!

Exercise 27–1 Using Parentheses (p. H-123)

Suggested revisions:

1. The new pear-shaped bottles will hold 200 milliliters (6.8 fluid ounces) of lotion.
2. World War I (or "The Great War," as it was once called) destroyed the old European order forever.
3. The Internet is a mine of fascinating (and sometimes useless) information.

Exercise 27–2 Using Brackets and Ellipses (p. H-125)

Suggested revisions:

1. Most people are willing to work hard for a better life. Too often, however, Americans do not realize that the desire for more possessions leads them away from the happiness they hope to find. William Henry Channing advised us "to live content with small means; [. . .] to be worthy, not respectable and wealthy, not rich [. . .]." Still, many people work longer and longer hours to earn more money and as a result have less time to devote to family, friends, and activities that are truly important. When larger houses, sport-utility vehicles, and wide-screen TVs fail to bring them joy, they find even more things to buy and work even harder to pay for them. George Santayana enjoyed the beautiful things of the world, but he understood that "private wealth [. . .] or [. . .] personal possessions [. . .] would take away [his] liberty." The cycle of acquisition can grind down the most optimistic American. The only solution is to realize how few material possessions people absolutely need to have. "Only when [a man] has ceased to need things," said Anwar al-Sadat, "can a man truly be his own master and so really exist."
2. Every human life is touched by the natural world. Before the modern industrial era, most people recognized the earth as the giver and supporter of existence. Nowadays, with the power of technology, we can (if we choose) destroy many of the complex balances of nature. Julius Nyerere, former President of Tanzania, points out that Africans are gravely concerned with the survival of their wildlife and its habitat because "[they] are an integral part of [Africa's] natural resources and of [its] future livelihood and well-being." With the power to destroy comes responsibility. "The overwhelming importance of the atmosphere means [. . .] that only by a deep patriotic devotion to one's country can there be a hope of the kind of protection of the whole planet, which is necessary for the survival of the people of other countries," warns anthropologist Margaret Mead. We are no longer merely nature's children, but nature's parents as well.

Exercise 28–1 Using Abbreviations (p. H-130)

1. Hamlet's famous soliloquy comes in act 3, scene 1.
2. AIDS has affected people throughout U.S. society, not just gay men and intravenous-drug users.
3. Mr. Robert Glendale, a C.P.A., is today's lucky winner of the daily double.
4. The end of the cold war between the United States and the Soviet Union complicated the role of the United Nations and drastically altered the purpose of NATO.
5. The salmon measured thirty-eight inches and weighed twenty-one pounds.

Exercise 29–1 Using Capitalization (p. H-133)

1. My aunt, Linda McCallum, received her doctorate from one of the state universities in California.
2. After graduation she worked there as registrar and lived in the San Fernando Valley.
3. She has pursued her interest in Hispanic studies by traveling to South America from her home in northeastern Australia.
4. Correct
5. After dinner we all toasted Grandmother's ninetieth birthday and sang "For She's a Jolly Good Fellow."

Exercise 30–1 Using Numbers (p. H-135)

1. *Fourscore* means four times twenty; a *fortnight* means two weeks; and a *brace* is two of anything.
2. Fifty years ago, traveling from New York City to San Francisco took approximately fifteen hours by plane, fifty hours by train, and almost a hundred hours by car.
3. The little cottage we bought for $55,000 in the 1970s may sell for $2 million today.
4. At seven o'clock this morning the temperature was already 97° Fahrenheit.
5. Angelica finished volume 1 of Proust's *Remembrance of Things Past*, but by the time she got to page 40 of volume 2, she had forgotten the beginning and had to start over.

Exercise 31–1 Using Italics (p. H-138)

1. Correct
2. *Deux yeux bleus* means "two blue eyes" in French.
3. Jan can never remember whether *Cincinnati* has three *n*'s and one *t* or two *n*'s and two *t*'s.
4. My favorite comic bit in *The Pirates of Penzance* is Major General Stanley's confusion between *orphan* and *often*.
5. In Tom Stoppard's play *The Real Thing*, the character Henry accuses Bach of copying a cantata from a popular song by Procol Harum.

Exercise 32–1 Using Hyphens (p. H-141)

1. Do you want salt and pepper on your roast beef sandwich?
2. Correct
3. Heat-seeking missiles are often employed in modern-day air-to-air combat.
4. *The Piano* is a beautifully crafted film with first-rate performances by Holly Hunter and Harvey Keitel.
5. Nearly three-fourths of the money in the repair-and-maintenance account already has been spent.

Exercise 33–1 Spelling (p. H-146)

You probably know about some of the benefits that exercisers receive, but did you know that improved mental functioning might be one of them? A recent study found that human subjects who took up aerobic exercise for three months grew new nerve cells — a phenomenon that earlier studies suggested was impossible. It appears that physical activity improves the flow of blood and proteins known as growth factors to the brain, causing nerve cells to sprout and connect. This growth is limited to a part of the brain involved in learning and memory, but the effects can be significant. The argument that exercise might help Alzheimer's patients remains controversial. By the time people develop that disease, their brains may be too damaged, and quick fixes are unlikely to help. Researchers advise that people get a checkup before committing to an exercise program. Then, they should get close to an hour of moderate to strenuous exercise for most days of the week. Couch potatoes, you now have more good reasons than ever to get up and get moving.

The Bedford Guide Readings at a Glance

The following table is designed to give you a ready overview of the readings in the eighth edition of *The Bedford Guide for College Writers*. Each reading is summarized and then briefly analyzed in terms of its point of view and rhetorical pattern. The last column estimates each reading's grade level based on the length of the words and sentences. This column, together with the summary and the number of pages, should give you a good idea of an essay's level of difficulty.

Essay	Location	Summary	Point of View	Rhetorical Pattern	Reading Level
Michael Abernethy, "Male Bashing on TV" (4 pages)	Ch. 25 Popular Culture	Abernethy criticizes the recurring images of male ineptitude on television.	First person	Evaluating Giving examples Proposing a solution Explaining causes and effects Arguing Taking a stand Supporting a position with sources	10th grade
Russell Baker, "The Art of Eating spaghetti" (3 pages)	Ch. 4 Recalling an Experience	Baker recalls how he discovered his vocation as a writer	First person	Recalling an experience/narration Describing	7th grade
John Barbieri, "Save Hydrogen for Later; Ethanol Power is the Viable Option for Now" (student essay) (2 pages)	Ch. 10 Proposing a Solution	The author argues for, and presents the benefits of, ethanol as an alternative fuel.	Third person	Proposing a solution Arguing Comparing and contrasting	12th grade
Dave Barry, "From Now On, Let Women Kill Their Own Spiders" (2 pages)	Ch. 24 Men and Women	Barry pokes fun at the inevitable mis-communication between genders.	First person	Arguing Comparing and contrasting Giving examples	11th grade
Sam Benen, "A Royal Mess" (student essay) (3 pages)	Ch. 9 Taking a Stand	Benen looks at the temptations and risks of online poker.	Third person	Taking a stand Arguing	9th grade

Selection	Chapter	Description	Point of View	Strategies	Grade Level
Judy Brady, "I Want a Wife" (2 pages)	Ch. 24 Men and Women	Brady describes the work performed by housewives and concludes that she herself needs a wife.	First person	Arguing Defining	7th grade
Suzanne Britt, "Neat People vs. Sloppy People" (2 pages)	Ch. 7 Comparing and Contrasting	Britt humorously analyzes the differences between neat and sloppy people.	First person	Comparing and contrasting Giving examples	8th grade
Jonathan Burns, "The Hidden Truth: an Analysis of Shirley Jackson's 'The Lottery'" (student essay) (3 pages)	Ch. 13 Responding to Literature	Burns argues that the story's impact is created by unsuspicious characterizations, harmless symbolism, and ambiguous descriptions.	Third person	Arguing Evaluating Responding to literature	11th grade
Jonathan Burns, "A Synopsis of 'The Lottery'" (student example) (2 pages)	Ch. 13 Responding to Literature	Burns gives a concise breakdown of the short story's events.	Third person	Responding to literature	7th grade
David Callahan, "A Question of Character" (4 pages)	Ch. 12 Supporting a Position with Sources	Callahan discusses how Americans have increasingly associated happiness with financial and material gain	Third person	Supporting a position with sources Evaluating Giving examples Taking a stand Arguing	12th grade

Essay	Location	Summary	Point of View	Rhetorical Pattern	Reading Level
Tim Chabot, "Take Me Out to the Ball Game, but Which One?" (student essay) (4 pages)	Ch. 7 Comparing and Contrasting	A student considers whether basketball should replace baseball as our national pastime.	Third person	Comparing and contrasting	11th grade
Yun Yung Choi, "Invisible Women" (student essay) (3 pages)	Ch. 8 Explaining Causes and Effects	A student discusses the effects of Confucianism on women in her native country of Korea.	First person	Explaining causes and effects Supporting a position with sources	12th grade
Kate Chopin, "The Story of an Hour" (2 pages)	Ch. 13 Responding to Literature	A woman resigns herself to the idea of her husband's death.	Third person	Recalling an experience/narration (fiction)	9th grade
Michael Coil, "Communications" (student essay) (2 pages)	Ch. 5 Observing Scene	Coil takes a closer look at a familiar part of his workplace	First person	Observing a scene Describing Recalling an experience/narration	8th grade
Annie Dillard, From An American Childhood (2 pages)	Ch. 27 Education	A poet and essayist recalls a childhood epiphany that guided her throughout her education.	First person	Recalling an experience/narration Describing	9th grade

Selection	Chapter	Description	Point of View	Strategies	Reading Level
Tamara Draut, "What's a Diploma Worth, Anyway?" (2 pages)	Ch. 27 Education	In today's economy, a bachelor's degree doesn't mean what it used to, the author argues.	Third person	Comparing and contrasting Evaluating Supporting a position with sources	12th grade
Barbara Ehrenreich, "Guys Just Want to Have Fun" (2 pages)	Ch. 24 Men and Women	Although women are now more likely than men to earn a college degree, a shift in corporate culture is continuing to favor men in the business world, the author argues.	First person and third person	Comparing and contrasting Supporting a position with sources	10th grade
David Gelernter, "Computers Cannot Teach Children Basic Skills" (3 pages)	Ch. 26 E-Technology	A prominent computer scientist challenges the widely held view that computers are always a "godsend" in the classroom.	Third person	Arguing Taking a stand Explaining causes and effects Giving examples Proposing a solution	11th grade
Nancy Gibbs, "Free the Children" (2 pages)	Ch. 23 Families	A mother writes in favor of giving children the freedom to savor summer days.	First person and third person	Arguing Evaluating Recalling an experience/narration	9th grade

Essay	Location	Summary	Point of View	Rhetorical Pattern	Reading Level
Terry Golway, "A Nation of Idol-Worshipers" (2 pages)	Ch. 25 Popular Culture	Golway laments America's obsession with the cult of celebrity, which is fueled in large part by shows like *American Idol*.	First person and third person	Arguing Taking a stand Giving examples	9th grade
Suzan Shown Harjo, "Last Rites for Indian Dead" (2 pages)	Ch. 9 Taking a Stand	A Native American writer argues for laws protecting Indian burial sites from desecration.	First person	Taking a stand Arguing Recalling an experience/narration Supporting a position with sources	12th grade
Harvard Magazine, "Creating Community, Online and Off" (5 pages)	Ch. 26 E-Technology	Blogging builds community among a university's students and faculty, according to the institution's alumni magazine.	Third person	Defining Giving examples Supporting a position with sources	11th grade
Shirley Jackson, "The Lottery" (7 pages)	Ch. 13 Responding to Literature	Tension builds imperceptibly as people gather for their town's annual lottery.	Third person	Recalling an experience/narration (fiction)	8th grade (mostly dialogue)

Reading	Chapter	Description	Point of View	Strategies	Grade
Robert Jensen, "The High Cost of Manliness" (3 pages)	Ch. 24 Men and Women	Jensen calls for abandoning the prevailing definition of masculinity, arguing that it is "toxic" to both men and women.	Third person	Defining Dividing and classifying Giving examples	12th grade
Stephen King, "Why We Crave Horror Movies" (2 pages)	Ch. 25 Popular Culture	A popular horror fiction writer argues that viewing horror movies helps curb our innate insanity.	First person	Arguing Evaluating	11th grade
Susan Brady Konig, "They've Got to Be Carefully Taught" (2 pages)	Ch. 27 Education	An event at her daughter's school prompts the author to question the emphasis that many schools place on teaching cultural diversity.	First person	Recalling an experience/narration Observing a scene	10th grade
Alex Koppelman, "MySpace or OurSpace?" (5 pages)	Ch. 26 E-Technology	A journalist reports on privacy concerns raised by cases in which students have been suspended from school or arrested based on their postings to social-networking Web sites.	Third person	Evaluating Interviewing a subject Supporting a position with sources	12th grade

Essay	Location	Summary	Point of View	Rhetorical Pattern	Reading Level
Dawn Kortz, "Listen" (student essay) (3 pages)	Ch. 6 Interviewing a Subject	Kortz creates a lively portrait of an elderly man who lives in Dodge City.	Third person	Interviewing a subject Describing Observing a Scene	9th grade
William Severini Kowinski, "Kids in the Mall: Growing Up Controlled" (4 pages)	Ch. 8 Explaining Causes and Effects	Kowinski discusses adolescents and their relationships to malls as quasidaycare and social outposts.	Third person	Explaining causes and effects Supporting a position with sources	11th grade
Ruth La Ferla, "Latino Style Is Cool. Oh, All Right. It's Hot" (4 pages)	Ch. 25 Popular Culture	A reporter explores the proud expression of Latino heritage and culture through fashion.	Third person	Describing Interviewing a subject Giving examples Supporting a position with sources	9th grade
Melissa Lamberth, "Overworked!" (student essay) (3 pages)	Ch. 12 Supporting a Position with Sources	Lamberth proposes shorter workdays or more time off to make workers safer, happier, and more productive.	Third person	Supporting a position with sources Evaluating Proposing a solution	11th grade
Jeffery M. Leving and Glenn Sacks, "Women Don't Want Men? Ha!" (2 pages)	Ch. 2 Reading Processes	Often, men are unfairly blamed for women's dissatisfaction with them, the authors argue.	Third person	Arguing Giving examples Supporting a position with sources	11th grade

Reading	Chapter	Summary	Point of View	Skills	Grade Level
Stephen Levy, From *The Perfect Thing* (2 pages)	Ch. 26 E-Technology	The author asks, "Has the iPod destroyed the social fabric?"	Third person	Describing Evaluating Observing a scene Supporting a position with sources	9th grade
Eric Liu, "The Chinatown Idea" (2 pages)	Ch. 5 Observing a Scene	Liu recalls a childhood trip to Chinatown in New York City.	First person	Describing Observing a scene Recalling an experience/narration	7th grade
Merrill Markoe, "Who Am I?" (2 pages)	Ch. 26 E-Technology	A comedy writer and author offers a humorous take on online personality quizzes.	First person	Evaluating Recalling an experience/narration	12th grade
Christy De'on Miller, "Give Me Five More Minutes" (3 pages)	Ch. 23 Families	The mother of an American marine killed in Iraq reflects on her loss.	First person	Describing Recalling an experience/narration	8th grade
Evelyn F. Murphy, "Why Not a Dollar?" (4 pages)	Ch. 24 Men and Women	Murphy uses sources to show that women's earnings aren't catching up to men's; in fact, she argues, the gender wage gap is widening.	Third person	Supporting a position with sources Giving examples Arguing Taking a stand	9th grade

Essay	Location	Summary	Point of View	Rhetorical Pattern	Reading Level
Dennis O'Neil, "Katrina Documentary Gives Voice to Survivors" (student essay) (2 pages)	Ch. 11 Evaluating	O'Neil considers what makes a documentary about Hurricane Katrina so effective and moving.	Third person	Evaluating Describing Interviewing a subject	12th grade
Tara Parker-Pope, "Custom-Made" (3 pages)	Ch. 25 Popular Culture	The author illustrates how global brands adapt their products and marketing tactics to appeal to local tastes	Third person	Giving examples Dividing and classifying	12th grade
Noel Perrin, "A Part-Time Marriage" (3 pages)	Ch. 24 Men and Women	The success of "part-time" relationships of divorced couples suggests that current conceptions of marriage need to be altered.	First person	Arguing Explaining causes and effects Proposing a solution	8th grade
James Poniewozik, "Why Reality TV is Good for Us" (5 pages)	Ch. 25 Popular Culture	Poniewozik defends reality TV shows against claims of exploitation.	Third person	Evaluating Comparing and contrasting Taking a stand Arguing Supporting a position with sources	10th grade

Selection	Chapter	Description	Point of View	Skills/Strategies	Grade Level
Anna Quindlen, "Evan's Two Moms" (2 pages)	Ch. 23 Families	A Pulitzer Prize-winning columnist argues that the time has come to legalize same-sex marriages.	Third person	Taking a stand Arguing Comparing and contrasting	11th grade
Anjula Razdan, "What's Love Got to Do With It?" (4 pages)	Ch. 23 Families	Razdan considers the place of arranged marriages in a culture devoted to romance.	First person	Comparing and contrasting Giving examples Supporting a position with sources	12th grade
Elaina Richardson, "Bono-Fire: U2's Brilliant Front Man Rocks Convention" (3 pages)	Ch. 6 Interviewing a Subject	Richardson gives insight into what drives this famous rock star and activist.	Third person	Interviewing a subject Describing	8th grade
Wilbert Rideau, "Why Prisons Don't Work" (2 pages)	Ch. 10 Proposing a Solution	A convicted murderer argues that our current prison system is a failure.	First person	Proposing a solution	11th grade
Richard Rodriguez, "Public and Private Language" (5 pages)	Ch. 27 Education	Rodriguez relates the personal experiences behind his views on bilingual education.	Third person	Comparing and contrasting Recalling an experience/narration	7th grade

Essay	Location	Summary	Point of View	Rhetorical Pattern	Reading Level
Carl T. Rowan, "Unforgettable Miss Bessie" (4 pages)	Ch. 27 Education	A journalist tells the story of a teacher who had a lasting impact on his life and on his view of himself.	First person	Recalling an experience/narration Describing	7th grade
Robert G. Schreiner, "What Is a Hunter?" (student essay) (4 pages)	Ch. 4 Recalling an Experience	Schreiner reconsiders his feelings about hunting and being a hunter.	First person	Recalling an experience/narration Describing Observing a scene	8th grade
Danzy Senna, "The Color of Love" (4 pages)	Ch. 23 Families	Senna, the child of an interracial marriage, explores her relationship with her white grand-mother.	First person	Comparing and contrasting Recalling an experience/ narration Describing	7th grade
Brent Staples, "Black Men and Public Space" (3 pages)	Ch. 24 Men and Women	A black man writes about how his presence affects other pedestrians at night.	First person	Recalling an experience/narration	10th grade
Seth Stevenson, "Wham! Bam! Buy a VW, Ma'am!" (2 pages)	Ch. 11 Evaluating	A media critic evaluates a car advertisement, explaining why it deserves a B grade.	First person and third person	Evaluating Giving examples Observing a scene	10th grade

Amy Tan, "Mother Tongue" (5 pages)	Ch. 23 Families	A Chinese American writer examines the effects of her mother's imperfect English on her as a daughter and as a writer.	First person	Recalling an experience/narration; Interviewing a subject; Explaining causes and effects	9th grade
Sherry Turkle, "How Computers Change the Way We Think" (6 pages)	Ch. 26 E-Technology	A psychologist explores how computer technologies are radically affecting our "habits of mind."	First person and third person	Explaining causes and effects; Taking a stand; Arguing; Evaluating; Supporting a position with sources	12th grade
E. B. White, "Once More to the Lake" (5 pages)	Ch. 23 Families	A father who takes his son to a favorite place from his own childhood experiences a startling revelation.	First person	Observing a scene; Describing; Comparing and contrasting; Recalling an experience/narration	8th grade
William Zinsser, "The Right to Fail" (3 pages)	Ch. 27 Education	Zinsser urges a reevaluation of what it means to fail.	First person	Defining; Giving examples	9th grade

Ancillaries to *The Bedford Guide for College Writers*, Eighth Edition

We've provided a large and varied ancillary package so that you can tailor your use of the book to fit your needs and those of your students. We recognize that not everyone uses *The Bedford Guide* the same way — or has the same classroom and institutional concerns. Our ancillary package gives you more flexibility in the way you teach the course. Each of these resources provides additional support in a key area; each gives you another option for reinforcing the concepts and skills that you consider central. Here's an overview.

ELECTRONIC RESOURCES

Never before have *Bedford Guide* users had access to a more extensive and innovative array of electronic resources, helping students with everything from planning and drafting to revising based on the comments of peers.

A Redesigned and Expanded Companion Web Site. The companion Web site (at <bedfordstmartins.com/bedguide>) has a cleaner, more uncluttered look while offering multiple routes of access to important information (by topic or keyword search). The site includes the following features:

- Interactive writing, research, and grammar practices, with new ESL exercises

- Readings and model papers

- New "Draft Doctor" feature: students pick a writing concern they have and then get suggestions for improving their papers, as well as links to related resources on the Web site.

- New links for authors featured in *The Bedford Guide*

- Research and documentation advice

- New peer review worksheets

- Classroom activities, syllabi, and other instructor tools, including new PowerPoint presentations on writing, research, and grammar

Premium Web content (including an e-book and peer review resources) is also available. These resources are described in the following sections.

A New e-Book. The e-book offers the complete text of the print book, with state-of-the-art tools and multimedia from the book's Web site built in. Students can highlight and annotate the readings, respond to writing prompts directly in the book, jump to interactive exercises, and bookmark sections for reference. Instructors can add their own materials — models, notes, assignments, course guidelines — and even reorganize chapters.

A New Peer Review Resource: *PeerSpace*. *PeerSpace* is a collection of confidence-building activities that teach best practices for peer review. Resources include an interactive simulation game, models, exercises, and assignments. When students are ready to put what they've learned into practice, they can use *Comment* (see below), a feature integrated into *PeerSpace*.

Comment for The Bedford Guide for College Writers (at <comment.bedford stmartins.com>). This Web-based peer-review software lets students share and comment on writing assignments. Instructors can create comments that link directly to specific passages in *The Bedford Guide e-Book*. Students who need more peer review help will find it in *PeerSpace*, integrated into *Comment*.

Re: Writing (at <bedfordstmartins.com/rewriting>). This free and open Web site collects Bedford/St. Martin's most popular and widely used online resources at a single address. It includes Exercise Central (more than 7,000 interactive online exercises), research and documentation advice, model documents, a tutorial on avoiding plagiarism, instructor resources, and more.

An Innovative New Online Course Space: *CompClass*. This easy-to-use online course space integrates all the innovative media supporting *The Bedford Guide* — the e-book, *Comment*, the book companion site, and more — with course tools designed specifically for the reading, writing, practice, and discussion that writing instructors and students do. *CompClass* also lets you add spaces designed for writing — blogs, journals, and discussion forums — and add your own course materials, customizing the site so that it reflects the way you teach. *CompClass* is *your* composition course space — whether you teach online, face-to-face, or a little of each.

Teaching Central (at <bedfordstmartins.com/teachingcentral>). This free and open collection of instructional resources is designed to meet the needs of all academic professionals, from first-time TAs to program directors. It includes online and print bibliographies for writing teachers, teaching advice and blogs, adjunct support, just-in-time classroom materials to help instructors plan and prepare, and information about Bedford/St. Martin's-sponsored workshops on technology, assessment, visual rhetoric, and more.

Exercise Central to Go. This CD-ROM offers hundreds of practice items to improve students' writing and editing skills. Drawn from the popular Exercise Central Web site, the exercises cover a wide variety of topics, from identifying effective main points and support to integrating and documenting sources to fixing grammar errors. No Internet connection is necessary.

Testing Tool Kit: A Writing and Grammar Test Bank. This CD-ROM allows instructors to create secure, customized tests and quizzes to assess students' writing and grammar competency and gauge their progress as the course progresses. The CD includes nearly two thousand test items on forty-seven writing and grammar topics at two levels of difficulty. Also, ten pre-built diagnostic tests are included. Scoring is instantaneous when tests and quizzes are administered online. A chart at the end of this manual correlates topics in *Testing Tool Kit* with chapters and sections of *The Bedford Guide.*

PRINT RESOURCES

Aside from the *Practical Suggestions* volume you're holding in your hands, *The Bedford Guide* is accompanied by other helpful print resources to aid your teaching and your students' learning.

Instructor's Annotated Edition of *The Bedford Guide for College Writers* puts information right where busy instructors need it: on the pages of the book itself. The marginal annotations offer teaching tips, analysis tips with readings, last-minute in-class activities, vocabulary glosses, additional assignments, and cross-references to other ancillaries.

Teaching Composition: Background Readings, third edition, edited by T. R. Johnson of Tulane University, addresses the concerns of both first-year and veteran writing instructors. This collection includes thirty professional readings on composition and rhetoric written by leaders in the field. The selections are accompanied by helpful introductions, activities, and practical insights for inside and outside the classroom. The new edition offers up-to-date advice on avoiding plagiarism, classroom blogging, improving online instruction, and more.

Study Skills for College Writers, by Laurie Walker of Eastern Michigan University, is a handy booklet full of activities designed to help underprepared students improve their study skills. It offers many practical tips and strategies for managing time, taking notes, taking tests, and accessing college resources.

Ordering Information

To order any of the ancillaries, please contact your Bedford/St. Martin's sales representative, e-mail sales support at sales_support@bfwpub.com, or visit our Web site at <bedfordstmartins.com>. Note that activation codes are required for the e-book, *PeerSpace, Comment,* and *CompClass.* Codes can be purchased separately or packaged with the print book at a significant discount.

When ordering an access card for premium Web site content (the e-book and PeerSpace) packaged with the book, use these ISBNs:

- with Reader, Research Manual, and Handbook (hardcover): ISBN–13: 978–0–312–47756–1; ISBN-10: 0–312–47756–2

- with Reader, Research Manual, and Handbook (paperback): ISBN–13: 978–0–312–47759–2; ISBN-10: 0–312–47759–7

- with Reader and Research Manual (paperback only): ISBN–13: 978–0–312–47753–0; ISBN-10: 0–312–47753–8

- with Reader (paperback only): ISBN–13: 978–0–312–47744–8; ISBN–10: 0–312–47744–9

When ordering an access card for *Comment* packaged with the book, use these ISBNs:

- with Reader, Research Manual, and Handbook (hardcover): ISBN–13: 978–0–312–47755–4; ISBN-10: 0–312–47755–4

- with Reader, Research Manual, and Handbook (paperback): ISBN–13: 978–0–312–47758–5; ISBN-10: 0–312–47758–9

- with Reader and Research Manual (paperback only): ISBN–13: 978–0–312–47752–3; ISBN-10: 0–312–47752–X

- with Reader (paperback only): ISBN–13: 978–0–312–47743–1; ISBN–10: 0–312–47743–0

When ordering an access card for *CompClass* packaged with the book, use these ISBNs:

- with Reader, Research Manual, and Handbook (hardcover): ISBN–13: 978–0–312–47754–7; ISBN-10: 0–312–47754–6

Ordering Information (continued)

- with Reader, Research Manual, and Handbook (paperback): ISBN–13: 978–0–312–47757–8; ISBN–10: 0–312–47757–0
- with Reader and Research Manual (paperback only): ISBN–13: 978–0–312–47751–6; ISBN–10: 0–312–47751–1
- with Reader (paperback only): ISBN–13: 978–0–312–47742–4; ISBN–10: 0–312–47742–2

When ordering *Study Skills for College Writers* packaged with your students' books, use these ISBNs:

- with Reader, Research Manual, and Handbook (hardcover): ISBN–13: 978–0–312–47696–0; ISBN–10: 0–312–47696–5
- with Reader, Research Manual, and Handbook (paperback): ISBN–13: 978–0–312–47691–5; ISBN–10: 0–312–47691–4
- with Reader and Research Manual (paperback only): ISBN–13: 978–0–312–47686–1; ISBN–10: 0–312–47686–8
- with Reader (paperback only): ISBN–13: 978–0–312–47680–9; ISBN–10: 0–312–47680–9

Correlation Chart: *The Bedford Guide for College Writers* and *Testing Tool Kit: A Writing and Grammar Test Bank*

The *Testing Tool Kit* CD-ROM available with *The Bedford Guide* allows you to create secure, customized tests and quizzes to assess your students' understanding of the writing and grammar concepts covered in the text. The CD contains nearly 2,000 questions grouped into sets on specific writing and grammar topics — 47 in all. You can administer the sets as is or mix and match them to create your own tests. Question sets are at two levels of difficulty so that you can pick just the right level for your courses and goals. Also included are ten ready-to-administer diagnostic tests.

The following chart correlates chapters in *The Bedford Guide* with topic sets in *Testing Tool Kit*.

Bedford Guide Chapter	Relevant Topics in *Testing Tool Kit*
17 Strategies for Stating a Thesis and Planning	Topics 1, 3 (Choosing/writing topic sentences) Topics 5–6 (Supporting a main idea) Topics 7–8 (Organizing support points)
18 Strategies for Drafting	Topics 14–15 (Introducing and concluding a paper) Topics 9–13 (Choosing transitions and correcting transition problems)
20 Strategies for Revising and Editing	See editing exercises throughout the CD.
29 Working with Sources	Topics 16–19 (Summarizing and paraphrasing sources)
32 Integrating Sources	Topics 16–19 (Summarizing and paraphrasing sources)
34 Documenting Sources	Topics 20–23 (Citing and documenting sources in MLA style)
35.1 Sentence Fragments	Topics 24–28 (Identifying and correcting fragments)
35.2 Comma Splices and Fused Sentences	Topics 29–33 (Identifying and correcting run-ons [fused sentences] and comma splices)
35.3 Verbs	Topics 35–36 (Identifying verbs) Topics 37–48 (Choosing correct verbs and identifying and correcting verb problems)
35.4 Subject-Verb Agreement	Topics 49–50 (Identifying subjects and verbs) Topics 51–54 (Identifying and correcting subject-verb agreement problems)
35.5 Pronoun Case	Topics 55–56 (Identifying pronouns) Topics 57–60 (Choosing correct pronouns and identifying and correcting pronoun-case problems)
35.7 Pronoun-Antecedent Agreement	Topics 61–62 (Identifying pronouns and antecedents) Topics 63–68 (Choosing correct pronouns and correcting pronoun-antecedent agreement problems)